Rajaji

— A —
Life

Rajmohan Gandhi

PENGUIN BOOKS

An imprint of Penguin Random House

PENGUIN BOOKS

USA | Canada | UK | Ireland | Australia
New Zealand | India | South Africa | China | Singapore

Penguin Books is part of the Penguin Random House group of companies
whose addresses can be found at global.penguinrandomhouse.com

Published by Penguin Random House India Pvt. Ltd
4th Floor, Capital Tower 1, MG Road,
Gurugram 122 002, Haryana, India

First published by Penguin Books India 1997

Copyright © Rajmohan Gandhi 1997

10 9 8 7 6 5

ISBN 9780140269673

Typeset in Garamond by SÜRYA, New Delhi

Printed at Repro India Limited

www.penguin.co.in

That they may know their roots —
for
Bharat and Shreya,
Vidur, Divya and Arjun,
Ananya and Anushka,
and siblings and cousins
joining their ranks,
great-great-grandchildren
of the subject of this book

Contents

Preface

To those knowing even a little about him, a biography of Rajaji or C.R., as Chakravarti Rajagopalachari was known, needs no justification. However, a word may be in order for the many for whom Rajaji's life is curtailed by time.

He was born in 1878 in a poor Tamil-speaking Iyengar family in a South Indian village called Thorapalli, not far from Bangalore and Hosur, and died in 1972 in Madras, now Chennai.

In the movement for Indian freedom he was Gandhi's southern general and at one stage regarded as Gandhi's heir. 'I do say he is the only possible successor,' Gandhi had said about C.R. in 1927. However, in 1942 Gandhi was to declare, 'Not Rajaji but Jawaharlal will be my successor.' Nehru was the nation's as well as Gandhi's choice as free India's first Prime Minister, yet in 1948 Rajaji became Governor-General and thus independent India's first Indian head of state.

From the late 1950s, when Rajaji was close to eighty, to the end of 1972, when he died at the age of 94, Rajaji was the period's most notable — and most quotable — dissenting Indian.

He crackled and sparkled. In 1962, when Nehru was alive, Rajaji was, at least to one person, 'by far the most interesting and lively man in all India.'[1] That from time to time he contradicted himself added to his liveliness.

This gifted wordsmith — and skilled administrator — was also remarkably prescient. When, in the 1950s, Nehru was luring everyone in India towards the 'socialistic pattern,' C.R. attacked the 'permit-licence raj' — the phrase was his — as a recipe for corruption and stagnation, and formed a political party, Swatantra, in support of an open economy and fundamental rights.

In 1971, within six weeks of a bitter electoral defeat at the hands of Indira Gandhi, he asserted that the policies of Swatantra were 'bound to become the Government's policies and programmes, if not now, some years hence.' The true if grudgingly acknowledged father of the economic reforms of the early 1990s is C.R.

In the 1950s he anticipated subsequent warnings regarding the global nuclear threat — and the power of China. Before independence he was the only Congress leader to admit the likelihood of Partition; and in 1947 he said that Pakistan might break up in about twenty-five years.

His capacity to be ahead of his times can be gauged also from what he said in 1921-2 about life after independence,[2] his 1961 call for state funding of elections ('Elections now are private enterprise, whereas this is the first thing that should be nationalised'[3]), and his 1970 warning about 'adventures in the manufacture of [a] small car'[4].

His lifespan joined far-apart ages. When he was born, the revolt of 1857 and, on the other side of the globe, the assassination of Lincoln were recent events; when he died, the twenty-first century had started impinging on people's minds.

He interests us also because in his case power did not translate into wealth.

Finally, a focus on C.R. is inevitably a welcome focus on South India, which features inadequately in stories of the Freedom Movement or of the post-1947 decades.

This book is a freshly written condensation of my two volumes on the life of C.R., the first of which came out in 1978 and the other in 1984. My sources were C.R.'s private papers, made available to me by his sons and daughters; the papers of Devadas Gandhi (my father and the husband of Rajaji's youngest daughter Lakshmi); the papers in different archives of several of C.R.'s contemporaries; the correspondence and writings of Gandhi in the *Collected Works of Mahatma Gandhi* and elsewhere; newspapers of the time, including *Kalki*, *The Hindu* and *Swarajya*; Rajaji's correspondence with his lifelong friend Navaratna Rama Rao; and recollections provided by numerous relatives, colleagues, adversaries, officials, journalists and other contemporaries.

They included G.D. Birla, John Brackenbury, Chellamma, Isobel Cripps, B.W. Day, Morarji Desai, Indira Gandhi, V.V. Giri, Ramnath Goenka, Lord Glendevon, R.V. Krishna Iyer, K. Kamaraj, Acharya Kripalani, T.T. Krishnamachari, S. Krishnamurti, Harold Macmillan, the Earl of Mar & Kellie, Minoo Masani, Mirabehn, Lord Mountbatten, John Munro, V.K. Narasimhan, Jayaprakash Narayan, Colleen Nye, Pyarelal, S. Ramakrishnan, Henry Ramsey, the family of Navaratna Rama Rao, B. Shiva Rao, C. Samachar, A.N. Sivaraman, Ian Stephens, C. Subramaniam, Margaret Tait, Mahavir Tyagi and Richard Wood.

In particular, this work owes a great deal to the prodding, help, information and insights provided by two close associates of Rajaji, T. Sadasivam and K. Santhanam — and by Rajaji's children, Krishnaswami, Namagiri, Narasimhan and Lakshmi.

For help at different times with research or translation I thank S.A. Govindarajan, D. Venkatesan, V. Ramaratnam, Neerja Chowdhury and K. Vedamurthy. I am grateful for the secretarial assistance received from Meher Ghyara, Linda Pierce and Usha Gandhi.

Thanks are also due to those who permitted me to study material in the following institutions: Tamil Nadu Archives, Madras; National Archives, New Delhi; Nehru Memorial Museum & Library, New Delhi; India Office Library, London; Gandhi Sangrahalaya, New Delhi & Ahmedabad; Rashtrapati Bhavan; the Prime Minister's Office; the Union Home Ministry; *Amrita Bazar Patrika* and *The Statesman*, Calcutta; *The Hindu* and *Indian Express*, Madras; and *Hindustan Times*, New Delhi.

A word on spellings. The English spelling of Rajaji's name varied during different phases of his life, from Rajagopalachar, favoured early in his career, to the usual Rajagopalachari, the respectful Rajagopalachariar and the rare Rajagopalacharya. The abbreviations most resorted to were Rajaji and C.R. These are freely used in the text. Indian towns have generally been given the spelling they had in the period under reference. Thus Madura instead of Madurai, and Cawnpore for Kanpur.

New Delhi, December 1996   *Rajmohan Gandhi*

1
Manga
1878-1915

Britain's presence in India seemed permanent in 1878, the year in which Chakravarti Rajagopalachari was born. Securing in 1876 the title of Empress of India, Victoria had sent a serene message to a Delhi assembly: 'We Victoria have been touched by the evidence of their (the Indians') loyalty and attachment to our house and throne.' She looked forward to 'yet closer affection' between 'ourselves and our subjects.'[1]

Good as well as greedy Britons had set foot in India. One of the best was Sir Thomas Munro, who reached Indian shores in 1780 as a 19-year-old seaman and died as the Governor of Madras in 1827. He understood the feelings of a subjugated race and observed that while 'the natives of British provinces may . . . enjoy the fruits of their labour in tranquillity, . . . none of them can look forward to any share in the civil or military government of their country.'[2]

Under a system devised by Munro, a South Indian village had a munsiff, or headman, who collected land tax, wrote reports for district officials, communicated and explained the Raj's orders to the villagers, drafted their petitions, and settled petty disputes. Chakravarti Venkatarya, father of Rajagopalachari, was the munsiff of Thorapalli village in a north-western corner of Salem district in Madras Presidency.

He was a Tamil-speaking Brahmin of the Iyengar or Vaishnavite variety. The quick-minded Brahmins of South India were and are a tiny part of the population, fewer than three in a hundred. An ancestor of Venkatarya figures in South Indian lore: Nallan Chakravarti. Living in a distant and unknown century, Nallan (the good) is said to have defied orthodox rules by performing the last rites for a dying wanderer from a lower caste. For a period Venkatarya's forbears had resided near the famed shrine of Tirupati, in Telugu country. From there they moved to the village of Pannapalli in the Balaghat plateau in the domain of the princes of Mysore.

The greater part of it about 3,000 feet above sea level, Balaghat was often visited by drought. Its population was sparse but diverse, speaking Tamil, Kannada, Telugu, Hindustani and Marathi. In 1792, when a number of adjoining pockets fell to the British, Balaghat stood unconquered; but seven years later, on the death of the Muslim prince, Tipu, it was ceded to the European powers. The British included Balaghat in the district of Salem in Madras Presidency and called it the taluk, or sub-district, of Hosur.

Around 1840, Narasimhachar, who would beget Venkatarya, moved fourteen miles from Pannapalli to the village of Thorapalli, also in Hosur taluk. He married a girl called Rangamma and lived in the house that her father, Srinivasa, who had no sons, had settled on her. Rangamma and Narasimhachar had three sons, of whom Venkatarya was the first, and three daughters.

Venkatarya was in his twenties when he became the munsiff of Thorapalli, which had about eighty dwellings at the time and a population of about 400. Thorapalli's red soil produced rice and ragi, coconut and mango. Venkatarya and his kinsfolk owned a few of its acres. Though the climate was dry and the trees scattered, Thorapalli's setting was not unattractive; on occasion the sun played picturesquely on clouds and low hills. Its dwellings crowded a rocky terrain that sloped quite steeply and was washed at its feet by a slender, shallow stream. Rangamma's house, now a national monument, lay on the higher slopes, where only Brahmins lived.

A humble house, the walls and floor are made of mud, the roof of bamboo and cheap tiles. The family lived and slept in a large central room with an opening in the roof to let the light in and a channel in the floor to let the water out. A room for eating, a kitchen, a bathing area and a twelve feet by six feet 'store' completed the house, adjoining which was a narrow seasonal well. In 1968 a descendant sold the house, almost in its original condition, for Rs 2,750.

Singaramma from Kuppam in Chittoor district, now part of the state of Andhra, was married to Venkatarya when he was fifteen. They waited many years before a boy, Narasimhachar, arrived. He was followed by Srinivasa and later, on 10 December 1878,[3] by their third and last child, Rajagopalachar. All births took place in the dark, windowless 'store' in grandmother Rangamma's house.

The two years from 1876 to 1878 had seen the worst of South India's recorded famines. When Lord Lytton, the Viceroy, journeyed from Calcutta, the capital of British India, to the affected region, he found that in Salem district alone 1,36,941 famine deaths had been registered. Mercifully, the north-east monsoon of 1878 brought 'the finest crop seen in the district.' 'Stocks were replenished, prices fell . . . and the weary officials were at last released from their heavy tasks.'[4]

Rajagopalachari's birth coincided with the revival of fortune. Called Rajan by his parents, the child went to the village 'school', played marbles on sandy patches beside the stream, frequented a tamarind tree, and on one occasion set fire to a clothes-line and watched the leaping flames until they were put out by an aunt invited by him 'to share in the entertainment.'[5]

Venkatarya must have demonstrated abilities, perhaps during the drought, for in 1883, when Rajan was four, he was named munsiff of Hosur, which was about six miles away. The promotion was noteworthy, for Hosur, known once for its silk, was the Raj's seat in the taluk, with a population at the time of over 5,000. Beyond Hosur lay Bangalore, the largest city in Mysore, a state ruled by Hindu princes who acknowledged British paramountcy.

Because of the clan and caste to which he belonged, Venkatarya usually went by the name of Chakravarti Iyengar. Tall, strongly built and light-skinned, he walked with a proud bearing. Typical of Brahmins, except for a tuft at the back, his head was shaved clean. Each morning he marked his forehead with a *namam* — a vertical line in red within a white U, generally applied by Vaishnavites. Barefooted at home, Venkatarya used leather chappals for going out, which was not yet a general Brahmin practice. The orthodox custom was to walk unshod or in wooden sandals, leather being thought unclean. But increasingly Brahmins were accepting chappals made by cobblers, giving rice or ragi in exchange.

As the Hosur munsiff, Chakravarti Iyengar's monthly salary was five rupees. Commanding prestige more than money, he was stingy with what he got. In a bid to shock him into loosening the purse strings, Singaramma once removed her ornaments and wore a widow's meagre attire.

Fluent in Tamil and Telugu, Chakravarti Iyengar had a fair knowledge as well of Sanskrit texts, which he read in the Telugu script. Though unable to speak English, Chakravarti Iyengar had access to Salem district's British officials, who on occasion asked him to accompany them in their horse carriages. He gave them uninhibited advice. Obeying tradition over food, Chakravarti Iyengar abstained not only from meat, fish and eggs but also from vegetarian items not cooked by persons of his caste.

Associating with white people conflicted with custom, for they ate beef. But they were rulers, and there was a convenient old belief that Vishnu's grace 'purified' a ruler, irrespective of who he was and what he ate. Previously enabling Brahmin administrators to serve the Muslim Tipu and his father Haider, this rationalization enabled an orthodox Brahmin like Chakravarti Iyengar to serve the Raj.

At Hosur's Government School, founded in 1858, the munsiff's son was not a diligent student, but the chief reason for this was the boy's acute myopia. He saw the blackboard as a blur in the distance and the teacher's writing on it not at all. When he asked his father for spectacles, the stern Chakravarti Iyengar refused. Nobody under forty-five wore glasses in Hosur, and he thought his son's request sprang from vanity.

Slow as he was to understand his son's handicap, the munsiff had spotted the boy's intelligence and saved money for his education. Hosur offered nothing after 'middle' school. However, Bangalore was near, and its British-run Central College prepared boys for matriculation and graduation.

The thin-faced, eagle-nosed village boy thrust into it, smaller than his peers, was all of eleven years old. The lad slept in a Brahmin hostel and took his meals (for two rupees a month) in an eating house run by a clansman. At thirteen he matriculated. His brothers, older than him by twelve and six years, did so at the same time, though not, it would seem, as Central College students.

Two other events occurred when Rajan was thirteen. The first was that he got his glasses. His life was transformed. He had not 'quite known,' until now, 'what green was.' And he found that the stars were not 'just a vague mist of light' but had 'points, and corners, and colours.' The second event was the start of a friendship. Navaratna Rama Rao was two years older than Rajan but junior to him at Central. Attracted by Rama Rao's brightness and by his familiarity with English literature, Rajan 'sought him out and left a letter in his room on the top of an eating house, asking for his friendship.'[6] He had risked a rebuff, but Rama Rao responded positively.

The two read a lot together, mostly Rama Rao — 'the greater connoisseur of us two,' as Rajagopalachari was to put it much later — reading for Rajan. They also 'laughed and enjoyed humour and talked metaphysics and educated each other.' In Rajagopalachari's words after Rama Rao's death, 'Our friendship was an astonishment and a mystery to our collegemates but they tolerated it and gathered round both of us.' It was to last nearly 70 years.

The favourite teacher of both of them, clearly first in 'a list of carefully prepared preferences,' was John Guthrie Tait. The Scot taught the boys 'to know and love literature.' More than that, 'careful in concealing his benefactions,' Tait became their 'beau-ideal of what was good and brave and noble in man.' The money his father provided him was nowhere near enough to meet Rajan's expenses in Bangalore. A college scholarship and Tait's personal gifts met the balance.

Studying for examinations went against Rajan's grain but Tait and John Cook, the Principal, obviously liked him and Rama Rao. To their surprise the boys were offered a cubicle within the college grounds for lodging. The favour was not extended to others, and the eight-foot-square space, 'luxuriously furnished with two benches which served as sofas by day and beds by night,' became a sanctum to which the proud lodgers admitted only a chosen few.[7]

Introduced to literature by Tait, Rajagopalachari was introduced by literature to liberty. A believer in the Raj and one of its finer specimens, Tait had, in retrospect, won Rajagopalachari only in order to lose him. For the moment, however, only the seed had been sown and neither teacher nor pupil seemed aware that it would grow into a thorn of revolt, as Tait would later view it.

Rajan and Rama Rao 'knew intimately and loved everything in the college, from the lawn and the cricket field to the venerable trees which bounded them . . . [and] the austere red college building with the gaunt clock tower keeping watch over it.' Since the college was affiliated at the time to Madras University, Rajan took his B.A. exams in the three subjects English, Science and Tamil at Madras, in January 1896.

'Having left everything until the last minute,' he sat up most of the night to swot up facts for the statics and dynamics papers the following day. Rajan's father, who was with him, ordered him to bed after he had finished with statics. Getting high marks in statics and a zero in dynamics, Rajan passed in science as a whole in the second division, with 218 marks out of 400. The periods assigned to Tamil had been devoted to amusement, and Rajan, destined to be acclaimed as a master of Tamil writing, failed his test in it. In English he was ranked fifth in the university. Despite his results in Tamil he was declared a graduate.

He decided to study law. This could be done in Madras. Though there was no separate law college, law was taught in the university's showpiece, the seashore Senate House. Completed in 1879, the ornate four-towered edifice with stained-glass windows sported European columns, Islamic minarets and Hindu decorative motifs.

Rajan's law course began early in 1896. His attire in class accorded with the rule laid down in 'The Calendar' of the university that 'graduates who are in the habit of wearing native costume shall be clothed in white, and shall wear either a white, red or black turban, which may have a gold border.' Because he had failed in Tamil, Rajan was also obliged, for the first two terms, to attend lectures in Tamil in the pink-domed Presidency College, 500 yards down the beach from Senate House. In January 1897 he narrowly passed the Tamil test, securing 46 marks out of 120. 'I am free at last from this Tamil devil,' he told his father.

His hostel, kept for students from Mysore by a certain Biligiri Iyengar, was located in an eighteenth century building called Castle Kernan. Also facing the blue sea, about a mile away from Presidency College, Castle Kernan was popularly known as Ice House; ice for chilling the whisky of British residents in Madras used to be brought round the Cape of Good Hope and stored in it.

Rajan still received occasional assistance from Tait. Sometimes, he would run on the inviting Marina sands for pleasure or exercise. Once he even had a brush with danger when, during a storm, a boat filled with students, including himself, almost capsized in the sea.

Queen Victoria celebrated her golden jubilee in 1897. *The Hindu*, founded in Madras two decades earlier, wrote: 'Everywhere Her Majesty's name is blessed and cheered to the echo by millions upon millions of voices of Hindus' (22.6.97).

The paper had exaggerated. In reality the bonds were not as warm. Formed in 1885 by a group of Indians and Britons, the Indian National Congress had been petitioning the white masters for representative government — with little effect. Wenlock, the Governor of Madras, had admitted injustice. In 1896 he had written to Lord Hamilton, Secretary of State for India in the British cabinet, that it was 'a monstrous shame that [the textile mills of] Lancashire should rule India' and that it was difficult 'to maintain that we rule India for the benefit of the Indians and not of England.'[8]

Rajan was attending an evening lecture in 1898 when a friend, G.A. Natesan, rushed in with a poster announcing the release of Bal Gangadhar Tilak, who had been sentenced for eighteen months after a trial for sedition that had made him a hero. The poster thrilled Rajan.

A telegram arrived at Ice House stating that Rajan's mother was ill. He hastened to join her. The last leg of the journey had to be done in a horse-drawn jutka. While engaging one he heard a Muslim driver say in Urdu to his fellows that the lad's mother was dead. Fearing confirmation, Rajan asked no questions as the jutka bumped along to the munsiff's house.

His ears had not deceived him. Singaramma was dead, a victim of cholera. Rajan accused his father of not taking care of her. 'In my hurt and shock I rebuked him,' he would later confess.[9]

Following Singaramma's death, there were marriage proposals for Rajan. Offers came from richer families. The munsiff was tempted but Rajan turned them down. 'You will end up marrying a poor girl,' Singaramma's sister told him. 'I want to marry a poor girl,' replied Rajan.

His mother had been raised in Kuppam, where slow trains between Bangalore and Madras briefly halted. Rajan knew that in a village called Lakshmipuram, two miles from Kuppam, lived Alarmelu Mangammal, Manga for short, whom Singaramma had thought would be suitable for him. The girl's father, Tirumalai Sampangi Iyengar, an itinerant priest of humble means, desired the match.

By previous arrangement, Rajan saw Manga offering worship in the Lakshmipuram temple. Charmed, he said he was willing. Sampangi Iyengar declared before guests that he would give Manga to Rajan. Next day, in Kuppam, in a modest courtyard decorated with flowers and plantain branches, while a priest recited ancient texts, the pair, bride behind groom, walked seven steps round the sacred fire, and Rajan took Manga's little hand in his.

Manga was just ten years old. The child-wife stayed behind with her parents. The groom returned to Madras for his studies. In January 1900, at the age of twenty-one, Rajan passed the Bachelor of Law exams — in the third division.

Chakravarti Iyengar hoped to see his son a judge one day. On Rajan's birth an astrologer had even prophesied a viceroyalty, which sounded absurd,[10] but a judgeship, which was big enough, was not impossible. The Bar could lead to the Bench. Father and son decided that the latter should set up practice in Salem, headquarters of the district to which Thorapalli and Hosur belonged, and the seat of the munsiff's ultimate boss, the Collector.

Salem town stands in a valley between the sizable Shevaroys in the north and lower hills on the southern horizon. At the turn of the century, when Rajan, soon to be called C.R. by friends and clients, arrived in Salem, it had a population of about 70,000.. Coffee had been successfully cultivated on the hills, but there was little industry of any scale in the town or near it. Thousands of Salem's lowly homes, however, echoed to the whirr of the handloom. Europeans frequented Yercaud, 4,500 feet above sea level in the Shevaroys. The town's Indian elite consisted of a handful of junior officials — senior posts were British preserves — and advocates.

Renting a home on the second street of the Agraharam, the Brahmin quarter, Rajan, very much his father's pride and hope, was soon joined by Chakravarti Iyengar, as he chose to retire and leave Hosur. His older sons were by now attached to the district administration and riding on mules to collect revenue and information.

Shortly after his arrival in Salem, C.R. was told that the case of his first client was unexpectedly 'on board.' Picking up a bicycle, he pedalled as hard as he could to the courtroom, opened with a remark that amused the English judge, and went on to win the case. It was the start of a reputation. Clients, including some accused of major crimes, began to make their way to his doorstep. Before the year ended, he had 'already defended [his] first murderer.'[11]

Navaratna Rama Rao, who had also studied law in Madras, acted for a while as C.R.'s junior. But either he was not suited for the Bar, or the Bar for him, for in about two years he returned to his native Mysore and joined its administrative service.

Twelve years old when she went to her husband's home, Manga gave birth to a boy, Krishnaswami, on the day following her thirteenth birthday. In less than two years, another boy, Ramaswami, was born. That Manga had to endure the pains of childbirth at so early an age would embarrass C.R. all his life.

In 1904-5, Japan inflicted defeats on Russia, destroying the notions of European invincibility and Asian impotence. Also in 1905, Lord Curzon, the Viceroy, announced that Bengal would be split, one part mainly Hindu and the other with a Muslim majority. Administrative convenience was the reason given, but many Indians saw a design to divide the communities. In protest, a campaign of boycotting British goods was launched.

C.R. was excited by Japan's victory and drawn by the stir against Curzon's step. His feelings were sufficiently strong for him to journey to distant Calcutta for the December 1906 session of the Indian National Congress, the largest political gathering witnessed in India till then.

Dadabhai Naoroji, India's Grand Old Man, was presiding. He asked for 'self-government, or Swaraj.' The twenty-eight-year-old C.R. glowed, but Pherozeshah Mehta, the 'Lion of Bombay,' who could speak with fire but was the leader of the Moderates, was perturbed. A Moderate-Extremist contest became inevitable. Standing with the Extremists, C.R. expressed himself in Patna's *Hindustan Review* of July 1907:

> Extremist forms of lawful agitation are . . . necessary to command the attention of the immovable statesmen who control the destinies of this country.

He added that while reform by instalments need not be opposed, there was 'a way of throwing crumbs' which created 'a debased canine nature of satisfaction without ambition' and had to be 'actively resisted and prevented.'

The trial of strength with the Moderates took place at Surat in western India, where the Congress met in December 1907. A fully involved C.R. took a number of southern delegates to Surat, paying for the journey of some. Steered by Mehta, the Moderates tightly controlled the platform. When Tilak, hero to C.R. and to large numbers of Indians, tried to raise a question, he was asked not to speak. Young Moderate volunteers tried to drag him down when he mounted the platform.

Unmoved and defiant, Tilak faced the audience with folded arms. Suddenly, a shoe hurtled through the air and hit Mehta. Pandemonium followed. Men rushed about shouting with fury and waving long sticks. C.R. saw the session break up in chaos. The Congress split, and Extremists like himself were ousted. The Moderates were to possess the Congress until 1915.

For articles in his journal *Kesari*, Tilak was sentenced to six years rigorous imprisonment. He was to spend the six years in a cell in Mandalay in Burma.

It was a pale Congress that met in December 1908 in Madras. Only those accepting in writing the Moderate creed could take part. C.R. fought for the right to attend without signing the creed. His bid failed, but so did an attempt by the Moderates to detach Salem from C.R.'s influence.

Repression was breeding violence. In April 1908 a bomb was thrown at a British judge in Muzaffarpur in Bihar; the judge survived but two Englishwomen were killed. Khudiram Bose was tried and sent to the gallows; in revenge the revolutionaries killed two officials and an approver.

Yet it did not appear that the bomb would frighten the foreigner away. In the years immediately following 1908, freedom seemed an unrealizable dream to C.R. and many like him. Raised high in 1905-6, their hopes now lay broken around them.

In 1906 Manga gave birth to a daughter, Namagiri. Their third son, Narasimhan, was born in 1909. Lakshmi, their second daughter and last child, was to come in 1912.

Wanting his clothes 'fresh and fine,' C.R. wore a silver-laced white turban, a white *panchakachham* (tied in five places) dhoti — the long cloth enclosing each leg separately — a black buttoned-up coat, and black socks and shoes. In a contemporary's view, 'from his very first year he had a roaring practice.'[12] Clients were paying him a thousand rupees for a case.

He liked the money, which looked even better when he remembered his boyhood, but his high fees were also a device for saving time, which he wanted for friends, for recreation, for politics, for 'social reform' efforts. He and his friends held converse on cultural, scientific and political questions. At a Book Club they formed they dissected new works. Songstress 'Salem' Godavari performed at a farewell party for a British judge.

There was sport: C.R. became a reasonable tennis player, had a shot at billiards and played cards; but after a dispute during a game he gave up cards for good. Buying a dogcart and horse, C.R. learnt to guide the animal. 'Baby,' a white horse, was sensitive — C.R. would recall in old age — to 'the gentlest and most delicate suggestions' from his fingers. Its hoofs announced to Salem streets that the lawyer was passing by in his dogcart. One day the 'untouchable' syce came running to C.R. and announced, 'Baby is very ill.' C.R. rushed to the horse. Baby just looked up, saw his master's face, and dropped dead.

A friend of C.R.'s during this period, R.V. Krishna Iyer, noticed in him knowledge — 'If there was any information lacking we used to go to him' — intelligence, and 'a tendency to take the opposite side even though inside he agreed with you.' Krishna Iyer, a lawyer himself, was told by another member of C.R.'s circle of friends, 'If you have a good case, don't discuss it with C.R. He will convince you that it is a very bad case.' Iyer also marked C.R.'s liberality. 'His hospitality became a byword. Donations to this cause and that cause, endlessly.'[13]

Guests often partook of the fare at C.R.'s home, where 'two very able cooks' were hired. Iyer adds that at the district court, three miles from the heart of town, the tiffin brought for C.R. was generally sufficient 'for at least ten persons' and shared with the advocates present.

His income growing, C.R. bought a larger house — a yellow dwelling with a margosa tree in front — on the first street of the agraharam, and furnished it with spring beds. A coach too superseded the dogcart.

Their own children were not the only youngsters in C.R.'s

and Manga's house. Nephews, cousins and Manga's brother were among the seven others who, over a period, lived under their roof and were educated in Salem. Manga, twenty in 1909, and the older children all played 'master' by turns, when they were expected to ensure that the younger children were bathed and fed on time and equipped for school.

Apparently Manga did not grudge looking after the wards that her husband had taken into the house. One of them, C. Samachar, told this author: 'I was not her son. I was her husband's cousin's son. Yet she treated me the way she treated her children.'

In a house brimming with youngsters, Manga had to be firm. Namagiri, or Papa as she was called, Manga's third child, had her breakfast withheld for two hours and more — 'until I had cleaned my mouth with tooth-powder.' At times Manga's patience snapped. Once she brought cinders from the kitchen-fire to threaten the boisterous children. Gripping her hand, C.R. led Manga back into the kitchen.

It was on a night in this period that a bullet fired by C.R. nearly killed an innocent man. A revolver beside him, C.R. was asleep on a bullock-cart trudging overnight towards Salem from the town of Namakkal, where he had argued a case, when a shout of '*panam*' (money) woke C.R. Thinking he had been accosted by a highway robber — dacoities were common on the route —, C.R. lifted his gun in the darkness and shot at the voice.

A man hearing the shot hurried with a lantern and C.R. saw in its light that he had hit someone posted at a toll gate. The bullet had pierced the man's forehead and come out behind the ear. C.R. took him in his cart to a hospital, found that the bullet had fortunately missed the man's skull, compensated him, and informed the police. A prosecution that followed resulted in C.R.'s exoneration, but his licence was taken away for a while.

From his earliest Salem days C.R. was lauded and assailed as a nonconformist. Opposition began with the Narayana Iyer incident. Accepted into the Raj's prized Indian Civil Service (ICS), Narayana Iyer had crossed the high seas, thereby violating a rule of orthodoxy. Because he had welcomed Narayana Iyer in his home, one of C.R.'s friends, Seshu Iyer, a lecturer, was also deemed guilty. A third offender was a priest called Krishna Sastri, who had performed a rite of absolution for Narayana Iyer.

Defending all three, and associating publicly with Narayana Iyer, C.R. initiated a monthly subscription for Krishna Sastri, whose income had been slashed by the social boycott.

Soon he fought for something more radical: the right of two 'panchama' or 'untouchable' boys to places in Salem's Municipal School. Despite a threat that the school's two hundred caste-Hindu boys would leave if the two 'panchamas' were admitted, C.R. insisted, and the Principal took the 'panchama' boys in. Their schooling paid for by C.R., the two did well, and the way was paved for more mixing.

Also controversial was a reformist marriage organized by C.R. It was unusual in three ways: one side was Vaishnavite, the other Saivite; the bride was a widow; she was also above the age of puberty. The Press published attacks on C.R., and his father concurred with them. The criticism only strengthened C.R.'s zeal, and at a social reform conference in Kurnool in 1910 he asked for a general acceptance of inter-caste marriages.

On the journey back from Kurnool, one of C.R.'s friends, Venkatasubba Iyer, accidentally let a valuable watch slip to the ground outside the moving train. While others commiserated or blamed, C.R. stared at the window — counting telegraph posts. At the next stop he gave the stationmaster the number he had counted: the watch was found.

C.R.'s interests were widening. At his instance, a young man called B.V. Namagiri started a Swadeshi store where only Indian goods were sold. A Hindustani course was arranged by C.R.; he and some of his lawyer friends attended it, and C.R. also learned the Urdu script. 'He was solicitous about Muslims,' Krishna Iyer would recall. Not all his friends liked it.

Slim of figure, light of skin, her height an inch under five feet, her long flowing black hair soft and straight, Manga had a slender attractive face. She looks shy and quaint in the only picture that exists of her, enlarged out of a group photograph taken in the home of her husband's friend Venkatasubba Iyer. Before leaving their house for Iyer's place, C.R. had daubed Manga's forehead with a fresh red tilak, the sign of a married woman. It was the second time that day that her husband had thus marked her forehead; he did it, and liked doing it, every morning, and Manga sought to keep the tilak unsmudged through each day.

Her plaited tresses were tied at the end with a thin strip torn off a plantain tree. Her blouses sleeved to the wrist, she wore nine-yard silk saris, often in a mixture of red and yellow.

Saturday was almsgiving day. Manga stored cereals for the purpose in tin vessels near the front door: rice for the Brahmins, and harder grain, ragi or kambu, for the others. And she enjoyed feeding her husband's friends, at home and on journeys. 'Mrs C.R. prepared and sent a basketful of sweets which all of us ate with relish,' Venkatasubba Iyer wrote in his diary in June 1910.

Narasimhan, the youngest of their sons, would recall another scene: 'A tiny pebble was found in the rice. Father sent for the cook and in complete silence presented the pebble to him. That was his reprimand.'

In 1911, when he was thirty-two, C.R. was elected to the Salem Municipal Council. A year earlier he had joined in the founding of the Salem Lodge of Freemasons where Indians fraternized with whites and members assisted the needy. 'I would like to send you to England,' C.R. said to Krishnaswami, when his oldest boy was ten. According to Krishna Iyer, C.R. was the first person to buy a car in Salem when in 1912 he acquired a French-built light-grey Darracq. Learning to drive it himself, C.R. also hired a Muslim chauffeur called Ghouse.

Though Manga had been reared in strict orthodoxy — for her parents any food not cooked by themselves was taboo — she accepted her husband's reformist ways, and was innovative herself. If C.R. was ill, she would not only send offerings to a Vaishnava temple but also give money to a sweeper for a Mariamman shrine and to Ghouse for a mosque.

On special days she drew brightly-coloured kolams on the

floor. For Navaratri, C.R. would set up rows of dolls in the early hours for Papa to see on waking; she was seven in 1913. Her sister Lakshmi arrived in 1912.

The mother now of three sons and two girls, Manga was in poor health. So was C.R., troubled by asthma; even in his early thirties he was spoken of as an old man. The periods when husband and wife were both well were rare. C.R. would teach the children during such spells, Manga joining as a pupil. When she came as a young bride, she could only read Telugu. Her husband taught her to read and write Tamil. 'Father asked us to write "Avvaiyar" in Tamil,' Namagiri would remember. 'Mother was the first to spell it correctly, and was delighted.'

She was not, however, always the meek wife. Krishnaswami has recalled: 'Father had returned late, as he at times did, from a marathon talking session with friends. Mother refused to let him in and shouted, "Go and sleep at Krishnan's (Krishna Iyer's) place." '

His home, friends and the courtroom did not wholly absorb C.R.'s soul. His emotions were also intertwined — involuntarily, he could not help it — with India's political condition. Pride and honour said that India had to be freed. But could it be? C.R. would recall before fellow-prisoners in 1930 that in his mid-twenties, when Japan was succeeding against Russia, he had day-dreamt about armed revolution but realized that it was 'a hopeless task to overtake' the Raj 'in the art of armed warfare.'

The cult of the bomb, practised in 1908-9, also held no promise. He could see that 'even if 20 or 30 [British] people were killed there were more people to take their places, firm, determined and perhaps worse people.'[14] As far as political change in India was concerned, C.R. was in despair.

Something, however, was animating South Africa. From 1906 onwards, newspapers had published items about a Gujarati barrister called M.K. Gandhi, who was battling there for the rights of Indians.

An Indian, deported from South Africa, called Asari had visited Salem in 1907, stayed awhile in C.R.'s home, and said,

'Gandhi is small in size but his heart is bigger than the Shevaroys you see from Salem.'[15] Then C.R. picked up, by chance, from the desk of a friend, Henry Thoreau's *Civil Disobedience*. It seemed to supply the theory for what Gandhi was practising.

Soon another book made an impact, Gandhi's *Hind Swaraj* or 'Indian Home Rule,' sent by a friend C.R. had met in Kurnool in 1910, in which Gandhi, calling himself 'Editor,' debated violence and nonviolence with a militant who was termed 'Reader.' Perusing it 'with very great avidity,' C.R. was struck by Gandhi's refusal to 'recognize the English as superior.' Writing the book's first Indian review, C.R. said, 'Naturally, "Editor" is the better debater.'

The suggestion was that the case for violence had not been argued well enough. Not yet 'quite convinced that the use of violence was wrong,' C.R. thought that Gandhi might be induced to lead the revolutionaries.[16]

Gandhi's doings in South Africa may have had a part in a walkout that C.R. led when he found separate enclosures for whites and Indians at a sports meet in Salem convened by the British Superintendent of Police. C.R.'s mood during this period is conveyed by a conversation later recounted by him to Rama Rao. On a train journey, an Englishman sharing a first-class compartment with C.R. said, 'It is a very hot afternoon.'

'Not hot enough,' C.R. replied. 'Not hot enough? What do you mean?' 'Not hot enough,' said C.R., smiling, 'to keep you gentlemen out of India.'[17]

However, the Raj's confidence was dramatized by the Imperial Darbar held in Delhi in December 1911, with George V on the throne, and by the calm response a year later to the hurling of a bomb at Lord Hardinge, the new Viceroy, while he led a procession on elephant-back along Delhi's Chandni Chowk.

Soon C.R. learnt that 'there was no hope of catching [Gandhi] into the movement of violence.' Gandhi's account of three prison terms served by him in South Africa, published in Calcutta's *Modern Review*, left no room for doubt. Then a missionary in Salem lent him a book on Gandhi by Joseph Doke, a Presbyterian minister in South Africa; it conveyed the same conclusion.

When in September 1913 C.R. heard that Gandhi's wife and young sons had been arrested for peacefully opposing a racial tax, he felt he had to do something. He reprinted *Mr Gandhi's Jail Experiences* with his own money and his own labour, treadling a press himself. C.R.'s introduction revealed the impact on him:

> Shall we sit happy in our homes, or shall we give only our tears? It is not given to all to exhibit the strength of M.K. Gandhi. He must be ranked with the avatars . . . Let us give up perhaps a few luxuries and support them . . .

Collecting Rs 1500, C.R. sent the money via Gopal Krishna Gokhale in Poona, who was in touch with Gandhi.

Rama Rao has left an account of a visit C.R. paid him in 1911:

> Then a sub-divisional officer in Shimoga district, I was camping in a village called Rajagonda Halli, miles off the main road, looking for refuge from a recent tragedy. I had run away from friends, whose expressions of consolation can often merely be a reminder of sorrow.

> 'One day, while I was finishing the morning's work, I saw someone approach my tent. Imagine my surprise and joy when I saw it was C.R.! He was covered with dust and sweat and looked dead tired, but his face was lit with that usual smile . . . He had pedalled his way there, doing forty miles in all that day. For four days he moved with me as I did the rounds of different villages . . .

> I had flown into a rage at one village, finding that my tent had not been set up. C.R. delivered a lecture to me: 'The peasants pitching your tent and helping you in other ways are working out of custom and convention, not for wages.'[18]

At the Salem courthouse, where in the hot months a servant raised a breeze by pulling a punkah, C.R.'s lot was to defend persons accused of murder, dacoity, forgery, or the like. Though, when he saw his father in action in the courtroom, the twelve-year-old Krishnaswami 'did not think much of a job where you were on your feet all the time,' C.R. was showing remarkable results. 'He won,' according to a lawyer who, for some years was a contemporary, 'practically all his cases,'[19] and a crack did the rounds that offences in Salem were growing because criminals had faith in C.R.'s skill.

His voice mellow, his thoughts clear, his questions brief, precise in argument, deliberate in delivery and forceful in advocacy, the turbaned, black-coated C.R. brought life to a courtroom the moment he rose to speak. No transcripts of proceedings in Salem courts when C.R. practised are available, yet a picture of his style emerges from the impressions of lawyers who watched him perform.

His cross-examination was sober rather than intimidating, but it was deadly. He would ask only a few questions, some appearing innocent or pointless. Yet 'the picture presented with the answers would normally demolish the case of the prosecution.'[20] Thus he obtained an admission from a forest officer, who had charged C.R.'s client with trespass, that 'he was at home making himself merry in the company of his wife and children at the very hour when he was ostensibly . . . rounding up the culprit cutting wood in the forest range.'[21] The method was equally effective in more important cases.

Proud of a favourite son, Salem circles before long claimed that 'even Nugent Grant could not come near C.R. in cross-examination.'[22] Grant was the (British) Lord of the Madras Bar. In outclassing competitors, C.R. was helped by his skill with the English language. Other qualities observed in him included 'a unique courtroom behaviour,' 'an intuitive power to attack the weakest points in his opponent's case,' and a strong memory.[23]

A judge before whom he appeared in Coimbatore later related how, at the outset, C.R. filed scores of documents 'giving their dates and details and explaining their relevancy.' On the judge asking how C.R. could narrate all the data without 'even a scrap of paper' in his hands, C.R. 'tapped his forehead with his forefinger and said, "My notes are here." '[24]

A principle that C.R. advocated and evidently practised was that a lawyer 'should not put the case at once to the judge but lead the judge little by little and let him feel that he has himself discovered the truth.'[25] The magistrates, on occasion 'sleepy' and 'irate,' as C.R. would recall, clearly respected him, and a Salem lawyer thought that 'the European judges liked [C.R.'s] short cross-examinations and to-the-point approach.'[26]

Clients 'generally felt that if C.R. handled a case it would surely end in success.' 'There was no sessions case or criminal appeal of any importance which was not handled by him,' and vakils who lost in lower courts assumed that 'once C.R. had taken on an appeal nothing more was needed.'[27]

Joining C.R. as his junior, K. Narasimha Iyengar, later a leader himself of the Salem Bar, received the following advice from C.R.: 'Fix your fee for a case in advance. Otherwise, even when the case is won, the client will think less about his success and more about the sum that he must pay.'[28]

If his own fees, levied, as was his custom, for a case as a whole rather than for a day of hearing, were large, the number of cases C.R. accepted was small. Still, many guilty men were saved by C.R.'s skill. Such men were not always penitent. A client rescued from the gallows approached him one day and said, 'Sir, I would like to have my knife back. It is an heirloom in my family.' C.R. drove him away. He was angry at the man, and at himself and his profession.

'I can understand,' he is reported to have said at the time, 'and even forgive, a harlot who sells her body for a price, but not a lawyer who prostitutes his intellect. I am looking forward to the day when I shall quit the profession.'[29]

The sweeping attack on his vocation could not have been his considered opinion, but his conscience was raising questions. The time would come when, in a different context, he would quit law.

The outbreak of the First World War saw the Moderate Congress cooperating with the Raj. They 'expressed its profound devotion to the throne . . . and its resolve to stand by the Empire at all hazards and costs.' The Congress had met in Madras. Extremists such as C.R. were still kept out. When Lord Pentland, the Governor, paid a visit, the deferential delegates cheered.

Early in 1915, C.R. fell seriously ill. A chill had turned into severe asthma and pneumonia. On 14 February his condition was judged critical. Calling on C.R., Venkatasubba Iyer found his 'friend explaining to his father how his assets should be distributed after his exit' and 'taking leave of his wife and children.' As he wrote in his diary, Iyer felt that the doctor's prognosis was 'probably right.'[30]

Dr Mathias, the district medical officer who had been a doctor and a friend to C.R. and his family, lost his self-control and began to weep. Namagiri would later recall that C.R. said, 'Dr Mathias has lost his head. Send for Dr Narayana Iyer.'

Manga herself had an alarming fever that night. However, resolved to pray suitably for her husband's life, she tidied up her room, unlocked the box containing her valuables, took out her best jewels, and gave herself the thorough 'head bath' that was decreed by custom. Then she wore the ornaments and one of her finest saris, and supplicated Lord Venkateswara.

If her husband recovered, she promised, she would offer the jewels to the Tirupati temple. That night C.R. slept well. The morning found him better. Manga's petition seemed granted and recovery came before long.

However, she was weakening herself and needed more air and space than the yellow house offered. Selling it for Rs 4,000, C.R. rented the ground floor of the Masonic Lodge at Sooramangalam, outside Salem town. The two-storey lodge stood on a slope in about an acre of arid ground, a lone tamarind tree emphasizing its barrenness.

One of its two large rooms became Manga's sick-room, the other C.R.'s study, where his desk, surrounded by law books, was lit at night by a kerosene lantern. Both rooms had punkahs. Chakravarti Iyengar, the children, Manga's mother, helping to nurse her daughter, and visiting relatives occupied three other rooms as well as the passage that ran along the middle of the house. A kitchen (where firewood was the fuel) and a room for dining, where the family sat on the floor to eat and where at night the two cooks slept, completed the residence.

Apart from the cooks and Ghouse the chauffeur, the staff at the Sooramangalam residence consisted of two men who drove a bullock-cart, looked after the bullock and three or four cows and washed the men's clothes, a woman who cleaned and swept, and a scavenger.

Daily, the bullock-cart was used to bring water from a well

three houses away. If water was needed for the kitchen, only one of the Brahmin cooks could draw it, not a cartman. Employing a watchdog, C.R. also took in a pair of pups; a duty of the cartmen was to find meat for the dogs.

There were wooden beds for Manga and Chakravarti Iyengar, the rest, including C.R., sleeping on mattresses on the floor. After dark, kerosene lamps, cleaned daily by a servant, spread the light they could in the different rooms.

Loved as well as envied among the women in her circle, the twenty-six-year-old Manga, we can assume, fondly shared C.R.'s hopes. We can picture him showing to Manga, and translating for her, the Gandhi booklet that he had printed, and perhaps describing Kasturba's prison-going. Did Manga know that destiny was pulling C.R.?

She was declining. There were occasions when, unable to walk to the kitchen or the dining-room, she had to be carried in a wooden chair. Resigned to their mother's long spells inside her room, the children would be delighted when she sat on the veranda, or talked to them. It was an event when she went with the others in the Darracq, Ghouse at the wheel, for little Lakshmi's ear-pricking at a Rama temple.

Virtually laying aside his practice, C.R. nursed her day and night. The Salem doctors having done all they could, he sent for a Bangalore physician, Dr Nanjappa, who advised placing steamed shawls on Manga's stomach. Someone else recommended goat's milk; a goat was brought to the house.

Sleepless nights were now frequent for C.R. After one such night, he was driven by a client on a motor-cycle for a case in Namakkal. C.R. returned home exhausted but with a money-filled briefcase. He opened it before Manga, hoping that the contents would cheer her. She looked at the cash and gave a sad smile.

On the afternoon of 22 August 1915, Manga asked Krishnaswami if he had eaten dal; it was what he liked. He said that he had, and Manga was happy. At six in the evening she asked Samachar to offer prayers at a temple in the town. By the time he returned she was very weak. 'Look,' said C.R., 'Chama has returned with prasadam.' She opened her eyes, nodded, and closed them again.

To comfort Manga, now in great pain, C.R. had taken her in his lap. After some time, his legs benumbed, he gently put her back on the bed. She said: 'I am such a burden. How long can you bear me in your lap? There must be a limit.' Ten minutes later, shortly after nine at night, she became still. 'Manga!' C.R. cried. 'Manga!' There was no response. She was dead.[31]

2

Hope

1915-19

C.R. was thirty-seven and could conceal his feelings. To thirteen-year-old Krishnaswami, the oldest of his children, he said, 'I'll have time for practice now.' But he was not calm inside. Before Manga's death, seeing her anguish and finding himself, as he said later, 'unable to relieve or share it,' he had 'rebelled against God's will.'[1]

Before long he came to terms with it; but self-reproach at what he called his 'breakdown ten minutes too early'[2] lingered. However, one of C.R.'s friends, T. Vijiaraghavachariar, wrote to Krishna Iyer: 'I have not come across in my life any man who nursed his wife with such care and loving attention and who tried to be such a source of courage and hope as C.R. during the last months of his wife's illness.'[3]

Now he had to be both father and mother to his offspring. It was a blessing that Manga's mother could stay on at Sooramangalam — Narasimhan was only six and Lakshmi three. Also needing care was C.R.'s father.

The Principal of the girls' section of the Salem Municipal School, an Englishwoman, was engaged to give painting lessons at Sooramangalam to Papa. The girl, dressed for school in an ankle-length skirt, shirt and short coat, also received tuition in English in the home of the British Superintendent of Prisons, from his daughter.

The boys went to school in round dark caps, shirts and

veshtis. On one occasion, knowing that Father was not at home, Krishnaswami got at the former's revolver and cartridges; aiming at the trunk of the tamarind tree, he pulled the trigger with the forefingers of both hands.

Manga had died before fulfilling her promise to donate her jewels to Tirupati. C.R. partially implemented it after her death. Taking Krishnaswami and Ramaswami to Tirupati for their *upanayanam*, the age-old rite initiating boys into a period of learning and discipline, he gave some of the jewellery to the temple. (The pieces that remained were not destined to stay in the family. In 1921, a servant called Perumal — God — removed the valuables, including her mother's jewellery, that Namagiri, married by then, was keeping.)

About a year after Manga's death, a client offered his daughter to C.R. 'I don't wish to have a sixth child,' C.R. replied. 'I am not going to marry again,' he added. The tone was final.

The War was still on. Indian troops fought for the Empire. Schoolgirls all over India, including Papa in Salem, were asked to knit for them. The endurance of brown soldiers in the winter battles of 1914-5 in France and Flanders won acclaim. Within India, however, those wanting to widen political rights were seriously curbed by the new Defence of India Rules.

Tilak, who had been released in 1914, offered a bargain: Indian recruits against a promise of Home Rule. To strengthen his negotiating position, he formed, in April 1916, a Home Rule League. Annie Besant, a radical Irishwoman who had made India her abode and Indian emancipation her mission, also popularized the Home Rule cry.

Gokhale and Pherozeshah Mehta, leaders of the Moderate Congress, had died in 1915. In the two years that followed, Mrs Besant, bursting with energy, and Tilak, physically weak but strong of will, held the political stage.

Gandhi, who had returned to India in 1915, was in the countryside, quietly sowing his strange seeds. They had germinated in South Africa, but would they in Indian soil? One of the first Indians to feel they would was C.R.

A paper he wrote in February or March 1916, 'M.K. Gandhi: His Message to India,' brings this out. Unlike Tilak and Mrs Besant, Gandhi had advocated unconditional Indian help to the Empire at War, thereby disappointing most Extremists. Not, however, C.R., who discerned that once Gandhi decided to oppose an injustice, he would fight harder than anyone else.

As C.R. saw it, Gandhi was prepared to attack not just the symptoms but the source and strength of the Raj — the civilization that sustained it. According to Gandhi, C.R. wrote, there was 'no use blaming the English, for they came and remain only because of us . . . By adopting their civilization, we retain them . . . But for [Indian] lawyers and judges and policemen, who are first cousins, no foreign rule would be possible.'

The solution was to expel the imported civilization, remembering, at the same time, that Indian weaknesses had produced 'child-marriage, baby-mothers, girl-widows, polyandry, inequalities of caste, prostitution in the name of religion [and] animal sacrifice.'

Above all, C.R. pointed out, Gandhi (referred to as Mr Gandhi in the paper) was ready to 'disregard unjust commands, laws repugnant to . . . conscience,' and to 'accept the penalty for [their] breach.' In South Africa, Gandhi had shown that 'there are no limitations to the power of human character with resolution and suffering.'

With prescience, C.R. said that whether or not Indians should turn to Gandhi's approach, pitting 'soul force'—the force of gladly invited suffering — against 'the force of arms' was 'a great question that has to be considered some time or other.'[4]

Seeing Gandhi for the first time in 1916, Jawaharlal Nehru, born in the UP of Kashmiri parents, found him 'very distant and different and unpolitical.'[5] Of Gujarati peasant lineage, Vallabhbhai Patel was playing bridge when Gandhi walked past him at Ahmedabad's Gujarat Club. Patel 'took stock of him, was not impressed and returned to the game.'[6] In 1917, in his province, the Bihari lawyer Rajendra Prasad watched Gandhi in action among the indigo peasants of Champaran. Abul Kalam Azad, the Bengal-based Muslim ideologue, met Gandhi first in 1920.

These five, C.R., Patel, Jawaharlal, Prasad and Azad, were to form, for nearly three decades, the core of Gandhi's political team. As Jawaharlal put it in a 1949 letter to Prasad, 'the public generally have looked up to us five persons' as 'the old guard.'[7]

Of the five C.R. was the fourth to meet Gandhi, Azad being the last. But C.R. was the first to note the glimmer on the horizon. One of the opening sentences of his 1916 paper said:

> Led by him, our brothers and sisters of South Africa had so acted that Indians may forget their unworthiness for a time and walk proudly in the world.

Meanwhile, also in 1916, he had joined Mrs Besant's Home Rule League and assembled a League unit in Salem. Congress met at Lucknow in December 1916 and asked for a proclamation from Britain that she would 'confer Self-Government on India at an early date.'

The Muslim League, founded in 1906, had been convened in Lucknow at the same time, and Congress and the League agreed on a scheme of self-government with quotas for Muslims in provincial legislatures and in a Central Assembly. The principle of the League's demand for a separate electorate for Muslims was conceded. Tilak, Annie Besant, and M.A. Jinnah, the League president, were the architects of the concordat.

Raised now by both Hindus and Muslims, the Home Rule slogan spread, despite stringent Press laws, to many parts of the land. Two Governors reacted on behalf of a perturbed Raj. In the Punjab, Sir Michael O'Dwyer accused Home Rule champions of 'revolutionary and subversive' intentions. And the Madras Governor, Lord Pentland, declaring that 'all thought of the early grant of responsible Self-Government should be put entirely out of mind,' referred to 'the possibility of coercive measures' against Home Rule campaigners.[8]

It was at Pentland that C.R.'s first public attack on a British official was directed. In a letter published in *The Hindu*, C.R. asked the Madras Presidency to express itself clearly 'so that there will be no mistake about what people think of His Excellency's pronouncement.' Reminding the Governor that in the agitation for Home Rule 'so far not a single act of violence or even technical illegality has been noticed in the Presidency,' he turned to the threat of 'coercive measures':

> Our consciences being clear, we can but await calmly the
> effect of such repressive measures on a people hitherto peaceful
> and law-abiding.

A protest meeting in Salem followed; 'the large representative
gathering' (it included Muslims) unanimously passed a resolution
moved by C.R., criticizing the Governor's 'astonishing and
unconstitutional attitude.'⁹

Pentland acted. Mrs Besant and her associates Wadia and
Arundale were interned in the Nilgiris on 16 June under the
Defence of India Rules. C.R. and his allies 'met informally' next
morning and convened a public meeting for the evening. Despite
heavy rain a large crowd assembled and cabled its protest to
Prime Minister Lloyd George. Next day the Salem Home Rule
League demanded Lord Pentland's recall.

Lloyd George's remedy was to ask thirty-six-year-old Edwin
Montagu to take the place of Austen Chamberlain as Secretary
of State for India. On 20 August, Montagu made an unexpected
declaration in London. 'Substantial steps' would be taken, he
said, in the direction of 'the progressive realization of responsible
government in India as an integral part of the British Empire.'
And on 16 September Mrs Besant and her associates were
released.

Her name now on most people's lips, Mrs Besant took a
train on the night of 20 September for Madras. To forestall
demonstrations of support, the Government banned the sale of
platform tickets at stops on the way. An important halt, which
came in the middle of the night, was Salem.

A fair crowd gathered at the station despite the lateness of
the hour. On its behalf C.R. asked for platform tickets. 'Not
being issued,' he was told.

'I will keep the crowd calm,' said C.R. 'Please sell the
tickets.'

'Sorry, they are not being sold.'

'You are depriving the railways of revenue,' C.R. argued.

'We have orders not to sell.'

The train came. 'Follow me,' said C.R., as he strode
towards the platform. The crowd followed him, welcomed Mrs

Besant, and remained calm. C.R. faced no consequences—the Raj did not want to add to his importance.[10]

But C.R. also had an ear for tunes other than of freedom. The felling of a Salem tree elicited a letter from him in the Madras *Mail*. In 1916 he launched, with some associates, the Tamil Scientific Terms Society, and edited the Society's journal, which proposed Tamil equivalents for terms in botany, chemistry, physics, physiology, astronomy, and arithmetic.

Though the journal died after four issues, C.R.'s interest in the subject survived. In subsequent years, he would write Tamil booklets with titles like *Can It Be Done In Tamil?*, *Chemistry on the Front Verandah*, and *The Domestic Life of Plants*.

The Empire asked India for fresh recruits in 1918, the fifth year of the War. India seemed willing to help, at a price, which was going up. Proclaiming the principle of self-determination, President Wilson had whetted India's political desires. Indian soldiers returning from the front were beginning to ask for equality of treatment. Inflation and shortages, products of the War, led to unhappiness.

Yet it looked as if a handsome political offer might satisfy Indian sentiment. It was known that an offer was going to be made. In October 1917, the Secretary of State, Montagu, arrived in India, the first holder of his office to do so. Touring and receiving deputations on a prodigious scale, he sparked off speculation on the degree of self-government that India would get.

Elected Congress President, Annie Besant altered her stance. She had hopes in Montagu. Urging India to help with the War, she dropped her pre-conditions. Unconditional support was Gandhi's stand too. 'Let the Montagu offer come,' said Tilak.

Sharing Tilak's views, C.R. fought against unqualified support when the South's politically-minded intellectuals gathered in Conjeevaram (Kancheepuram) for the Madras Provincial Conference of May 1918. With this conference C.R. leaves the periphery of Indian politics and mounts the stage.

Sarojini Naidu, the poetess, was presiding. Mrs Besant proposed a resolution of unconditional support. An amendment to make the support conditional was moved by S. Satyamurti, who would soon become prominent in South Indian politics and in the Central Assembly.

Backing Satyamurti's amendment, C.R. reminded the gathering of Tilak's stand. In a thrust aimed at Mrs Besant, he added that popular opinion 'should on no account be subordinated to the changing views of a few leaders.' Annie Besant defended her position. When hands were counted, 140 were for Satyamurti's amendment and 118 against. From Mrs Besant's side, however, came a demand for voting against a roll-call.

C.R. at once objected. Plain-clothes policemen were present. While hands raised by a seated flock were almost anonymous, 'ayes' pronounced when names were individually called would expose supporters of the amendment.

Mrs Naidu ruled in favour of a roll-call. The result was a tie, each side obtaining 118 votes. Fear had neutralized 22 participants. Mrs Naidu's casting vote went against the amendment, amidst loud cries of 'shame.'

Unafraid, C.R. had stood up to Mrs Besant. He had also been alert, instantly seeing through the roll-call plea. Also, his persuasive powers had been in evidence. Writing to *The Hindu*, a Tinnevelly (Tirunelveli) lawyer said that he had seen that C.R. could 'convert many others.' Another participant, K.S. Venkataraman, left Conjeevaram with the impression that 'if there was to be a leader who could lead the South as Tilak was doing in Upper India, it was none other than C.R.'[11]

In June came the reform document, the Montagu-Chelmsford Report, named after the Secretary and the Viceroy, and soon to be known as the Montford Report. It proposed partial self-government for the provinces, worked by elected legislatures and 'Cabinets' of Indian Ministers. However, vital subjects were reserved for the Governor and the Executive Council that he nominated, and Members of the Council were to be far more influential than Ministers of the Cabinet. And Central powers were not to be shared at all.

What to Montagu was a leap appeared a crawl to many Indians. Not, however, to the Moderates, who welcomed the Report. To counter them a Nationalists Association was formed in the South, with Kasturiranga Iyengar, editor of *The Hindu*, as chairman and C.R. as secretary.

C.R. declared that Congress now had to think about 'the form of agitation . . . that we should organize in order to compel more genuine reforms.'[12] Madras sent a fair contingent of Nationalists to Bombay, where Congressmen gathered from all parts of India for a special meeting.

The session's leading lights were the candid Chittaranjan Das, Bengal's foremost lawyer, and the dignified Madan Mohan Malaviya of the United Provinces, spokesman of the conservatives. In a demonstration of unity, Malaviya moved a resolution first drafted by Das. Modified by C.R., the resolution reminded the Government of the Lucknow Scheme for Home Rule and termed the Montford reforms 'disappointing and unsatisfactory.'

'This thin Madrasi,' said Das, pointing to C.R., 'put a comma here, a semicolon there, inserted a phrase here, removed one there . . . and within a few minutes he was able to give us an acceptable resolution.' C.R.'s role delighted the Madras contingent. 'Returning home,' K.S. Venkataraman would recall, 'we felt as if we had conquered an empire.'[13]

It was reported that Tilak, with whom C.R. talked in Bombay, had said that Salem was too small a place for the forty-year-old C.R. In any case, Kasturiranga Iyengar urged C.R. to make Madras his base, while his paper, *The Hindu*, noted that 'very great enthusiasm prevailed' at a political conference that C.R. organized in Salem, with '300 delegates and 1,500 visitors present.'[14]

Increasingly playing a political role, C.R. was also elected, in June 1917, Chairman of the Salem Municipal Council. Though the rules permitted a municipal council to select a chairman from outside its ranks, the provision was rarely used. In 1917 Salem had reasons for doing so. Plague had afflicted the town. Also, an extension to the town had been planned.

The courtroom giving him only partial satisfaction, C.R. was willing to accept the challenge involved in the Chairmanship. In the first year of C.R.'s term, the municipality earned Rs 94,794, of which Rs 35,392 came from house tax and Rs 33,346 for water and drainage. Tolls fetched about Rs 10,000. In the next year the town's income rose to Rs 1,14,852.

Running a few schools and a hospital were some of the municipality's chief concerns. (In 1917 there were 671 deaths from plague in Salem, 115 from imported cholera and 108 from small-pox.) The civic body was expected, too, to supply water to the town, remove its refuse, clean and light up its streets, and, if possible, add to its classrooms and dispensaries. However, its resources were pitifully inadequate.

His council did not even have the money, C.R. was to complain, to pay a doctor for a periodical examination of Salem's schoolchildren, scarcely a multitude at the time. Reporting to the provincial government, Davis, Salem district's British Collector, wrote that C.R. sought 'to put [the municipality's] finances in order, even at the cost of much harshness.'[15] When a clerk appointed by him reported a second illness within the space of a few days and asked for long leave, C.R. ended his services, observing that 'the municipal office cannot afford to employ a sickly person.'[16]

Salem Extension owed something to C.R.'s initiative. Before he was thought of as Chairman, he had argued in Madras for the municipality's right to acquire land at the edge of the town. When the municipality auctioned sites in the Extension, C.R. bought a plot himself. Three months later, he became Chairman.

Gavel in hand, he auctioned a fresh batch of sites. Profits from the auctions helped reduce the town's accumulated arrears.

During his spell as Chairman, C.R. selected, for lifelong opposition, two demons: liquor and untouchability. Liquor was pauperizing Salem's handloom weavers. At C.R.'s prodding the Municipal Council asked the Government to curtail its availability. Persuaded by C.R., the weavers made a similar appeal at what *The Hindu* described as 'two remarkable meetings' (15.11.17).

A joint council that included E.W. Legh, the Collector,

C.R., and Sweeting, the Police Superintendent, then decided that the number of arrack shops in Salem should go down from fourteen to six, with none in the centre of town. The hours of sale were reduced, and the employment of women inside liquor shops banned.

Three incidents revealed C.R.'s stand on caste. One involved a preacher belonging to a depressed caste, Swami Sahajananda, who visited Salem in 1917. A feast for the Swami was arranged in the home of C.R.'s friend Yagyanarayana Iyer, the Brahmin principal of Salem College. The Chairman attended.

Iyer had committed, and C.R. had abetted, a social crime. The horrified majority of Salem's Brahmins ostracized the two and other Brahmin accomplices. Excluded at weddings and funerals, they were also told that priests would not conduct annual ceremonies for the dead in their homes. To reduce reliance on priests, some of the culprits memorized the religious texts themselves.

The second incident was related to water. In different wards of the town, the municipality's employees turned on the water taps every morning and turned them off every evening. In July 1918, one of the employees, an 'untouchable', was assigned to the public tap in the agraharam.

This had been the doing not of C.R. but of one of his close friends, the engineer responsible for the town's water supply, A.V. Raman. All the same, an 'untouchable' was defiling the Brahmins' water. There was an outcry. A hundred 'respectable and responsible ratepayers' asked the council to move the employee to another ward, and letters in *The Hindu* attacked C.R.

As *The Hindu* wrote, 'There was a sensational meeting of the municipal council.' 'A number' of "untouchables", the paper added, 'crowded round the meeting hall.' Inside, a Brahmin deputation pressed its view. The council was evenly divided. C.R. cast the Chairman's vote to keep the employee in the agraharam. As a result, C.R. would later recall, Brahmin widows 'cast looks of hatred' at C.R. A friend asked him, 'Do you wish to kill my grandmother? She has not eaten for two days.'[17]

C.R. was unyielding, and after a while the resistance subsided. Hurdles again arose when he wanted to send two 'untouchable' students to Salem's Technical Training School. The Indian headmaster and the European inspector were unwilling to take them but an insistent C.R. again had his way.

Goaded by his conscience, C.R. was taking an attitude in 1917-8 that K. Kamaraj, Chief Minister of Madras from 1954 to 1962, would characterize as 'revolutionary at that time.'[18] Among those offended by it was the Chairman's father. Discovering once that his grandson Narasimhan, then six, had consumed lemonade in the home of an Anglo-Indian official, violating the caste code, Chakravarti Iyengar berated the boy, but C.R. told Narasimhan, 'You have done nothing wrong.'

Chakravarti Iyengar wondered whether a priest would preside at his cremation, but there is no record of his asking his son to retrace his steps. In the father's feelings about his son, pride and admiration outweighed disagreement.

There was no controversy in Salem regarding C.R.'s sense of duty. As unpaid Chairman he was spending six hours a day in the municipal office, forgoing professional earnings, and combining in himself the twin roles of a Municipal Chairman and an executive officer or Commissioner of the future.

A year after C.R. had become Chairman, Legh, the Collector, told the Madras Government that C.R. was giving 'personal attention to public business,' and R.A. Graham, Secretary in the Madras Government, minuted 'the energy and ability of the Chairman' of Salem municipality.[19] Seven months later, at the end of January 1919, C.R. resigned his position.

Attending the council for the last time (he had chaired over fifty of its meetings), C.R. spoke of the 'liberal and sympathetic attitude' of Legh, who was leaving Salem. C.R. added that Legh was 'not one of those who believed that they could not serve under Indian ministers responsible to the people of this country.' Here C.R. was explicitly anticipating Swaraj, for which, in retrospect, his role at the head of the Salem council was a useful apprenticeship.

By July 1919, the ex-Chairman of the Salem municipality had not only actively joined an agitation against the Raj; his role was known to the Raj's officials. Nonetheless, in a confidential note to the Government of Madras, Salem's new Collector, E.A. Davis, wrote that month of C.R. as a person ·'of whose work I have heard nothing but good.'[20]

Withal, he was a lawyer, though his practice had been curtailed. And it was as a lawyer that he drew attention throughout the South in 1918-9.

Dr P. Varadarajulu Naidu, a popular Tamil speaker, had been arrested and charged with sedition for remarks addressed to a few thousand mill-workers in Madras. C.R. defended Naidu, whose trial commenced in Madura, now Madurai, in September 1918. The large crowd that gathered outside the court was fired at; two were killed. Next day, ignoring a machine-gun placed atop the courthouse and the marching of the military up and down the town, 25,000 assembled to protest.

South India remained interested in the proceedings which lasted until April the following year. Throngs daily waited outside the courtroom and the papers reproduced every word uttered inside.

The sedition law sanctioned prosecution on the recommendation of the Governor-in-Council. The Madura public prosecutor, C. Krishnan Nair, showed the court a telegram from Ooty, the Presidency's summer capital; that, he said, was the authority for Naidu's arrest.

'Does the telegram prove the sanction of the Governor-in-Council?' C.R. asked Nair. The prosecutor admitted that it did not contain sufficient proof. It was on the case's merits, however, that C.R. wanted to win. He disputed the text of Naidu's speech given to the court and, according to *The Hindu*, 'showed how the report was inaccurate.'

Quoting other Indian lecturers, C.R. demonstrated that Naidu had 'treated in far milder language' than theirs 'matters of the deepest importance to us.' Even the Government's version showed that Naidu had not challenged India's connection with the Empire; this, C.R. maintained, ruled out sedition.

The day before a three-week vacation, giving the judge a list of witnesses on whom he proposed to rely, C.R. made a plea that the names be kept confidential during the vacation. He feared improper influence on his witnesses.

Judge: It is always my practice to give the list [to the other side].

C.R.: Whatever might be the practice in this court, it should not be held valid in the present case . . .

Judge: I do not see any reason to deviate from the practice.

C.R.: This is the first case of its kind. I do not think Your Honour has decided such cases.

After a marathon defence, C.R. left the 'judgement in the care of Your Honour's sense of justice, religion and conscience.' Though S.V. Nargunam, the magistrate, heard him with courtesy, C.R. did not expect an acquittal. A man like Nargunam, both a judge and a district officer under the Collector, could hardly decide against the Government in a sedition case.

Soon after the trial began, C.R. aired his misgivings. At a Home Rule meeting in Madura, he asked: 'How could they possibly expect, when the Crown was so directly . . . against the accused person, that the accused person could have a fair . . . trial at the hands of a Magistrate who . . . held the appointment at the pleasure of the Crown?'

The Government wanted to sue C.R. for contempt of court but dropped the idea. It would have alienated the public afresh and added to C.R.'s popularity.

Nargunam pronounced as expected, sentencing Naidu to 15 months' rigorous imprisonment. An appeal went to the Madras High Court, where three judges, of whom two were British, acquitted Naidu, without discussing his speech, on the technical ground that C.R. had spotted at the outset: lack of proof of the sanction of the Governor-in-Council. The Salem advocate tasted victory and fame.[21]

As 1919 opened, India seemed a reliable, even if dissatisfied, member of the Empire. The War had ended the previous November. Meeting in Delhi in December, Congress congratulated the King and reaffirmed their loyalty to him.

Anxiety emanated, however, from the recommendations of

a committee on sedition headed by an English judge, Sir Sydney Rowlatt. These included, for suspected seditionists, arrests without trial and trials without appeal; a two-year prison term was proposed for offences like carrying a seditious pamphlet.

Their eyes fixed on the Montford Reforms, many Congressmen chose not to see the Rowlatt hazard, but C.R. was perturbed. In January he complained that the proposals 'have not received a tithe of the attention which the Reform Scheme has been honoured with,' adding that 'even our Bar Associations have not thought fit to examine the proposals, which threatened to set aside all legal traditions . . . not temporarily but for all time.'

The remarks were made at Trichnopoly, or Trichy, where he presided at a Home Rule League conference. He anticipated, in his short (and remarkably Gandhi-like) address, many of the key elements, short-term and permanent, of the struggle that was to come. 'Never allow yourself to be injured or insulted,' he exhorted. 'Stand up for your rights always.' 'We lost our liberties,' C.R. added, 'by reason of weaknesses in national life.'

His most important remark, however, related to what he called 'this disastrous legislation' — the Rowlatt proposals. Said C.R.:

> The matter is serious enough for an anxious examination of the principles and propriety of *opposing it with the entire soul-force of the nation*.[22] (Author's italics.)

The Rowlatt sword fell on 6 February 1919. Two Bills were introduced in the Imperial Legislative Council in Delhi. Non-official members opposed the measures with eloquence and logic, but the decision of the nominated majority was a foregone conclusion.

Political India could lament. It could warn. Could it do more? One man had the grit to turn dismay into defiance. Though quite seriously ill at the time, Gandhi decided to pit satyagraha, or soul force, against the Bills: he would refuse, he declared in the second week of February, to obey the Bills if they became law.

A month earlier, C.R., who was yet to meet Gandhi, had

asked for the technique that had seemed to work in South Africa to be applied in India. Even before they met each other, the two had embraced the same thought.

In January 1919 C.R. made up his mind to migrate to Madras. Salem limited his growing public role. Many had reminded him of this fact, including Kasturiranga Iyengar, and men such as K.S. Venkataraman who looked up to him. 'You have won after all,' he told Venkataraman towards the end of January.

Kasturiranga Iyengar told C.R. that a house in Madras he owned on Cathedral Road was available. Informing Iyengar that he would rent it, C.R. also proposed that Gandhi, who by mid-February was asking for signatories to a pledge of resistance to the Rowlatt Bills, be invited to Madras. Gandhi could stay with him, C.R. added.

Iyengar sent a letter inviting Gandhi, who was glad to get the word. Though, on 24 February, six persons in Ahmedabad, including Barrister Vallabhbhai Patel and Sarojini Naidu, signed the pledge along with Gandhi, and a Satyagraha Sabha had begun functioning in Bombay, top-ranking Congressmen had on the whole avoided him. They were not sure about satyagraha.

Madras offered Gandhi an opening. Though still shaky in health, he decided to take it. He was in Delhi, where he had gone to plead with the Viceroy, Lord Chelmsford, against the Bills. Consideration of one was postponed, but the other was a sufficient fetter.

Gandhi's secretary, Mahadev Desai, was with him on the long journey from Delhi to Madras in the middle of March. On the train Desai informed Gandhi that the man behind the request from the South was C.R. We do not know how Desai knew.

C.R.'s last weeks at Sooramangalam had been busier than ever. He resigned as Municipal Chairman but would return home late, and read. Wanting to draw his attention one night, Papa, then twelve, asked him, 'Are you reading for a law case?' Her father smiled and said, 'I am reading about breaking laws.'

'We are going to Madras,' he announced one day. Early in

March 1919, accompanied by Papa, Narasimhan, aged nine, Lakshmi, six years old, and Manga's mother, who had continued to look after Lakshmi, C.R. boarded the train for the Presidency's capital. His father as well as Krishnaswami, sixteen, and Ramaswami, fourteen, who had to complete the term at Salem College, were left behind with C.R.'s brother Srinivasa. Also left behind was a house slowly rising on C.R.'s plot in the Extension.

Built on two floors and surrounded by coconut and mango trees, the Cathedral Road house in Madras, for which C.R. paid a monthly rent of Rs 230, stood where the Chola Hotel stands today. Two cooks were found. Ghouse brought the car. Bundles of law books were carted from Salem. C.R. furnished his study on the upper floor with a desk and chairs made in the School of Arts; a sculptured chest of drawers with brass handles went against the wall.

Dressed in a rough white handspun and handwoven or khadi kurta and a khadi dhoti and donning the white cap that he had recently designed, a weary Gandhi arrived in Madras on the morning of 18 March. Desai was with him. C.R., who had signed Gandhi's satyagraha pledge the previous day, stood inconspicuously in the welcoming group at the station.

In the evening the news came that the Legislative Council in Delhi had passed one of the Rowlatt Bills. Only the Viceroy's assent remained. Then what? Satyagraha, Gandhi had said. Yet how precisely would one disobey the Rowlatt law? An unjust order not to attend a meeting or enter a town could be disobeyed, but the Rowlatt law was a threat, not an order. How did one fight a threat?

Gandhi wrestled with the question. For the first two days of his stay in Madras, Gandhi did not know that the bespectacled lawyer who was around was his host. Informed that the bungalow belonged to Kasturiranga Iyengar, who had sent him the letter of invitation, Gandhi thought he was the editor's guest.

Correcting Gandhi, Desai also advised him to cultivate C.R., 'who,' as Gandhi would recall afterwards, 'from his innate shyness kept himself constantly in the background.'[23] Gandhi acted on Desai's advice. For three successive days he and C.R.

discussed the Rowlatt law.

Word that Lord Chelmsford had signed the Bill was received on 22 March. Early next morning, while, as Gandhi put it, he was still in the 'twilight condition between sleep and consciousness,' an idea came to him, as if in a dream. An hour or so later he told C.R. about it:

> We should call upon the country to observe a general hartal. Satyagraha . . . is a sacred fight . . . Let all the people of India, therefore suspend their business on that day and observe the day as one of fasting and prayer . . . It is very difficult to say whether all the provinces would respond to this appeal of ours or not but I feel fairly sure of Bombay, Madras, Bihar, and Sind.

C.R. 'was at once taken up' with the suggestion of his guest, who drafted a call to the nation.[24] Gandhi had found the next step and was at peace. On 25 March, two days after Gandhi left Madras, the city's Commissioner of Police informed the Government of the opening of a branch of Gandhi's movement 'in the home of Mr C. Rajagopalachari, late of Salem.'

He had learnt, the Commissioner added, that a few invited to become secretaries of the Madras branch were 'reluctant to accept the nomination on some ground or other.'[25] This was understandable. Gandhi's proposal was untried; it could also land sponsors in trouble. It was C.R., 'late of Salem', who became secretary of the Satyagraha Sabha of Madras and who moved, at a meeting on 30 March, the resolution asking the South to observe the hartal.

The appointed day, 6 April, was wonder. Nobody knew quite how it all came about. Almost the whole of India, from one end to the other, towns as well as villages, observed a complete hartal.

C.R. marvelled. He had not imagined this outcome while proposing Gandhi's southern visit. Referring to Madras, he wrote in *The Hindu* (7.4.19): 'As if by magic the whole city was stilled to prayer.' In the evening, he added, 'it was one surging mass of humanity' from 'Napier's Bridge to San Thome' that gathered on the beach, listening to speeches relayed by human voices from a series of spaced platforms.

An intelligence officer named Moore submitted an identical report to the Government:

All shops, big and small, were closed. Coffee hotels and vegetable and milk-stalls were also not open. Vendors of curd were not seen, and even the women who sell rice cakes in the morning did not do so today.

Moore said, too, that the crowd on the beach was 'unanimously considered to have been the largest gathering . . . on such an occasion in Madras.'[26]

A week earlier C.R. had spoken of 'Mr Gandhi.' Now he employed a phrase that some, including the poet Tagore, were using — Mahatma. 'The fiat of the Satyagraha Mahatma,' said C.R. in *The Hindu*, (7.4.19), 'had been observed by all of India, by the high and the low, as if he had all the armies and the police forces . . . of the Indian government behind his word.' 'Can soul force,' he asked, 'be any longer denied?'

Within days the movement entered another phase — of peaceful and open sale of banned books, provided they were free from violent thoughts. These included the Mahatma's *Hind Swaraj* and his translation of Ruskin's *Unto This Last*.

In Madras, with C.R.'s help, a sheet that was deliberately unregistered, *Satyagrahi*, was published. In a leaflet dated 12 May, preserved in the Raj's archives, C.R. said:

Let it be clearly understood that we would oppose such legislation vesting in the executive Government the absolute right to suspect and imprison without trial even if the Government is democratic and purely Indian, and not bureaucratic and foreign . . .[27]

C.R. now cut the chains that were tying him. For all their value, the courts were sustaining the Raj. This was Gandhi's view and in theory C.R. had agreed. Now he ended his practice, before quite beginning it in Madras. The law books carefully brought from Salem were never unpacked.

Also, he would cease wearing his finely textured clothes. Following Gandhi, he and his children would wear khadi, which would spread across India as the livery of revolt and a symbol of identification with the lowly.

When one day a large green roll of coarse thick fabric turned up at home, seven-year-old Lakshmi asked her father if it was a carpet. It was not. She and her sister and brothers were going to be clothed in it.

3

Battle

1919-21

Hindus and Muslims were acting as one — Gandhi was invited to speak in a Bombay mosque, and Swami Shraddhanand, leader of the Arya Samaj, in Delhi's Jama Masjid. The breadth of opposition hurt the Empire's prestige, which received a stunning blow in April 1919 in Amritsar, the holy city of the Sikhs.

The Punjab had been tense for some time. Methods used to recruit soldiers and raise loans for the War had caused resentment. On their part, the British were disposed to believe rumours of an Afghan invasion.

The April hartal, enthusiastically observed all over the province, passed off fairly peacefully in Amritsar, but hostility was in the air. Two Congress leaders, Dr Satyapal, a Hindu, and Dr Saifuddin Kitchlew, a Muslim, pressed Gandhi to visit the Punjab and be a calming influence.

However, annoyed by the hartal, Sir Michael O'Dwyer, the Punjab's Governor, prevented the Mahatma's entry. On 10 April, Gandhi was taken off his train at the Punjab border and compelled to return to Bombay under escort; for part of the journey he was confined in a goods train.

O'Dwyer also had Satyapal and Kitchlew arrested and removed from Amritsar. A procession of protesters was fired at. In revenge, the infuriated crowd killed five or six Englishmen in their offices, and Miss Sherwood, a schoolmistress, was assaulted.

Next day, Amritsar was taken over by General Reginald Dyer, a professional soldier born in Simla. He prohibited meetings but the ban was proclaimed only in English. On the afternoon of 13 April, over 10,000 people, Sikhs, Hindus and Muslims, assembled at Jallianwala Bagh, a public ground enclosed on three sides by five-foot-high walls. Speakers sat on a platform on the open side. Not many in the audience were aware of Dyer's ban, and none had firearms.

Suddenly, the meeting barely begun, Dyer appeared with 50 rifle-carrying Gurkha and Baluchi soldiers, occupied the speakers' platform, and — without asking the audience to disperse — ordered fire. His men obeyed, for ten death-filled minutes. The trapped gathering could only shriek and fall in heaps. Almost every bullet got a man; according to official figures, 379 were killed and over 1,100 injured.

O'Dwyer imposed martial law throughout the Punjab. In Amritsar, Dyer decreed that any Indian passing along the street where Miss Sherwood was attacked would crawl, Indians on vehicles or horses would dismount at the sight of a British officer and salaam him, and hundreds of students would walk 16 miles a day for roll-calls. Violators were flogged at a public whipping post. Elsewhere in the province men were stripped and beaten, and in two places groups of peasants were bombed from the air. A non-existent revolutionary plot was crushed.

Two days before the Jallianwala killing, C.R. had assailed the bar against Gandhi and said that if anyone could 'keep the satyagraha movement true to its principles it is Mr Gandhi'(*The Hindu*, 11.4.19). Later, he claimed that the Punjab violence would have been averted had the Mahatma been allowed to enter the province.

The Mahatma, however, divided the blame between the Raj and his countrymen. The latter had rioted in Bombay and Ahmedabad because he was forcibly turned back at the Punjab border. Shocked at their violence, Gandhi fasted in Ahmedabad for three days and restored peace.

As for the Punjab, though sharing the view that his visit there might have averted the tragedy, Gandhi was disturbed by the province's two-sided violence. He concluded that he had committed a 'Himalayan blunder' in launching his campaign without disciplining the masses. The satyagraha was suspended.

In a letter to C.R., Gandhi explained that 'the spiritual cause of the temporary setback' was the satyagraha's impurity. In a subsequent letter Gandhi revealed his reliance on C.R. and the closeness established between the two:

> I have written so much in order to share with you my inmost thoughts as they came to me this morning. It is now 6.30 a.m. For on you and the few we are will be the burden.[1]

Though C.R. noted that 'ardent spirits' were 'disappointed and dispirited'[2] by the suspension, his regard for Gandhi had increased: the Mahatma was plainly interested in his struggle's integrity. However, Willingdon, Pentland's successor as Governor of Madras, called Gandhi a 'Bolshevik.'[3]

In London some tried to take a balanced view. In a private cable to the Viceroy, Montagu, Secretary of State for India, said:

> I have never heard of a case in which the appearance of Gandhi has not had a tranquillising effect. It certainly had in Ahmedabad and Bombay during the recent riots . . . So far as I can hear, Gandhi is a man who has always kept his word.[4]

But the sahibs in India saw things differently. According to a later British view, they had 'stiffened into amoral solidarity: Englishmen backed each other right or wrong.'[5]

Indians sympathetic to the Raj were horrified by Jallianwala. Tagore renounced his knighthood. In July, the Raj formed a commission under Lord Hunter to sift the Punjab evidence. Congress set up an inquiry of its own, to be conducted by Gandhi, Motilal Nehru, the successful Allahabad lawyer, and C.R. Das of Bengal.

First Rowlatt, then the Punjab and finally Khilafat struck at the concept of Empire. The Allies were considering the terms to be imposed on Turkey, defeated in the War along with Germany. The Sultan of Turkey was the Khalifa, or head, of the faithful; the vast majority of Indian Muslims gave him allegiance and recognized his suzerainty over the Arab lands that contained Islam's holiest sites.

David Lloyd George, the British Premier, had said that the Allies were not 'fighting to deprive Turkey of the rich and renowned lands of Asia Minor.'[6] Depending on this assurance, a number of Indian Muslims had swallowed their reluctance and soldiered for the Empire against Turkey.

Now, in August 1919, it transpired that Britain meant to end the Khalifa's suzerainty and give control over the holy places to Arab chieftains. To Indian Muslims this was a betrayal and a sacrilege. Seeking to undo the wrong, they found a champion in Gandhi — and also in C.R.

A believer in Hindu-Muslim partnership from his South African days if not earlier, Gandhi had been heartened by signs of entente during the anti-Rowlatt agitation. To him the chance that the Khilafat question offered for cementing the Hindu-Muslim relationship and weakening if not ousting the Raj was 'not going to recur for the next hundred years' (*Collected Works* 18:180).

As over Rowlatt, the Congress was slow to respond to Gandhi. C.R., however, was once more on the Mahatma's wavelength. Later he would recall a conversation that took place at the start of the Khilafat stir. 'Is it not a beautiful thing,' he said to Gandhi, 'that India could present the spectacle of one religion not merely tolerating but actually fighting for a sister religion?' Apparently Gandhi's 'eyes flashed' as he replied, 'Isn't it beautiful?'[7]

In August 1919 C.R. made his first Khilafat move by initiating a resolution at the Madras Provincial Conference in Trichy, demanding that Islam's holy places remain with the Khalifa. Reminding the audience that some Muslim leaders arrested during the War for alleged pro-Turkish sympathies were still in jail, including the outspoken brothers Shaukat and Muhammad Ali, C.R. warned that many Muslim newspapers 'had been gagged' and that 'Muslim feeling in India ran high' (*The Hindu*, 22.8.19).

His doings were not all political — the mathematician, Ramanujam, as yet insufficiently recognized and struggling, was his house guest for a month. But C.R. was being watched, and in November the Government of Madras informed Delhi that C.R., still described as 'a Salem vakil,' had persuaded the

Hindus 'with the result that on the 17th [of October] most of the shops and the Bazaar were closed.'[8]

To the Raj a Hindu-Muslim alliance was neither natural nor welcome. But it began to take shape. The Khilafatists met in Delhi towards the end of November to consider steps if their fears materialized. Gandhi was asked to preside. Searching for a suitable riposte on behalf of Hindu and Muslim India, Gandhi came up with 'non-cooperation.'

Not yet spelt out, non-cooperation seemed a weapon of sharp edge. However, Britain's terms for Turkey were not final as yet and Gandhi was prepared to wait for a revision.

In December 1919 Congress met in Amritsar, the venue reminding people that Jallianwala remained to be redressed. Gandhi noted two positive signs — the Ali brothers were released while the Congress was meeting, and the Rowlatt Act, while not repealed, was not being used.

For the Amritsar session, C.R. made his first journey to North India. Motilal Nehru presided but Gandhi was the central figure. The Ali brothers arrived straight from prison, Muhammad Ali announcing that he was holding 'a return ticket.' The phrase would be repeated by thousands in the years to follow.

The resolution on Jallianwala proposed at Amritsar called for the removal of Dyer from his command, the resignation of O'Dwyer, and the recall of the Viceroy; it also expressed hope that the Hunter Commission would recommend justice.

For Gandhi this was not enough. He asked the session to include a condemnation of the Indian excesses of April. This was a hard pill and Gandhi had to fight for its acceptance. It was true, he said, that 'the Government went mad at the time.' But, he added, 'we went mad also.'

Then, in a sentence, he defined successful satyagraha: 'Do not return madness with madness but return madness with sanity, and the whole situation will be yours.' The pill was swallowed.

Congress agreed to work the [Montford] Reforms Act, which had just come into force, while expressing disappointment at its inadequacies. The sword of non-cooperation, bared for a brief moment over Khilafat, lay quiet and unnoticed in its sheath in Amritsar.

C.R. played no part in shaping the resolutions. For him Amritsar was an opportunity to meet men who would be colleagues in the future — among them the Nehrus, father and son; Das, whose friendship he had made the previous year, and Rajendra Prasad of Bihar.

Invited by Prasad to Patna, C.R. visited Benares on the way, buying a sari there for Papa. He was accompanied to Patna by Devadas, the Mahatma's nineteen-year-old son. On returning to Madras, C.R. posted twenty-three books to Devadas — on literature, science, geography, and Greek, Roman, English and Indian history. Writing what he himself described as 'a schoolmaster's letter' to Devadas, C.R. said: 'Remember that the last one or two letters in a word have the same right to be legible as the rest.'

Before his trip North, C.R. had shifted, with his children and father, to a smaller house, 'Venkata Vilas' on Luz Church Road in Mylapore. They were living on his savings, and economies were called for.

Early in 1920, an explanation of Jallianwala prepared by the Punjab Government — the accused party, in Congress eyes — was released in Britain. C.R. urged the Congress to publish its findings speedily.

Drafted by the Mahatma and published on March 25, the Congress Report concluded that there was no Indian conspiracy, that Martial Law was unjustified, and that Jallianwala was a 'calculated' and 'unparalleled' piece of inhumanity. It was later claimed that 'not a single fact' stated in the Congress Report 'was ever disproved.'[9]

All over India the demand for redress grew. Appointed Convener for Madras Presidency of the Congress's Jallianwala committee, C.R. strove to mobilize southern opinion over the Punjab.

His task was aided by the Hunter Commission's Report,

published at the end of May, which confirmed the grim facts but drew weak conclusions. Indian resentment was roused on both counts. Dyer was relieved of his command after the Report, but O'Dwyer and other Punjab officials emerged unscathed. The justice for which Gandhi and the Congress had nursed a hope was missing.

Shocks followed the disillusionment. The House of Lords passed a resolution justifying Dyer, and British admirers gave him a sword of honour and 20,000 pounds. On the Khilafat front, a Muslim deputation was reminded by the Viceroy that Turkey had drawn the sword for Germany.

Muhammad Ali went to London and called on Lloyd George. 'Germany,' he was told by the British Premier, 'has had justice, pretty terrible justice. Why should Turkey escape?' *Young India*, Gandhi's journal, replied that 'the terrible, stern justice for Turkey must be tempered with the pledged word ... of the British Empire' (31.3.20).

A month earlier, C.R., conveying to Gandhi his assessment that 'the Khilafat question is assuming most serious proportions,' had advocated 'a big agitation in India.'[10] On 19 March, Gandhi, C.R. and several Muslim leaders addressed a meeting in Bombay.

At this meeting Gandhi declared that his loyalty to the Empire was evaporating. If adverse decisions over Khilafat were not corrected, he would unsheath non-cooperation. Some Indians broke with the Raj even before Gandhi gave the signal. The first to do so was Hakim Ajmal Khan, Delhi's noted physician and leading figure, who returned his medals at the end of March.

C.R. pushed the agitation in the South, pledging Hindu support to the Muslims at a 9 April meeting in Madras. Muslim businessmen gave him blank cheques.

India learnt on 14 May the final terms imposed on Turkey and the Khilafat by the Treaty of Sevres. They were as harsh as feared. Later in the month the Hunter Report came out, followed by the House of Lords' approbation of Dyer. Simultaneously repelling Muslim and non-Muslim India, the Raj had generated a tide that Gandhi would ride.

An all-India Khilafat committee voted for non-cooperation

under Gandhi's guidance, but a Congress committee meeting in Benares at the end of May was more cautious. It shifted the onus to a special session in Calcutta in September. Gandhi decided that he would not wait for the Congress's approval: preceded by a day of fasting and prayer, nonviolent non-cooperation would be launched on 1 August by him and his Khilafat friends.

In all his bids, the Mahatma received C.R.'s instant understanding and wholehearted loyalty. At times, as we saw over Rowlatt, C.R. seemed to anticipate if not to prod Gandhi. And if a disciple, he was frank with his master, who seemed to treat C.R.'s views with respect. The text of Gandhi's telegram referred to in the following letter of 12.6.20 from C.R. to the Mahatma is not on record, but we may surmise that it indicated acceptance of 'out-of-turn,' candid advice given by C.R.:

> My dearest Master, Had your telegram. Words fail me altogether. I hope you have pardoned me. Yours most sincerely, Rajagopalachar.

Acknowledging C.R.'s concern for his integrity, the Mahatma would call him 'my conscience-keeper.'

In July, in a private report to Delhi, the Madras Government described C.R. as 'conspicuous' among 'the most energetic public advocates of noncooperation.' A Madras Provincial Conference had recommended non-cooperation; the Government informed Delhi that 'this result is regarded as due to the exertions of C.R. Achari.'[11]

C.R. needed to exert himself, for non-cooperation had influential opponents in the South. Some Hindus held that a Muslim cause was not necessarily an Indian cause. The Moderates and Mrs Besant were opposed in principle to the new policy. Other prominent intellectuals had been looking forward to the Councils spelt out by the Reform Act of 1919.

C.R. himself had been ready to see some usefulness in the Councils. He had signed, and probably helped draft, an election manifesto of the Congress' Nationalist party, of which he was a secretary. But by the time the manifesto was published, he was well on the way to non-cooperation.

Under Gandhi the country's politics, and the nature of Congress, was being changed. An elite debating society, doubtless patriotic and often brilliant, was being converted into a mass movement just when it could have taken over the gleaming Councils. Not all liked the conversion.

Besides being unexciting in comparison with elections, non-cooperation carried a risk of discomfort and prison terms. A secret report that went on 1 July from Madras to Delhi said that some leaders opposed non-cooperation for 'fear of the logical results with regard to themselves.'[12]

Then there was caste. South India was in fact witnessing two struggles, one against the Raj and the other against Brahmin influence. C.R. sought to convince the South's non-Brahmin majority that the struggle against the Raj included a fight for social justice.

At the end of March he had urged a conference of schoolteachers 'to fight the caste spirit and work for the removal of untouchability so that the nation would achieve Brahmin/non-Brahmin and Hindu-Muslim unity' (*The Hindu*, 1.4.20).

On 6 April, at a meeting to remember the previous year's hartal, C.R. asked that the chair be given to the non-Brahmin writer, T.V. Kalyanasundara Mudaliar, even though the latter had shortly before backed a resolution 'not to return any Brahmins to the Legislative Council' (*The Hindu*, 8.4.20).

Hitherto, Congress leadership in Madras, Moderate or Nationalist, had mainly come from Brahmins. Founded in 1917, the Justice Party attacked Brahmin domination and Congress in the same breath. Supporting the Montford Scheme, the Justice Party hoped to capture power in the 1920 elections. Since a Congress boycott of elections would suit the Justice Party, Madras's Congressmen were chary of non-cooperation.

Finally, there was opposition to C.R. from a quarter of another kind. His old teacher, John Tait, called C.R. to College House in Madras on 31 July, on the eve of non-cooperation. He was surprised, Tait said, that C.R. should get mixed up in an 'unconstitutional and superstitious' movement like Khilafat.

The former pupil heard Tait with respect but was unrepentant.[13]

Forty minutes after zero hour on 1 August 1920, Lokamanya Tilak died in Bombay, his health sapped by diabetes and years in prison. Stirred by his death, all of Bombay seemed to turn out for the final procession. Gandhi and Shaukat Ali were among those shouldering the bier. To C.R., Tilak's passing came as a personal blow.

On 1 August the Mahatma returned, not without a pang, the medals the Empire had given him for organizing ambulances in South Africa and London. Now, he said, he harboured 'neither respect nor affection' for the Government. In reply the Viceroy called non-cooperation 'the most foolish of all foolish schemes,' but the Indian people rallied round Gandhi in unprecedented numbers.

C.R. invited him to Madras and Salem. Over 50,000 heard Gandhi on the beach. While in Madras he called on C.R.'s ailing father at 'Venkata Vilas.' C.R.'s children were curious and also anxious about the encounter, for their grandfather had promised that if Gandhi ever met him, he would hear a mouthful for having 'ruined the entire family by mesmerizing my son.'

However, when Gandhi arrived, the ex-munsiff, dressed in his best and rising with an effort, joined his palms in a courteous welcome and told the Mahatma, who had bowed before him, that he was happy with what his son was doing. As soon as Gandhi left, the youngsters demanded an explanation from grandfather. 'He mesmerized my son and today he mesmerized me,' said the ex-munsiff, adding, 'Let him come again, I will have it out with him.'[14]

Banter apart, two anxieties remained. In obedience to the non-cooperation call, Krishnaswami and Ramaswami had been removed from the Raj's colleges and Narasimhan from his school; how were these grandsons going to be educated? Secondly, the ex-munsiff feared that non-cooperation would bring the shame of a prison term to his son.

Arresting C.R. was considered by the Government of Madras, but Delhi advised that 'a premature prosecution of the leaders could result in making martyrs of them.' It clarified, however, that 'association with Mr Gandhi, the apostle of nonviolence, will not confer immunity from prosecution on even the most prominent of his co-workers.'[15]

The Mahatma's visit did not convert non-cooperation's principal opponents in the South. However, C.R. received the support of a group of young lawyers who heeded Gandhi's call and gave up their practices; and the Provincial Congress Committee accepted non-cooperation in principle though not the steps proposed by Gandhi.

Congress's national body was to decide on non-cooperation at a special session in Calcutta in September 1920, presided over by Lala Lajpat Rai, the Punjab leader who had spent the War years in America. C.R. arrived at the head of some 200 Madras delegates on a train placarded as 'The Khilafat Special.'

The Congress establishment was keen to defeat the Mahatma. Bipin Chandra Pal, a central figure in the protest against Bengal's Partition, C.R. Das, and others attacked Gandhi's proposals; only Motilal Nehru broke ranks with the old guard. But Gandhi swayed the assembly, which by 1855 votes to 873 adopted his agenda.

Its items were a surrender of titles bestowed by the Raj; a boycott of official ceremonials, of the elections announced for November, and of foreign goods; and a gradual withdrawal by students and lawyers from the Raj's schools, colleges, and courts.

The Government voiced the hope that 'the sanity of the classes and masses alike would reject non-cooperation,' but in November evidence came that at least the masses were embracing it. Almost two-thirds of India's electors — many millions, despite the limited franchise — stayed away from the polls.

Waiting until noon at 'a freshly swept polling station' near Allahabad, where 'the presiding officer with his assistants sat at his table with his freshly printed electoral roll,' Sir Valentine Chirol, the British observer, saw not a single voter.[16]

In Madras C.R. led the boycott, his car, still driven by Ghouse, carrying a 'Vote For None' sticker. Abstention in the South was fair, even if not spectacular.

The Calcutta decision was ratified in December when Congress met in Nagpur for its annual session. Spending Rs 36,000 from his pocket, Das had brought 200 delegates from Bengal and Assam in a bid to reverse the decision. But after an all-night discussion with the Mahatma, Das himself succumbed — and moved the resolution declaring non-cooperation! Lajpat Rai seconded it.

Nagpur altered the creed of Congress. The previous goal of 'Self-government within the Empire' was replaced by 'The attainment of Swaraj . . . by all legitimate and peaceful means.'

Also changed was the constitution of Congress. The new scheme, prepared by Gandhi, provided for democratically elected committees at all levels — the village, town, taluk, district, 'province' and all-India. The provinces were linguistic areas not necessarily coinciding with the provinces of the Raj. Thus, Madras would have a Tamil Nadu Congress Committee and a separate Andhra Pradesh Congress Committee.

The All-India Congress Committee (AICC) would choose a Working Committee, which would be the decision-making and round-the-clock arm of the Congress, consisting of the President, the General Secretary, the Treasurer, and about a dozen others. Elected annually by the provincial units, the President would be first among equals and no more.

Nagpur raised C.R. to national leadership — he was chosen as a General Secretary for the coming year. Also drafted as General Secretaries were Motilal Nehru and Dr M.A. Ansari, a leading Muslim figure from Delhi.

Inaugurating the practising revolt, the Mahatma had enjoined strict nonviolence in implementing his negative and positive programmes. The boycotts were to climax in mass civil disobedience, perhaps in a refusal to pay taxes.

The positive targets to be achieved were a Rs 1 crore fund in Tilak's name, to be used for national activities, two million charkhas for spinning yarn, and one crore members for the Congress. Hindu-Muslim partnership and the elevation of untouchables were the broader goals. Also sought, in a lower key, were the spread of Hindi/Hindustani and the prohibition of liquor.

As the first step, the visit of the Duke of Connaught, the King's uncle, who was to inaugurate the legislatures, was boycotted. Three thousand Calcutta students walked out of their institutions. 'National' educational bodies were formed in Ahmedabad, Patna, Benares, Maharashtra and Calcutta.

Withdrawn from their schools, Krishnaswami and Ramaswami, C.R.'s sons, engaged themselves in promoting khadi in and around Salem. A Swadhinata Vidyalaya (Independence College) started in Madras at C.R.'s initiative, 'open,' as *The Hindu* put it, 'to students withdrawing themselves from college classes and desiring to complete their equipment for national service or as teachers in national schools' (8.3.21). The Raj's response was to warn municipalities against supporting any 'national' college.

Hindus and Muslims fraternized in hitherto unheard of ways. At Id, Muslims did not sacrifice cows. Courts continued to function and the vast majority of lawyers attended them. Yet an impressive number opted out, entering a life of uncertainty and poverty.

Das and Motilal Nehru led the exit. C.R. had stopped practising before non-cooperation was formally launched. Vallabhbhai Patel in Gujarat and Rajendra Prasad in Bihar were among others who gave up lucrative practices. In June 1921, C.R. announced that in the Tamil country 36 lawyers, including T. Prakasam, a barrister who would play an important role in South India, had left the courts.

As Indian opposition to the Raj gained momentum, Gandhi's close colleagues were the Ali brothers, Lajpat Rai, Motilal Nehru and his son Jawaharlal in the North; Das and Abul Kalam Azad in Calcutta; Patel in Gujarat; Prasad in Bihar; and C.R. in the South. The Mahatma had assembled a talented team.

To Gandhi's feats of generalship all over India, C.R., travelling ceaselessly and speaking at meetings and through the press, lent valuable support.

He made time, however, to arrange the marriage of Namagiri, now nearly fifteen, to Varadachari, who was a journalist in Rangoon. C.R. had wanted Papa to wait but friends of her age had husbands, and her father's constant travelling had made her insecure and keen on marriage.

After the wedding, which took place in Tirupati, C.R. moved from 'Venkata Vilas' to 'Gem,' on Poonamallee High Road, a smaller and less expensive lodging. He had been realizing that 'living on my little savings . . . in Madras . . . is simply an "irrational", as they say in Mathematics.'[17]

By the middle of 1921, 'Gem' too was given up; the Darracq, the chest of drawers and the desk and the chairs obtained from the School of Arts were sold; Ghouse was sent away; and C.R. was back in Salem, staying in his bare house in the Extension.

In a ten-day period, Congress membership in the Tamil area went up from 8,000 to 30,000. A new provincial Congress committee, loyal to C.R., came into being in July.

Leading Brahmin intellectuals, including S. Srinivasa Iyengar, who had resigned as Advocate-General of Madras to join the Congress, Kasturiranga Iyengar, and A. Rangaswami Iyengar, editor of the Tamil daily *Swadesamitran*, opposed him; but C.R. secured the support of three prominent non-Brahmins, Ramaswami Naicker, the future founder of the Self-Respect move. T.V. Kalyanasundara Mudaliar, editor of *Navasakthi*, and the man he had defended in 1919, Dr Varadarajulu Naidu. Backed in addition by the Muslims, C.R. was able to take Madras to the battlefield.

The liquor front saw progress. The Madras Government informed Delhi that 'the decrease in revenue is likely to be considerable . . . The recent sales of arrack shops have been boycotted.' Five months later, another report admitted 'a comparative failure in the sales of toddy shops through the

Presidency,' and acknowledged that 'the preaching of noncooperation and in some cases the picketing of liquor have contributed largely to this result.'[18]

The Moplah riots, among the most tragic in modern Indian history, took place in 1921 in Malabar, then part of Madras Presidency. Muslims with a trace of Arab blood, the Moplahs, many of them tenants of Hindu landlords, had a tradition of fanaticism.

In February 1921, C.R. and Yakub Hassan, a Khilafat leader from Madras, visited the Moplah region with the declared aim of preaching nonviolence. However, the Government put a ban on their public speaking. Smelling danger, C.R. asked the public 'not to fall into the trap set by repression and commit violence' (*The Hindu*, 23.2.21).

Poorly led, the Moplahs blundered. Alleged insults to their religious guides suddenly brought them into rebellion in August — first against the Government and then against the Hindu landlords. 'Independence' was declared, arson and murder took place, and some Hindus were forcibly converted.

The Raj moved thousands of troops into the area. In the full-scale military action that ensued, 2,339 were killed and 24,167 convicted of rebellion or lesser crimes, figures withheld till much later.

Beginning with the struggle over Rowlatt, Hindu-Muslim trust had grown hearteningly all over India. The Moplah outbreak injured the trust. Stories of forced conversions spread across the country, and movements for strengthening the Hindu community were launched. Some of these movements in turn caused disquiet among Muslims.

In April 1921 Lord Reading, the former Rufus Isaacs, ex-Attorney-General and Lord Chief Justice in the UK, succeeded Chelmsford as Viceroy. He sent for Gandhi; they had six talks spread over thirteen hours. C.R. expected nothing new or striking from the talks but he did not share the apprehension of some that Gandhi would be softened by the new Viceroy.

The Mahatma was achieving astonishing results. He had come close to the Tilak fund target and recruited six million members for Congress. Young men in thousands enrolled in the National Volunteer Corps. Khadi-clad shock troops of Swaraj penetrated squalid villages and industrial slums, teaching spinning, promoting literacy and deprecating drink and untouchability.

India was astir — and altering. One way in which C.R. helped was by explaining Gandhi's moves. As *Young India* put it, C.R.'s introduction to *Freedom's Battle*, a collection of the Mahatma's speeches and articles, provided 'crushing replies' to 'the stock objections against noncooperation.'

Had Hindus gained by worrying about Muslims in the Middle East? Yes, said C.R.: 'The Indian support of the Khilafat has, as if by a magic wand, converted what was once the pan-Islamic terror for Europe into a solid wall of friendship and defence for India.'

Was not non-cooperation negative? No, it was building unity among Indians. 'Even if we had no grievances against this Government, noncooperation with it, for a time, would be desirable in so far as it would perforce lead us to trusting and working with one another . . .'

He also dealt with the plea for a 'constitutional' path to freedom: 'An Act of Parliament can never create citizens in Hindustan. Liberty unacquired, merely found, will on the test fail like the Dead Sea Apple' (*Young India*, 6.4.21).

By July 1921 the tempo was high. Turkey's Sultan had become a British puppet. Kamal Ataturk was leading his country's nationalists against the Treaty and fighting a British-backed Greek invasion. In fiery speeches in Karachi, the Ali brothers called upon Muslims in India to leave the police and the army.

To end dependence on foreign cloth, bonfires of imported textiles took place. Gandhi himself set a pile alight in Bombay on July 31, claiming that he was diverting the public's hatred from (British) individuals to inanimate things.

When he heard of the Moplah outbreak, Gandhi decided to go to Malabar with Muhammad Ali. On their way, at Waltair, Ali was arrested. Shaukat's arrest followed. The Karachi speeches were cited as the reason. At Trichy, C.R. standing beside him, Gandhi declared that had he been in Karachi he would have backed the brothers.

On the train between Trichy and Madura, Gandhi showed C.R. a statement he had prepared, announcing that he was reducing his raiment to a waist-to-knee length of cloth. This would be, said the Mahatma, in mourning for the arrest of Ali, and in identification with India's poorest. It would also answer the objection about khadi's cost; his new khadi dhoti would be cheaper than a standard-length dhoti of imported cloth.

Though he 'employed all kinds of arguments to dissuade the Mahatma,' C.R. failed. 'I am absolutely clear about the correctness of the step I have taken,' Gandhi told him.[19]

The sartorial change interested the Raj. From Madras, Governor Willingdon wrote to the Viceroy: 'I hope he would not die of pneumonia as a result! Though his demise might save us all a lot of trouble.'[20]

The Ali brothers' arrest intensified the fight. Gandhi, told to keep out of Malabar, wrote that 'sedition has become the creed of the Congress,' and added that noncooperation 'deliberately aims at the overthrow of the Government' (*Young India*, 29.9.21). Yet the Government did not lay hands on the Mahatma, for fear of the people's reaction.

Early in October, C.R. joined a gathering in Bombay of leaders from all over India. In a manifesto the leaders said that it was 'the duty of every Indian soldier and civilian to sever his connection with the Government and find some other means of livelihood' (*Young India*, 6.10.21).

After daring the Government to do its worst, the Mahatma and C.R. travelled together to Sabarmati, Gandhi's Ashram outside Ahmedabad. The 1919 hospitality was being returned, and there were walks and talks at the Ashram.

About seventy-five years old, his health eroded by diabetes, Chakravarti Iyengar struggled against a fever and asked for

'Rajan.' C.R.'s boys sent their father a wire. There was a moment of recognition when C.R. arrived, after which Chakravarti Iyengar went into delirium. Proud, thrifty, and hopeful of major things from his son, he had overcome to a large extent the unhappiness he felt when C.R. gāve up practice. On 20 October 1921 he passed away.

By then C.R. had suffered another loss. His eldest brother, Narasimhachar, at 54, his senior by 11 years, suddenly died two days before his father. Sending Krishnaswami to his brother's rites, C.R. arranged his father's obsequies. These possessed the odour of sanctity, with proper priests serving; Iyengar's fear of a caste boycott at his last rites proved false.

His responsibilities as Gandhi's colleague and General Secretary of Congress had restricted C.R.'s times with his ailing father. Years later, looking back on this period, C.R. would tell the author that he harboured dissatisfaction with his filial role; he thought he could have done more as a son, without injury to the cause.

When the Ali brothers were awarded two years' rigorous imprisonment, the Mahatma announced that he would lead mass civil disobedience in Bardoli. The people of Bardoli, a taluk of Surat district in Gujarat, would simply refuse to pay taxes.

'When the Swaraj flag floats victoriously at Bardoli,' said Gandhi early in November, 'then the people of the taluk next to Bardoli . . . should seek to plant the flag of Swaraj in their midst. Thus, district by district . . . throughout the length and breadth of India, should the Swaraj flag be hoisted.' But he warned that he might stop the movement if there was violence.[21]

The Prince of Wales arrived on 17 November. India observed a hartal on the day but violence in Bombay sullied its success. Those welcoming the royal guest were attacked in the streets; the riots and the police reaction took 58 lives. An eyewitness to mob scenes, Gandhi said that the Swaraj he had seen stank in his nostrils. He fasted until the non-cooperators made peace with the cooperators — and postponed the Bardoli rebellion.

Troubled by the violence, C.R. suggested to the Mahatma that boycotting the Prince was 'a political manoeuvre,' involving no sacrifice. Gandhi replied: 'You do not understand the pain I suffered in not meeting the Prince.'[22]

To the Raj, the hartal was an act of defiance. Though not yet ready to arrest Gandhi, it banned, in different parts of the country, the volunteer organizations of Congress and the Khilafat.

Thousands peacefully and openly defied the bans, filled the Raj's prisons, and looked forward to sounds of triumph from Bardoli.

When the Madras Government issued an order forbidding meetings, C.R. declared that he would disobey it. Leaflets were printed announcing that he would address a meeting in Vellore on 14 December. Over 5,000 gathered to hear him. C.R. asked them to maintain communal unity and to 'keep to the path of nonviolence under all provocation' (*The Hindu*, 15.12.21).

At eight the next morning he was served with summons. 'I feel today as young as yourself and so buoyant,' he wrote at noon to Devadas.[23] He was brought to trial at 4.00 p.m. but the prosecution was not ready, and the case was adjourned for four days.

His sons were in the Salem Extension house, under the care of his brother Srinivasa, who was also looking after the children of the deceased Narasimhachar. Lakshmi, now nine, was with Namagiri and her husband Varadachari in Rangoon.

Sending the addresses of his children to the Mahatma, C.R. informed him that he would ask for the full sentence. 'Good,' Gandhi wired back. 'Hope you will get maximum penalty.'[24] On 18 December C.R. wrote to Devadas:

> Think of me and pray for me . . . that I may not lose faith and hope. We are in great times.
>
> Bapu is like a trunk shorn of all hands and feet. All his companions in all provinces including even little me have simultaneously decided to run away into prison voluntarily.
>
> You don't go to prison. You should remain free for work outside. Harilal (*the Mahatma's eldest son*) has cheated you by going first.[25]

After the judge sentenced him for three months, C.R. wrote to Gandhi: 'I feel am realizing the object of my life as I am approaching the prison' (*Young India*, 12.1.22).

4

Jail
1921-22

C.R. was locked up in a cell in Vellore Central Jail. As the key was carried away he was conscious, he wrote in a diary, of a 'rather strange and new' feeling, which however gave way to another thought. 'For the first time' in his life he felt that he 'was free, and had thrown off the foreign yoke.'

He had taken with him some clothes, a pillow, a thick sheet, a shawl, a flask, a quire of paper, and a few books — the Mahabharata in Tamil and English, the Bible, the *Kural*, a Shakespeare volume, *Robinson Crusoe*, and a work on Socrates.

While waiting to be escorted to prison, he had written to Gandhi that he hoped to find India free when he came out, and the Mahatma therefore pursuing his 'normal vocation — research in dietetics.'[1]

Entered from a veranda, C.R.'s solitary cell was 11 ½ feet long and 8 ½ feet wide; at its highest point the arched roof was 10 feet from the floor. A 4 feet by 1 ½ feet barred opening in the rear wall, just below the roof, brought the smell of urine from a drain outside. Though the cell door had a barred portion through which light and air could enter, there was not 'the least movement of air' inside. Flies infested the cell by day and mosquitoes by night.

A brick platform was the bed; a straw mat and a blanket provided by the jail formed the 'mattress' over which C.R.

spread his sheet. Four feet from the bed lay two uncovered mud vessels which served as chamber-pot and commode at night. The open pots did 'not make the place sweet.'

Prisoners awaiting execution occupied neighbouring cells. They cursed, wailed, clanked their chains, and at times prayed through the bars.

To begin with, the cell was totally dark after sundown. On the fourth night, which was Christmas Eve, C.R. lit a candle from a packet given to him by a fresh arrival, Mahomed Ghouse. In the diary that he had started, the source of much of this chapter, C.R. noted, 'Never did I see a candle give such quiet holy light before.' The following morning he wrote: 'It is Christmas day for our rulers. May the Spirit of Christ purify their souls and give them Light.'

His food, for some weeks, was rice gruel (of which he took only the liquid) at about 6.30 a.m. and rice and kolambu around 11.00 a.m. and again around 5.00 p.m. The kolambu, 'unparalleled in horrid taste,' contained radish root and leaves, chillies, tamarind, salt and oil, and also 'dirt, grit, hair, wool and all sorts of things.'

Along with other prisoners C.R. was let out of his cell for meals and ate standing or sitting on his toes at a filthy spot under menacing crows; it was 'like beggars being fed.' After a while, however, the food improved, and C.R. was granted the option of eating in his cell.

On the fourth day, he had been given his 'medal': a disc bearing his number, 8398, and the dates of his entry and release. He wore it round his neck. No newspapers were allowed, but each month C.R. could write and receive a letter and have an interview. Though other imprisoned activists were not allowed to meet him, conversation was possible over a meal in the open or on the way to the privy or to a bath at the prison well — and when a violent eruption of boils sent C.R. to the foul-smelling prison 'hospital.'

By the last week of December, more than 20,000 civil resisters were in jail, and Gandhi declared that Bardoli was ready to cease paying taxes. This would be the climax. The jailed C.R. was chosen as the Congress' General Secretary for another year, and Gandhi gave his opinion in *Young India* that C.R. 'knows the science of Satyagraha as no one else perhaps does' (12.1.22).

On 14 January C.R. availed of his first interview. His son Krishnaswamy, his brother Srinivasa, and Dr T.S.S. Rajan of Trichy were allowed to meet him. C.R. learnt of his reappointment and of the effective though violent hartal observed in Madras when the Prince of Wales visited the city. A mob had damaged the Wellington Cinema, which hoisted 'loyal' flags, and another crowd had prevented Sir Thyagaraja Chetty, leader of the office-holding Justice Party, from leaving his house.

The Government was controlling the Press, C.R. was told, but Rajan added that even as they were meeting in jail an All Parties Conference for reconciling Congress and the Government was being held in Bombay. This news gave C.R. no joy. In his diary he wrote: 'Cutting down our demands or suspending the Congress programmes would be unthinkably wrong just now, when victory is nigh.'

The Bombay conference urged the Mahatma to postpone his Bardoli step, and the Government to release those arrested, withdraw the bans, and convene a Round Table Conference. Gandhi put off Bardoli till 1 February but the Viceroy rejected the Bombay proposal.

On 29 January, 4,000 khadi-clad Bardoli resisters, some of them veterans of the South African struggle, pledged their readiness to stop paying taxes and 'to face imprisonment, and even death . . . without resentment.'[2]

On 1 February the Mahatma sent Lord Reading an ultimatum: if in seven days there was no declaration that prisoners would be released and the Press freed, the Bardoli tax-strike would commence. The Viceroy replied, on 6 February, that the Government would stand firm; next day Gandhi sent a rejoinder. India was agog.

Though he did not know of these moves, the incarcerated C.R. shared his compatriots' suspense and expectancy. His censored monthly letter could not contain 'politics,' and C.R. had to content himself with saying to the Mahatma on

24 January: 'I guess you have not started for Bardoli and Anand yet' (*Young India*, 9.2.22).

After informing Gandhi that his asthma was persisting and that his weight was down from 104 lbs. to 98 lbs., C.R. pulled the Mahatma's leg:

> Your eyes would flow with delight if you saw me here in my solitary cell spinning — spinning not as a task imposed by a tyrant faddist, but with pleasure.

C.R. also managed to convey his longing for a bigger entry into the Raj's prisons:

> This Ashram is very much less congested than yours at Sabarmati and I wish more people understood the real advantage of this retirement and discipline.

Gandhi published the letter in *Young India* under the heading, 'From his Solitary Cell.' In an accompanying note, he wrote:

> When you are locked up in a cell, . . . the air in a short time becomes thick and foul with your own exhalations. And you are doomed to rebreathe your own emissions. The least that humanity demands is that C. Rajagopalachari should have, if he has not, all the fresh air he can get day and night.

Three weeks after the Mahatma's remarks were published, the Raj moved C.R. to a general ward.

By then the climax had proved to be a stunning anti-climax. On 13 February, at his second interview, C.R. learnt from Ramaswami Naicker that the Mahatma had called off the Bardoli offensive.

A small police party with little ammunition had fired at a procession of non-cooperators in an obscure place called Chauri Chaura in eastern UP; when their ammunition was exhausted, the policemen had taken refuge in their outpost. Enraged, some in the procession set fire to the outpost; the fleeing constables were hacked to pieces. Twenty-two policemen were killed.

Learning of the incident the day after he had sent his

rejoinder to the Viceroy, the Mahatma was struck dumb. He felt that through Chauri Chaura God had spoken. Though the number of arrests had gone up to 30,000, though Bardoli was eager, the action had to be cancelled.

'Let the opponent glory in our humiliation or so-called defeat,' said Gandhi, who was convinced that 'the cause will prosper by this retreat' (*Young India*, 16.2.22).

Thus ended a bid about which the Governor of Bombay at the time, Lord Lloyd, said: 'He (Gandhi) gave us a scare. Gandhi's was the most colossal experiment in world history, and it came within an inch of succeeding.'

When he learned of the stoppage, C.R., for all his dislike of violence, was shocked and hurt. 'Victory was nigh,' he had said and believed. There was dark defeat instead. The Mahatma, he thought, had erred. In his diary C.R. wrote:

> In spite of my tenderest and most complete attachment to my master and the ideal he stands for, I fail to see why there should be a call for stopping our struggle for birthrights [because of] every distant and unconnected outburst.

'The opponent would glory in our humiliation,' Gandhi had anticipated. Rousing C.R. before dawn on 15 February, the Jailor jubilantly told him that 'noncooperation had gone to sleep' and that Gandhi had 'cried halt to civil disobedience.' A stung C.R. counter-attacked about the Jailor's treatment of prisoners.

Reflection brought some consolation. C.R. acknowledged that 'in seclusion and without materials' he could 'not judge well.' 'With the mass mind a retreat' was undoubtedly 'a great handicap,' yet 'God leads us right where logic may not.' The news that in penance for Chauri Chaura Gandhi was fasting for five days turned C.R.'s unhappiness with the Mahatma into anxiety for his health.

Four months later, after he was free and had gathered facts and perspective, C.R. would laud the stoppage:

> In February last, when the probability of violence stared us in the face, firmly believing in Nonviolence as the essential condition of liberation and progress, in spite of every temptation that urged us to advance and fully realising all the losses and risks which sudden halt involved, we deliberately chose to stop our aggressive activities.

In his fellow-prisoners and some of the servants C.R. found 'devotion and brotherliness' but 'no love such as my heart wants.' He treasured the interviews, to which one or more of his boys came, 'chewed and consumed every line and word' of the monthly letters from his children, and fought homesickness by comparing his 'insignificant share of suffering' with the deprivation of others.

He referred tenderly in his diary to Manga (without ever naming her) and to his mother:

> Somehow my poor mother haunts my mind and sweetens my thought today. She could not imagine that her fond child, her pride and hope, would be in a common gaol, imprisoned and locked up under a 9 ft. arch.

> Yet another soul there was who has now passed away from this earth, from whose mind too the idea was farthest, that I should ever be in prisons, a fate from which, to her delight and pride, I had saved so many of my clients.

On another occasion he wrote:

> Today, as I was at my evening prayer, the sweet music of the village *nagaswaram* that came from some happy home in the hamlets lying outside the prison wall, brought with it such an irresistible rush of happy recollections that I could not for long get them out. The music of these pipes is to me, and I suppose to every man and woman in this land, a sound that brings on its back a world of sweet recollections, a *vahana* (vehicle) of happy youth, of joy and hope.

> These thoughts render me weak. All my strength is needed for the battle, and I cannot afford to let my mind wander thus

into the garden of sweet flowers that yield only tears. All that I shall say to my God is, if she is anywhere and is still subject to pleasure and pain, keep her happy and free from pain or sadness; and give me strength to endure and to perform my duties.

He daily rose at 5.30 a.m. and retired at about 8.30 p.m.; the time in between was consumed by spinning, reading, writing the diary, translating into Tamil the 'Trial and Death of Socrates,' cleaning his cell and the aluminium eating dishes, washing his thick khadi clothes, and praying.

Boils in the legs, a fever, and stomach disorders troubled him. Talkative warders filling 'the night with noise,' bugs, mosquitoes that stung 'sharply through thick khaddar,' and, above all, his asthma gave him sleepless nights. On 17 February he wrote:

> Passed a night of real terror . . . Sat up like a ghost, and found some relief in lighting my candle and heating some water on it for sipping.

As the weeks passed, C.R.'s food improved. Every morning, a Sikh prisoner-cook, Nidhan Singh, was allowed to bring, along with a Vande Mataram greeting, two thin chapatis for C.R., instead of the rice porridge; bread and milk (at midday) and milk or buttermilk and sago (in the evening) replaced rice and the kolambu that had repelled him. On occasion he even had butter and raw tomatoes. 'I don't think a prince can enjoy a better breakfast,' he wrote.

In the diary Major Anderson, the British Superintendent, is described bitterly as the Prison King. 'None at all,' was his reply when C.R. asked if newspapers would be allowed in, and interviews had to stop 'at the exact minute.' With time, however, the Major became 'friendly and considerate'; on his part, C.R. conceded that 'any limitations in [Anderson's] liberality of conduct are due to interference from above or absence of scope in the codes and rules.' He also helped resolve confrontations between Anderson and other convicts.

Next in rank to Major Anderson was the Jailor. Without provocation he had hit a prisoner, Subba Rao. C.R. persuaded the Jailor to apologize to the victim in front of witnesses. When

Subba Rao said that 'Providence brought about the incident so that it may change the Jailor's heart,' a moved C.R. wrote:

> How beautiful is the path of charity and love, once we gather wisdom and strength to walk on it . . .

An acting Jailor 'came and made a long confessional history of his official and private life' to C.R., and the junior doctor, of whom C.R. had written that he was 'more a jailor than a doctor and more a tyrant than anything else,' dropped entirely 'the manner which was so repulsive.' 'Insults of the grosser variety are gone,' C.R. noted.

Shortly after C.R.'s arrival at Vellore, a poor Moplah, tears welling 'from his manly eyes,' had said: 'We feel so cheerful and hopeful when we see big and rich people coming into jail like you.' Other Moplahs told C.R. that they would gladly serve four more years if that would remit his three months.

Vellore brought C.R. 'in the closest contact with some of the best Andhra types,' and he noted that Andhra had sent more prisoners, more recruits to the 'National Army,' than the Tamil country.

There were also the Sikhs, including Nidhan Singh, 'the indefatigable, decorous, brave and patriotic Sikh prisoner' who took seriously ill before C.R.'s release, and the 'cheerful' life-prisoner Hira Singh, who had tried to escape from Hazaribagh Jail where, 'for six years, he says, he never saw the sun.' C.R. 'promised to write to Hira Singh's brother Ram Singh.'

Occupants of neighbouring cells were described in the diary:

> Just now there is a young Mussalman lad of Ambur, sturdy, bright, and handsome, as made by God, and condemned . . . for some outburst of animal spirits, some assault in company with friends, as he says, or it may be for a more serious deviation from the law . . . A heavy wooden door is drawn across the iron bars of his cell door amd bolted, so that God's light and air may not reach him . . .

> On the other side . . . are four young men awaiting death by the gallows . . . always sitting close against the cell door, for

it is the nearest approach to freedom and light . . . They watch, and sometimes, I believe, jeer at me in natural jealousy, as I move about without a guard, enjoying comparative luxuries such as going to the tap for a bath, or wash my dish, or bring water, and pass in front of them, a Brahmin . . . clean, and in white clothes, as if to mock at their condition.

Four condemned prisoners, with whose 'foul abuse and oft-repeated attempts at humour and . . . prayers of desperation' C.R. had become familiar, were hanged during his term. For one of them C.R. had drafted an unsuccessful mercy petition, and all four had become part of his life:

Appadurai, the butler, is to be hanged tomorrow. Night after night, I used to hear the chatter of gallows friendship. 'The Sepoy' would cry, 'Appavu, Appavu!, Nagiah, Nagiah!' and they would carry on a conversation, each from his own cell . . . 'Nagiah!' ceased for some months past: for the poor fellow was hanged one fine morning. For some days, the leader in the conversation, the Sepoy, was talking of Nagiah being in Heaven and eating his full meal with God — eating is the chief event in prison . . . From tomorrow 'Appavu!' also will disappear . . .

The Sepoy too disappeared (facing death bravely, C.R. was told) but not before the jail authorities, prodded by C.R., had given him the food he wanted. Execution without notice and religious assistance outraged C.R.:

Without ministration of religion or prayer or any thoughts of God [the condemned prisoner] is seized one morning when he does not expect anything like it, and taken away, arms bound, and there at the gallows his legs are fettered and a cap put over his head and in a few minutes the platform goes down and he is despatched . . .

The jail authorities won't give a single thought to whether Appadurai may not make peace with God before he yields up his life . . . They are only concerned with getting the execution done without any hitch on the day fixed.

In the solitude of prison, C.R. reaffirmed to himself his view regarding non-cooperation with an alien government:

> To refuse to cooperate in the process of reducing ourselves to
> foreign rule . . . is the natural law and instinct. We forgot this
> law of national life, and cast our minds into the terrible slough
> of unfelt slavery.

If non-cooperation was right, so was nonviolence and the
elimination of hate:

> The purest determination and freedom from all stain of anger
> on our part is necessary to produce the beautiful effect of
> suffering and love.

That C.R.'s own soul was generous to the antagonist comes
across from the diary:

> The music and din of the wedding in the Jailor's house is
> sweetening the air as I sit praying in my cell . . . I fancy I see
> the busy crowd of men, women and children hurrying up and
> down and helping to make the noise and happiness of the
> wedding . . . Can't we teach every man and woman and child
> to pray for more love and yet more love being sent down?
>
> I regret many of the unkind and uncharitable thoughts that I
> have allowed myself about these unfortunate jail officials
> without giving them a sufficient chance to change their attitude
> or create a better understanding betweeen us.

Another entry reveals C.R.'s spiritual curiosity:

> In spite of strenuous prayers the vision of the true God has
> not yet come to me. It is a hard task to keep the wandering
> mind steady, and even after that the mind does not find its real
> objective but dwells on family, self, friends and country, and
> formulates desires instead of purifying itself.

A passage in the diary was often to be quoted, for its foresight,
after freedom:

> We all ought to know that Swaraj will not at once or, I think,
> even for a long time to come, be better government or greater
> happiness for the people. Elections and their corruptions,
> injustice, and the power and tyranny of wealth and inefficiency
> of administration will make a hell of life as soon as freedom
> is given to us. Men will look regretfully back to the old regime

of comparative justice, and efficient, peaceful, more or less honest administration. The only thing gained will be that as a race we will be saved from dishonour and subordination.

C.R.'s release was preceded by an event he apprehended — the arrest of the Mahatma. Early in March, the AICC ratified the stoppage announced by Gandhi, but not without murmurings against his moves. Some Congressmen voiced doubts about civil disobedience. Finding non-cooperation irksome, and disconcerted by the abrupt halt of the aggressive campaign, a section of the Khilafat leadership withdrew its loyalty from Gandhi and offered it to the Raj.

Emboldened by the weakening in nationalist ranks, the Raj finally laid hands on the Mahatma. He was arrested at Sabarmati Ashram on 10 March and tried for sedition in Ahmedabad. Pleading guilty, Gandhi said that preaching the Government's overthrow had become his duty. Judge Broomfield sentenced him for six years.

On 12 March C.R. wrote in his diary: 'We had news today that Gandhiji was arrested. The news was received fairly calmly, and we resolved on a 36-hours' fast and prayer.' Joint Hindu-Muslim prayers were held in the evening. Non-political convicts 'instinctively came and joined.'

It was on the day of his release that C.R. heard of Gandhi's sentence:

Learnt that Pilate gave six years S.I. to Christ. God gave us a man to lead us, but the Government claim the right to take him away . . . Their will be done!

Parting from his jail 'family' was sad for C.R. On 20 March Major Anderson accompanied him through the gates and asked if the jail did not look better from outside.

'The inside is not so bad as it is thought to be,' replied C.R.

'Don't come again,' said Major Anderson.

5

Hero
1922-25

C.R. and Devadas were the first to interview Gandhi in Poona's Yeravada prison. On 1 April, cross-examining jail officials and the Mahatma, C.R. prised out particulars that Gandhi had chosen to ignore. The Mahatma had a flimsy blanket for a mattress and was using his clothes and some books as a pillow. Locked inside his solitary cell at night, he was denied newspapers and made to petition for religious books.

Rejecting the Mahatma's advice, C.R. informed the Press of his findings, and asked the Raj's officers to realize their 'privilege of being custodians of a man greater than the Kaiser, greater than Napoleon . . . ' (*Young India*, 6.4.22).

The regime tried to refute C.R.'s allegations; his rejoinder was devastating, and in a private letter to New Delhi the provincial government admitted that C.R. had won the debate. Gandhi's circumstances improved: C.R. had thus done for the Mahatma in Yeravada what Gandhi had done for him in Vellore.

In April, C.R. commenced editing *Young India*, an arrangement advised before his arrest by the Mahatma. Though the journal continued to be printed in Ahmedabad, the editor functioned from Salem.

India was confused and demoralized. The confusion was caused by Gandhi's decision to call off the battle when he held the advantage, the demoralization by his arrest.

Noticing the change in the atmosphere, Gandhi had proposed a new strategy before he was arrested, a switch to a phase of preparation, of training through constructive work. 'All our energy' should be concentrated, he counselled, 'on the tasteless but health-giving economic and social reform' (*Young India*, 2.3.22).

Yet efforts for khadi and Hindu-Muslim unity and against drink and untouchability were unexciting alternatives to revolt, and many Congressmen, including C.R., craved for disobedience. Others, however, questioned the practicability of disobedience and non-cooperation. Indirectly at first and later openly, they proposed a return to pre-Gandhian constitutional protest — agitation within the Raj's rules.

The Raj made a number of fresh arrests in the first half of 1922. Editors and publishers were among the victims. There were other restrictions: a few days after his release, C.R. was ordered not to take part in a mass meeting called in Trichy.

This was hard to take, and C.R. suggested to the provincial Congress that 'if normal Congress work is rendered impossible or extremely difficult by orders of magistrates,' civil disobedience should be considered (*The Hindu*, 10.4.22).

In his eve-of-arrest remarks the Mahatma had discouraged even this 'defensive disobedience.' However, the Raj was informed by an intelligence officer that, influenced by C.R.'s advice, Congress's Tamil Nadu and Andhra committees were 'in favour of defensive disobedience on a very large scale.'[1]

Shorn of numerous imprisoned members, the AICC met in Lucknow in June, its proceedings guided by the recently released Motilal Nehru and C.R. It endorsed, with no marked enthusiasm, Gandhi's constructive programme, and asked a six-member Civil Disobedience Enquiry Committee (CDEC) to tour the country and explore the possibilities of disobedience.

Besides Nehru and C.R., the committee included Congress's acting President, Hakim Ajmal Khan (Das, the President, was in prison), Dr M.A. Ansari, Vithalbhai Patel, and Kasturiranga Iyengar. C.R.'s position was clear. In *Young India* he wrote:

> The demand for individual civil disobedience is becoming irresistible . . . The injunctions (discouraging disobedience)

> issued by Mahatmaji ... are straining the loyalty of
> Congressmen to the utmost (8.6.22).

Yet many rank-and-file Congressmen were exhausted, and some
influential voices spoke of other avenues. Mrs C.R. Das suggested
(with the approval, it was said, of her jailed but accessible
husband) that non-cooperators should consider capturing
'provincial councils, where . . . their task would be to obstruct
all work, good or bad' (*Young India*, 4.5.22).

Among the pro-council forces were all-out cooperators,
'responsive' ones who would cooperate only if the Government
was positive, and 'wreckers from within.' What they had in
common was a coolness for the constructive programme and for
disobedience. Together they proposed an invasion of the
councils.

C.R.'s chief concern now was to combat the new doctrine.
'Those who do not believe in . . . noncooperation,' he suggested,
'should form themselves into a distinct and separate party
(within the Congress) and work along the lines of their own
faith' (*Young India*, 22.6.22).

What the pro-council factions wanted, however, was to
capture the Congress. A battle thus ensued betwen the 'pro-
changers,' who wanted Congress to enter the councils, and the
'no-changers,' led by C.R., who wished to adhere to the boycott.

For some months the CDEC tour took the heat out of the
controversy. From his 'cabin in the steamboat as it throbs in
its course up the great' river, C.R. wrote of the 'forest-clad hills
and broad-bosomed Brahmaputra' of Assam, which he was
visiting for the first time.

Adding that 'Assam's greatest beauty is the family loom,' he
contrasted the 'sisters in Assam, . . . plying the shuttle and
making garments for themselves and their children,' with the
'highborn ladies' elsewhere in India 'laboriously picking and
choosing from the silks exhibited in the bazaar' (*Young India*,
17.8.22).

At times sending four or five pieces a week to *Young India*,
he asked, 'What became of the Bombs?' and answered: 'It is the

Mahatma's hold and the truths he . . . drove home into the mind of India that have . . . made secret crime a thing to be ashamed of' (22.6.22).

It was 'a mistake,' he wrote in another piece, 'to lay undue emphasis on Indianisation':

> The self-respect of India does not depend on the colour . . . of its officers. It depends on the complete control which the representatives of the people of India have over the officers . . . Then it matters little whether [the bureaucracy] is composed of Englishmen or Scotchmen or Indians (24.8.22).

Here C.R. anticipated his own role fifteen years later when as a democratically chosen Premier of the Presidency he would be served by Indians, Scots and Englishmen.

A section in Congress urged a boycott of all goods from Britain and a preference for imports from other countries. To C.R. this was 'the road from one prison to another, not to emancipation.' Moreover, singling out British goods for a ban would suggest malice (*Young India*, 2.11.22).

C.R.'s writing reflected the thinking of the Mahatma, whose release seemed to be C.R.'s chief desire in 1922. The thought that Gandhi 'at the age of 53 [had] to rot in jail for six long years' agonized C.R. 'What is outraged love doing?' he asked, and exhorted Indians 'to marshall their invincible strength' to secure freedom for Gandhi (*Young India*, 7.9.22).

As the Mahatma's interpreter, he was asked if physical force in self-defence was permissible. C.R.'s answer was, 'No one may surrender to wrong.' But violence for political objects was out (15.6.22).

Noting that the public debt was 'increasing at a pace that should alarm all honest administrators,' C.R. made the radical proposal that Congress should 'give notice that any further loans floated on the sanction of the present . . . sham legislatures of India will be repudiated' (*Young India*, 17.8.22).

Turkish developments were partly pleasing but chiefly disconcerting. Kamal Pasha defeated the Greeks. Many Indians shared what C.R. called the 'joy of the East in finding itself strong,' (21.9.22) but Kamal also deposed the Sultan and abolished the office of the Khalifa. Swept away along with the Khalifa was a major fuel for the nationalist drive, Khilafat.

The CDEC submitted its report on 30 October. Unanimous in the view that the country was not ripe for mass civil disobedience, endorsing but not proposing limited disobedience, the CDEC was evenly divided on the question of council entry.

Vithalbhai Patel, a council enthusiast from the start, was supported by Ajmal Khan and, to C.R.'s disappointment, by Motilal Nehru. For a while C.R. feared that Ansari too would desert him, but in the end Ansari and Iyengar joined C.R. in advising that the council-boycott should continue.

On one issue, the proposed boycott of all British goods, which he opposed, C.R. found himself in a minority of one. But he felt he 'would be doing grave wrong if [he] did not stand by Mahatmaji's oft-emphasised view' (*Young India*, 23.11.22).

Leading the attack on the council-boycott, Das, who was released in August, Motilal Nehru and Vithalbhai Patel were men with resources and of acknowledged stature. Das, in addition, was Congress President. C.R., on the other hand, was a comparatively new political figure groomed in the unprepossessing town of Salem.

Though a General Secretary, he commanded no 'bloc' or faction and possessed but little influence on moneyed men. But he had *Young India* and he owned a sharp intellect. His arguments were not easy to refute.

Elections, he pointed out, would cause 'a fatal drain on resources,' drawing off funds, men, time and talent from constructive work, which was preparation for the next round of battle. Also, competition for seats and offices would intensify caste and communal feeling. 'Wreckers from within' were reminded by him that the bureaucracy had ample powers to rule, through certificates and ordinances, without the legislature's assent.

Moreover, said C.R., members elected to councils on Congress tickets might ignore or defy Congress instructions; there could be 'a gradual corruption and disintegration of the

Congress organisation.' Besides, elections would 'surely place the policy of the Congress in the hands of the wealthy and their friends' (*Young India*, 30.11.22).

The first trial of strength took place in November, when the AICC met for six days in Calcutta, but a decision was postponed to the end-December annual session of the Congress at Gaya.

Das and Nehru mounted an impressive effort to bring their supporters to Gaya. To Satyamurti, who with Srinivasa Iyengar and Rangaswami Iyengar comprised the trio campaigning for council entry in the South, Nehru wrote:

> It is now time to work hard to see that persons in favour of running elections are returned as delegates in large numbers . . .
> If we can count on the support of even one-fifth of the delegates from Tamil Nadu, Andhra and Karnataka, victory will be certain.[2]

On the sandy banks of the Phalgun, not far from the Bodhi tree under which, 2,500 years earlier, Gautama had become the Buddha, the delegates gathered. A profusion of white tents, a cluster set apart for the leaders, had sprung up to house them.

Lodged in a tent among the mass of the delegates, and not among the 'leaders,' C.R., 44, bespectacled and dressed in a white kurta and dhoti with a folded *angavastram* draped over one shoulder, was a focus of attention. So were Das, the President, and Nehru.

Discussions went on for days. Formal meetings were followed each night by informal but crucial talks at the different tents. C.R. would go to Das' and Motilal Nehru's; Nehru came to his. For his unflinching loyalty to Gandhi and his programme, and because of a similarity in appearance, C.R. was satirized by opponents as the 'Deputy Mahatma.' Gaya as a whole, however, called him Rajaji, a form coined by Mahadev Desai, Gandhi's secretary.

An early issue was the proposal to boycott British goods. Many of the no-changers were sufficiently embittered against the Raj to support this departure from Gandhi's view, and the CDEC, we saw, had voted five to one for such a boycott. But C.R. fought pluckily against it, and the Subjects Committee voting, though going against him, was surprisingly close: 146 to 129.

At the open session the voting was reversed. C.R. was to cherish this result all his life, describing it at the time as 'proof that the nation holds fast to the teachings of its imprisoned leader in spite of every temptation' (*Young India*, 11.1.23). Rainy, Chief Secretary of Bihar-Orissa, informing Delhi of C.R.'s victory, reported that his words against a boycott of British goods had 'created a deep impression.'[3]

He easily carried Gaya on debt repudiation. His scheme had been called 'clearly Bolshevik,' 'immoral' and 'outrageous.' It was 'immoral and outrageous for any government to borrow beyond the capacity of the people it purports to govern,' C.R. retorted. Clarifying that only future loans would be repudiated, he said that borrowings 'till now . . . will be deemed a lawful charge' (*Young India*, 7 & 21.12.22).

On the council question, Gaya heard the powerful oratory of Das and Nehru. Vithalbhai, Srinivasa Iyengar and Satyamurti ably supported them. Not expected to win, C.R. countered them.

Courteous, quickwitted and sure of his stand, he was in irresistible form. A voice from the audience urged him once, while he was speaking, to move forward in order to be seen better. 'I cannot show my back to the revered President,' replied C.R.

But he could cause the defeat of the President's policy. Das and Nehru were worsted in debate and votes. C.R.'s resolution retaining the council-boycott was passed by 1,740 votes against 890.

'Great was their (the no-changers') enthusiasm and the hero of the day was the Madras leader, Mr Rajagopalachari,' Subhas Bose would comment.[4] Prafulla Chandra Ghosh, a future Chief Minister of Bengal, would observe: 'Mr Rajagopalachari became the leader of the Congress at Gaya.'[5]

'The limelight into which the votes have thrown me does not suit my temperament,' wrote C.R. (*Young India*, 18.1.23). Liking it or not, he stayed in prominence for another year, striving to protect Congress from the fascination of councils. In the end he was unsuccessful.

Das, who vacated the Congress chair following the Gaya voting, and Motilal Nehru launched a Swaraj party within Congress, with Das as president and Nehru as secretary. The Swaraj party would aim, they said, to capture the councils.

Was the Congress splitting? Abul Kalam Azad, released in January 1923, made an immediate compromise bid; he was joined by Jawaharlal Nehru, also lately freed. 'Forced,' as *Young India* put it, 'to accept the [Swarajist] revolt as a fact and make terms with the rebels,' C.R., Vallabhbhai Patel and Rajendra Prasad asked the AICC, meeting in Allahabad at the end of February, to accept a truce.

C.R. moved and Motilal Nehru seconded a resolution calling on both sides to suspend, until 30 April, all propaganda for or against the councils.

Accompanied, and translated, by Prasad and Devadas, a now well-known Rajaji spoke to large crowds in the Central Provinces, Bihar, Bengal, the Punjab and Sind. His theme was Gandhi's constructive programme. Years later, with characteristic modesty, Prasad would recall:

> It was my privilege to join him and also translate his speeches . . . which, while giving me an opportunity of learning a lot, also saved me the trouble of delivering . . . speeches of my own, which, I doubt not, would have fallen flat after his brilliant performance.[6]

In Jubbulpore (Jabalpur) in the Central Provinces, their visit provided an opportunity for the sort of defensive disobedience that C.R. had been looking for. To welcome C.R. and his friends, the municipal committee wanted to hoist the national flag over the Town Hall; the District Magistrate vetoed the plan. After C.R. spoke to the thousands 'who had angrily gathered,' local citizens resolved to disobey the fiat.

'The Flag Calls You,' C.R. enjoined in *Young India* (23.3.23), adding:

> We cannot get a cleaner or a more beautiful battlefield . . . We should get ready for a severe struggle round this flag.

Ascending the well-guarded Town Hall tower peacefully was however a problem. A month later the Central Provinces Government offered a plainer opportunity for disobedience: it banned a street procession with a flag.

A defiance campaign was organized by Jamnalal Bajaj, a rich Marwari who was a trusted disciple and a generous supporter of the Mahatma. Flag in hand, hundreds from all over India, including many southerners enlisted by C.R., trooped to Nagpur, where they were arrested.

Taken into custody in June, Bajaj was awarded eighteen months in jail and a Rs 3,000 fine. To realize the sum his car was attached but not a man in Nagpur would buy it; it was sold, finally, in Kathiawad.

The 'flag satyagraha' ended when the Raj allowed Congressmen to carry the flag along a route earlier banned, with Congress agreeing to declare after one procession that the satyagraha was over.

So who won? Reading, the Viceroy, said to Peel, Secretary of State, that the terms seemed to provide 'evidence that persistent pressure on Government is not devoid of results.'[7]

Stimulated by the response to the flag satyagraha, C.R. thought of defensive disobedience by 10,000 Congress volunteers, but the ingredients for success were absent. Congress was to wait until 1928 before reapplying the pressure of disobedience.

Meanwhile, the Hindu-Muslim relationship was souring. Campaigns of conversion and reconversion had divided the communities, especially in the Punjab. C.R. noted that Hinduism, 'a non-proselytising religion, is flapping its wings in Punjab and has frightened Islam.' ' "If you may fly, why not I," says she.' Cautioning Hindus against inviting Muslim ill-will, he said that as a Hindu he had a 'birthright to speak harshly to my Hindu brethren' (*Young India*, 5.4. & 3.5.23).

C.R. was missing the Mahatma. In April 1923 he went to Poona's prison gates to welcome Shankerlal Banker, Gandhi's fellow-prisoner, who had been released after a year. Though Banker brought no advice from the Mahatma, who was against counselling from jail, meeting him cheered C.R. He felt that Banker's soul had been 'polished by a masterhand' during his 13-month obligatory retreat in Gandhi's company (*Young India*, 31.5.23).

In July C.R. learnt that because of his 1921 conviction he had been expelled from the Masonic Lodge by its District Grandmaster, who happened to be one of the Raj's senior officers. Some Lodge members in Salem resigned in protest, and a bitter C.R. retorted in *Young India* that he had been freed from one of 'the governing caste's many instruments for political domination' (12.7.23). Five years earlier, serving as a Lodge Master, he had thought differently.

The Swarajists gained new support during Congress's internal truce. At a Bombay meeting in May, the AICC passed a resolution disallowing propaganda against councils. This was a violation of Gaya and produced a strong reaction from C.R.:

> We cannot submit. All Congressmen and Committees have to decide whether they will accept the AICC's decision or the Congress resolution. (*Young India*, 31.5.23)

He, Vallabhbhai, Prasad and three others resigned from the Working Committee. Categorically, he declared in *Young India* (7.6.23):

> We have worked this policy (constitutionalism) for forty years, and at no time did it seriously threaten the life of the Bureaucracy. The only policy and the only programme that frightened the British lion are the policy and the programme that we adopted at Calcutta in 1920 . . .

> If we have not yet succeeded in getting up the requisite capacity to carry it out . . . it is a problem of work and time. It is not for us to throw away the new weapons and take to bows and arrows again.

Defying the Bombay resolution, C.R. began the 28 June issue of *Young India* with the words, 'Don't Vote.' The Swarajists, meanwhile, were placarding the country with calls to vote for them in the November elections. Das and C.R. embraced each other when Das visited Salem, but the exchange of fire did not cease.

C.R.'s fightback had some effect. When it met again in July in Nagpur, the AICC refused, after a speech by him, to censure the provincial Congress committees of Tamil Nadu, Karnataka and Gujarat for criticizing the May decision. This led to the resignation from the Working Committee of Jawaharlal Nehru, who had asked for the censure.

The Congress was now speaking with two voices. To end the confusion, some of C.R.'s friends asked at Nagpur for a special plenary. Despite Swarajist opposition, the proposal was carried. Abul Kalam Azad was chosen as the President.

Das, however, indicated that he would not accept an adverse verdict. This ruled out a reaffirmation of the Gaya decisions, for few in Congress were ready to lose Das and Motilal Nehru. Even C.R. was not.

He hoped that Muhammad Ali, who was about to emerge from prison, would influence Das and Nehru against councils, and other no-changers hoped that an Ali-C.R. combination would preserve non-cooperation.

C.R. shattered the second hope by announcing that he would not attend the special session! He claimed he was exhausted: 'I have been putting my feeble frame to a great strain. I have kept the flag flying only until stronger hands could reach and hold it aloft and firm . . . '

But apparently a bigger factor was an insinuation (we do not know by whom) that he desired power. 'My struggle with talented and powerful opponents is given the name . . . of low intrigue,' he complained. He would 'quietly withdraw . . . from places and positions of seeming power,' including the *Young India* editorship, if only to prove to himself that he did not care for power (*Young India*, 16.8.23).

His colleagues protested. By retiring, said one of them, C.R., who had 'dared to fight for Bapu's flag against the concentrated onslaughts of erstwhile friends and open foes,' would weaken Gandhi's cause (*Young India*, 6.9.23).

Ali delivered the second blow. He advocated a compromise

whereby Congress in Delhi repeated its dislike of councils but permitted council entry to those desiring it. . 'Life is all through one second best,' Ali told Mahadev Desai (*Young India*, 4.10.23).

Wiring C.R. for advice, Desai had informed him of Ali's stand. C.R., in his own words, 'threw up the sponge at once.' In a telegram he said:

> When Maulana Muhammad Ali, who holds stronger views than myself regarding councils, who holds in his broad chest the heart of Islam in India — when even he . . . gave up the fight, it was final.

C.R.'s telegram reached Delhi just before Vallabhbhai was to commence a speech. Patel told the session:

> We are all soldiers. There is no leader. But there is one man with a clear head and clear thinking who has sent this message which I will read to you.

After reading C.R.'s telegram, Patel added, 'I have nothing more to say,' and sat down.

Abandonment of council-boycott produced a deep grief in believers in non-cooperation. 'Remembering the hope of the dawn and the power of the day,' and 'now fated to watch the last dipping of the sun,' they were mournful, as George Joseph, an ardent no-changer who had given up his law practice in Madura and was on the Working Committee, admitted. Joseph, who was asked by C.R. to take over the *Young India* editorship, added:

> Since the days of the Calcutta Special Congress, Gandhism has won all along the line . . . It is good for everybody to be beaten.

What concerned C.R. as much as the Delhi compromise was a call by the session for a boycott of all British goods. This rejection of the Gaya line was, in his view, a repudiation of Gandhi. According to C.R., the 'easy' doctrine now being preached was 'not love, but hatred . . . not self-suffering but cleverly-organized embarrassment of the enemy.'

Recalling a Bengal leader's words in November 1922 that

'our national work cannot be based on love but must be built on hatred,' C.R. spelt out what he thought Gandhi had prescribed:

> . . . suffering, maximum; love of the enemy, true and genuine, the love and pity that filled Christ's eyes with tears as he was led to Golgotha, not suppressed hatred finding legal and constitutional shape.[8]

C.R.'s acceptance of the Delhi compromise contributed to the estrangement of two of his close colleagues, E.V.Ramaswami Naicker and S. Ramanathan, from him and the Congress. The former, spoken of as E.V.R. and, later, Periyar, would head a militant anti-Congress and anti-Brahmin movement in the South.

The Congress met in Cocanada (Kakinada) in December 1923 for its annual session. In November, the Swarajists had secured several seats in provincial councils and in the Central Assembly.

On his way to the session, C.R. was joined in his second-class compartment at Bezwada (Vijaywada) station by P.C. Ray, the distinguished scientist who was to open a khadi exhibition at Cocanada. After studying C.R. for a few moments, Ray said, 'Frail, fragile, frame.' 'Yes,' C.R. at once agreed, 'and there is a fourth "f" — a failure.'[9]

Cocanada, presided over by Ali, reaffirmed the Delhi compromise. Embittered men on both sides needed calming, and C.R. averted an unpleasant incident by leading an angry Motilal Nehru off the dais.

There was talk of a Das-C.R. pact. C.R. moved and Das seconded a resolution declaring that non-cooperation remained the Congress policy. That was the theory. In practice, the Swarajists were permitted council entry, though as Swarajists rather than as Congressmen.

On occasion C.R.'s mind would leave the heated controversy and dwell on pleasanter scenes. On 22 November he wrote in *Young India*:

> Have you seen a little white child smiling and opening its blue eyes wide with pleasure when the ayah's dark baby comes to join it in play? . . . I never could tire of looking at the beautiful

frontispiece in an edition of *Uncle Tom's Cabin* that was with me — little Eva hanging a wreath of roses round the good Negro's neck and sitting down on his knees, laughing.

C.R. was conferring in Salem with four visitors when, in the second week of January 1924, he heard that the Mahatma had been operated for acute appendicitis. Such operations were not, at the time, routinely successful. A worrier at the best of times, C.R. was anxious when he and his visitors — Jamnalal Bajaj, Shankerlal Banker, Maganlal Gandhi, the Mahatma's 'right hand' at his Sabarmati Ashram, and Mathuradas Tricumji of Bombay — began a tour of the province to promote khadi.

Their first call was at the village of Pudupalayam, south-west of Salem, where they were welcomed by Ratnasabhapati Gounder, a landlord whose late father had been C.R.'s friend and client. 'If you teach my sons English,' the father had once said to C.R., 'I shall present you a village.' The offer was not taken up, but under C.R.'s influence Gounder had become a Congress supporter, a teetotaller and a khadi wearer.

Listening to the visitors' hopes about khadi, Gounder said he could put a four-acre coconut grove at C.R.'s disposal. The travellers looked at the grove and moved on.

In Poona, meanwhile, though the electricity failed and he had to work by torchlight, Maddock, the Raj's Surgeon-General for Bombay, had successfully removed the prisoner Gandhi's appendix. 'Too happy for words,' C.R. wired Devadas.[10]

On 27 January C.R. called on Gandhi, their first meeting in two years. The reunion must have been touching. In his diary, Mahadev Desai, who was present, would only write, 'There are things of the heart too sacred for disclosure.'[11]

Finding the Mahatma reduced to almost half his size, C.R. was struck dumb. Gandhi, lying on his bed, went on the attack, charging C.R. with indifference to *his* health. He should learn, Gandhi told C.R., from the British: had not Asquith gone on a Mediterranean cruise soon after the War began? In obedience to Government and Gandhian rules, politics was not discussed.

On 5 February, Gandhi was unconditionally released because of his health. 'We are now in a changed world of gladness and hope,' C.R. said in a telegram to the Mahatma, who went to Juhu-on-the-sea near Bombay to recuperate.

Narasimhan, 14, and Lakshmi, 11, were being coached at Salem Extension by a pair of tutors, with C.R. also helping when he could. Krishnaswami, C.R.'s oldest boy, was now a journalist on *Swarajya*, a Madras daily started by T. Prakasam; Ramaswami had found a place in the National Medical College of Bombay, which trained students like him who had left Government colleges.

Ramaswami met Gandhi in Juhu. Thereafter the Mahatma wrote to C.R.:

> It is now 3.30 a.m. I have hardly slept during the night after 12.00. You are one of the reasons.

> I had a chat with your son last night. Incidentally I asked him whether he wrote to you and you to him in English or Tamil. When he told me it was English, the information cut me to pieces . . .

> You are my greatest hope. Why this, as it seems to me, grave defect? If the salt loses its savour, etc. What are the Tamil masses to do if her best sons neglect her? . . . With deepest love, M.K. Gandhi.[12]

After thus chastizing C.R., the Mahatma had Ramaswami write a letter to his father in Tamil. Attached to the letter was a note from Gandhi:

> The son has begun before the father. That is as it should be. You can see how the discovery has preyed on my mind . . .[13]

To C.R. the castigation was 'hardly distinguishable from supreme happiness.' He wrote to Devadas:

> I have written to Bapu . . . that he saw but one fault. What shall he or I do about the hundred other[s]? What have I that I may offer to my beloved master, except a hundred faults?[14]

As for Tamil, C.R. was to produce, in course of time, works both popular and literary in it. Gandhi intervened, too, in the matter of C.R.'s health. His asthma, C.R. had written to

Devadas, was giving him 'unsleepable nights'; it was 'like an occupancy tenant who won't be evicted.'

Gandhi sent two Ashram members, one after the other, to nurse C.R. — Shivaji Bhave, brother of the scholar-ascetic, Vinoba Bhave, and Surendra Gupta. Though C.R. was embarrassed at having 'to keep young and good souls for serving me physically,'[15] Shivaji and Surendra — massaging, fetching and carrying — restored their patient's health.

The health of Congress concerned both the Mahatma and C.R. In 1920 Congress had been converted from a talking shop into a fighting body. Now it seemed to be reverting to speech-making. To restore rigour to Congress, C.R. and Gandhi came up with the novel idea of replacing the four-anna fee for Congress membership with a levy of self-spun yarn.

Under the title, 'A Condition of Congress Membership,' C.R. aired the idea in March 1924; Gandhi fully backed it. What drill was to the soldier, and churchgoing to the Christian, C.R. and Gandhi wanted spinning to be to a Congressman.

Assailed as queer and undemocratic, the 'spinning franchise' was proposed by Gandhi in June, adopted with alterations in December, and made optional in September 1925.

A Gandhi proposal that the no-changers should fill party posts while the Swarajists concentrated on the councils was shelved under fierce Swarajist opposition when the AICC met in Ahmedabad in June 1924. Another Gandhi resolution condemning the murder of an Englishman in Calcutta narrowly escaped defeat.

In Gandhi's words, Ahmedabad 'defeated and humbled him.' He decided to yield what he had thought crucial, the council-boycott, for something more precious, tolerance among Congressmen. He would stoop in order to conquer the Swarajists, and let them control Congress.

C.R. saw the rationale. In March he had written, 'The best and only course open is to let the Swarajists work their dear plan to the full . . . and then discover the blind alley they are in.'[16] But he was not as ungrudging while stooping as his chief, and was disappointed that the Mahatma had not crushed the Swarajist revolt.

While expecting the Swarajists 'to retrace their steps when experience has disillusioned them,' Gandhi recognized nonetheless, as he wrote to C.R., that they supplied 'a felt want' and represented 'a large section of people who want petty relief.'[17]

Asking Gandhi to shoulder the Congress Presidency, C.R. had written him in July 1924: 'The masses still feel that you alone must lead.'[18] With the Swarajists saying the same thing, Gandhi agreed to preside at the December session.

At the end of September, Gandhi announced that he would fast for 21 days as penance for the Hindu-Muslim violence of 1924. To be at Gandhi's side, C.R. went to Delhi. Gandhi was staying at the home of Muhammad Ali for the period of the fast. C.R. had questioned Gandhi's capacity to survive the self-inflicted ordeal, but found, as he wrote to Devadas, that 'the Mahatma smiled and talked as if he had been taking his milk and fruits every meal every day.'[19]

Delhi's disturbed climate improved as a result of the fast, but C.R. had noticed a hardening in senior Muslim leaders. To Devadas he added:

> I am afraid I am a changed man as regards the Mussalman leaders . . . I see no change of heart in them. They have not realised the least bit the psychology of the fast — that Bapu is in deepest grief over the ingratitude of the Mussalmans and the sufferings of the Hindus . . .

> I shall return, I fear, from Delhi with altered mind in regard to the most essential things . . . A long period of suspension of all Swaraj activities is before us.

Hindu-Muslim trust, a jewel mined in 1919-20, was cracking.

Despite Gandhi's efforts to calm him, C.R. was not at peace about the Swarajist ascendancy. They wanted, he thought, 'all

the prestige of the Congress to be theirs, unshared by others ...
[and] they want Bapu, of course, for without him what prestige
is there for the Congress?'[20]

As for Gandhi, however, his fight was with the Raj, not
with the Swarajists. When some Bengal Swarajists were arrested,
including young Subhas Bose, Gandhi not only protested strongly;
he resolved to strengthen the Swarajists.

He would suspend non-cooperation and agree that the
Swaraj party was in the councils 'on behalf of the Congress.'
The concession was spelt out in a pact he signed with Das and
Motilal Nehru. On their part the Swarajists accepted the 'spinning
franchise,' while Gandhi agreed that the yarn earning membership
of Congress did not have to be self-spun.

Gandhi's pact with Nehru and Das grated on C.R., who
told the Mahatma that the saving clause made 'a mockery' of the
spinning franchise.[21] Answering that the pact was 'a bold
experiment in nonviolence,' the Mahatma added: 'Cheer, boys,
cheer. No more of idle sorrow.'[22]

At Belgaum in December 1924, when Gandhi took the
Congress chair for the first and last time, it was C.R. who
moved, despite all his grievance, the resolution in favour of the
amended spinning franchise. 'I depend on the judgment of the
Guru ... and I feel at ease,' he explained (*Young India*, 15.1.25).

To the Mahatma his surrender to the Swarajists was also useful
for testing the no-changers. If they really believed in constructive
work, they would gladly yield their Congress positions to the
Swarajists. Their duty was 'self-effacing, silent and sustained
service, without grumbling and without the expectation of
reward' (*Young India*, 17.11.24).

C.R. was dropped from the Working Committee. Where
would he 'self-effacingly' serve? C.R. had an answer.

He would tear himself away from his house in Salem
Extension and put his roots down in a scarcely-known village:
he would move to the patch in Pudupalayam offered by
Ratnasabhapati Gounder. There he would raise an Ashram and
practise, with any willing co-workers, the gospel of constructive
work.

He would train khadi workers there, and work to attack the grip of untouchability and the hold of liquor. The Mahatma, with whom C.R. discussed the idea in Belgaum and, after the session, in Sabarmati, gave his blessing; and Jamnalal Bajaj, who had endowed a 'Gandhi Seva Sangh' to assist rural service, indicated that some money might be available.

A Bangalore meeting on 10 January, when, as he put it himself, C.R. spoke in his 'finest propaganda style and kept the audience laughing,' tempted him to 'tramp the country all over India and address such meetings as of old.' But he had given Gandhi his word to 'settle down at Pudupalayam.'[23]

On 6 February 1925 the Ashram was 'opened' and C.R.'s feet set on a rough and almost unmapped path.

Around the Ashram, granite hills rose from an undulating earth. A fortress erected by Tipu, a reminder of bygone strength, looked down from Sankaridurg hill, 12 miles north of Pudupalayam.

Tipu's British successors had built a railway line through Sankaridurg; but from there to Pudupalayam it was a dusty three-hour bullock-cart journey past ragi and cotton fields, palm trees and roadside shrines. Half-way, at Tiruchengode, stood an imposing rock, two thousand feet high, its bosom sheltering an ancient Ganesa temple. From Tiruchengode town, officials of the Raj administered about a tenth of Salem district, including Pudupalayam.

The village of about 150 dwellings did not even have a letter box. The red rocky earth around it was responsive to rain, but the latter by no means made a yearly appearance. Familiar with famine and superstition, the sweltering hamlet of Pudupalayam nevertheless possessed two advantages for C.R.

Firstly, Gounder, its landlord, was his ally. While giving the promised four-acre plot he had also seen to the erection of half a dozen thatched mud huts that comprised the Ashram. Secondly, around Pudupalayam lived numerous weavers who owned their cottage looms, as also ex-spinners, all women, who retained their spinning-wheels. They had been forced, after the advent of factory yarn, to consign these wheels to their attics.

But when the women heard that the Ashram was willing to supply cotton and pay them for spinning it into yarn, they brought their old wheels down and dusted them.

From the start the Ashram defied untouchability. Five 'untouchable' boys were enrolled as members, eating and living with the rest. An instant boycott ensued, and it looked as if Ashram members and their accomplices, the Gounder family, would have to live without milk or vegetables, or only with what one milkman was surreptitiously supplying.

A rumour that the Ashram would be torched proved to be false, but it caused its members to be trained in fire-fighting, a skill later used to tackle fires in nearby 'untouchable' settlements.

Narasimhan, 15, and Lakshmi, 12, were now part of C.R.'s new multicaste family of seventeen Ashramites. Along with Narasimhan and Lakshmi, C.R. occupied one of the thatched-roof huts until another hut with a tile roof was ready. An iron safe containing the Ashram's cash was also kept here.

The 'big room' in the new dwelling was 12 feet by 5 feet; two tiny rooms next to it, one of them serving as a kitchen, completed the hut. A Madura lawyer who had given up his practice, N. Narayanan, was the Ashram manager. In charge of khadi production was C.R.'s young colleague from 1920, K. Santhanam.

For most members, the Ashram meant a new lifestyle: open-air prayers before dawn and at sundown, with all Ashramites participating; coarse meals shared by all together; encounters with snakes and scorpions; hours spent in trying to relieve the lives of the debt-laden, liquor-hit, and rejected poor.

For the last goal, the Ashram's principal weapon was khadi. The women of the villages were enabled to spin. The weavers were persuaded, slowly and not without difficulty, to use handspun yarn, which being thicker, less even and more fragile than factory thread was harder to shuttle across a loom. The end-product, khadi cloth, was energetically hawked.

To begin with, the women spinners earned between a rupee and a rupee and a half a month; this sum, miserable even for the time, was yet often a quarter of what a family made. Within two months, a thousand women living in twenty villages around the

Ashram were spinning. By August 1925, 70 weavers were using handspun yarn.

Next in importance was the battle against liquor. On many a night a decorated cart pulled by a pair of bullocks (picked by C.R. at a cattle market) would carry him and some other Ashramites to neighbourhood hamlets. On reaching a village a drumbeat from the cart would announce the visit. A throng would surround the cart, peer at petromax-lit drawings depicting the fate of men who drank, and would listen to Ashram songs. Then the bullocks would be goaded to heave again for a repeat performance at the next village; five or six villages could be covered nightly.

Congress's national leader of 1922-3 thus became, in 1925, an itinerant preacher in an obscure corner of the South. He was making a mark, for liquor agents soon tried to break up his meetings. Personal work followed propaganda. Importuned by a woman beaten by a drunken husband, C.R. sent for the man, the cobbler Veeran.

Veeran denied drunkenness. 'You were drunk last night and hit your wife,' C.R. again charged. 'No sir, it is not true,' repeated Veeran. Placing in Veeran's hands a pair of chappals that he, Veeran, had made, C.R. said: 'Swear on these chappals that you are telling the truth.'

Veeran fell at C.R.'s feet, owned up and vowed never again to touch liquor. Nor did he, till he died. Well before his death, Veeran took charge of the Ashram's footwear unit.

Schools came up, first in Pudupalayam for the children of Ashramites and of adjoining hamlets, with C.R. as one of the teachers, and then in the quarters of 'untouchables' in different villages; the Ashram strove, not always successfully, for mixed classes in these.

Old wells were renewed and new ones dug where the 'untouchables' lived; fortunately, an Ashram inmate was a water diviner. Every week, Ashramites scrubbed and fed 'untouchable' children in nearby hamlets and dispensed modest medical aid. Until a doctor was enlisted, C.R. himself diagnosed and prescribed.

Also, C.R. and his friends drafted letters from aggrieved villagers to officials and helped sort out some of their disputes.

When a warning from C.R. to the police chief in Tiruchengode resulted in policemen returning the bribes they had extorted in the village of Molipalli, the Ashram's prestige soared.

Lakshmi, thirteen at the time, would later recall an exchange. Her father was perched on a ladder in their hut, fixing a mesh to keep cats out. Thinking that he might fall, she said, 'Chinnan is around. Can't he do it?' 'So it doesn't matter if Chinnan falls and injures himself?' C.R. asked. Born in the 'low' washerman caste, Chinnan was C.R.'s cook and helper.[24]

Yet C.R. was no pamperer. In the view of Chagan, a Muslim spinner who was an early Ashramite, every worker 'was very careful in doing his allocated work lest he incurred Periya Ayya's (the Big Master's) disapproval.'[25]

Crushed by debts and forfeiting his land, Chinna Gounder drove the Ashram cart. In 1973 he told the author that shortly after he was hired C.R. had said to him: 'I won't accept your thumb impression, you will have to learn to write your name.' Later, Chinna Gounder did that, and went on to pay off his debts and redeem his land.

Visiting the Ashram six weeks after it opened, Gandhi observed that 'a little touch of kindness, a little touch of humanity and love' had made the 'untouchables' 'one flesh with the whole Ashram.'[26]

Early in 1925, Gandhi and Shaukat Ali had gone to Kohat in north-western India to inquire into a riot that had caused the Hindu minority to flee. The two did not agree on what had happened. *Young India* published their separate reports. The partnership of the Mahatma and the Ali brothers was coming to an end.

In June, C.R. Das suddenly died in Darjeeling. Gandhi responded to his passing away by prescribing a Swarajist mould for Congress. The spinning franchise, C.R.'s pet, was made optional.

Sweating for khadi in the baking hinterland — in accordance, he thought, with the Mahatma's deepest wish — C.R. felt offended. To him the declaration virtually amounted to Gandhi joining the Swaraj Party. He poured out his embittered feelings to Devadas:

> I wish I had been a private gentleman, pure and simple — and
> I should then have been less of a fool than I am now. Why
> should this poor yarn franchise be made to die this slow and
> lingering death? I would prefer to kill it at once.[27]

This was crossed by a letter to C.R. from Gandhi:

> You are . . . perhaps the nearest to me. My innermost being
> wants your approbation of what I am doing and thinking. I
> cannot always succeed in getting it, but it craves for your
> verdict . . . [28]

Gandhi's words melted and overwhelmed C.R. He wrote to
Devadas:

> Can I bear the great weight of his love? . . . I have replied that
> I approve of all that he has done. The truth is my fits of
> opposition are temporary outbursts of Adam. My soul has
> been surrendered long ago and I cannot but agree.[29]

In September, when the AICC met in Patna, the Swarajists
accepted Gandhi's offer and at last obtained control over the
whole of Congress. Spinning would go on, it was agreed, under
the aegis of a new body, the All India Spinners' Association
(AISA). C.R., Vallabhbhai, Rajendra Prasad and Jamnalal Bajaj
were made members of the AISA executive.

Zealous though he was in his rural work, C.R. at times
missed the old life. 'I pine to see you all,' he said in a letter to
Devadas. He even followed cricket:

> Do not think I have not been following the quadrangular
> match. Today's exciting news at this far corner is up to the
> close of the Europeans' second innings. I do feel that the
> Hindus will make the 355 runs somehow and win. (14.8.25)

As the year reached its end, an occasion arose for C.R. to break
the letter of his pledge to boycott the courts. An 'untouchable'
who had entered the temple of Tiruchannur near the famed
Tirupati shrine was apprehended by the police, prosecuted for
insulting religion, and sentenced to a Rs 75 fine or a month's
rigorous imprisonment.

Incensed by the conviction, C.R. acceded to a request to

argue the appeal. However, he would not call himself 'a defence lawyer' or wear the required turban and coat. Covering his head and shoulders with a khadi sheet to show respect to the judge in Chittoor, he obtained permission to argue as the accused's friend.

The old advocate was alive and kicking inside C.R. He felt, as he argued, that he had 'never stopped practice these seven years.' All that the outcaste had done, said C.R., 'was to steal the Lord from the temple, keep him in the casket of his heart, and walk away.'

Was that, asked C.R., a crime? Was adoration an insult? Moreover, C.R. pointed out, no witness had deposed that his religious feelings had been wounded by the outcaste's entry.

The accused was acquitted.[30] The contagion caught on. Another 'untouchable' similarly charged was also acquitted. But the non-cooperator conscience had been shocked. Some Ashramites frowned at C.R.'s 'return' to the polluted courts, but he was defended by the Mahatma. C.R., wrote Gandhi,

> would have been like a Pharisee if he had sat there still, gloating over the sanctimonious satisfaction of noncooperating, while the accused could have been discharged by his intervention.[31]

6

Ashram

1925-29

The Mahatma's efforts to strengthen the Swaraj Party failed. Obstruction was a difficult policy to maintain in the face of the prizes the Raj was offering.

After Motilal Nehru accepted a nomination to the Skeen Committee on cadet training, and Vithalbhai Patel became President of the Central Assembly, Tambe, a Swarajist leader in the Central Provinces (C.P.), went a step further and joined the provincial Executive Council.

Nehru condemned Tambe's action and was promptly counter-criticized by other Swarajists. By the end of 1925, the Swarajists were obstructing one another, not the Raj.

Though his warnings regarding councils had been proved right, C.R. saw a role for the Swarajists sitting there: they should demand prohibition. If the Raj came in the way, a lively political issue would emerge. 'A poor man's question like drink is the best fireworks even such as they (the Swarajists) want,' he said to the Mahatma.[1]

S. Satyamurti, a prominent Swarajist, replied at first that Swaraj was the only issue, adding: 'I would rather be a member of a free nation of drunkards than belong to a slave nation of teetotallers' (*The Hindu*, 1.1.26). Pointing out that 'a definite struggle will bring matters to a head,' C.R. succeeded, as he put it in a letter to Mahadev Desai, in 'samjhaving' Satyamurti and the Madras Swarajist chief, Srinivasa Iyengar.[2]

In return for the Swarajists' adoption of prohibition, C.R. agreed, in a public statement, to assist them in elections due later in 1926. This alignment, which accorded with Gandhi's position, was probably also influenced by the worsening caste climate in the South.

C.R. thought that the prohibition plank, promising relief to the mostly non-Brahmin poor, would counter the Justice Party's propaganda that Congress, still led in the South by Brahmin Swarajists, was anti-Brahmin.

However, C.R.'s support of the 'Brahmin Swarajists' incurred the displeasure of two influential non-Brahmins who had been his comrades for some years, E.V.R. and Varadarajulu Naidu, and also of *Justice*, the organ of the non-Brahmin party. Hitherto, as C.R. said in a letter to Mahadev Desai, he had been 'a great favourite with the Justice people' (6.2.26).

'Your central work,' Gandhi wrote to C.R. in March 1926, 'is to develop the Ashram you have established. Everything else is subsidiary.' By this time over 2,000 women around the Ashram were adding precious coins to their families' means.

At the end of March C.R. felt he could afford a quick trip to Bihar and Ahmedabad. Rajendra Prasad had requested him to address the students of Patna National College, which had been started in 1920-1.

In Patna he explained that he was not 'hiding himself amidst spinners and weavers.' The truth was that they had lost a round of battle against the Raj because the capacity to suffer, which was their cannon, had been exhausted. Now, in places such as his Ashram, they were making more cannon for the future.

On the way back to his Ashram, before a large gathering in Ahmedabad, he again used a military expression. The spindle, he said, was the Indian masses' pistol.

By the summer of 1926, 30,000 spinners were employed in making khadi in Tamil Nadu, but the Marathi-speaking region was cooler towards it. In this bearish territory C.R. achieved a breakthrough. At Nagpur's Tilak National College he challenged students to live in the villages, ply the wheel and wear khadi.

Two students of the Government-run Morris College were

in the audience; they pressed C.R. to speak at their college. With the Principal, a Mr Cheshire, in the chair, C.R. talked about destitute villagers:

> Can you move these people from their homes? ... You must find employment at their very doors ... You do not solve the problem of hunger by industrialising India, but by making it industrious.

True, C.R. admitted, khadi was more expensive than mill cloth, but it was indecent to wear the latter. Not caring for the poor was indecency.

'You are a hawker, sir. What are your wages, may we know?' a student asked. 'No wages, my friend,' C.R. answered, 'but the satisfaction of feeling that I have persuaded some of you to wear khadi.' 'It is a retrograde step, sir,' the smart student rejoined. 'Yes,' C.R. agreed amidst loud applause, 'as retrograde as asking a dishonest man to go back to honesty.'

'Never was the effect of a speech more instantaneous,' wrote Mahadev Desai. Mr Cheshire offered to wear khadi himself, as did a number of students. Many yards of cloth were bought on the spot, and a Students' Khadi Union was formed.[3]

The Swaraj Party was bruised afresh in 1926. A group opted for 'responsive cooperation' and formed the Indian National Party (INP). In August, Lajpat Rai left the Swarajists and helped Pandit Malaviya start the pro-Hindu Independent Congress Party. This was a reaction to Muslim assertions: Muhammad Ali had said that he prayed for the day when he would convert Gandhi to Islam.

Motilal Nehru, making his first approach to C.R. after the Gaya split, and Srinivasa Iyengar, who was chosen Congress President for 1926-7, sought C.R.'s help in the November elections. Iyengar had requested C.R.:

> [to] bestir yourself and help support Congress prestige and organisation which are being shattered deliberately in Maharashtra, C.P. and U.P. by rebellious persons ... A word by you at this time will have a very welcome effect.[4]

While not getting embroiled in North Indian quarrels, C.R. made a strong appeal to the Madras electorate to vote for Congress, i.e. Swarajist, candidates. United under Iyengar's vigorous leadership, the Madras Swarajists fared well, winning more seats than the Justice Party, but not so their colleagues in the rest of the country. In the U.P. and the Punjab, the party was routed.

Pledged against becoming ministers, the Madras Swarajists kept Justice out by declaring support for a ministry of Independents led by C.R.'s friend and neighbour in Tiruchengode, Dr P. Subbaroyan.

At C.R.'s suggestion, an exhausted Gandhi spent over three months in 1927 in Mysore state, first in Nandi Hills, 35 miles from Bangalore, and then in the latter city. In both places he was the Maharaja's guest; C.R. was his constant companion, along with Narasimhan and Lakshmi. Kasturba, Mahadev Desai and Devadas also joined Gandhi's party, which reached Nandi in the second half of April.

At Nandi's altitude there were 'wonderful cloud effects at sunset' and the climate was bracing. In two weeks the Mahatma turned the corner and the spring in his gait returned. C.R. acted as 'jailor,' keeping Gandhi's visitors at bay and terminating his interviews.

A lawyer doing the cooking, a barber dressed in khadi, a chief medical officer and his wife clad likewise — sights such as these fed the Mahatma's spirits. C.R. ushered in visitors: the Right Honourable V.S. Srinivasa Sastri, Iyengar the Congress President, Sir M. Visvesvaraya, ex-Dewan of Mysore, Sir Mirza Ismail, the Dewan, and so forth.

From Sir Mirza, the Mahatma and C.R. obtained the assurance that the state's officials and employees were free to wear khadi.

Despite the number of callers, it was a relaxing, enjoyable time. When the Mahatma protested at the restrictions on his walks, talks and writing, C.R. replied: 'I am the jailor, but the prisoner can dismiss me at any moment. Yet so long as I am the jailor, I must take the necessary precautions' (*Young India*, 12.5.27).

In Nandi, C.R. did a bit of writing — a short story and a dialogue, both on the theme of khadi. A pessimist predicting that khadi would die because it was expensive was told that patriotism would sustain it (*Young India*, 26.5.27):

> Don't you abstain from meat as a Brahmin, though beef is cheap and nourishing? Is it economy? You marry your girl at 12. Is it wisdom? Do you not yield to custom, good or bad? You spend money on useless ceremonies and on poor relations . . . Is it economics or only sentiment?

Thomas Hood was quoted by C.R. in aid of khadi:

> No alms I ask, give me my task;/Here are the arms, the leg,/ The strength, the sinews of a man/To work, and not to beg.

Commenting on Tagore's 'Jana Gana Mana,' C.R. said to Devadas in Nandi, 'I find the poem limited. Why victory only to India? Why not to humanity?'[5]

Early in June, they moved to Bangalore, where Gandhi, Kasturba, C.R. and the rest — nearly 50 in all — were looked after at the Maharaja's Kumara Park estate by his employees — 'my brothers and sisters, not servants,' as Gandhi said of them.

Hundreds attended Gandhi's daily prayers, and others called on him. Continuing to function as Gandhi's jailor, C.R. had the Kumara Park mains switched off when, despite several polite hints, a distinguished visitor did not get up to leave.

C.R. did a brisk trade in khadi. Ladies came, absorbed the khadi message and 'came in again, but entirely changed, in the new khaddar sarees they had purchased' (*Young India*, 30.6.27).

A milestone in the khadi story was the South India Khadi Exhibition, conceived by C.R., that opened in Bangalore at the end of June. Women spinners from Karnataka, Andhra and Tamil Nadu demonstrated their art. The progress of khadi was demonstrated through maps and charts, and spinners competed before the thousands of visitors. They scanned the charts, made notes, watched the khadi being made, and purchased the fabric and the charkha that created it.

Khadi-clad South Indian actors rendered on stage the story

of Kabir, the saintly weaver-poet, in what Gandhi said was 'exquisitely pronounced' Hindi. It was the first time in years that he or C.R. had seen a play.

The response to the Exhibition delighted Gandhi, but he made a significant remark about his plans to K. Srinivasan, editor of *The Hindu*, 'If I am spared, I shall certainly enter again the political arena. It will then be a fight to the finish' (*Young India*, 16.6.27).

As C.R. put it to Mahadev Desai, Mysore's ruler, Krishnaraja Wodeyar, 'wished to have the privilege of doing all he [could]' for Gandhi,[6] yet the Maharaja, dependent on the Raj that Gandhi was committed to fighting, could not afford to meet him. In a signal of support, however, the Maharaja sanctioned a khadi centre in Badanval village near the city of Mysore. Six men for the centre were sent for training at C.R.'s Ashram, and the state's Industries Department made 1,500 charkhas.

The area around Badanval was dry and needed a source of income besides farming. Its women could spin. The Pudupalayam story was repeated, and khadi took off in Mysore. The state's example was followed a year later by Hyderabad.

For four months, a recovered Gandhi, supported by C.R., stumped much of South India and Ceylon, bringing to every stop the gospel of khadi. Crowds, eager and large, were instructed and often uplifted. On occasion the travellers were touched — in Arni, a few 'untouchables', almost completely naked, gave C.R. a five-rupee note for khadi, and in Madras, cobblers who had heard that Gandhi's sandals were tattered, made a new pair for him.

A few of the Mahatma's interviewers in the South told him that C.R. could not be trusted, for he was a Brahmin. Gandhi's response went beyond defending C.R. In Karaikudi he said that C.R. was his 'only possible successor.'[7]

Meanwhile, there was a development which took both C.R. and the Mahatma by surprise. Devadas and Lakshmi fell in love and wanted to marry. In Bangalore Devadas gave C.R. a letter requesting his daughter's hand.

C.R.'s closeness with Devadas, as we have seen, went back to early in 1920, when he travelled with C.R. from Amritsar to the U.P. and Bihar. He was not quite twenty then. Devadas had first met C.R., and presumably Lakshmi, ten months earlier in Madras, where he was teaching Hindi, just after C.R. had moved to Madras from Salem. Lakshmi was just seven then.

C.R., as we have found, often confided in young Devadas and at times communicated with Gandhi through him, as at other times he did through Mahadev Desai. When Gandhi was jailed in Poona, C.R. and Devadas had visited him together. Clearly, there was warmth and trust between the two.

But when Devadas's feelings towards C.R. grew into, or helped kindle, or were joined by, love for Lakshmi, C.R. at first did not know what to think. He liked Devadas greatly, and the idea of an alliance between his daughter and Gandhi's son must have thrilled him. Yet, arranged rather than love-marriages were the norm around him.

Moreover, Devadas was not a Brahmin. Even more importantly, in the autumn of 1927 Lakshmi was only fifteen. C.R. discussed the matter with his daughter and also with Gandhi. Lakshmi told her father, as C.R. would later relate to the author, that while she would not marry Devadas without her father's permission, he should not expect her to marry anyone else.

Caste was not a serious issue with either C.R. or Gandhi, but Lakshmi's age was. The two fathers wanted to be sure that it was true love rather than infatuation. Lakshmi was told by her father and also by Gandhi that she should test the truth of her love. No doubt most Indian girls were married by the time they were her age, but she should wait. And while she waited, there should be no contact — no meetings and no letters.

Devadas, twenty-seven, was similarly adjured. He returned to North India. Obeying the injunctions, he and Lakshmi were to wait for four years for parental permission and another two years for marriage.

C.R. called Gandhi's 15-day Ceylon tour 'an unprecedented triumphal march' (*The Hindu*, 28.11.27). Welcomed with devotion and affection by the Ceylonese, the Mahatma did not lose his frankness. To Indian businessmen in Colombo he said:

> Let your scales be absolutely correct, your accounts accurate. I hope you regard every woman in this land as your own sister, daughter, or your mother.

Sophisticated Sinhalese women gathered in a stately drawing-room were addressed thus:

> My hungry eyes rest upon the ornaments of sisters whenever I see them heavily bedecked . . . Do you know the hideous condition of your sisters on plantations? . . . Their service will deck you more than the fineries you are wearing.[8]

Tamil plantation workers 'poured in,' wrote C.R., 'to see Mahatmaji in their thousands and made many a hillside alive with men and women' (*The Hindu*, 28.11.27). Gandhi warned them against liquor.

Raising money for khadi was one of C.R.'s aims in Ceylon. At Jaffna, the last halt on the island, he crossed his target of Rs 1 lakh. He had also collected numerous orders for khadi.

After returning to India on 30 November 1927, the Mahatma went to Andhra and Orissa, and C.R. to his Ashram. The Bania and the Brahmin, master and disciple and yet comrades, had been with each other for seven months. It was, and would remain, their longest spell together.

For three years after the Ashram's opening, the front against the Raj had been quiescent. Suddenly, and unwittingly, the Raj breathed life into it.

Summoned to Delhi in November 1927 from the deep South, the Mahatma was told by Lord Irwin, the Viceroy, that a statutory commission led by Sir John Simon would tour India and make constitutional recommendations. Gandhi told the Viceroy that this piece of news could have been sent to him in a one-anna envelope.

He also noted, as did most Indians, that the Simon Commission was going to be all-white. The Empire was willing to inform Indians but unwilling to trust them. Political India boycotted the Commission. Across the land the cry was raised, 'Simon Go Back.'

C.R. attended Congress's annual session held in Madras in December 1927 but took no part in the deliberations of what still was a Swarajist Congress. He was present because the Mahatma was. Gandhi spoke on khadi; C.R. translated him into Tamil. For two more years C.R. was content to remain off-stage politically, but in March 1928 he momentarily appeared on the stage.

Jawaharlal Nehru, recently returned from a trip to Europe and Russia, was advocating 'foreign propaganda.' Writing in *Young India* (1.3.28), C.R. urged realism. 'The Indian fight against Britain,' he wrote, 'if it is to be by nonviolent means, depends entirely on its own strength and can never be converted into an international affair.' What was needed was not 'propaganda, foreign or domestic,' but 'solid constructive work and internal strength.'

Internal strength was soon demonstrated by the peasants of Bardoli in Gujarat, where the 1921 struggle would have climaxed but for the Mahatma's abrupt cancellation of it. Refusing to pay an enhanced land tax, the peasants and their families saw their lands and cattle confiscated but did not give in. In August 1928, after five months of struggle, the increase was virtually scrapped and much of the seized property returned. The Raj had yielded.

The hero of Bardoli was Vallabhbhai Patel, who had organized the peasants. C.R. had offered to join Patel on the battlefield but Gandhi wanted the struggle to remain a local one. Hailing 'a wonderful victory,' C.R. said that 'Vallabhbhai's part in Indian history has been great.'[9]

Gandhi meanwhile experimented with his diet and pondered a European invitation. C.R. wrote to him: 'I did get very angry when I read your last letter about almond paste and coconut milk. Knick-knacks like these are totally inadequate substitutes for bread and milk.'[10]

As for Gandhi visiting Europe — the Mahatma wanted C.R.

to 'say without fear or favour what you will have me do' —
C.R. advised against it. He thought that morale in India would
be hurt.

Stories from C.R.'s pen continued. Gandhi found them
'touching' and published them. They generally involved
'untouchables' and Gandhi hoped they would 'melt some stony
"touchable" heart' (*Young India*, 12.1.28). C.R.'s translations of
verses from the Tamil saint-poetess, Avvai, and Subramania
Bharati, the poet laureate of the Tamil country who had died in
1921, also appeared in *Young India*. The Bharati translations
were C.R.'s retort to the Madras police seizing 2,000 copies of
a collection of Bharati's patriotic songs.

The contributor C.R. and the editor Gandhi did not always
see eye to eye. The Mahatma turned down a piece by C.R., now
untraceable, on the Hindu-Muslim question on the ground that
the views expressed were 'entirely unseasonable.' C.R. was
advised to 'keep them under lock and key for the time being.'
Replied C.R.:

> I fully expected that you would put an embargo on such stuff.
> That is why I called the article 'Unsold Stock'; and unsold it
> is and you advise that it should not even be exposed for sale.[11]

There were phases in 1928 when C.R. seemed depressed. He felt
'dilapidated,' he once wrote to Gandhi, and in another letter in
May he said:

> Your letter has not helped me to attain the peace which you
> intended it should do. I see your love and your reasonableness.
> But peace must come from within. As yet it is like a parched
> throat only causing pain if you try to find moisture and
> swallow.[12]

The parched area around the Ashram did not give any cheer;
there was a continuous drought. Nor was C.R. satisfied with the
pace of the khadi movement, though he noted, objectively, that
a lost industry had been revived in the neighbourhood, and that
'a number of half-starved families were getting a few more
mouthfuls of food' (*Young India*, 23.8.28).

The Mahatma hoped that C.R. would have the 'patience to

wait for a century . . . and the desire to succeed tomorrow.'[13] In fact, C.R. wondered whether the future would see selfless workers to sustain khadi, and whether the Ashram was not 'like a foreign mission among the people' (*Young India*, 23.8.28). Yet it is a fair surmise that C.R.'s depression was linked to his absence from the political stage.

As for khadi, C.R. himself pointed out in May that while the textile industry had given employment, after a long innings and a huge investment, to four lakh people, khadi, in four years and with a tiny fraction of the investment, had given supplementary work to one lakh in their own homes (*Young India*, 24.5.28).

Not limited to khadi, his Ashram gave impromptu medical relief, in a 19-month period, to 28,095 patients, and fought the drought that had sent women to the bottom of wells from where they tried to scoop water with coconut shells. Jowar bought in Mysore state was sold at half the cost to about 250 worst-hit families (all of whom were 'untouchables') within a three-mile radius from the Ashram.

The freight for this grain was high, and the railways refused a concession, but donations sought through *Young India* sustained relief for 35 weeks.

The Congress session held in Calcutta at the end of 1928 heralded a return to Gandhian ways. At the Mahatma's instance Motilal Nehru presided, though some had desired Vallabhbhai's chairmanship in recognition of his Bardoli feat. Unable to mount a struggle without Gandhi, the politicians were asking the Mahatma to return to the helm.

In turn, Gandhi summoned C.R. On his part C.R. tried to enlist Annie Besant's cooperation for the struggle of civil disobedience that now seemed possible. She had kept out of the 1920-1 defiance. C.R. assured her that violence would be prevented by restricting civil disobedience this time to trained volunteers. For a moment it looked as if Mrs Besant would enter the fray but the moment went and she chose to stay out.

In Calcutta, where C.R. and the Mahatma stayed together,

a younger set of leaders led by Subhas Bose and Jawaharlal criticized the willingness of a committee headed by Jawaharlal's father Motilal to tolerate Dominion Status for India.

Gandhi proposed a compromise: Congress would ask for complete independence if London did not commit itself within a year to freedom for an Indian Dominion. After accepting the compromise in committee, Bose and Jawaharlal opposed it at the open session, an about-turn that elicited blunt words from the Mahatma:

> You may take the name of independence on your lips but all your muttering will be an empty formula if there is no honour behind it. If you are not prepared to stand by your words, where will independence be?[14]

As C.R. saw it, Dominion Status versus complete independence was an 'issue which nobody takes as real.'[15] He agreed with Gandhi's appraisal:

> Dominion status can easily become more than Independence, if we have the sanction to back it. Independence can easily become a farce, if it lacks sanction. What is in a name if we have the reality? A rose smells just as sweet whether you know it by that name or by any other (*Young India*, 6.9.28).

Endorsing the Gandhi formula, Calcutta proclaimed that non-violent non-cooperation would be revived at the end of 1929 unless the Raj satisfied the Congress demand by then.

Could a sanction be forged in a year? Congress set out to enroll and train cadres through a burst of constructive activity. Prohibition was settled upon as a principal form of this activity and placed, by a Working Committee resolution, in C.R.'s charge.

Yet, to C.R., prohibition was more than a means to an end. He persuaded the All Parties' Conference (APC) convened in Calcutta alongside the Congress to accept it as an end in itself. A prohibition clause was inserted in the constitution the APC proposed for India.

Gandhi generated fervour for khadi and against foreign

cloth. In March 1929 there was a ten-minute shower of foreign cloth before him in Calcutta: the mountain of fabric was then set ablaze. As in 1921, the Mahatma argued that he was transferring the nation's resentment from 'men to things' — to foreign cloth.

But some of his compatriots had other ideas. Saunders, the Assistant Police Superintendent of Lahore, had been shot dead in December 1928. Two bombs and a heap of pamphlets were thrown in April 1929 at the Central Assembly floor, without injury to anybody, from the visitors' gallery.

Two prisoners of the Raj, Wiziya, a Buddhist monk in Burma, which, at the time, was administratively linked with India, and Jatin Das, arrested over Saunders' murder, died following marathon hunger-strikes against prison conditions. Gandhi's letter on the subject to C.R. showed his desire for the latter's approval:

> I am wholly against hunger-strikes for matters such as Wiziya and Jatin died for. Any expression of such opinion would be distorted and misused by the Government. I therefore feel that my silence is more serviceable than my criticism. Do you not agree with my judgment of the hunger-strikes and with my consequent silence?[16]

C.R.'s reply is not traceable but we may infer that he supported Gandhi on both counts.

The Mahatma's return to the centre of national affairs was a signal for Madras to seek C.R.'s leadership. There was keenness for battle in Vedaranyam in Tanjore district, where a Madras provincial conference was held in the first week of September 1929, but C.R. and Vallabhbhai, who together toured South India for a fortnight after the conference, counselled patience till the end of the year.

C.R.'s mood became brighter. In a letter he wrote in February, the Mahatma could read 'unrestrained joy.'[17] While not referring to his spirits, an English participant at a conference C.R. attended at Red Hills near Madras noted 'the soundness and brilliance of his exposition and the courage and simplicity of his life.'[18]

Though what Gandhi called C.R.'s 'ingenuity' (*Young India*, 28.3.29) was evident in Tamil Nadu's lead in khádi production — in 1927-8 it supplied more than a third of the national output — the drink demon had drawn a greater share of C.R.'s energy. He used two platforms — Congress, and the Prohibition League of India, of which he became honorary general secretary, succeeding a Briton, Revd Herbert Anderson. At the instance of G.D. Birla, the industrialist, Gandhi had asked C.R. to accept the post.

By April 1929 a national scheme for prohibition prepared by C.R. had been adopted by the Congress executive. Under this scheme every province would have a prohibition unit, attached to the provincial Congress Committee, and every taluk an organizer who would create anti-drink sabhas in towns and villages. A sabha could picket liquor shops or dissuade bidding at auctions where liquor vendors bought licences, and also sponsor healthy entertainment to draw off the tempted.

Against liquor, C.R. drafted pledges, composed lyrics, designed a flag and arranged demonstrations. He trained a team and countered objectors. Political moderates, cautious about Congress, joined C.R. on the platform of the Prohibition League. He linked up with Lord Clwyd, the British temperance enthusiast, and welcomed to Madras 'Pussyfoot' Johnson, famed for his silent nocturnal raids on liquor joints in America.

He brought out two magazines for the cause, *Prohibition*, the League's quarterly, and *Vimochanam* (Release), a Tamil monthly. Though *Vimochanam* came out only ten times, it left a mark on Tamil journalism, presenting the poor man's misery 'vividly and with infinite pathos' and becoming, at least for one reader, 'the symbol of how large the human spirit could be, and how good.'[19]

In his 1929 engagements diary, C.R. recorded the dates, places and serial numbers of his prohibition talks. There were 62 speeches in all, the last delivered by him as president of the

Temperance Conference held along with the Lahore Congress of December 1929, which was chaired by Jawaharlal Nehru. Jawaharlal called C.R. 'the unquestioned leader of the prohibition movement in India.'[20]

The Raj blew hot and cold over prohibition. While a village munsiff in Salem district, accused of taking pledges against drink from 'untouchables', was suspended for a year, the Madras Government, pressed by public opinion, allotted Rs 5 lakhs for temperance education. Informing the Raj of his Ashram's anti-liquor credentials, C.R. coolly asked for a share of this sum. Of course, he did not get it, and had not expected to.

Late in 1929, however, Madras's Excise Commissioner, E.B. Cotterell, visited the Ashram and recommended to Government the creation of a dry area around it. This had been C.R.'s demand for some time. The Government agreed to close 53 toddy and arrack shops in the Tiruchengode and Rasipuram taluks.

The dry zone experiment lasted three years. The area's 'untouchables', whom liquor had hit the hardest, were weaned. But by April 1933 all the shops that were closed down were reopened in retaliation for the civil disobedience that C.R. would lead in 1930 and 1932.

Someone had written that Gandhi's southern India collections had been made over to C.R. who was maintaining idle Brahmins with them. Seated on the veranda of his hut, C.R. was working on a suitable reply to the calumny when he was disturbed by a woman in rags. Crying 'Swa-a-mi, my Swa-a-mi,' the woman, clearly an 'untouchable', fell prostrate before him.

C.R. thought she would beg. She did not. Her husband, she said, had borrowed five rupees from a moneylender, paid ten as interest, and died. Now the moneylender was threatening that if she did not return the five rupees he would break up her daughter's wedding, to take place in a few days.

'Go on with the wedding,' C.R. told the woman. 'If the moneylender interferes in any way, come and tell me at once. Do not fear.' After the woman left, C.R. sent a warning that restrained the moneylender.

He also tore up the article he was writing in self-defence. The .libel against him, he wrote in *Young India* (11.7.29), was nothing against 'the miseries of these defenceless people.'

On occasion, however, he felt obliged 'to sing my own heroism' and to tackle those who charged that he was not going far enough in reform. In October 1929 he wrote:

> I claim to be a greater changer than many that now beat up a great deal of dust. I have been an out-caste among my relations for the last twenty years. I have done and am doing things which my clamorous friends have not, I believe, in their own persons attempted.

The lines occur in a postscript to a short story by him about the hazards of a 'two-anna, two-minute' court marriage. Reformism was tinged with caution. While agreeing that 'to stand still is death; change alone is life,' and 'wanting Hindu marriage reform in many desirable respects,' C.R. held out for 'the continuance of the religious form,' which made for 'strength and durability in the marriage tie.'

'I confess,' he continued in the postscript, 'that I have discovered in myself a strong element of Conservatism.'[21]

On 31 October 1929 Lord Irwin announced that a Round Table Conference (RTC) of British and Indian statesmen on India's future Constitution would take place in London, and conveyed what appeared to be a commitment from Britain:

> I am authorised on behalf of His Majesty's Government to state clearly . . . that the natural issue of India's constitutional progress . . . is the attainment of Dominion Status.

Welcoming the Irwin declaration in a joint manifesto, Gandhi, Malaviya, Mrs Besant, Motilal Nehru and some others asked whether the proposed RTC would result in India acquiring Dominion Status. On 23 December, a few hours after escaping unhurt from a bomb explosion, Irwin informed the Mahatma and four others calling on him in Delhi that the promise sought could not be offered.

The ball was back with Congress, now gathered in Lahore for its annual session.

7

Vedaranyam
1929-31

At the Lahore Congress, where a fight was in the air, C.R. watched with approval the return of the Mahatma as an active general and was pleased at the council-believers' admission of failure. Jawaharlal, 40, presided.

C.R. had wanted Gandhi to take the chair. However, resolved to give it to the younger Nehru, Gandhi turned down the idea. He also secured the withdrawal of Vallabhbhai, favoured by five of the Provincial Congress Commitees. Conscious of Subhas Bose's and Jawaharlal's leftist inclinations, the Mahatma expected Nehru's nomination to help Congress unity and to keep Jawaharlal in check.

He extolled Jawaharlal's qualities but added that youth had to let its energy 'be imprisoned, controlled and set free in strictly measured' quantities. And he assured the older men that a Congress President was 'not an autocrat . . . He can no more impose his views on the people than the English King.'

Moved by Gandhi, Lahore's cardinal resolution defined the goal of Congress as complete independence, asked the Swarajists to resign their legislature seats, and authorized the AICC to launch civil disobedience when it thought fit. This was comfortably passed, but when Gandhi asked Congress to conngratulate Irwin on his escape and to appreciate the Viceroy's efforts, Subhas Bose opposed him. Losing narrowly in a vote,

Bose walked out and, with the support of Srinivasa Iyengar, formed the Congress Democratic Party.

C.R. and Patel were lodged next to each other in tents. It was bitterly cold, especially for those from the South, but, as Sitaramayya would record, 'the heat of passion and excitement, . . . the flushing of faces on hearing the beat of the war-drums, . . . was in marked contrast with the weather.'

At midnight on New Year's Eve, 300,000 men and women, including C.R. and his son Narasimhan, now twenty and a delegate from Tiruchengode, gathered on the banks of the Ravi to watch Jawaharlal hoist free India's tricolour.

Congress was to unleash an attack, but how? How would it sponsor nationwide disaffection against a system still extremely powerful, and keep the rising nonviolent? A new Working Committee, which included C.R. and Patel, considered the question and named Sunday 26 January as independence day. On that date the people of India were asked to take a pledge which termed submission to alien rule 'a crime against man and God.'

In Wardha, on his way back from Lahore, C.R. said that India would shortly 'pronounce talaq to Britain.' He spoke also of 'two great sins' — one, 'the Government's sin,' the sale of liquor, which made beasts of men, and the other, 'the people's sin,' untouchability, which treated some as worse than beasts (*The Hindu*, 11. & 15.1.30).

On 26 January, the appointed day, no speeches were made anywhere. This was in accordance with Gandhi's instructions. The flag was hoisted, the pledge read out, and audiences asked to raise hands if they subscribed to it. Place upon place that Sunday morning was a forest of hands.

The councillors were getting the message. Though a few Swarajists were hesitant still, 172 members of legislatures, including 30 at the centre, resigned by February.

All over the South, C.R. drew huge crowds. He advised: 'Do nothing wrong in the eyes of God, but resist injustice. Resist, not by bringing a heavy stick down on your opponent's skull, but by suffering the penalties imposed by him for your resistance.'

He ridiculed: 'The British say, "Swaraj is good for us, not for you, and because you are so wicked as to ask for it, we must cure you by locking you up." '

And he challenged: 'The hour is struck for all of us to cast away our dearest attachments and to make a supreme effort again.'

'We must all die, but let us not leave the struggle to our children,' he said in Tiruppur; and in Salem in early February he spoke of freedom 'in our lifetime.'[1]

Gandhi, meanwhile, had been 'furiously thinking' for a plan of action. It had to be defiant and sacrifice-demanding to attract the 'secret, silent, persevering band' of young men lured by violence. It had to be nonviolent; he was sworn to the creed. And it had to be uncomplicated so that all freedom-desiring Indians could adopt it.[2]

Suddenly it came to him: break the salt law. By taxing the manufacture and sale of salt the government was hurting 'even the starving millions, the sick, the maimed and utterly helpless.' To deny the Government this inhuman tax, the people, he felt, should make their own salt.

Some like Jawaharlal were mystified by the choice of salt, but C.R. harboured no doubts. He told a big gathering in Sholapur:

> You may say, 'Hello, this is a funny thing. All along he was telling that if we made khaddar we will get swaraj, now he says we must make salt also.' Buying salt means accepting this government and owing allegiance to it. Making salt is refusing to owe allegiance to government.

At Tuticorin he said:

> A people [who] rise in revolt . . . cannot attack the abstract constitution or lead an army against proclamations and statutes but have to capture a stronghold here, a stronghold there, seize an arsenal here and destroy a fortification there.

As in armed conflicts, so also in civil resistance, you must give up the general and apply yourself to the particular. Civil disobedience has to directed against the salt tax or the land tax or some other particular point . . .

Moreover, the salt tax was a cess on necessity, bloating the price of a gift of nature that should not cost more than 'the cost of removal.'[3] To no one's surprise, Congress asked C.R. to organize disobedience in the Tamil country.

The Mahatma moved. He wrote to the Viceroy, asking not for complete independence, not even for early Dominion Status, but simply for a repeal of the salt tax, adding that if the law was not reconsidered, he and his Ashram co-workers would break it.

At Gandhi's request, a young English Quaker called Reginald Reynolds, dressed in khadi, delivered the Mahatma's letter at Viceroy's House. This was Gandhi's way of showing that his attack was aimed at British rule, not at Englishmen.

The Viceroy's four-line reply said that Gandhi was inviting 'danger to the public peace.' 'On bended knees I asked for bread,' the Mahatma commented, 'and I have received stone instead.' Gandhi added that it was his 'sacred duty' to break 'the mournful monotony' of the 'prisonhouse peace' that India enjoyed.

He would perform this duty, Gandhi declared, by marching the 241 miles from his Ashram at Sabarmati to Dandi, a village on the West coast, and breaking the salt law there. He would take with him 78 colleagues, all ready for suffering and pledged to nonviolence.

Early on 12 March, the Mahatma and his fellow-marchers prayed and set forth.

So began what a Briton has called 'the weirdest and most brilliant political challenge of modern times.' Adds Geoffrey Ashe: 'The English laughed, their Indian flatterers echoed them, the intellectuals of Congress were bewildered . . . and the great motionless crust of India began trembling.'[4]

'It is not salt but disobedience that you are manufacturing,' C.R. perceptively wrote to Gandhi (8.3.30)[5].

Adding that he had been considering a different focus for the South — liquor — C.R. raised with Gandhi the possibility of a dramatic 'march from Cape Comorin to a single picketting centre, getting volunteers on the way.' In the end, however, he conceded the advantage in 'a unified attack all over India.'

After touring the province 'to see how the land lies,' he announced (*The Hindu*, 18.3.30): 'I have decided that we should start the campaign in this province on the salt issue.'

The crowds at C.R.'s meetings were unusually large and his speeches were going down very well, one in Madura producing, in *The Hindu's* words, a 'great impression on the public mind.' (15.3.30)

Before launching the southern campaign, he went to Gujarat for Congress meetings and to see the walking Mahatma. There were no waverers. left in Congress. The response to Gandhi's march had converted them. The satyagraha was ratified. Now it had to be spread. A pledge framed by C.R. for Tamil Nadu satyagrahis was circulated for use in other provinces. It said:

> I believe in nonviolence as an article of faith for the achievement
> of Swaraj . . . I shall patiently and willingly undergo all
> penalties including imprisonment . . . May God help me (*The
> Hindu*, 27.3.30).

On 23 March C.R. joined the trekking Mahatma in the village of Buwa, north of the town of Broach and almost halfway to Dandi. C.R. was not sure that the Mahatma, at his age, would survive the physical exertion of the march and of the imprisonment that would follow. Fully expecting to earn a fair prison term himself, C.R. thought that this meeting with Gandhi in a rough hut in the hot hamlet of Buwa might prove to be his last. When it ended, C.R. found himself reluctant to leave.

On 5 April the Mahatma reached Dandi with his followers and camped near the shore. Next morning, early, he bathed in the ocean, walked to where the salt lay thick and 'scooped some of it up with his fingers' and then he 'straightened and held it over for all to see: the treasonable gift of God.'[6]

Indians now knew what they should do — make, sell or buy salt illegally. In large numbers they proceeded to do so. The person who did not know what to do, to arrest Gandhi or to 'ignore' his defiance, was the Viceroy. Meanwhile revolt erupted in the far North and the deep South.

A complacent Madras Government had informed Delhi that 'very few people . . . seem to have definitely committed themselves to take part' in C.R.'s march and that 'the question of funds may prove an additional stumbling block.'[7]

C.R. had decided that his marchers would walk about 150 miles from Trichy to a town on the Tanjore seaboard, Vedaranyam, which possessed convenient salt swamps and had a merchant called Vedaratnam Pillai who was willing to host a battle.

Ten days before the march, the Tamil Nadu Congress Committee unanimously made C.R. its president. Though he had made it clear that only those ready for long prison terms, even for death, qualified to join, he had to turn down volunteers; the Raj's assessment was wrong.

The eventual regiment — the 'hundred gems,' as they came to be called — included a man from each Tamil district, seven youths resigning jobs in Bombay, eight from C.R.'s Ashram, an engineering college lecturer and a railway official, the last two also sacrificing their posts.

Tanjore's astute and energetic Collector, J.A. Thorne, promised the Raj an 'ignominious failure' of the march provided he was authorized to arrest all those feeding or housing the marchers for 'harbouring criminals,' and to arrest C.R. as soon as he entered the district. 'I apprehend no great difficulty dealing with the sheep once their shepherd is gone,' he wrote to Madras.[8]

The Collector's game plan was to cut off food and shelter for the marchers. 'I shall take pains to see that they meet with increasing difficulties and discomforts,' he asserted. If somehow they managed to reach Vedaranyam, there he would 'prevent their getting accommodation.'

Assessing C.R. as 'probably the ablest and certainly one of the most intransigent' of the South's leaders, the Raj nonetheless reasoned that arresting C.R. before he violated any law would 'confer on him the cheap martyrdom that he and Mr Gandhi desire.'[9] But Thorne was authorized to arrest 'harbourers.'

His warning that 'harbouring' would invite a six-month sentence and a fine was carried on Tamil leaflets, declared by beat of drum and in the Press. Retorted C.R.: 'The satyagrahis are prepared to lie under the sky or starve on Tanjore soil . . . We pursue our advertised plans' (*The Hindu*, 11.4.30).

Precisely at 5.00 a.m. on 13 April, the day of the Tamil New Year, a figure of medium height with a bald oval head, a staff in his right hand and a haversack across his shoulder, emerged outside a house in Trichy cantonment. He was joined on the road by 96 others who stood in rows of two, most of them in caps and holding staves. As they stood in silent prayer, C.R.'s daughter Lakshmi and another girl applied the vermillion mark of blessing and luck on each forehead.

Hundreds had assembled at the dim hour. When the marchers took their first deliberate steps, there was a complete hush; tears trickled down some faces. After a few seconds the notes of a song could be heard: '*Kathiyinri, Rathaminri*' — 'No sword, no blood.'

A reporter walking in step sought C.R.'s comment on Thorne's order against 'harbouring.' 'Thorns and thistles cannot stem this tide,' said C.R. However, at Koviladi, on the second day, the party found the *chhatram* — pilgrims' inn — barred and bolted against them. C.R. was invited to a private home and the rest slept on the bed of the Cauvery.

'Stretching out everywhere, the Cauvery serves us like a great friend and mother,' C.R. wrote to his children. 'She assists with our lodging and our washing. On her sands thousands, including large numbers of women, attend our meetings.'[10]

In the halts that followed, the marchers were joyously hailed. More important, they were fed and housed. Thorne's directives, reinforced in places by face-to-face warnings from the Collector, were defied or defeated — at one halt, bundles of food were hung on trees the marchers could not miss. Eventually C.R. had to appeal against pampering the satyagrahis.

Walking five miles in the morning and five in the evening — past rice-fields or groves of banana or coconut, with the Cauvery, flowing seaward, often by their side — they carried with them their larger message. At stops they fraternized with 'untouchables' and refrained from entering temples from which the latter were barred, swept village streets, and spoke up for Hindu-Muslim unity and against drink. And at two crowded meetings a day they preached the gospel of nonviolent revolt.

Reporting on the 'extraordinarily vigorous propaganda' along the route, Thorne argued with his seniors 'with all respect' that he had been right in proposing C.R.'s early arrest. He added that 'harm to the prestige of Government has been done by the march.'[11]

At Tanjore town, Thorne's post of command, a brother and sister gave, in C.R.'s words, 'shelter and noble hospitality,' but in the morning his heart sank when he found nothing arranged for a meeting scheduled for later in the day. No one, C.R. was told, was willing to offend Thorne.

A lawyer finally offered C.R. a rickety old table; with the help of the lawyer's gardener, C.R. had it moved to the meeting site. Not a soul was to be seen there, and C.R. prepared himself for 'a miserable failure,' and to 'yield to [Thorne] at least in one battle.'

But when C.R. and his team marched down at the appointed hour, they saw a surging mass of humanity. The twenty thousand present observed 'complete silence' for a minute, and then, 'with a heart moved to the depths,' C.R. spoke.[12]

At Kumbakonam, Pantulu Iyer, ex-member of the Legislative Council, kept all the marchers in his home for two nights and fed them. He was jailed for six months. Some government servants who were in the welcoming crowd at Semmangudi lost their jobs.

Ramachandra Naidu, who had fed the satyagrahis at Tiruthuraipoondi, was picked up by the police from the meeting addressed by C.R. that he was attending. The thousands who watched Naidu being arrested remained calm: Gandhian teaching had been imbibed.

A mighty crowd was waiting in Vedaranyam, reached on 28 April, the sixteenth day of the march. C.R., tired but smiling, declared that he would break the salt law on the 30th and expect others to break it after him; in an aside, he prophesied that the police arresting the satyagrahis would one day serve them.

The next day, settled in a camp erected by Vedaratnam Pillai, the marchers fasted and prayed. So did, in fellowship, many others in the province. And C.R. formally wrote to Thorne of his intention to violate the law.

By now all India was astir and the Raj had reacted. *Young India* and *Navajivan* were banned by an ordinance. Jamnalal Bajaj was sentenced for over two years. Jawaharlal was in prison. A police bullet had hit Jairamdas Daulatram, Working Committee member from Sind.

From 23 to 28 April the town of Peshawar, lying on the historic invasion route from Central Asia, was in control of the Khudai Khidmatgars ('Servants of God') led by Abdul Ghaffar Khan. Scores of the followers of Ghaffar Khan, pledged to nonviolence, were killed by machine-guns, but unarmed Muslims escaped on one occasion when the Raj's Garhwali soldiers, who were Hindus, disobeyed an order to fire at them.

The sun had not yet risen over the Bay of Bengal on 30 April when C.R. and 16 fellow-marchers set out towards the Edanthevar salt swamp, a couple of miles from the Vedaranyam camp. Almost immediately after they reached the swamp, bent down and picked up some salt, the district's police superintendent, Govindan Nair, backed by other officers and 50 constables, was on the scene.

C.R. and others holding salt were told to surrender it. On their refusal, Nair arrested C.R. To prevent demonstrations of sympathy, Thorne had arranged for a quick, secluded trial in a salt shed near the sea. When the prosecutor fumbled for words, C.R. helped him out.

The judge, Ponnuswamy Pillai, was composed when he pronounced six months' rigorous but broke down and wept while signing the jail warrant.

Some minutes after C.R. was put on a train for Trichy, a

small white man entered his compartment and extended his hand to the prisoner. It was Thorne.

To him C.R. said: 'Your plan was bold, but you forgot that we are in our own country.' Thorne smiled and replied, 'Yes, we have each tried to do our best and our worst.' Then he ordered coffee and refreshments for C.R.[13]

On the train C.R. wrote to Lakshmi: 'My dear child, I am getting leave . . . Pray to God for our battle's success.'[14]

The next day, shops were closed and business suspended throughout the Tamil country. At Vedaranyam, the cycle of gathering salt, seizure by the police, and a fresh gathering continued for weeks despite a series of selective arrests. Thorne hoped to frighten away the ranks without having to arrest them. Sticks were brought down on fists, and salt forced out. But the 'sheep' stood their ground and kept collecting. Only when Thorne ordered wholesale arrests was the cycle broken.

Including the marchers, 375 were arrested for revolt in Tanjore district. In secret reports to Madras, Thorne said that C.R. had 'had something of a triumph, even Mohamedans and Adi Dravidas "(untouchables)" taking part in the receptions.' He noted, too, that C.R. 'throughout maintained excellent discipline among his followers, . . . always adhered to nonviolence . . . and refrained from the arts of demagogy.'

Added Thorne: 'If there ever existed a fervid sense of devotion to the Government, it is now defunct.'[15]

Forty-five minutes after midnight on 5 May — within five days of C.R.'s arrest — two oficers holding pistols and thirty rifled policemen surrounded Gandhi's straw hut in Karadi, three miles inland from the Arabian Sea. Gandhi was arrested under an 1827 regulation that did not require a trial. At ten minutes past one, after being allowed to pray, Gandhi was put in a lorry and driven more than 200 miles to Yeravada Central Jail in Poona.

On 21 May, 2,500 satyagrahis under the leadership of Sarojini Naidu and Manilal Gandhi, the Mahatma's second son, raided the Dharasana salt works. They were pitilessly beaten, and arrested, by a force of 400 Indian policemen commanded by six British officers. Two died and 320 were injured but not a hand was raised by the peaceful army.

In an even bigger raid on 1 June in Wadala, 15,000 took part. Irwin admitted to the Secretary of State in London that he was 'surprised at the dimensions the movement had assumed.'[16] The shunning of foreign cloth was now virtually complete. Imports of cotton piecegoods were down by 75 per cent, khadi sales up by nearly 60 percent. Liquor sales were curbed by a growing corps of women pickets.

The Raj fought back with wholesale arrests, lathi charges, press censorship, and ordinance rule. Between mid-April and December-end, Irwin ruled through ten ordinances, an 'arbitrary rule . . . wielded by no previous Viceroy.'[17]

In June the AICC and the Working Committee were declared illegal. But India was changing. A parallel establishment was growing. The queues ready for jail were endless and now increasingly formed by women. A city like Bombay had two governments, the majority, including businessmen and workers, obeying the illegal Congress. When Congress proclaimed a hartal, silence fell on the streets.

In Gujarat, the recently released Vallabhbhai led a successful no-tax campaign among the peasants. Rather than pay the land tax, 80,000 of them left their villages for temporary camps in the princely state of Baroda.

To the extent that prison would allow, C.R. followed these developments. He spent three weeks, as convict number 5557, in Trichy Central Jail where at six each evening he was locked inside a small cell in which the only 'means of ingress of air' was 'a small ventilator about 2 feet by 1 foot, barred and wirenetted.'[18] From Trichy C.R. was moved for two weeks to the Madras Penitentiary and thence to Bellary Central Jail.

The summer is long, hot and exacting in Bellary, but C.R.'s four months there offered some satisfaction. He was in the company of intelligent young satyagrahis. They were eager to learn, and C.R. was glad to teach. The jailor, who 'knew how to deal with gentlemen as well as to keep within the rules,' allowed C.R. to hold classes and prayer meetings.

The young men chose the subjects: the lives of great men, of trees and bees, stars and atoms; also Bolshevism, untouchability and the national debt. One of the 'students' took down the talks in shorthand; they were published in 1931 as *Chats Behind Bars*.

C.R. would turn a dry fact, e.g. the distance of stars, into a memorable picture:

> When you look at a dim star you see not what is there now, but what was there before Buddha was born. The light started then and has taken all the time up till today to reach your wondering eyes... All the history of India has taken place in the interval.

He described how trees yield fruit:

> The beautiful little insects, the flies, the bees and the ants carry the essence from one flower to another, and thereby trees fructify. Don't imagine these little insects are enemies to the flowers. They are the priests who perform their marriages.

Satyagraha had to be guarded against misuse:

> Suppose Srinivasa Sastri and Sir Tej Bahadur Sapru go on hunger strike so that the Mahatma may withdraw his obdurate demands? Can Mahatmaji's heart allow Sastriar to commit suicide, and therefore is he to give up the claim on behalf of India? . . . I warn you, enthusiastic young men who have found a new weapon in satyagraha, against [its] misuse.

Concerned by 'a pressure of concentrated hatred upon a particular people, the Brahmins,' he told the men:

> I belong to that hated caste . . . But I want you . . . to avoid all hatred and pursue the method of love in social reform.

Nationalism was not enough:

> The satyagraha experiment . . . . is not a mere nationalist experiment for getting our own liberty. God will help it . . . only if India's battle is a step in the progress of the whole world.

Though a battle raged outside and he was part and parcel of it, C.R. showed no bitterness:

> The labour of yours will be spoilt if we . . . swerve even an
> inch from nonviolence.

At the final 'class' the day before his release, he said, 'Outside
. . . they cannot see or understand me truly as you, my dear
friends, have done,' and added:

> I am naturally an impatient man. I thank you for all the
> patience you have shown me in spite of my constant harsh
> behaviour towards you.

Admonishing the men 'to be considerate' to the jail staff, he
asked them to return to their cells at lock-up time without
waiting to be told. Discipline would lead to 'strength in civil
disobedience .. . . when we want it.' Pleading against any
demonstrations of affection — 'I don't want to break down,' he
explained — he rose and stepped away.[19]

On his release C.R. attacked the new ordinances but also
called them 'fresh vitaminous dishes' offered by the Viceroy. At
meetings in Madras he asked for a 'dynamic spirit' of revolt.[20]

His words were too much for the Governor, George Stanley,
who rebuked officials for allowing 'a notorious agitator' like
Rajagopalachari to address meetings.[21] This description of C.R.
was new, and an indication of the Government's loss of temper.

Two weeks after his release C.R. was asked to enter into a
Rs 500 bond for peaceful behaviour. Before a crowded court in
Madras, he refused. On 25 October he was sentenced for a year.

The Mahatma, serving his term in Poona, sent a characteristic
leg-pulling message. 'Write to Rajaji,' said Gandhi, addressing a
colleague, 'and tell him that generally I do not write to eminent
leaders and therefore I will not write to him either. But I
remember him every day.'[22]

Lodged first in the Madras Penitentiary, C.R. was later back
for a while in the Bellary Jail, where a cat he had befriended
seemed glad to see him, and then removed to Vellore, his
1921-2 'home'.

In Vellore he had the company of leaders and activists from
the Telugu, Malayalam and Tamil districts. A fellow-prisoner,
G. Ramachandran, wrote in his diary:

> There were extremists . . . and hot disputes and occasionally
> exercises in violent language and action. But most of such
> violence became subdued as soon as Rajaji came on the scene.

Ramachandran noted that while in appearance 'cautious and
even timid,' and 'physically . . . skin and bone with almost no
flesh,' C.R. was 'fearless.' Also, 'in any crowd in a few minutes
he would be the focus of all attention.'

Asked in Vellore whether the Mahatma approved of his
fondness for coffee, C.R., according to Ramachandran's diary,
replied: 'If this is the only thing I do that Bapu disapproves and
my only sin, I shall be on my way to heaven.'[23]

His spirit unsullied by imprisonment, he sent a Christmas
day wish to Anderson, his colleague on the Prohibition League,
'that all bitterness should cease and we may all be united in the
bonds of friendship — a free India and a Christian Europe.'[24]

Among the Raj's advisers were those who wanted even firmer
measures, but Irwin was now thinking differently. In December
he said in Calcutta:

> We should, I am satisfied, make a profound mistake if we
> underestimate the . . . meaning of nationalism . . . and for this
> no complete or permanent cure had ever been or will be
> found in strong action by the government.

When a few weeks later he said that he recognized 'the spiritual
force which impels Gandhi,' officials in Delhi raised their
eyebrows.[25] Something more unexpected was in store for them;
it also surprised nationalist India. The doors of selected prisons
opened on 26 January 1931, exactly a year after Congress's
independence pledge in Lahore, and Gandhi and their colleagues,
including C.R., were let out.

8

Stigma

1931-33

They met in Allahabad, where Motilal Nehru was dying. C.R. had come to visit him at his sickbed. Used to affluence, Motilal had cheerfully borne the rigours of battle. C.R., 20 years younger, had often differed from him; his lifestyle, bordering on the austere, contrasted with Nehru's. Some thought that Motilal looked like a Roman emperor; C.R. preferred Socrates as a model.

After Gaya, where they had clashed directly, C.R. had moved to an ashram and the Pandit to the Assembly. But they had met again on the battlefield, and Motilal had finally agreed that councils were futile. 'There is no hope in that line,' he had told C.R.[1]

When he died, C.R. observed, 'The nation has lost one of its grandest figures' (*The Hindu*, 6.2.31).

Responding to their release, the Working Committee members authorized the Mahatma to negotiate with the Viceroy. When Gandhi asked for an interview he was summoned right away. The Working Committee accompanied him to Delhi.

Lord and Lady Irwin had just moved to their new mansion, an immense edifice of red sandstone, designed to suggest the Raj's grandeur and permanence. There, on 17 February, the Viceroy received Gandhi, enabling Winston Churchill, MP, to utter an alarm that 'Mr Gandhi, a seditious Middle Temple lawyer now posing as a fakir' was 'striding . . . up the steps of the viceregal palace' while still conducting a defiant campaign and 'parley[ing] on equal terms with the representative of the King-Emperor.'

Hope alternated with despair during the fortnight in which Irwin and Gandhi conferred. At home in conference as in combat, the Mahatma obtained a Pact. A role was also played by C.R., who 'quietly laboured with skill and persistence,' as B. Shiva Rao, the journalist, would observe.[2]

With C.R.'s help a compromise over the salt law was evolved: residents of regions close to the salt swamps were allowed to collect their own salt and to trade in it in their own areas. C.R. sold the compromise to Sapru and Jayakar, the Liberal leaders who functioned as the Raj's intermediaries, and to influential members of the Raj's civil service like B.Rama Rau and Akbar Hydari. In Shiva Rao's assessment, C.R. had a part, too, in persuading Gandhi to accept the compromise.

Ian Stephens, a British official who would become editor of *The Statesman*, met C.R. in the home of Akbar Hydari. Later he recalled:

> Mr Rajagopalachari I took to; kind, moderate, wise, he much attracted a young Englishman. If Congress people can be like this, I thought, what's all the fuss about; why this Indo-British political squabbling?[3]

If the Delhi negotiations shed some light on C.R.'s assets, their chief outcome was an increase in the prestige of the Mahatma and the Viceroy. Their agreement, described officially as the Irwin-Gandhi Pact and by Indians as the Gandhi-Irwin Pact, by no means conceded all that the Congress had fought for in the previous year. Independence was not mentioned at all in the Pact, and even the salt law was only modified, not withdrawn.

Yet India thrilled to the Pact because it acknowledged parity between the Viceroy and the Mahatma. For Congress this intangible prize was worth all the preceding exertion. Significantly, Churchill complained that 'the lawless act' had 'now been made lawful' and appeasement extended to those who had 'inflicted such humiliation and defiance as had not been known since the British first trod the soil of India.'[4]

There were tangible gains also. Apart from the salt compromise, these included a clarification that as long as the public was not coerced or obstructed, picketing would be allowed — 'under the eye,' as Sitaramayya would record, 'of the very policeman who was till yesterday jumping upon [those picketing] like a wolf on a fold.'[5] Also, all prisoners were to be released, apart from the Garhwalis who had disobeyed their officers in the NWFP and some men in Sholapur who had briefly 'taken over' the city. And the bans on Congress committees were to be lifted.

While acknowledging that 'Swaraj was not won' by the Pact, Gandhi felt that a 'second door to Swaraj was opened' by it.[6]

Congress met in Karachi in April. Following Gandhi's advice, C.R. and his Working Committee colleagues elected Patel as President. Karachi ratified the truce and authorized Gandhi's participation as Congress's sole representative in the Round Table Conference scheduled in London for later in the year.

When C.R.'s name was missing from the Working Committee announced by Patel, some southern delegates publicly protested. Addressing one of them, Patel said: 'I withdrew it on his behalf. I know Mr Rajagopalachari more than you do.'[7] Vallabhbhai was implying that C.R. did not need the distinction of membership to assist the Working Committee.

C.R.'s stock was in fact high. In Masulipatam on the Telugu coast, where C.R. addressed 'a vast gathering' in June, Sitaramayya, a future President of Congress, said of C.R.: 'He is recognized by one and all to be the foremost of Gandhi's lieutenants' (*The Hindu*, 28.6.31).

At Vedaranyam, where residents now made their own salt, victory was celebrated. Pointing to an old woman who had brought food for the satyagrahis a year earlier and whose pot had been seized by the police, C.R. said: 'Today she comes again with joy and pride . . . We have won the battle' (*The Hindu*, 3.6.31).

For a short while after the truce it almost seemed as if Congress had obtained a say in the Government, and in a letter to the Mahatma, C.R. even spoke of a 'Gandhi-Irwin Pact administration.'[8]

Senior officials showed a new courtesy. When C.R., who had resumed the presidentship of the TNCC, complained to the Madras Chief Secretary that mail addressed to the party office was being censored and delayed, Cotton, the province's top civilian, answered the letter the day after receiving it, signing himself — to the previous year's 'notorious agitator' — 'I have the honour to be, sir, your obedient servant,' and stating that the complaint 'will be enquired into.'[9]

In July 1931 the Madras Government indicated that it would view favourably a plea for reduced taxes from small landholders affected by a fall in agricultural prices. When C.R. argued that the distance of 100 to 150 yards that picketers of liquor and foreign-cloth shops in Tanjore were being asked to keep was unreasonable, the Collector of Tanjore agreed not to enforce it.

Yet C.R.'s hope of an emerging Raj-Congress partnership that might lead to a transfer of power proved to be illusory. Powerful segments of the Raj resented the Pact and regarded it as a blunder. They received full support from Irwin's successor as Viceroy, Lord Willingdon.

Encouraged by his outlook, officials tried to rescue the Raj from the implications of the Pact. The Collector of Madras, a man called A.R. Cox, assailed picketing. Said C.R.:

> If Mr A.R. Cox had been Viceroy of India, he would never have signed the Gandhi-Irwin settlement and permitted picketing, . . . however peaceful it might be promised to be. But Mr Cox is not Viceroy, he is only Collector of Madras, a responsible subordinate administrator (*The Hindu*, 21.7.31).

After Cotton, the Chief Secretary, died at his post, C.R. felt, as he wrote to Gandhi, that the successor seemed 'determined to put me down' and 'push all representations on behalf of the

Congress to the district magistrates.'[10]

The Excise Commissioner of Madras claimed that the unaggressive picketing allowed by the Pact could not include the picketing of auctions where the Government sold licences for liquor vendors. C.R. challenged this interpretation and, before the Government backed down, asked the public to defy it. Gandhi conveyed C.R.'s protest to the Government of India, which advised Madras to yield.

At lower levels, village headmen were warned against giving 'lodging and food and other conveniences to Congress volunteers who come to picket toddy and arrack shops in the villages,' because 'it has come to our notice that by reason of this . . . shopkeepers have no sales.'[11]

When liquor vendors tried to defeat picketing by selling outside the prescribed hours and at places other than their stalls, officials connived at the illegalities. But picketing was winning the day. A single volunteer, national flag in hand, could stop sales at a liquor shop merely by standing near it.

In June, C.R., with a sense of triumph, wrote to his friend 'Pussyfoot' Johnson of 'desolate public houses, mere ghosts of their former selves.' 'Tavern after tavern [is] being abandoned,' he informed Mary Campbell, an American missionary and temperance worker.[12]

Despite the Government's auctioneering, about 3,000 out of the 9,000 liquor licences in the presidency were still unsold in September 1931. Against an estimated Rs 150 lakhs, liquor licences fetched only Rs 50 lakhs in 1931.

Yet C.R. did not merely want shrunken drink revenues and deserted liquor stalls. He wanted these without disorder or violence. Firm with his own side, he instructed picketers to ask for Swaraj but, in view of the truce, not attack the Government; to boycott foreign cloth, 'German and Italian' as well as British, and not British goods as such; and 'whenever there is a doubt' as to the rules of peaceful picketing, to 'err in favour of the Government.'[13]

In the Congress leadership there was none keener than C.R. to work the Pact, which to him was an example of 'what two God-fearing men could achieve though history places them in opposite camps.'[14]

But Willingdon was different. Enjoying the company of Indian princes but disliking Gandhi and the Congress, he seemed determined to stamp out what he felt the Pact had condoned: the mentality of disobedience.

By August Congress had lost faith in the Raj's sincerity towards the Pact. Its experience in Gujarat contributed to the disillusionment. Hardship was in store for the peasants there who had withheld taxes during the struggle and whose lands had been seized.

In many cases seized fields had been sold by Government to third parties. Original owners sought the help of officials in negotiations to buy back their lands. This was denied. C.R. charged: 'Not only is there no assistance from officers, but actually incitement is offered to resist negotiations' (*The Hindu*, 17.4.31).

With the truce crumbling, the Mahatma wondered whether there was any point in his attending the Round Table Conference (RTC) in London, the more so since Willingdon had vetoed the participation of Dr M.A. Ansari, who headed the Nationalist Muslims. Irwin had earlier said that Ansari could join.

Anxious that Gandhi 'goes to the London conference with the Hindu-Muslim problem solved,' C.R. had advised: 'If the Mussalman community wants protection, the Hindus must give all that is demanded' (*The Hindu*, 20.4.31). What, prodded by C.R., Congress offered was rejected by Muslim leaders like Jinnah.

Nonetheless, and despite the enfeebled truce, C.R. saw merit in Gandhi going, if only to influence the British public. At talks in Simla, Gandhi found the Viceroy 'bereft of all grace.'[15] Willingdon offered nothing beyond a small concession over an inquiry on the treatment of the Gujarat peasants.

Even so Gandhi agreed to sail for London. He would woo the people of England. Many assumed that he would take C.R. with him. But the Mahatma wanted C.R. to serve from India. In a letter to C.R. he said (28.8.31):

> There are two men whom I would like by my side in London, you and Jawaharlal. But I feel that even if both of you were

available I must not have you by me. You will both help me like the others by being here. Only, your presence with me would have lightened my burden.[16]

Young India was once more placed in the care of C.R., who was asked to assume the title of editor if absence from India disqualified Gandhi. Significantly, Gandhi also instructed that if 'opinion among our own coterie differs, C.R.'s should be the final voice.'[17] C.R. received a letter (30.8.31) from Patel, the Congress President:

Bapu has gone and I feel so terribly lonely that I don't know what to do. In his absence the burden of carrying on negotiations with Government . . . falls on me and I am so ill-equipped for that kind of work that the burden is too much for me.

I suggested [to Bapu] that if you could stay with me for the short period of his absence from India, it would be a great relief. He agreed with me, but was in doubt about your being able to leave your province, but asked me to write to you about it.[18]

C.R. felt unable to act as requested. Picketing had spread all over his province. Without vigilance it could easily slide into disorder. Also, he had his daughter Namagiri, who was ill with lung and nervous ailments, to look after; in July he had fetched her from Rangoon. He wrote to Patel:

Just like the province I am in charge of, my family also has no second-in-command. You must not be angry with me but forgive.[19]

He looked after *Young India*, and carried on tussles with the Raj, from his Ashram. When the salt concession was suddenly withdrawn from two taluks of Ramnad district on an allegation of 'extensive removals of large quantities of salt to distant places,' he demanded to know why the public had been denied a chance to disprove the charge.[20]

And he prepared a prohibition manual for Congress and a drama on drink, censured a temple that had leased its trees for tapping toddy, attacked the devadasi custom ('I detest the practice of attaching woman servants to temples, pledged to, celibacy, who have become by accepted practice prostitutes'[21]), and shot arrows at untouchability.

In June 1931 he joined in a demand that 'at least . . . all streets, places of worship and sources of drinking water' be opened to 'the so-called untouchable castes.'[22] And in December he went to Guruvayur in the Malayalam country to assist a non-violent bid to open for all the doors of its famed temple, closed for centuries to the 'untouchables.'

To a proposal for a postponement of the battle against untouchability until freedom was achieved, C.R. replied:

> I would like to know if any persons quarrelling over the ownership or enjoyment of any piece of land would postpone their suit until the Swaraj fight is finished.[23]

Tamil Nadu responded to C.R.'s leadership with discipline. There were virtually no incidents of which the Raj could complain. In Madura, in October, picketers were hit by lathis. To prove that the assaulted volunteers had kept to the agreed code, C.R. at once proposed an inquiry by Robert Foulkes, an English resident of Madura.

Simultaneously, he wrote to Vaidyanatha Iyer, president of the Madura district Congress committee:

> The men in Madura, I fear, do not know how to do a thing quietly . . . I fear you must have started with a flare of trumpets. I wonder if you did not have a procession and shouts and demonstration (*The Hindu*, 7.10.31).

The letter to Iyer and the offer of arbitration by Foulkes were published in the Press. When Iyer protested, C.R. explained that he had raised his 'severe' questions in order to obtain 'a conclusive denial.'[24] The Raj rejected the offer relating to Foulkes. To C.R., and many others in the province, this was proof that his picketing volunteers had been wrongfully beaten.

C.R. was proud of their type. They were, in his words, 'mostly poor workmen' who 'get nothing out of this . . . and are not paid salaries.' With 'every kind of corrupt influence and temptation around them, no one,' said C.R. 'dare utter the calumny that they have been bribed or corrupted' (*The Hindu*, 29.8.31).

In a letter he sent to the editors of the South in November 1931, C.R. claimed that the Congress movement was 'stronger in our province now than anywhere else in India.'[25]

The RTC failed as expected. Indian divisions were magnified at it. The British Press portrayed the Mahatma as a caste Hindu leader who could not speak for Muslims or the 'untouchables'.

Ambedkar demanded separate electorates for the 'untouchables'. Claiming that such a move would split Hindu society and solidify prejudice, Gandhi said he would resist it with his life.

Several seas away, C.R. wrote that Ambedkar's demand was the 'most unkindest cut of all,' adding, 'Well might our Caesar cry, "Et tu, Brute," and his mighty heart burst in grief at this' (*The Hindu*, 17.10.31).

British elections held while the RTC was on made the Labour leader, Ramsay MacDonald, Premier once more but heading a coalition where Conservatives were powerful. C.R., who had speculated whether Irwin would be made Secretary of State for India (he was not), wrote:

> I do not think it matters what British Cabinet is in power. The conflict is British interests against Indian interests . . . The British occupation came and developed uniformly under all parties. The retirement must also be [of] the same sort (*The Hindu*, 25.8.31).

Before the RTC dissolved, C.R. wrote: 'Whatever might happen, Mahatmaji's visit to England will not have been a waste' (*The Hindu*, 17.10.31). The effort was not in fact wasted. Independently of the conference at St. James's Palace, Gandhi held a dialogue with the people of England, meeting them in an unending sequence of gatherings, visiting them in their homes, and getting through to a large number. Even in Lancashire, hurt by the Indian boycott, there were cheers for him.

In November 1931, Patel led a move to make C.R. Congress President. 'It is your turn this time,' he wrote to C.R., adding,

'You must be prepared to bear the burden.'[26] C.R. said that Gandhi should combine the de facto and de jure positions and take the chair. When he found that Gandhi was opposed to this, C.R. proposed Prasad's name. A diffident Prasad wrote to C.R.:

> I really feel that we have very difficult times ahead and we
> want a man at the helm of affairs who will not waver or falter.
> I do not find that I can do it and am anxious to serve under
> another like you.[27]

The TNCC proposed C.R.'s name. The session was due to be held in Puri in Orissa, where too the provincial Congress committee recommended C.R.'s election. Discouraging the idea, C.R. said he felt disqualified 'on account of my ignorance of Hindi.'[28] Moreover, Gandhi had not asked him to preside.

Willingdon saved Gandhi the task of choosing. The Puri convention was not held, and it was not until October 1934 that a Congress session was again allowed. By Gandhi's choice, it was chaired by Prasad.

To return, however, to the end of 1931: the Indian scene had worsened during Gandhi's absence. In Bengal there was a sequence of repression and violence. In the UP it looked as if a 'no rent' campaign would start. In the NWFP there were restrictions on Ghaffar Khan and his brother. Finding the Gujarat inquiry one-sided and superficial, Patel broke off from it.

The spirit of the Pact was dead. Willingdon and Willingdonites were in control. As C.R. wrote to Patel: 'All over, Government has tightened the reins or rather let go the reins and have asked officials to do whatever they like.'[29]

C.R. disfavoured the 'no rent' campaign in the U.P. and opposed the terrorist methods used in Bengal by some of the Raj's foes. But the repression that India was soon to experience was wholly out of proportion to Congress indiscretions or excesses in Bengal.

Even while Gandhi, returning, was on the high seas, Ghaffar Khan and Jawaharlal Nehru were arrested. Ordinances virtually ending civil liberties were imposed in the NWFP and the UP.

Along with Kasturba and Patel, C.R. went to the *Pilsna* that brought Gandhi to Bombay and gave him the news. Immense crowds welcomed Gandhi back but his days of freedom were numbered.

Swift and sharp the blows fell. The Mahatma was arrested before dawn on 4 January. After a few hours Patel and the Working Committee were taken. C.R. was not a member but would not wait long.

With a series of ordinances the Government sought to silence all opposition. Congress organizations were banned. Meetings were forbidden. Press censorship was imposed.

India hit back. Thousands defied the ordinances; by the end of February 1932, the 1930 figure of political imprisonments had been crossed. The lock had replaced the Pact.

For all concerned, including the Mahatma and C.R., the six-day interval in Bombay between Gandhi's return and his arrest had been fateful, exacting and void of leisure. But in it time had been found for the two friends to reach a decision on the future of Devadas and Lakshmi.

The young persons had now waited for more than four years. During this period they had faithfully observed the conditions of no meetings and no letters. Gandhi and C.R. agreed to permit and bless their marriage. But wedding day was distant yet. Lakshmi and Devadas would not marry while their fathers were in prison, and in any case Devadas was soon to be arrested himself.

On 9 January 1932, C.R. courted arrest. Accompanied by S. Satyamurti, he cruised slowly in a taxi along crowded streets in Madras and distributed a Tamil leaflet, *The Satyagraha Fight*. As the leaflet called for a boycott of foreign cloth, C.R. was violating Ordinance V of 1932, which prohibited picketing and 'molestation.'

When a police inspector asked C.R. what he was doing, C.R. handed him a copy of the leaflet. Four vans filled with police emerged. One of them blocked C.R.'s taxi, and C.R. was told that he and Satyamurti were under arrest. After they were removed, police dispersed the crowds that had gathered by opening a water-hose on them — a tanker too had been brought on the scene.

Two days later C.R. and Satyamurti were tried. In his statement to the court C.R. said:

> I molested no one and loitered nowhere. I did distribute handbills asking the public not to help economic exploitation by a power that refuses us our national right to rule ourselves.

He was sentenced for six months. Over a thousand Tamils followed him and Satyamurti into prison.

Lodged, to begin with, in the Madras Penitentiary, C.R. found that the jail officials had a harsher spirit than what he had previously encountered. Soon, however, he was shifted to Vellore — his third sojourn there.

Here C.R. explained the devotional verses of the Alwars to fellow-prisoners and read Upton Sinclair and Thomas Hardy and also Thomas Kempis's *Imitation of Christ*, which, as he wrote to Devadas, he found 'truly beautiful.'[30]

C.R. added that prisoners around him were 'making good progress' with Hindi, with some 'gurgling away at Urdu too.' He himself was advancing in Sanskrit, helped by a political prisoner from Kerala, Narayana Menon.

> Sanskrit grammar is too beautiful for mortals like me, but I have all the same done the first book of Hitopadesa and I am doing Panchatantram, starting at the fourth book.

Rules for interviews were hardened in the course of C.R.'s term in Vellore. A thick screen was placed between the prisoner and his visitor. When a protest C.R. made on the prisoners' behalf went unheeded, the prisoners responded by forgoing interviews.

Eleven days before he was to be released, C.R. learned that his daughter Namagiri's husband Varadachari had suddenly died in Trichy. It was Namagiri ('Papa') who had been ailing, but typhoid and pneumonia claimed Varadachari, who had come from Rangoon to look after Namagiri.

'Papa is his (Rajaji's) dearest child,' the Mahatma correctly observed.[31] C.R. received a wire from him: 'You stand in no need of consolation from us. God must be your rock.' Gandhi's message for Namagiri was, 'Remember you are daughter of brave father.'[32]

On 9 July C.R. was released. Early in August, in a fifty-minute talk, he fruitlessly probed the Madras Governor, Sir George Stanley, for a way out. At the end of August C.R. referred in the Press to 'the torment of these eight months' and said: 'The hopes of honourable and fruitful negotiations were shattered in January.'[33]

With the arrest on 22 August of Dr Saifuddin Kitchlew, C.R. became — in accordance with instructions left by Patel before his arrest in January — Acting President of Congress.

Their spirits affected by the deadlock, Congressmen needed a fresh inspiration. From behind prison walls Gandhi provided it.

Two months after being arrested, Gandhi had learnt that London was proposing separate electorates for the 'untouchables' — the Depressed Classes, as the Raj termed them. The Mahatma wrote to Sir Samuel Hoare, Secretary of State, that, as he had indicated at the RTC, he would fast unto death if the plan was implemented.

In August, nonetheless, through the so-called Communal Award, London announced that it was arranging a separate electorate for the 'untouchables'. Gandhi's response was to declare that his fast would commence on 20 September.

A worried C.R., wanting, as he put it, to 'obstruct the sacrifice,'[34] sought interviews with Gandhi. The Raj refused permission. C.R. wired the Mahatma a request to desist. Gandhi replied:

> No cause for distress. On the contrary, I expect you to rejoice
> that a comrade of yours has this God-given opportunity for a
> final act of Satyagraha in the cause of the downtrodden.[35]

Was it proper for Gandhi, C.R. wondered, 'to threaten to die if ignorant and superstitious men did not decide within a fortnight to be wise and courageous?'[36] Answering a fresh plea from C.R., and sending 'love and yet more love,' the Mahatma expressed confidence that the former would 'soon see the light out of the darkness.'[37]

There were two ways of saving Gandhi's life. London could go back on the Award, or caste Hindus and 'untouchables' together could agree to an alternative. Hurdles across the second avenue were formidable. C.R. felt that satyagraha 'may, in spite of its glory, fail to move age-long ignorance and superstitious power.' 'The only hope now left for us,' he thought, was that 'the policy of the British Government may be revised.'[38] London, however, clarified that in the absence of an agreed alternative it would keep to the Award.

Then the unexpected happened. In a bid to earn, if they would give it, the trust of the Depressed Classes, Hindu society looked afresh at its settled customs.

C.R. prodded Hindu society. Because he was Acting President of the Congress, close to the Mahatma, and a Brahmin, his was a three-fold responsibility. At his suggestion, 20 September was marked by fasting in countless homes, including many where 'untouchables' lived.

Once the fast started, Hindu leaders were allowed to meet Gandhi to explore a solution. Seizing the opportunity, C.R. discovered that Gandhi was not only prepared but keen to give the 'untouchables' more seats in legislatures than London had given them in the Award. But he wanted them to give up the separate electorate.

C.R., Ambedkar and others negotiated with a weakening Gandhi who lay on a white hospital cot under a mango tree inside the Yeravada Jail campus. Ambedkar was prepared to go along with Gandhi's proposal if seats were reserved for 'untouchables' for at least 25 years, and for longer if a referendum after 25 years showed that the Depressed Classses wished to retain them. However, Gandhi wanted a poll on the question in five years.

'Five years or my life,' said Gandhi. After a long discussion with his colleagues, Ambedkar said he could not agree to anything less than ten years. The way out was conceived by C.R., who asked Ambedkar if he would leave the time-table to be decided by mutual agreement in the future. Ambedkar agreed.

Hastening to Gandhi, C.R. conveyed his solution, adding, 'I have done it on my own responsibility, taking it that you cannot but agree.' The Mahatma listened with care, asked C.R. to repeat his solution, and expressed himself in one word, 'Excellent.'

What became known as the Poona (or Yeravada) Pact was now rapidly drafted and signed. Both wings of the Depressed Classes, one led by Ambedkar and another by M.C. Rajah, consented to it. Malaviya agreed on behalf of the caste Hindus. C.R., other Congressmen on the spot, and Liberal leaders like Sapru and Kunzru also signed it.

C.R. and Ambedkar exchanged pens. The cabled text reached London on a Sunday. The Prime Minister was at a funeral in Sussex. On his return to 10 Downing Street, he conferred with Hoare till midnight.

On Monday morning word was received that the British Cabinet had accepted the Yeravada agreement. Still, it was not until Colonel Doyle, the Raj's Inspector-General of Prisons, showed Gandhi an official piece of paper signifying acceptance that he broke the fast.

From the shade of a mango tree inside a prison a starving man had imposed his will on an Empire. More important, in order to save the life of its loved representative, Hindu society was at last admitting its injustice, and trying to deal with it.

Orthodox priests dined with the 'untouchables'. Worshippers at a Bombay temple voted 600 to 1 for opening it to 'untouchables'. By 2 October over a hundred temples in the country had been opened to them. On 1 October an Untouchability Abolition League was launched. On 1 November, the Madras Legislative Council asked the Government to legislate in favour of temple-entry.

The Economist of London (1.10.32) thought that the fast was 'the most important event that has occurred in the history of Hinduism for centuries.' 'Before our very eyes the wonder has happened,' said Tagore.[39]

When the fast ended, C.R.'s primary feeling was one of relief. By Hindu reckoning the day that followed was Gandhi's birthday; C.R. termed it a day of 'veritable rebirth.' Some weeks later he reflected on the anxiety he had entertained:

> As for Socrates's friends it was difficult, so it was difficult for me too to remember that the goose can never be killed. I thought the body was the goose . . .

And he added:

> The inhumanity [of untouchability] is so great and the superstition so obstinate that the death of the most loved . . . among us cannot be too great a price . . .

In the end, that drastic remedy was not asked for. Ambedkar would say that C.R. 'came to our rescue when we were almost at a breaking point and had it not been for his ingenuity probably the agreement would not have come into being.'[40]

9

Switch

1932-35

If the Gulf within Hinduism was being bridged, why not a bid to unite Hindus and Muslims? The thought entered the minds of several including C.R. and Shaukat Ali.

In November 1932 a Unity Conference was held in Allahabad. C.R.'s veteran friend C. Vijiaraghavachariar of Salem presided. Leading Muslims turned up to meet Hindu counterparts; from the UK, Jinnah advised the Muslims to settle if the terms were good. The Sikhs, too, were represented.

C.R., Acting Congress President, proposed joint electorates and reserved legislature seats for Muslims and Sikhs. The conference accepted this application of the Yeravada formula, agreed to a 32 per cent Muslim quota in a national assembly, and endorsed the separation of Sind, which had a Muslim majority, from Bombay Presidency.

Describing the settlement as 'the beginning of a new epoch of complete harmony,' C.R. felt that it was Gandhi's 'fast that had changed . . . the hearts of the stoutest champions of particular interests' (*The Hindu*, 18.11.32).

Others also saw a turning-point. Rajendra Prasad thought that the settlement was 'laying the foundations of true nationalism and freedom.' Shaukat Ali expected 'the overwhelming majority of Muslims' to accept the terms, and Azad hailed the outcome as one of the biggest achievements in Indian politics (*Free Press*, 20.11.32).

Alas, the jubilation was premature. The Hindu Mahasabha as well as prominent Muslim bodies rejected the Allahabad package. Greatly disappointed, C.R. would later describe the repudiation of the Allahabad agreement as a major tragedy of Indian politics; he seemed, in particular, to blame Pandit Malaviya's alleged coolness towards the package.[1]

Allahabad seemed a brief diversion from the struggle against untouchability, which focussed, at this time, on the right of the Depressed Classes to enter temples.

During Gandhi's fast a conference of Hindus had resolved that social and religious equality, including temple entry, would be guaranteed to 'untouchables' by 'one of the earliest acts of the Swaraj Parliament,' if it was not conceded before Swaraj. On breaking his fast, Gandhi had said: 'I would hold myself hostage for the due fulfilment of the resolution.'[2]

Although in September two temples in Madras had been opened to the 'untouchables', or Harijans (People of God), as they were increasingly called, the South was resisting. Despite efforts, the gates of the Guruvayur temple near Calicut had not yielded.

Caste Hindus around Guruvayur seemed hesitant. Kelappan, a local reformer, wanted to fast on the issue. Gandhi asked him to put off the step and offered to fast himself if that remedy was required.

If they did not want Gandhi to fast, Guruvayur's caste Hindus had to show their support for reform. C.R. asked them to do so through a referendum. Nearly 28,000 adult caste Hindus were living in the temple's vicinity; C.R. would strive to influence them in favour of reform.

But if he was to devote himself to Guruvayur, C.R. announced, he could not remain Acting Congress President as well (*The Hindu*, 5.12.32). He therefore handed over the Congress burden to Rajendra Prasad.

The Guruvayur temple's trustee, by tradition, was the Zamorin of Calicut. A year earlier, shortly before he died, the then Zamorin had asked the Governor of Madras to prevent the temple from 'falling a prey into the hands of these iconoclasts.'[3]

The Raj sympathized with the Zamorin and his successor but learnt from Russell, the Collector of Calicut, that C.R.'s speeches were 'swinging the mass of popular opinion towards temple entry.'[4]

When votes were tabulated at midnight on 24 December it was shown that 56 per cent of the caste Hindus supported Harijan entry, 9 per cent opposed it, 8 per cent were neutral, and 27 per cent said nothing. This was a clear mandate for reform. In two meetings in Yeravada on 29 December, C.R, supported by Kelappan, was able to persuade Gandhi to abandon his fast.

However, the temple doors did not open. The Zamorin claimed that the shrine was private and not bound to respect public opinion. When one of the South's Sankaracharyas publicly supported the Zamorin, C.R. commented that the Sankaracharya 'could not release himself from the orthodox prison in which he is interred' (*The Hindu*, 12.12.32).

The Zamorin had also said, with some justice, that the laws of the Raj stood in his way. It seemed possible for two orthodox individuals to obtain an injunction against Harijan entry even if the trustee favoured it.

New legislation was called for. At C.R.'s urging, P. Subbaroyan prepared a Bill for the Madras Council enabling a majority of a temple's devotees to regulate entry into it.

Without the Viceroy's sanction, however, the Bill could not be discussed in the Madras Council. After C.R. had spent an hour with him, the Governor of Madras agreed to 'support the request for sanction.'[5]

A vehement opponent of councils was now turning to them and to a Governor. Informing Devadas that he was having to call again on the Governor, C.R. wrote: 'What a shame! But there it is, I have no time to think out conundrums. I go straight at it.'[6]

But he went to Yeravada and asked Gandhi whether, for the sake of the Harijan movement, he should not claim exemption from civil disobedience. Replied Gandhi:

Those who have the slightest doubt in their minds ought to give the benefit of the doubt to their initial pledge of civil disobedience. But if you feel you have a clear call, and it seems that you do, you must do Harijan work.[7]

The Viceroy, meanwhile, had ruled that provinces could not deal with religious issues. The battle now shifted to the Assembly in New Delhi where, at C.R.'s instance, Ranga Iyer, an elected member, put forward two Bills. One sought to prohibit disparities or discrimination against 'untouchables', the other to bring to the whole of India the benefits of the abortive Madras Bill.

At the end of January 1933, the second Bill obtained the Viceroy's sanction for discussion. C.R. went to Delhi to enlist the support of legislators. His task was difficult. Orthodoxy was opposed. Malaviya was against the Bill, and Muslims in the Assembly were unclear whether to support the reform or merely watch the Hindus quarrel.

The Government, on its part, first tried to block discussion of the Bill and then encouraged opposition to it. The end, to come later in 1934, was pathetic. Faltering in face of orthodox pressure, Ranga Iyer withdrew the Bill.

Outside the Assembly, however, the Bill had not only registered the necessity for reform; it had given Congress a much-needed public platform at a time when bans, detentions and censorship had virtually silenced its voice.

Not all Congressmen welcomed the Harijan movement or C.R.'s preoccupation with the Bill. 'Reform,' it was alleged, was weaning men away from a political fight. In his prison, Jawaharlal Nehru thought that C.R.'s Assembly effort was strange and blameworthy.

As for orthodoxy, it was unsparing in its attacks on Gandhi and C.R. Predictably, the Mahatma defended C.R. in his new journal for social reform, *Harijan*, which the Raj allowed Gandhi to edit from prison. C.R.'s work with the MLAs, the Mahatma said, was 'highly necessary' (*Harijan*, 18.2.33).

C.R. was in his element lobbying the Assembly members. The columnist Pothan Joseph referred to C.R.'s 'talent of adjusting his plea to the humour of his opponents' and added:

If the Viceroy invites him to address a meeting of his executive
council on the subject, the Government themselves would
adopt the Bills . . . (*Hindustan Times*, 23.2.33)

By now a White Paper of the Raj, a precursor of the Government
of India Act of 1935, had announced how India would be
governed in the future. There would be a federation at the
centre, to be joined, the Raj hoped, by the princely states.
Provincial legislatures, elected under a fairly wide franchise,
would enjoy substantial powers, but Governors or the Viceroy
would have the right to veto them in certain fields.

The electorate would be divided by religion, Sind and
Orissa would become provinces, and Burma would be formally
separated.

Still banned, Congress could not discuss the scheme.
Attempts to hold a session in Delhi in 1932 and another in
Calcutta in 1933 were broken up by the Raj's police. However,
Congressmen could individually react to the White Paper.

None liked it, but it was clear that before long they would
have to choose between complete boycott and a measure of
cooperation, however distasteful. The promotion of the Temple
Entry Bill suggested that the latter course might be chosen.

Asked in February 1933 if Congresss thinking on councils
was changing, C.R. replied:

It is never to be imagined that the Congress will hold on to
any policy fanatically (*The Tribune*, 19.2.33).

True, C.R. and the Mahatma were at this juncture speaking only
for themselves. Yet C.R. had only recently served as Acting
Congress President, and *The Statesman* (24.2.33) recalled that he
'had been second in command in the camp of the Mahatma for
a number of years.' His words were rather more than a straw
in the wind; and Congress in fact had taken its first slow steps
towards the council doors.

At the end of April 1933 Gandhi told his Yeravada companions
that on 8 May he would commence a 21-day fast for the

effectiveness of his Harijan movement. Because of his increasing age, the anxiety of Gandhi's contemporaries in relation to his fasts grew with each succeeding one.

'One thing is clear to me,' observed C.R., 'and that is he could not survive a fast for 21 days' (*The Hindu*, 4.5.33). Patel, the Mahatma's companion in prison, agreed. Calling on Gandhi at Yeravada, C.R. used stronger words:

> You have lost your sense of proportion. You have a great fondness for conducting experiments. You are now experimenting with death . . . Can you show me even one person who approves of your step?

'Andrews,' replied Gandhi. C.R. shot back: 'Andrews does not even know how to lock a room and he is talking about locking one's life.' Evidently, the Briton's reputation for worldly wisdom was not high. Gandhi rejoined that he had to listen to his heart.

At this C.R. prescribed a medical examination to see if Gandhi could stand a 21-day fast: Gandhi had said he wanted to live, not to die. Shankerlal Banker, who was present at the conversation, backed the idea, but Gandhi said a medical test would show lack of faith.

'You are then conceding nothing and claiming infallibility,' charged C.R. Replying with some heat, Gandhi said: 'You shall not thus undermine my conviction and my faith . . . I cannot agree to any examination of me by doctors.'

Regretful some hours later that 'even on the eve of a purificatory fast I gave way to anger against my dear friends,' Gandhi wrote out an apology:

> My dear C.R., You are dearer to me than life itself. I wounded you and Shankerlal deeply. It is no use my saying, 'Forgive me.' Your forgiveness I have before the asking. But I will do the very thing that I resisted like an ass. I will submit to the examination, . . . provided, of course, the Government permit it . . .

Next day C.R. went laughing to Gandhi and said:

> There was no occasion for the apology, the irritation was more on our side than on yours, and we have now decided to

have no examination (*Harijan*, 13.5.33)

Asking India to pray, C.R. added: 'Let prayer melt into sleep and sleep wake up with prayer. Let us not waste time in foolish merry-making' (*Harijan*, 20.5.33).

The day his fast began, 8 May, Gandhi had been released — because, the Raj said, of 'the nature and objects of the fast and the attitude of mind which it discloses.'[8] The Mahatma's response to the release was to suspend civil disobedience for a month and to ask the Government to free its prisoners and withdraw its ordinances.

To have used the release to prosecute a fresh campaign of defiance would have been ungracious and also unrealistic, for the forces of Congress were tired. Breadwinners had gone to jail for long periods in 1930 and 1932; many were still inside. Donations to Congress were banned, and its funds seized or exhausted.

It was time for a fresh look at Congress strategy. Shortly after the fast ended, Gandhi and C.R. had two sessions together. They reached four conclusions.

One, the mass struggle should come to an end. Two, it might be necessary before long, though not immediately, to 'think of taking power in our hands,' even under 'the constitution they (the British) are framing.' Three, a small number should keep up the struggle on a higher level of intensity. Finally, a letter asking for an interview should go from Gandhi to Willingdon, even though 'we will get the same reply from the Viceroy.'[9]

Even a selective protest would of course lead to imprisonment again. The Mahatma and C.R. decided that while the two of them and Kasturba were out of prison, the marriage of Lakshmi and Devadas should take place. C.R. wrote a letter:

My dear Ba, . . . We do not know how long Bapu may be free and available to us, and when a similar chance may, if not utilised now, occur again. So, however hurriedly and quietly it may have to be done, we decided that the wedding may be

gone through now . . . I hope you will approve of the idea.
I am bringing Lakshmi and Papa when I go to Poona about
12th June and with your concurrence I hope God will enable
Lakshmi to become formally and finally your own child on
some auspicious day thereafter. With love and regards, I am,
ever yours affectionately, Raja.

On 16 June 1933 the marriage was solemnized in Poona in the
home of Lady Premlila Thackersey. The Mahatma insisted on
shortening the guest-list; even Ramdas, Devadas's brother, was
not invited; and Lakshmi was asked by Gandhi to return the silk
saris that friends had presented to her.

Yet a dream that had felt so true and yet seemed so elusive
was fulfilled. Lakshmi's joy, and that of Devadas, knew no
bounds.

At twenty past midnight on 15 July, C.R. went to a Poona
telegraph office to transmit Gandhi's request for an interview
with Willingdon. The Viceroy replied that he was unable to
grant it.

To this expected rebuff, the response of Gandhi, C.R. and
M.S. Aney — Congress's Acting President since January 1933,
when his predecessor, Rajendra Prasad, was arrested — was
selective civil disobedience. On 1 August, Gandhi, Kasturba,
Mahadev Desai and 30 others marched together from Sabarmati
to the village of Ras. This was in violation of a law against
unauthorized processions; they were all arrested.

Three days later Gandhi was released but ordered to reside
within the limits of Poona city. On his refusal to do so he was
arrested again and sentenced for a year. Released early because
he seemed seriously ill, Gandhi, recovering slowly, declared that
he would restrict himself to the Harijan movement, abjuring
protest or politics until August 1934, when his sentence would
have ended.

Selective disobedience was not popular. It did not find
favour, the Madras Government reported to New Delhi, at 'a
secret Congress meeting' held in Trichy where C.R. 'tried to
ascertain' the party's mood.[10]

But C.R. knew where his duty lay. Early in August he wrote to Stanley, the Governor:

> No one would have been gladder than myself had an honourable settlement been reached, but . . . I am one of those who have pledged themselves to struggle.

Charging that the Raj's officials had sabotaged the Gandhi-Irwin settlement which they 'did not like,' C.R. said that as the interview with the Viceroy sought by the Mahatma 'was refused, . . . the struggle had to be resumed' (*The Hindu*, 7.8.33).

C.R. informed the Governor that he would be violating the law on 7 August in Tiruchengode. Before five that morning, C.R. and 16 others, including a Muslim, a Harijan, and two women, walked from the Ashram to the foot of the Tiruchengode temple. There, C.R. advised a boycott of foreign cloth. Then, followed by a police party, the group marched along the town's principal streets, distributing handwritten leaflets.

When they were walking outside the Taluk Office, the local seat of the Raj, a voice from behind them announced their arrest. 'Turn right,' the voice ordered. They obeyed, and entered the building, where a trial was immediately held. Asking people not to buy foreign cloth was his right, C.R. told the court. All the accused were sentenced, under the Criminal Law Amendment Act, to rigorous imprisonment for six months. A bus under police escort took the party to Salem prison; from there the men were sent to Coimbatore Central Jail and the women to Vellore.

The day after his conviction, C.R. learned that Devadas had been arrested at New Delhi station, where he had arrived with Lakshmi, and sentenced for six months. Devadas explained to the police that he had come to Delhi to take up a post with the *Hindustan Times*, but refusal to sign a pledge against disobedience fetched him a prison term.

Lakshmi, 21 and married for no more than seven weeks, would now be on her own in a strange city, but friends provided shelter. C.R. wrote to his daughter:

> I send my love and joyful appreciation of the brave manner in

which you have accepted what has happened. Man proposed but the Chief Commissioner (of Delhi) disposed. God knows better than we do what is good for us. We should be grateful for the wonderfully devoted and affectionate friends that surround us everywhere. (12.8.33)

To Devadas he wrote:

God always arranges things better than we can ever hope to do with our limited vision. You will always be near me in spirit until we meet again in body. I am full of joy at Lakshmi's chance to show courage. (12.8.33)[11]

In Coimbatore Jail C.R. had the time to translate the *Kural* into English and to continue the Sanskrit studies he had begun on his 1932 'vacation.' In a letter to Devadas he said: 'I will not be at any time anything more than a baby in [Sanskrit]. Yet I do feel satisfied with even the baby's knowledge.'

Newspapers sympathetic to Congress were not allowed inside prison. However, C.R. wrote that he was 'thriving on the bitter tonics' of the Madras *Mail* and the *Times of India*, which were British-owned.

His letters from prison — he was permitted to send one every fortnight — contained ideas for promoting Hindi, pushing khadi sales, and providing relief to flood-hit Harijans in Salem, and messages for MLAs regarding the Temple Entry Bill.

It was also, inevitably, a contemplative time, producing some sensitive lines. To a missionary acquaintance he wrote (24.9.33):

My dear Rev. Popley, . . . I have had plenty of time and opportunity for reflection since we met last. How absurd it was for me to spoil your nice and kind visit to the Ashram with that controversy over conversions. I am really ashamed.

We do not know what that controversy was. To someone called Tirunarayana Iyengar who seemed to nurse a grievance, C.R. wrote (1.11.33):

I give you my word of honour that I have not... done anything to injure you . . . On the contrary, I ever tried to be helpful to you. I do not ask for gratitude for this, for I am more beholden to you than you to me if all accounts are cast.

His temperance friends, Herbert Anderson and Mary Campbell, had sent good wishes. Their word, C.R. replied, had 'softened these walls and these bars and these locks.' Solitude drawing out his warmth, he wrote to his Ashram flock:

> Behave like brothers . . . See one another's good points and do not emphasise bad points.

> Be kind and considerate to the poor and illiterate folk . . . They toil for the country in a truer sense than we do. Time is their most important asset; therefore, they should not be kept unnecessarily waiting . . .

> I hope the hospital and the store are worked so as to be more and more useful to them. Little children however dirty and ill-clad should be treated as you want your own children to be treated by others.

Annie Besant, the doughty Irishwoman, died in September. Another blow to C.R. was the repeal of prohibition in the U.S.A. To Anderson he sent a message: 'America is gone. It is a great calamity to those who are struggling to outlaw Alcohol through State action.'

The Mahatma, meanwhile, was launched on a tour in the Harijan cause. C.R. sent word out bidding him South, where orthodoxy continued strong. He wanted 'the appeal of [Gandhi's] personality' to reach 'the common folk so that the opposition of the sophisticated hypocrites may be undermined.'

Accepting the invitation, Gandhi also indicated that his visit South would continue beyond C.R.'s release. On the morning of 6 February 1934, C.R. was discharged. He motored at once to Tiruppur, fifty miles away, where his friend the Mahatma was.[12]

Gandhi's southern tour arrested the slide in Congress morale. The tour's primary aim, to sap orthodoxy on the Harijan question, was not political. But the tour drew such crowds that Congressmen found their confidence returning.

Having urged the tour from behind bars, C.R. was delighted. He called it, in a letter to Devadas, 'an unprecedented success, . . . a royal triumphal march, . . . a crushing reply to those who thought that Bapu was becoming unpopular,' and felt sure of its impact 'in regard to politics also' (27.2.34).[13] To his friend Herbert Anderson C.R. wrote:

> Far from Mahatmaji's attitude in regard to the untouchables reducing his hold over the masses, what I have seen in every place with my own eyes indicates that at no time was his hold over the people greater than now. (28.2.34)[14]

In Bihar, the Raj and Congress worked together for relief after a calamitous earthquake in January 1934. The Mahatma had gone there, and the funds collected on Congress's behalf were larger than what the Government could gather.

A horrible asthma attack caused C.R. to write to Devadas that 'bathing is an exertion, sitting is tiresome, talking is a trouble and on the whole living is a punishment' (15.3.34). He was still recovering when, from Bihar, Gandhi announced that disobedience would be suspended.

Though Gandhi reserved for himself the right to disobey, he asked the Congress to suspend disobedience, and to allow those of its members inclined to enter councils to do so. In a cable to Andrews in England (6.4.34), Gandhi said that civil resistance, 'an appeal not to fear but to heart . . . should evoke not resentment but sympathy.' Yet it had 'evoked repression.' He would now confine it to himself.[15]

C.R. was informed by Chandrashanker Shukla, who was serving as Gandhi's secretary, that it was Gandhi's belief that the suspension would give 'much-needed respite to civil resisters who are today tired' and enable them to emerge 'stronger and more equipped for the next battle whenever it comes.'[16]

To Vallabhbhai Patel, Gandhi wrote, referring to the charm that councils held for many Congressmen, that it was but 'right that those who daily attend legislatures in their thought should do so physically as well' (18.4.34).[17]

The switch in strategy did not surprise C.R. We have seen that he and Gandhi had agreed on it in their talks in Yeravada almost a year earlier Wiring his agreement to Gandhi, C.R.

proposed that Congress should control the councils, and Gandhi should control Congress. Merely allowing Congress's Swarajists to enter councils was insufficient and even hazardous. C.R. affirmed this in a letter to Gandhi (21.4.34):

> My dream is that if this parliamentary party is organised properly and guided by you it can work out a state of things in the provinces equivalent to that we brought about under the Gandhi-Irwin Pact, of which the Civil Service has such a wholesome fear.[18]

Gandhi agreed to C.R.'s suggestion for an AICC meeting for endorsing the new line, even though Patel, the President, was still in prison.

Yet could the AICC, a banned body at this time, meet? Treating Gandhi's announcement as a truce offer, which is doubtless how the Mahatma wanted it treated, the Raj let it be known through Haig, the Home Member in Delhi, that an AICC meeting called to ratify Gandhi's decision would not be disallowed.

The AICC met in Patna in the Mahatma's presence, confirmed the suspension of disobedience, and agreed that Congress, rather than Swarajists on behalf of Congress, would enter the legislatures.

Sitting in prison, Jawaharlal Nehru thought that Congress had lost face. In his diary he wrote that Gandhi's announcement 'bowled him over,' and he feared he would have to break with the Mahatma.[19]

Patel, on the other hand, fell in with the decision. As for C.R., his reaction was expressed in a letter to Mathuradas Tricumji (24.4.34):

> I do not think we look small at all. Withdrawing a movement of sacrifice is often necessary and should not be deemed a matter for shame . . . Our record is good . . . It is the government that ought to be ashamed and will be ashamed when history is written.

> The situation is now different from what it was in 1922. I think we should now go into the elections on behalf of the Congress . . . Nobody can prevent the adoption of civil resistance by the Congress at any future time.[20]

He was urged to enter the Central Assembly, for which elections were due at the end of 1934. Lala Dunichand, a Punjab Congressman, wanted to ask Gandhi to 'spare' C.R. for the Assembly,'[21] and K.M. Munshi made a similar plea to the Mahatma. To Munshi, Gandhi wrote: 'Rajagopalachari, Rajen Babu, etc., will probably stay out.'[22]

But speculation did not die down. To scotch it, C.R. allowed himself to be quoted in *The Hindu* (18.5.34): 'There was no chance of his being persuaded to stand for the Assembly and there was no occasion therefore to seek Mr Gandhi's advice on the subject.'

But he would guide Congress on parliamentary matters. One of the trickiest issues was the Raj's Communal Award, which granted a separate electorate to Muslims and allotted them a third of the Central Assembly seats. While most Muslims wanted Congress to endorse this Award, a section of Hindu Congressmen led by Malaviya and Aney wanted an explicit rejection of the Award.

Congress responded by 'neither accepting nor rejecting' the Award. This was not good enough for the Malaviya group, which broke away to form the Nationalist Party.

Wisdom was also needed on Congress's stand towards its Socialist group, constituted in 1934 at the initiative of Jayaprakash Narayan and others. On the Socialists' behalf, M.R. Masani sought the cooperation of C.R., who replied that the Government was the common foe; the Socialists should 'do nothing to lose the support of any important section.'[23]

In June 1934, the Raj lifted its bans on various constituents of Congress, but the NWFP's Red Shirts, led by the Khan brothers, were not covered by the withdrawal. Pointing out that each Red Shirt volunteer was 'sworn, Quran in hand, to nonviolence,' C.R. alleged that the Raj wanted to tell Muslim supporters of Congress that, 'nonviolence or not, they must suffer for joining Congress.'[24]

What did the unpredictable Gandhi mean by retaining his own right to disobey? Would he court arrest again after August? Meeting Gandhi in Wardha, C.R. argued that he should not, and he urged Ansari, chairman of the Congress Parliamentary Board, to 'prepare tasks of great importance that enlist Gandhiji's presence outside prison.'[25]

Though agreeing not to seek arrest—'It is fairly certain that he will NOT go to prison,' a relieved C.R. informed Devadas (30.8.34) —, the Mahatma said that he was 'thinking of retiring from Congress.'

One of Gandhi's reasons was the 'stifling effect' of his personality on expression of opinion in Congress. Members did not say what they felt about khadi, councils or socialism. Gandhi wanted them to be frank, and he wanted Congress's different factions to find their levels.

As he wrote to Bhulabhai Desai (24.8.34), C.R. was afraid that Congress's election programme 'will crumble to pieces' if Gandhi were to quit.[26] To the Mahatma he wrote:

> If you can think you can retire from the Congress now and keep it and yourself both or either politically important, . . . you will surely be disappointed (28.9.34).[27]

Gandhi had explained himself to C.R.:

> I do not retire to a cave. I hold myself at everybody's disposal. Where is the difficulty? Can you not see the unnaturalness of the present position? Everybody feels the suffocation . . . I wish you will not worry (13.9.34).[28]

As so often before, C.R. acquiesced. 'Mahatmaji's proposed withdrawal from the Congress,' he explained to an English friend, was more 'in the nature of a judicial separation than a divorce.'[29]

In June 1934, a bomb attempt on Gandhi's life misfired. Orthodox foes of his Harijan campaign were behind it. Prophesying, C.R. claimed that the bomb's message was clear:

> I shall not fly only at the throat of the British magistrate but also at Gandhiji's. If you give me room I shall fly at my brother's and sister's also (*The Hindu*, 29.6.34).

Before Willingdon's crackdown, C.R. and Prasad had both been nominated for the Congress Presidentship by provincial committees; each had urged the other to accept the post. Now, in 1934, Gandhi offered Prasad the crown, telling him (18.9.34) that C.R. 'cannot now be chosen.'[30] One reason was that C.R. was shouldering the parliamentary programme.

When in October 1934 Congress met in Bombay under Prasad's chairmanship, Gandhi formally withdrew, but the vast gathering rose to signify loyalty to him. In substance if not in form, the link between Congress and the Mahatma was to continue.

Twice during this session C.R. and the Mahatma found themselves on opposite sides. From prison Jawaharlal had suggested that the UP be named Hind in Congress's discourse, and Gandhi endorsed the proposal. Yet Hind was India to many, and C.R. pointed out that 'if Hind was adopted as the name for [the] UP many changes would have to be made in songs and national cries' (*Bombay Chronicle*, 29.10.34). The suggestion was defeated.

Jayaprakash Narayan and Minoo Masani asked for proportional representation in committees of Congress for groups such as the one the Socialists had formed. C.R. opposed them. So did Patel. But the Mahatma surprised his close colleagues by supporting the J.P.-Masani proposal, which was carried.

Yet the Gandhi-C.R. relationship was intact. In a letter to B.C. Roy of Bengal, who was unhappy at not being included in the new Working Committee, the Mahatma said (30.10.34):

> You know how I have three times suppressed Rajagopalachari, or rather how Rajagopalachari has allowed himself to be suppressed. Rajagopalachari has certainly gained, and if today he is most useful in the parliamentary struggle in the south, . . . it is due to this self-denial.[31]

C.R. had grudged the days that had to be given to the Bombay session — he was immersed body and soul in the November elections. He had had a part in writing Congress's national manifesto and composed the individual manifestos of some candidates; he was raising money, organizing publicity and teaching candidates to fill out forms; and he was attacking and counter-attacking the opponents of Congress.

Madras had 16 seats in the Assembly, but since three were reserved for Muslims and one each for the Depressed Classes and landholders, only 11 general seats were available for Congress to contest. Its principal foe was the Justice Party, which was in office in the province and preferred by the Raj, and which attacked Congress as pro-Brahmin.

Orthodoxy was another Congress foe. A leaflet on its behalf said:

> Do not yield to the siren voice of Mr Rajagopalachari . . . In the name of Brahma, Vishnu and Siva . . . we exhort you to teach those who wish to interfere with our religion a lesson they will never forget . . . Will you vote for God or for Mr Rajagopalachari and his Congress nominees?[32]

Whatever God thought of it, the public voted for C.R. and his candidates, who won all the eleven seats. 'You have reason to be proud of your marvellous achievement,' Patel wired C.R.[33]

The fear of C.R. that the Mahatma's withdrawal would hurt Congress fortunes at the hustings had been falsified, and in a letter to an English friend a rejoicing Gandhi referred to 'the wonders [Congress] has worked during the elections with the least amount of expenses.'[34]

C.R.'s response to the triumph was businesslike. He asked the winning candidates to send him the names, with addresses, of all those who had assisted their effort, and to remember that 'our success is no disgrace for our opponents.'[35]

Including a dozen or so Nationalists of the Malaviya school, Congress had 61 members in the 146-strong Assembly. What C.R. described as the ENO group (Europeans plus Nominated plus Officials) had 47; these were backed by 16 or so loyalists, representing landholding or other privileged interests.

Pro-Government and Congress votes were thus more or less evenly balanced. The result of a division generally turned on the attitude of a bloc of 16 Muslims legislators led by M.A. Jinnah.

In 1935 C.R. spent several weeks in Delhi, along with Prasad, in a bid to enlist Jinnah in a united front. However, the League leader's terms were termed 'impossible' by C.R.[36] In a letter to C.R., Jinnah had stated (19.3.35):

> The Congress should accept the Communal Award by an express declaration till a substitute is agreed upon by the communities concerned. On this basis I think a solid united front can be secured.[37]

This Congress could not do, though it was prepared, despite objections from Malaviya and his friends, to withhold 'rejection' of the Award. The result was that often the Jinnah group either abstained or voted with the Government against Congress. Still, there were times when a defeat was inflicted on the Raj.

10

'Fall'

1935-37

The first quarter of 1935 saw an edgy C.R. He had his reasons. He had been questioned on his Ashram's financial health by Kishorelal Mashruwala, president of the Gandhi Seva Sangh, to which C.R.'s Ashram was affiliated. Mashruwala implied that the Ashram was likely to face a Rs 28,000 loss, and C.R. was asked about a loan the Sangh had given to the Ashram.

Claiming that the Rs 28,000 figure was an 'unfounded estimate,' C.R. wrote to Mashruwala:

> If it is not possible to let the Ashram function autonomously and if it becomes necessary to withdraw the loan given for khadi work, I am quite prepared to let the institution be wound up . . . [Or,] you could run the Ashram directly . . . The time has come when I should be relieved of the charge.[1]

This correspondence was followed by a letter from Gandhi. Because of his involvement with three by-elections to the Madras legislature, all won by Congress candidates, C.R. had missed a Wardha meeting of the Seva Sangh trustees, of whom he was one. The Mahatma wrote to him:

> You must attend these meetings regularly or not be in these bodies at all. I feel sore about it. (2.3.35)[2]

The letter burst a dam. C.R. sent in his resignation as a trustee — and asked for Gandhi's leave to quit the AICC, the

Working Committee, the All-India Parliamentary Board, the presidentship of the TNCC, and the charge of the Ashram, the lot! He was weary and longed for rest, he explained.

'Not so fast, nor so cheap,' replied the Mahatma (9.3.35), adding, 'There can be no weariness, no rest for you or me. Our rest has to come in the life hereafter, if at all.' When C.R. repeated his yearning, Gandhi wrote back (24.3.35):

> You may give up posts of responsibility, but you dare not give up responsibility so long as there is breath in you.[3]

Obviously C.R. had been feeling aggrieved. Making a guess, K.M. Munshi asked Gandhi whether not being made Congress President could have upset C.R. After directly questioning C.R., Gandhi wrote to Munshi that there was 'no such reason as you suspect' (2.5.35)[4]. However, it is possible that disappointment on the score was felt by C.R. — and then quickly slapped down.

Besides, C.R.'s heart was increasingly in the legislature. We have no evidence that in early 1935 he harboured a wish to play a role there himself, but his zeal was unmistakable in the elections of 1934 and the by-elections of 1935, and we will shortly see what happened in 1937.

In any case, he was genuinely tired. To Prasad he wrote of a 'weariness of flesh and spirit' and a desire to be relieved 'for a good long time if not once and for all,' and to Patel of 'a chronic mood of disappointment,'; it was 'an irresistible mental craving for a holiday,' he said in a letter to Agatha Harrison, a friend of India in England.[5]

His colleagues protested. 'Do not imagine,' Prasad wrote to C.R., 'that it is a matter of form with us when we insist on your continuing.' Patel used stronger language:

> You have done us a great injustice. We all have frail bodies, but none of us has the right to leave others in the lurch. What right have we . . . to seek solitude . . . after having made several young men in the country to sacrifice their all? I do not understand you, but I know you are very obstinate. (15.3.35)[6]

To talk with Gandhi, Patel and Prasad, C.R. went to Wardha. After eliciting a promise that C.R.'s help 'would be available whenever needed,'[7] Gandhi and the others yielded to C.R.'s request.

He was permitted to shed, for a period, all his positions, but Patel extracted C.R.'s consent to being retained on the Parliamentary Board — after assuring him exemption from meetings until he felt restored. The Mahatma and Patel had desired that C.R. should follow Dr Ansari, who had resigned for health reasons, as the Board's chairman; the burden now went to Vallabhbhai.

Describing C.R. as 'the leader of the Congress fight for freedom,' the TNCC accepted, on 11 May 1935, C.R.'s resignation as its president. An editorial in *The Hindu* (13.5.35) regretted the withdrawal of one who 'in the public estimation stands second only to Gandhiji among the nation's leaders.'

Feeling 'as free as a bird,' (*The Hindu*, 13.5.35) C.R. sought his strength back, resting with his son Krishnaswami in Madras, or in his Ashram, where he tried his hand at bee-keeping. Part of the 'vacation' was devoted to writing a commentary on the Gita.

In three months, however, he was obliged to spend some weeks in Delhi, where Lakshmi had just given birth and Devadas was laid low with typhoid. Accompanied by Lakshmi and her two children, C.R. stopped in Wardha on his way back.

By this time Patel had thought up a plan: C.R. should succeed Prasad as Congress President. At Wardha, the Mahatma put the plan to C.R., who turned it down as impossible. To Patel, Gandhi wrote (13.9.35) that C.R. was 'in no condition just now to accept the crown,' being still 'extremely tired.'[8]

With C.R.'s consent the Mahatma made the offer of the Presidentship to Jawaharlal, who was in Europe, where his wife Kamala lay ill. 'Jawaharlal is willing,' Gandhi wrote to C.R. at the end of September.[9]

By the second week of October C.R. was willing to involve himself politically again. He wrote to Gandhi (8.10.35):

I was and I am still doubtful about Jawaharlal's fitting in with the parliamentary programme and policy. While I readily agreed, and had in fact anticipated you in my own mind, that . . . we could not pitch on a better choice for the Congress president's place this year, . . . I could not but feel very doubtful about his dealing with the parliamentary policy in the right way.[10]

Congress, C.R. added, should be ready to take office and prevent 'reactionaries and anti-nationalists' from continuing in power.

Visiting Madras for an AICC meeting in October that C.R. did not attend, Prasad, calling himself 'an usurper of the place which is rightly [C.R.'s],' said that C.R.'s judgement was 'faultless': in 1922 he had courageously opposed the councils; now he was equally courageously advocating office-acceptance (*The Hindu*, 18.10.35).

At the end of January 1936, C.R. attended a Congress meeting in Karaikudi and proposed that the TNCC recommend Nehru's name for the Congress chair. This was agreed to. Other provinces also suggesting his name, Nehru was formally elected.

Though back in action, C.R. was reluctant to resume charge of the TNCC. He supported the re-election of Satyamurti, who had become president on C.R.'s retirement. The re-election was not entirely smooth; reporting to Delhi, the Madras Chief Secretary referred to the possibility of 'a breach between the Brahman and non-Brahman elements of Congress.'[11]

Division was feared at the Lucknow session of the Congress. Jawaharlal, presiding, favoured socialism and opposed the idea of acceptance of office in provinces. The reverse was the inclination of C.R., Patel and Prasad. But unity prevailed, aided by the presence of Gandhi. Though formally out of Congress, Gandhi was willing to guide.

Prudently, a decision on the issue of office acceptance was put off. Nehru named a Working Committee in which the non-socialists — or the Gandhi-ites, conservatives, or the right wing, as they were variously called — predominated. It included C.R., Patel and Prasad.

Two months after Lucknow, C.R. said: 'The British perhaps hope for a quarrel among Congressmen . . . But we hope to disappoint them' (*The Hindu*, 19.6.36). 'Independence first' was C.R.'s simple formula for unity, and, in fact, Nehru's as well.

An open letter that Kasturba Gandhi wrote in the autumn of 1936 to her son Harilal, following an announcement that he was embracing Islam (the conversion was to prove temporary), touched C.R. 'It is liquid Mother-lava,' C.R. commented to Mahadev Desai, 'ancient pathos pouring out from the volcano of maternal anguish.'[12]

By declaring that they would stay out of it, the princes of India blocked a federation at the centre envisaged by the Raj in the 1935 Government of India Act. The abortion of the federation, which was to be British-controlled, did not distress C.R., but he resented the princes' opposition to an all-India entity. 'The only solution is to wipe out the yellow patches,' he is supposed to have said, referring to the princely states, which were coloured yellow in maps of the period.[13]

Provincial elections were due at the end of 1936 or early in 1937. Congress was all set to contest them, but C.R. wanted a further step. With his approval, the TNCC urged the AICC to declare that Congress would accept office.

Then a sensitive nerve in C.R. was touched. Despite an appeal by him, his friend and Congress colleague, T.S.S. Rajan, who represented Trichy in the Central Assembly, organized the defeat of Congress's official candidate in an election for the chairmanship of the Trichy municipality.

To this indiscipline C.R.'s response was nothing less than to resign — from the national Working Committee, from the Parliamentary Board, and from the TNCC. He even wanted to resign his membership of Congress, but Patel persuaded him against severing that primary link.

Duni Chand of the Punjab Congress welcomed C.R.'s step

as 'shock treatment' against indiscipline, but everyone else protested. Kripalani, the AICC General Secretary, said that C.R.'s action was 'in excess of what the situation required,' and a correspondent wrote in *The Hindu* that it was 'not right for a general to flee from his post on account of slight defections in the camp.'

Patel spoke of 'a serious blow to the whole nation.' Censured by the Working Committee, Rajan resigned his Assembly seat and regretted that for the first time 'in over 20 years' he had disobeyed 'the greatest Congress leader of South India'; but he defended his role in the local election.

Patel, Prasad and Nehru remonstrated with C.R. at a Working Committee meeting in Bombay, following efforts that Prakasam and Satyamurti had made in Madras, but C.R. insisted that though he would 'remain a Congressman,' he would 'cease to participate in Congress politics.'[14]

Following this decision, he was, by turns, both troubled and calm. To Bhulabhai Desai he wrote that an 'ugly crisis' had affected him. Though feeling he could have done nothing else, he had let colleagues down. He asked Desai to 'make up' for his 'naughtiness' (22.8.36).[15]

'What will you do?' he was asked. 'I have some interests in life other than politics,' C.R. replied. 'I have immediately some sick people to attend to (his second son Ramaswami was among them) . . . I shall not die of ennui. In fact politics left me no time for many things for which my soul craved' (*The Hindu*, 24.8.36).

He completed the commentary on the Gita begun a year earlier, observing that Krishna's words in the Gita were not 'a recruiting sergeant's declamation.'[16] He wrote short stories. And he turned to the Upanishads, finding their ancient authors 'as much inspired by constructive doubt as the most modern men of science.' To C.R. the heart of the Upanishads' teaching was that 'the good is one thing, the pleasant another.'[17] In a letter to Mahadev Desai, he wrote:

> I believe with Bapu that most of our mythological stories are allegories, including the Ramayana and the Mahabharata.

> Only I don't believe in the attempts sometimes made to weave
> a systematic allegory running throughout a book. I think it is
> a wild collection of isolated and valuable allegories.[18]

Congress needed a President for the coming year. Nehru indicated
that he was willing to be chosen again, but two men were
extremely keen for C.R. to wear the crown. One was Patel, who
saw that a C.R. nomination, overdue in any case, would lead to
a withdrawal of Jawaharlal's. The other was Satyamurti, who
thought that with C.R. as President Congress was bound to
accept office, a policy Satyamurti had long been advocating.

Primary membership of Congress sufficed for elevation to
its chair, which is why Patel had insisted that C.R. retain it. He
urged Gandhi to draft C.R. In a letter to the Mahatma, Satyamurti
did likewise. Enclosing what Satyamurti had penned, the
Mahatma wrote to C.R. (21.11.36):

> My dear C.R., . . . Read Satyamurti's letter and give me your
> decision. Needless to tell you that Sardar is desperately anxious
> for you to wear the thorny crown.
>
> I shall be pleased if you will, but I have no heart to press it
> on you.[19]

However, C.R. could not say, within three months of having
'retired,' that he was willing; and there is no evidence that he
was.

Though urged by supporters, Patel declined to be a candidate
himself. After consultations with Gandhi, he asked Congressmen
to re-elect Nehru. Patel added, however:

> The Congress does not part with its ample power by electing
> any individual no matter who he is . . . I can visualise that
> office-acceptance may be desirable. There may then be a sharp
> division of opinion between Pandit Jawaharlal and myself.

So Nehru, who clarified that his re-election would not necessarily
be a vote for socialism, was given the crown for the third time.

C.R. went to Travancore, where the young Maharaja, encouraged
by his Dewan, C.P. Ramaswami Iyer, had by a proclamation

thrown open all the temples in the state's charge to the Harijans.

At a meeting in Trivandrum, C.R. was described as 'the author of the temple entry movement' (*The Hindu*, 30.11.36).

The proclamation had stirred him. Offering sacred ash to 40 young Harijan boys, he took them to the famed Sri Padmanabhaswami temple, which had not seen 'untouchables' for a thousand years.

'God be thanked,' C.R. said, 'and may your Maharaja live long. This is the happiest moment of my life.'

If Congress won the elections in Madras and accepted office, who would head its government? Satyamurti was a candidate but in a party election Muthuranga Mudaliar had defeated him, and there was a question whether Prakasam, who led Congressmen in the Telugu districts, would serve under Satyamurti.

Perturbed by the possibility of a bitter rivalry among Madras's Congressmen, Patel saw C.R. as the answer. So did many in the South, including *The Hindu's* Kasturi Srinivasan, the Liberal leader, T.R. Venkatarama Sastri, P. Subbaroyan, the former First Minister who had recently joined Congress, and Kala Venkata Rao of Andhra. A bid was launched to enlist C.R.

In the middle of December 1936, Patel, visiting the South, talked with C.R. during the short stretch between Renigunta station, where C.R. had joined him, and Madras. The talk obviously had some effect, for on the following day C.R. said at a Madras meeting that his retirement did not mean that he would 'continue to sit at home' if he found 'that [he] should resume active work' (*The Hindu*, 15.12.36).

At Trichy, Patel told local Congressmen that if 'they had not forced him to resign, Mr C. Rajagopalachari would have been unanimously elected President of the Congress long since' (*The Hindu*, 16.12.36). After delivering the rebuke, Patel proceeded to Faizpur in Maharashtra for Congress's annual session. C.R. returned to the Gita, on which he lectured in Madras on 24 December.

On 16 January *The Hindu* announced that C.R. would 'come out of his retirement' and enter the Assembly elections. 'Leading Congressmen both in this province and elsewhere have long been pressing him,' the newspaper added. In Bombay, Patel declared that C.R. would stand from the University constituency. Satyamurti, who had hoped to represent that seat, had stepped aside, Patel added (*The Hindu*, 17.1.37).

Five days earlier, C.R. had said to Gandhi, who changed trains at Madras station en route to Travancore: 'I am under pressure.' The two met again on 22 January when Gandhi stopped in Madras on his way back from Travancore. 'Ah,' said Gandhi, 'now I know what you meant by pressure.' 'What do you think of my decision?' C.R. asked. 'You are free to do as you like,' replied the Mahatma.[20]

C.R. liked the idea of entering the Assembly, but he had only recently, and categorically, 'retired.' For some days he was embarrassed. 'I am glad I have not got any communication from you making fun of my sudden fall,' he said in a letter (21.1.37) to Devadas, adding: 'I have been rushed into it and I have hardly four weeks to win all the elections . . . '

The 'fall' was welcomed all over the South and beyond. 'Arjuna resumes the bow,' said the *Mahratta* of Poona. On 19 January he filed his nomination. Two came forward to oppose him, P. Narayana Kurup and S. Rajagopalan, the latter promising to prevent the Harijan reform that C.R. had sponsored.

The seat had 8,109 voters. C.R.'s canvassing consisted of a single press statement, in which he asked his voters to 'bless an experiment in poor man's electioneering' and pardon his not sending even a letter to all of them, for that 'would mean nearly a thousand rupees' (*The Hindu*, 25.1.37).

C.R. conducted the Congress campaign from the bare floor of his son Krishnaswami's modest new house in Tyagarajanagar. Prakasam and Satyamurti ably backed him. The main opposition was from the Justice Party, which had been in office for years.

But this time the franchise was wider than it had ever been, and Congress was in the fray for the first time. In speeches across the province, C.R. said that votes against Congress were votes for national dishonour.

Votes for Congress went into yellow boxes, votes for Justice into red ones. When all ballots were counted, Congress had won 159 seats, Justice 16, the Muslim League 10. C.R. received 5,326 votes, Kurup 372, Rajagopalan 270. The Raja of Bobbili, the outgoing Chief Minister, lost to V.V. Giri of Congress by a margin of over 5,000 votes.

'The magnitude of the Congress victory was greater than I or anyone else expected,' Lord Erskine, the Governor, wrote to George V.[21] C.R. spoke of 'the irresistibility of a just cause' (*The Hindu*, 2.3.37).

Congress had won in most parts of India, not just in the South.

Madras's Congress legislators met on 10 March to elect their leader. Prakasam, chairing the meeting, proposed C.R.'s name. Loud and prolonged applause broke out. 'I take it that you are for electing Mr Rajagopalachari unanimously,' Prakasam said.

'Yes,' said voices from everywhere. When Prakasam formally put the proposal to vote, cries of 'All' rent the air.

Addressing the legislators, C.R. said that he would break down if he recalled 'the adventurous days when Mr Prakasam and he first conversed together about the great and wonderful programme laid down by Mahatma Gandhi,' and added:

> Anybody who is anxious for any office proves that he is unfit for that office. It is easy to fast on an Ekadasi day sitting on a plank; it is difficult to fast sitting in the Modern Cafe. (*The Hindu*, 11.3.37)

The MLAs wanted to know whether Congress would accept office. 'The chances are fifty-fifty,' C.R. told them, adding that they should obey the AICC's decision. But they could make their recommendation to the AICC. The MLAs voted in favour of taking office. So did the TNCC and the Andhra Pradesh Congress Committee. Most of the South's taluk and district committees of Congress had done so already.

However, Nehru, the Congress President, had said at Faizpur in December that 'the only logical consequence of the Congress policy . . . is to have nothing to do with ofice or ministry.'[22] Thinking differently, the Mahatma was ready to counsel acceptance provided the Raj gave an assurance that Governors would not use their special powers against the advice of Ministers.

Meeting in Delhi in the third week of March, the AICC

disagreed with Nehru and authorized office-acceptance if Gandhi's condition was met.

At meetings with Erskine, C.R. probed the Raj's willingness to satisfy Gandhi. The Governor, who was of aristocratic Scots lineage, independent, hopeful of a rising career in British politics, and head of the presidency since 1935, probed C.R. He had heard of him as 'a wholehearted disciple of Gandhi' with 'a visionary and impractical turn of mind.'

However, after their third meeting, which Erskine found 'very amicable,' he wrote to Linlithgow, the Viceroy, that he 'liked the old boy.'[23] C.R. asked if the Governor would give a written assurance that his special powers would not be used unless orders were issued by the Viceroy or the Secretary of State.

The Viceroy, whose advice Erskine sought, ruled that out. Instead he asked the Governor to find out from C.R. if Congress would be satisfied by a statement from Erskine that he would be 'ready to work with any party taking up office.' C.R.'s reply, given after consulting Gandhi, was that this would not be enough.

In Madras and six other provinces, Governors formally invited the leader of the Congress legislature party to form a government. C.R. and his counterparts formally sought the assurance that Gandhi had stipulated. When it was not forthcoming, they said they could not accept office.

In Madras, Erskine asked Srinivasa Sastri, the Liberal leader, if he would form a caretaker government. Saying that he was old and ill and that accepting the offer would make him unpopular, Sastri refused. However, Sir K.V. Reddi, asked next by the Governor, agreed.

The caretaker ministries satisfied no one. Ready to settle with the Raj for somewhat less than Gandhi's minimum, C.R. went to the village of Tithal on the Gujarat coast to confer with the Mahatma. Gandhi said he wanted a sign from Britain that it would cooperate.

The Raj showed movement. In the House of Commons, Zetland, the Secretary of State, uttered encouraging words. Then the Viceroy gave Britain's formal response to Gandhi's demand:

There is no foundation for any suggestion that the Governor is free, or entitled, or would have the power to interfere with the day-to-day administration of a province outside the limited range of the responsibilities specially confided to him.

This sufficed for Gandhi. When the Working Committee conferred in Wardha, C.R. argued for taking office. No one opposed him, not even Nehru. Gandhi had convinced Jawaharlal against defying the rest. On 5 July 1937 the Working Committee sanctioned the formation of ministries.

Two days later, C.R., five times a prisoner of the Raj, was sent for by Erskine and asked to form a cabinet. C.R. agreed and became Prime Minister (that was the designation used) of Madras. His life had entered a new phase. Now he would govern. Interrupted during the War and enriched, in 1947, by freedom, the phase would last until 1954.

For the present he was launched into an unusual experiment of a dual relationship with the Raj, combining trust and struggle, participation and opposition.

'You know how my hope is centred in you,' said the Mahatma to him in a telegram. 'May God bless your effort.'[24]

11

Premier
1937-39

He was 58, five-foot-five and wholly bald except at the back of his oval, bespectacled eagle-nosed head. The eyes — if you saw them — were serious and sad-looking but were protected from scrutiny by thick dark glasses. The face was hard and austere except when it broke out in a grin. The baritone voice was always calm, the speech always distinct, the words always interesting. Each day this Iyengar Brahmin widower wore exactly the same dress: a kurta, dhoti and folded shawl of clean white khadi, the fabric of revolt and reform.

Now, in July 1937, after nearly two decades of a struggle that had earned him five spells in prison and a reputation for unpredictable actions and a quick keen mind, C.R. was Premier of Madras Presidency, which extended to Mangalore and Calicut on the Arabian Sea, and Vizag on the Bay of Bengal.

Though the Act of 1935, under which he had become Premier, reserved some key areas (e.g., the appointment of judges to the High Court) for the Governor and the Viceroy, C.R. possessed powers that no Indian had held in Madras for a century or more. He and his Ministers could borrow and tax, release and imprison, hire and fire. His new status was understood by the liveried peons of Fort St. George, the Raj's southern headquarters, when they saw Sir Charles Cunningham, the head of the Presidency's police that had arrested C.R. in the past, waiting in an ante-room for an interview with him.

A Premier's prestige surrounded C.R. but he and his colleagues in government and the legislature refused to take the emoluments set by the Raj. Instead of the Rs 56,000 per annum specified for a Premier, C.R. drew in all Rs 9,000 a year, inclusive of allowances for rent and transport. His government did not provide Ministers with houses, but he had the use of an official car, one of six bought at Rs 3,000 a vehicle. C.R. was 'a miser' over public funds, Erskine, the Governor, wrote to Linlithgow, the Viceroy.[1]

The Congress-Raj compact was tricky. It required former victims of the Raj to rule a province through officials who had been their masters in the past (and were quite likely to be their masters again in the future), and in conjunction with a Governor who could, on certain grounds, veto their measures. While Congress wished to use the compact to weaken the Raj, the Raj hoped that 'the gulf between us and Nationalist India [would] diminish as the cooperators become absorbed in the problems of administration,' as the Marquess of Zetland, Secretary of State for India, said in a letter to the Viceroy.[2]

Congress Premiers had to prove themselves impervious to the charms of office — hence the low salaries — but equal to its demands. And they needed to be moderate and bold at the same time, the former to obtain the cooperation of officialdom, the latter to keep faith with the Indian masses.

When C.R. announced, in his first measure, that buttermilk would be added to the diet of prisoners, the thousands of activists who remembered the inadequate rations of their prison terms were pleased, and the Raj was not specially bothered. But officials tried to block C.R. when he said he would release political prisoners, including some convicted for violent deeds but now disavowing violence. The Viceroy murmured misgivings to the Governor, but C.R. had his way. In his first month in office, 38 political prisoners were discharged.[3]

In early utterances as Premier, C.R. referred to the Raj's officials as 'my comrades in the permanent public service' (*The Hindu*, 20.8.37), and renounced 'rancour or prejudice against any group or class or individuals for anything done or suffered in the past.' 'I want the entire service, including the police, to look upon me as a friend,' he added (*Indian Review*, Aug. 1937).

In speaking in this vein C.R. was alone among the country's popular leaders, but his words placated the Raj's white officials who had the capacity to cripple the transition. 'I am the snake-charmer of British Imperialism,' C.R. told Erskine.[4] With Sir Charles Brackenbury, the Chief Secretary, he hit it off particularly well. The Governor reported to Linlithgow that C.R. 'has struck up a great friendship with the Chief Secretary, which is certainly reciprocated.'

Soon after assuming office, C.R. made Brackenbury a gift of a length of khadi: the Chief Secretary wore a suit made of it. 'The news tickled the imagination of the people . . . In homes, in buses and trams, in clubs and cafes, people discussed nothing else' (*Triveni*, Oct. 1937).

C.R. took trouble also over J.B.L. Munro, the under secretary in the public department, which was in the Premier's direct care, as were home and finance. Munro would later recall:

> Everything seemed to be going nicely until I read the report of a speech by a Minister attacking the I.C.S. . . . I wrote a hot-blooded little minute to the Prime Minister through the Chief Secretary . . . I was told that the P.M. wanted me. He said that . . . the Minister would make a speech which would put things right (and he did so the same evening) but that I must remember that an express train full of steam might occasionally run past the platform. Then he gave me a grin and said, 'Next time you feel like that, Munro, go and have a cold bath!'[5]

C.R. saw Munro in his home when he was running a high fever and arranged a spell for him in Ooty's cool climate.

Both Gandhi and the Viceroy seemed concerned about the long hours that C.R. was putting in. Linlithgow wrote to the Governor that 'he hoped sincerely that Rajagopalachariar will not overdo things,'[6] and the Mahatma told C.R., 'The world won't go wrong if you took an hour's rest during the day.'[7] 'Make your father rest,' Gandhi advised C.R.'s children. As in the past C.R. countered by urging 'a definite plan of compulsory rest' on the Mahatma. In a letter to Mahadev Desai which was also meant for Gandhi, C.R. admitted that he was ill: 'my fingers tremble and often I get wearied and at night I go to bed with a feeling of fever.' Rest, however, was 'simply impossible.'

Yet, being at long last in a paid job, even the arduous one of a Premier, removed some of the worries of his widowed daughter Namagiri and son Narasimhan, who lived with him. C.R. could say to Desai: 'I have never had a happier atmosphere and peace at home, these many years.'[8]

Relations feeling their way with C.R. about possible jobs were rebuffed. When one of them called on him in Madras, the Premier greeted him with the question, 'Have you come for jobs for your sons?' 'No, no,' the relative lied, 'I just came to see you.' Returning to Bangalore, he told his family, 'I have come back without opening my mouth.'[9]

Bal Gangadhar Kher, the Premier of Bombay, asked C.R. about a disagreeable rule that said that Governors, who were all British, should preside at cabinet meetings. Replied C.R.: 'It is too early to judge. I am on the saddle but my feet are not in the stirrups yet.'[10] Soon afterwards the solution suggested itself: while the Governor presided over formal meetings lasting five or ten minutes, the real cabinet would take place in the Premier's office.

C.R.'s ingenuity was also tested by a popular demand for the removal from Mount Road in Madras, of an 1861 statue of General Neill. A hero of the 1857 Mutiny in British eyes, Neill was remembered as heartless by Indians. Minuting, 'There are more ways than one of keeping a historic monument or memorial,' C.R. ordered the statue's removal and, simultaneously, its preservation within the precincts of the Government Museum; the order was quietly carried out in the darkness of a November night.[11]

A circular drafted by C.R. informed district magistrates that the release of prisoners who had been guilty of violence did not mean that violence was to be condoned. An impressed Erskine wrote to the Viceroy that C.R.'s wording was 'in substitution for a considerably milder draft that had been put up by the Chief Secretary.'[12]

Neither C.R.'s conciliatory tone towards the British nor his concern with law and order was liked by Jawaharlal Nehru and Subhas Bose, at this stage the heroes of the Congress Left. Nehru protested about C.R.'s style to the Mahatma. The latter replied:

'I fear that often when the Congress is in power it will use language which its predecessors have used and yet the motive will be different.'[13] C.R. had a better equation with Patel, who found it natural on occasion to travel to Madras 'to consult [Rajaji] on several matters,' as he put it (*The Hindu*, 1.1.38).

Soon after assuming office, C.R. barred employees of local authorities from joining the Congress or any other party. Nehru, who was the Congress President, objected. 'Is the Congress organisation going to become a camp follower of the government?' he asked C.R. 'It was impossible,' replied C.R., 'conscientiously to permit the employees of the local boards to become members of the Congress party simply because we were in office. It would be a scandal.'[14]

In November 1937, S.S. Batlivala, a Bombay socialist, was given a six-month sentence in Vellore for incitement to violence. Leftists in Congress and outside were indignant. Nehru, it seems, asked C.R.: 'Do you mean to say that if I come to Madras and make a similar speech you would arrest me?' 'I would,' C.R. apparently replied.[15]

Nehru asked the Congress Working Committee to direct Ministries to obtain the Committee's clearance for political arrests or prosecutions. But the Committee was unwilling to go so far. While advising Ministers not to object to criticism, it acknowledged their right to act against incitement to violence.

If he was wooing the British, C.R. also strove to defend the frontiers of his autonomy. Thus he objected to the draft of the Governor's first speech to the legislature following Congress's assumption of office. Erskine asked the Viceroy for the latter's 'full support in preventing this invasion of the discretionary power of the Governor' but was advised by Linlithgow to exclude 'matter which might have a controversial or argumentative tinge.'[16]

C.R. claimed a 'right' to see files on subjects assigned by the 1935 Act to the Governor's own domain, but Erskine was unyielding. 'Nobody,' the Governor minuted, 'either a Minister or Secretary, can advise me in regard to matters in which I exercise "my discretion." '[17]

Selected by Premier Stanley Baldwin for the Governorship, 'Jock' Erskine, a bespectacled and stocky Scot and a son of the

Earl of Mar and Kellie, had been an MP before coming to Madras and expected a place before long in the British Cabinet. He had been anti-Congress and pro-Justice before the 1937 elections but he liked C.R.'s wit and reasonableness and enjoyed dealing with one whom he described as 'a big figure' belonging to 'the inner ring of the Congress.'[18] To King George V, Erskine sent this account of C.R. (29.12.37):

> As to the Premier himself, I get on quite well with him, but he is an odd mixture ... He is an idealist and his main object in life seems to to get India back to what it was in the days of King Asoka. He runs the whole show and if anything were to happen to him we should be all over the place ... [19]

On his part C.R. had a warm spot, nourished by memories of his teacher John Tait, for the Scots, and he liked Erskine's sense of humour. However, the tussle between Congress and the Raj and the jealous attitude of both C.R. and Erskine towards their rights ensured tension. Always more than willing to rule without Ministers, Erskine from time to time gave the Viceroy a fair idea of the money Governor's rule would save, and a less realistic estimate of the response Governor's rule might get.

Erskine spent three months in a year in Government House on Mount Road, the mansion Clive's son had used, three months in Guindy Lodge — the present residence of Tamil Nadu's Governor, first acquired by Sir Thomas Munro in 1821 for use as the Governor's country house — and six months in Ooty.

C.R. lived in a modest dwelling on Bazlulla Road in the suburb of Mambalam. Jamnalal Bajaj, friend and supporter of Gandhi, C.R. and others, had bought the house for C.R.'s use and rented it to him. (Five years later, when Bajaj died and C.R. was in political wilderness, the Bajaj family transferred the ownership of the house to C.R. The house stood next to the home of C.R.'s son Krishnaswami, who was on the editorial staff of *The Hindu*).

Namagiri, C.R.'s widowed daughter, kept house for him. From seven in the morning there were visitors — officials, partymen, and others. C.R. received them in the small 'swing room' into which the front-door opened, named after the most prominent item of furniture in it. He would sit on the swing, the visitors in chairs, if they were trousered officials, or on straw mats on the floor. From 9.30 to 4.30 he would work in Fort St. George, with a ten-minute interruption for coffee and an idli or two brought from home.

In C.R.'s ten-man Cabinet, T. Prakasam, V.V. Giri and Gopala Reddi represented the Telugu districts, and P. Subbaroyan, T.S.S. Rajan, S. Ramanathan, Muniswami Pillai and C.R. the Tamil areas. Pillai, in addition, was a Harijan. From Malabar C.R. took Ramana Menon, replaced by C.J. Varkey following Menon's death. Yakub Hasan was the Cabinet's Muslim member. Subbaroyan alone had previous ministerial experience; and Prakasam was the only colleague to question some of C.R.'s decisions.

For most of his colleagues C.R. was a mentor and a backstop. Besides leading them, he was apt on occasion to do their work even before they showed their unfitness for it. 'Why do you try to mind the portfolios of others?' Gandhi asked him. 'I have not acquired the art of controlling my swabhava,' C.R. replied.[20]

The Assembly sessions were held in the University Senate House, familiar to C.R. from his college days. The Speaker, Bulusu Sambamurti, a Telugu lawyer who had discarded his practice to join the Gandhi-led movement, would come to the House in a dhoti with a sheet draped over a bare chest. The opening day's proceedings have been described in *Triveni* (Oct. 1937):

> The hall was filled with khaddar-clad ladies and gentlemen in as many types of unconventional attire as one could imagine. The few Europeans present looked almost apologetic for the clothes they were in. The people at last seemed to be tenanting the central seat of power.

Members spoke in Tamil, Telugu, Malayalam, Kannada, Urdu and English. Except when a member interpreted a colleague, there was no translation — the House would not hear, Sambamurti ruled, the voice of an outsider. C.R. instructed MLAs in the art of speaking into a mike and in the culture of parliamentary politics.

At the first session he asked the Speaker to ensure the

opposition's rights and his partymen not to make personal references to any opposition member. Congress MLAs speaking of Europeans in India as 'parasites' and 'bloodsuckers' were rebuked by him, and when a Minister was found absent, C.R. delivered an open reprimand.

'I consider the opposition strong and important and I respect it. That is why I have accepted so many amendments.'[21] This remark by C.R., made during the debate on his Debt Relief Bill, was both true and misleading. While ready to accept improvements, C.R. was unwilling to yield on a core issue, and he disarmed the opposition with his courtesy.

On 1 October 1937 — within three months of Congress taking over — Salem district, C.R.'s own, went dry, and a programme of gradual extension of prohibition was announced. Despite the loss this entailed in excise, which along with land revenue formed the bulk of the government's income, C.R. presented a balanced budget in 1937 and was to do so again in the two following years.

There were misgivings over the dry law. Drinkers would surely violate it by making their own brew or by buying grog made illicitly by others. And were there officials to enforce the law? C.R. found a remarkable one from the ranks of the ICS, A.F.W. Dixon, 'a tall popular officer determined to make prohibition a success though no teetotaller himself.'[22]

Dixon and most other officials stuck loyally to a convention that C.R. proposed: officials in a district going dry would neither drink within its confines nor ask for a permit, which was easily available to Europeans pleading habit and somewhat less easily to Indians pleading addiction.

Salem's officers could, however, go to Bangalore for a drink, a detour to which C.R. did not object. Clubs could apply for licences to keep liquor for sale to permit-holding members; bishops and priests were authorized to keep wine for religious purposes; and hospitals could stock brandy. A sense of proportion was thus retained. When C.R. heard that a magistrate had fined a European Rs 500 for a dry law violation, he reduced the penalty to five rupees.

Such was Dixon's zeal, and such the climate of the time, that in the dry law's first year there were only 110 cases of illicit distillation and no more than 170 of illicit tapping of toddy palm; there had been 265 and 470 cases, respectively, of the offences in the previous (and wet) year. Employers spoke of a fall in absenteeism and a rise in real earnings among their workers. After four months of prohibition, Dixon reported that 'conditions have changed to a remarkable extent' in 'thousands of homes.' 'Domestic brawls have ceased, a sufficiency of food is available, and the grip of the money-lender has relaxed.' A Madras University study of the first year of the dry law suggested that over 200,000 persons formerly paying the drink bill were no longer doing so, while a report of the Annamalai University referred to 'a phenomenal improvement.'[23]

Erskine wrote to the King that prohibition had 'succeeded far better than was expected' and that 'there has been a great diminution in the consumption of alcohol in the Salem district.' He noted that the public had 'calmly acquiesced' in 'the forcible removal' of its liquor. 'Your Prime Minister seems to have plenty of character,' the King's secretary wrote back, adding that the news of prohibiton had 'particularly interested' the King.[24]

To C.R. the dry law was part of a bigger programme of influencing the countryside. He hoped to popularize games, ballad and bhajan singing, folk dances, street dramas and the cinema, and tea and coffee. However, he was unable to forge instruments for achieving the interesting vision.

The Telugu districts of Chittoor and Cuddappah went dry a year after Salem, and North Arcot in the Tamil country followed a year later, all three witnessing, though perhaps to a lesser extent, the gains that had come to Salem. But illicit tapping and distillation seemed also to increase. However, no study pronounced the experiment a failure when in October 1939, in the aftermath of the declaration of war, the C.R. Ministry was to resign.

The Debt Relief Bill that C.R. piloted with passion was strongly opposed. Damdupat was the broad principle laid down by him: if, in interest and principal instalments, a farmer had paid back more than twice the principal, his debt would stand cancelled. (We should mark that the rate of inflation was zero at the time.)

Sir A.T. Pannirselvam of the Justice Party termed the Bill a cheap device for winning the sympathy of 'the poorer people, who are naturally more numerous.' Leading the European block, W.E.M. Langley complained that approaching the Assembly not 'claws and all, as a lion,' but disarmingly, C.R. was bringing in 'pale-pink socialism or even communism' through the Bill. Krishnamachari said it was a balm, not a cure: debts would accumulate again. He also regretted the absence of detailed statistics to justify the Bill.

C.R. likened Krishnamachari's criticism to 'laughing at a bullock cart because it was not a motor car [or] at our feet because we have bought a bicycle.' As for statistics, C.R. said that 'if mosquitos had to be escaped in Madras, it was better to buy a net in time, before the statistician could collect figures as to the distribution of mosquitos between Mylapore and Triplicane.'[25]

The Hindu's columns in November and December 1937 were filled with protests assailing the measure as 'un-Hindu' and likely to 'frighten away credit.' Close to 300 amendments were proposed in the Assembly, which sat well into the night while discussing the Bill for four days. It was passed more or less as C.R. wanted it.

Bombay copied C.R.'s Act and Sikandar Hyat Khan, Premier of the Punjab, termed it 'a lead' (*The Hindu*, 19.7.38). Though, as C.R. admitted, the Act did not help the agricultural labourer, the tenant was relieved. C.R.'s hope to 'devise and introduce a measure to emancipate' the rural labourer as well (*The Hindu*, 1.2.38) was not to be fulfilled.

Over its life of two years and three months, the Rajaji Ministry gave modest subsidies to handspinners and to what C.R. called 'the valiant handloom,' took water to dry villages, built rural roads and dispensaries, remitted land revenue in areas hit by cyclone or drought, and halved grazing fees. It negotiated a settlement — C.R. playing a personal part — with the states of

Hyderabad and Mysore for the use of river waters, and helped launch the Tungabhadra scheme.

Thermal plants were initiated in Bezwada and Vizag in the Telugu districts; power from the hydro stations of Pykara and Mettur was taken to eight additional Tamil districts. In towns new sums were spent on drainage, purification of water and prevention of disease: the Ministry's Public Health Act was the first of its kind for a province. Buttermilk, newspapers, radio sets and Fuller's earth for washing clothes were made available to prisoners. Teaching Hindustani was financed in 125 secondary schools. Most expensively, four districts went dry, depriving the government of large sums in excise.

Savings and new levies paid for all this. The transfer of the government each summer to Ooty was stopped, and C.R. fixed lower salaries for new entrants to some provincial services.

'It must be remembered,' Erskine wrote to the Viceroy, 'that the Premier is a terrible miser where public funds are concerned.'[26] For travelling expenses in the province in his first eight months in office the Premier claimed the princely sum of Rs 400!

For his second budget, C.R. received Rs 21 lakhs as Madras's share of the all-India income tax. It was the first time that the tax was shared with provinces, and opposition MLAs called the 21 lakhs 'a windfall.' Retorted C.R.: 'It is a return of stolen property. Is the land revenue which comes with the hot tears of the farmer the only legitimate revenue of the province, and not the income tax?'[27]

In 1938-9, C.R.'s hungry eye found an unearmarked nest-egg of over Rs 40 lakhs that had accumulated in the Minor Ports Fund, into which ships using the Presidency's smaller ports had over the years been paying fees. C.R. coolly employed the sum to overcome a financial crunch caused by cyclones, floods, a monsoon failure and an influx of refugees from Burma. Terming this sum a windfall, he added:

Was the failure of the monsoon a windfall? Was the cyclone a windfall? Was the huge remission that had to be given a windfall? If misfortunes befall us, God also sends us a windfall. It should not be grudged.[28]

His most important innovation was the sales tax, levied by him — for the first time in Asia — in 1939. First he imposed a tax on the sale of petrol and tobacco, then on the sale of electricity, and finally a general sales tax of half-an-anna in the rupee — a 3 per cent levy — payable on sales by anyone with a turnover of over Rs 10,000 a year.

While C.R.'s ingenuity was praised, his new taxes were fiercely opposed by Justice and pro-business MLAs. The Premier's answer was that the levies shifted a load from the poor to the not-so-poor, and from the peasantry to urbanites.

He incurred some unpopularity in the Andhra country by accepting the report of a white judge, Horwill, exonerating officials involved in a disturbance in the town of Chirala. 'Down with Horwill Report!' chanted young men at a meeting C.R. addressed in Guntur. 'I have accepted it because it is right,' replied C.R. 'You cannot intimidate me,' he added. 'Every act of the administration cannot be disposed of by a crowd.'

This was hardly palatable, but the Guntur audience cheered C.R. when he said: 'Andhra Pradesh is the birthright of the Andhras as much as Swaraj is the birthright of the Indians.'[29] The statement was necessary, for it was being rumoured that C.R. had sent a secret letter to London arguing against a separate Andhra province.

The truth was that in the Assembly and to the Raj C.R. had declared his clear support for a separated Andhra. In a memorandum to Zetland, he and his Ministers had asked for steps for its creation. When the Secretary of State expressed his inability to accede to the request, C.R. wrote to him again:

> There can be no stable administration of the province unless
> it is divided as desired by the people of Andhra . . . In the
> interests of sound administration, the demand of the people .
> should be granted.[30]

It was, however, the issue of Hindi, or Hindustani, as C.R. preferred to call it, which harassed the Premier the most. His

Ministry had introduced its teaching in standards six to eight in 125 schools. Students could choose either the Nagari (Sanskrit) or the Urdu script, and it was clarified that failure in Hindustani would not block a student's promotion. 'It was chutney on the leaf,' said C.R., 'taste it or leave it alone.'[31] He claimed it would equip southerners for jobs across India.

But he had underestimated both the sentiment against the northern tongue and the opposition's ability to exploit it. Hindustani was successfully portrayed as an alien, Aryan import which the South's Brahmin minority with its supposed Aryan links might accept but which the sons of the soil, the Dravidians, must oppose.

The initiator and leader of the anti-Hindi movement was E.V.R. Naicker, who had started as C.R.'s ally in Tamil politics and was now his opponent. Called E.V.R. until he was named Periyar, the Big One, Naicker was chairman of the municipality of Erode while C.R. was chairing its counterpart in Salem. C.R. had enlisted him in Gandhi's non-cooperation battle, but E.V.R. resigned from Congress after the Mahatma suspended his campaign in 1922.

As soon as the Hindustani policy was articulated, E.V.R. attacked it from public platforms and Justice men censured it in the Assembly. Opponents went to C.R.'s public meetings with black flags and shouted slogans against Hindi, Brahmins and the man himself. In Trichy, sandals and shoes were thrown at a platform where C.R. sat.

Demonstrators shouted slogans outside schools teaching Hindi and also outside C.R.'s Bazlulla Road house. Prakasam told the Assembly that life had become 'intolerable' for those living in that house.[32] Though C.R. claimed that he possessed 'one ear that works and another that is deaf,' enabling him to 'sleep in a market if necessary, by having the wrong ear up,'[33] we can be certain that he was personally affected.

That the agitators were parodying satyagraha also outraged C.R.; the Gandhians had never sought to embarrass opponents. C.R. thought, too, that the anti-Hindustani agitators were fostering permanent communal hatred, thereby 'annoying the national heart.' Their language affronted him: they were describing some people — C.R. told the Assembly — 'by caste, by their sacred thread, by the tuft of the hair on their head' and had descended to an 'intolerable' standard of 'scurrilousness . . .' . personal libel, and . . . references to the physical processes of physiological regeneration.'[34]

How was he to deal with them? They could not be booked for posing a threat to a breach of peace, for violence was not really threatened by their noise. There was a law against nuisance, but it sanctioned only a trifling punishment and was moreover powerless against the instigator—'the man who comes on a bicycle and fixes the boys,' as C.R. described him.[35]

In the circumstances, C.R. ironically and unwisely turned to Section 7 of the Criminal Law Amendment Act, offences under which were non-bailable and which the Raj had used to combat Congress's picketing of cloth and toddy shops. In a note recommending Section 7 to Brackenbury, the Chief Secretary, C.R. said: 'Those who are organising this [campaign] will not like the application of the penal law and if they see that the arm of the law is long enough, the business will come to an end.'[36]

Erskine warned C.R. that using the penal law might prove 'undesirable from his party's point of view.' (He told the Viceroy, however, that it was 'no business of mine to keep the Congress party popular.')[37] *Indian Express* and *Swadesamitran*, both friendly to Congress, urged a repeal of the Act, and in a *Harijan* article the Mahatma suggested that C.R. remove the 'obnoxious' features of the controversial law. But C.R. was not willing to yield.

The leader of the Muslim League group moved a resolution asking the Ministry 'to stop its policy of repression' against the demonstrators. Supporting the resolution, Pannirselvam claimed that for the Tamilian Hindi was 'a foreign language, foreign in words, script, culture and tradition' and recalled that the Criminal Law Act had once been 'an anathema' to C.R.

The opposition, replied C.R., was 'grievously disappointed' that 'this inconsistent Prime Minister says that he will use this Act, this repression, and will hinder the course of defiance [conducted] in parrot-like copy of Congress methods.' Added C.R.: 'This disappointment, I say, they deserve.' He went on:

Repression is the word used. Congressmen used the word not . . . when people were prosecuted or tried or arrested but [when they] were beaten and bones were broken. Even then not we but others used it.

Not even the vilest abuse that I have read with these eyes, printed in literature, multiplied by the tens of thousands, has been made the subject-matter of prosecution. Has a single procession been stopped? Has a single demonstration been ordered not to be conducted?[38]

Yet Section 7 continued to be applied, and C.R.'s foes were strengthened, as Erskine had foreseen.

By the end of January 1939, 683 persons in all, of whom 36 were women, had been convicted, for terms ranging from six weeks to a year, as a result of the anti-Hindustani agitation, including 173 prosecuted for their activity in front of the Premier's house. One of those arrested was a young man called C.N. Annadurai, destined to become one of the South's most popular leaders.

Satyamurti and Sarvepalli Radhakrishnan, the philosopher-educator, urged C.R. to make Hindustani an optional subject or to provide a conscience clause giving parents the right to withdraw their children from Hindustani classes, and Gandhi supported the suggestion. Claiming, however, that no parent had asked for such a right, C.R. turned down the idea. To the Mahatma he wrote: 'My objection is not pride or prestige. I do not wish to yield to the misuse of satyagraha. Bear with me.'[39]

Bombay followed the southern lead and introduced Hindustani, and Vallabhbhai Patel came out with support for C.R.'s policy, but E.V.R. registered at least partial success: in elections to the Madras municipality in October 1938, Congress lost several seats.

When the demonstrations began, C.R. had thought that 'it would be unnecessary in all probability to proceed against others if we book E.V.R. Naicker.'[40] But he changed his mind, and for five months no action was taken against Naicker. In November 1938, however, he was prosecuted.

By this time plans had been made to install E.V.R. as the president of the Justice Party. His arrest, and the one-year sentence he received, made him a martyr to his followers. Every morning the newspaper edited by his brother announced in big type the number of days their leader had passed in prison; E.V.R. became Periyar; and a fiery address sent from jail was read out at the Justice convention.

Calling Brahmins 'mosquitos,' 'bugs' and 'Jews,' the Periyar said that abolition of the reign of priests was more urgent than abolition of zamindari. Kumararajah Muthiah Chettiar, leader of the opposition, claimed at the rally that E.V.R.'s arrest had awakened the masses; separating Brahmins from Tamils, Pannirselvam called the former interlopers in the Tamil land. *The Hindu's* report of the rally referred to a 'hymn of hate' (29.12.38).

When questions were raised in the Assembly about the Periyar's detention in Bellary, C.R. said:

> It is a good jail. I claim to be a personal friend of Mr Naicker,
> though a very bitter political opponent. He knows that I am,
> as far as I can be, kind and considerate to him.[41]

In May 1939, when he was released on medical grounds, E.V.R. said: 'I have received exceptionally kind treatment.' (*The Hindu*, 23.5.39). By this time, however, the anti-Hindi movement had lost its intensity.

The Justice Party prized a 1935 decision to increase progressively the proportion of non-Brahmins in government services. Soon after assuming office, C.R. pledged that this policy would not be altered. His Ministry extended concessions to applicants from educationally or socially backward groups, Muslims included: they qualified with lower marks, paid a smaller fee, and could enter at a higher age.

While defending the concessions, which did not, however, satisfy the Justice group in the Assembly, C.R. asked members to 'remember how hard it was for them in school to get a few marks' and 'to enter the skin of those young men who have come out with brilliant records from the university and professional colleges and are sent away because a man of a particular community who has passed the age limit and is inferior perhaps in qualification gets the job.' And he warned against allowing 'this communal talk to become the daily pabulum in this House.'[42]

Subhas Bose was the Mahatma's choice for Congress President in 1938-9, succeeding Jawaharlal. The selection did not thrill C.R., who would have preferred someone less radical in this phase of an understanding with the Raj. When Bose suggested that the Premiers meet with him, and Kher of Bombay sought C.R.'s advice, the latter wrote: 'I should myself prefer to be left alone . . . If called, however, I fear I must go and cannot decline the invitation.'[43]

Among other issues which engaged C.R. were corruption and censorship of literature preaching violence.

Finding that legal proof of corruption was difficult to obtain, C.R. came up with the formulation that

> a corrupt official will be dismissed or removed without definite proof of a specific act of corruption if there is cumulative evidence that he was suspected in a number of instances to be corrupt.[44]

After *Viduthalai*, an E.V.R. mouthpiece, alleged that proceedings against certain butter manufacturers for adulteration were being withdrawn because they were Congress supporters, C.R. found that while there had been no withdrawal, frequent postponements had taken place. Ordering expedition, C.R. minuted: 'The case should not end in smoke or a nominal fine.'[45]

While lifting many of the restrictions imposed by the Raj on books and journals — among the beneficiaries was E.V.R.'s brother Krishnaswami, editor of *Viduthalai* —, C.R. retained curbs on literature preaching violence. Told in the Assembly that some volumes proscribed in Madras were circulating legally in the UP, he observed: 'Thank you. I will get in touch with the U.P. Government.'

Madras Customs detained a copy of 'Soviet Communism' by Sidney and Beatrice Webb and sent it to Fort St. George for instructions. A Home Department official suggested confiscation but his senior disagreed, terming the book 'a serious study, not mere propaganda.' It went up to the Chief Secretary, Sir Brackenbury who minuted: 'It is a good book. If we have not got it in the Secretariat Library, we might get it.'[46]

Sir Cecil Fabian Brackenbury was the son of a vicar and three years younger than C.R. In the future C.R. would warmly recall this gaunt, lean and idealistic man, a hard-working teetotaller who was loyal to the Raj but believed in Indian self-government. Candid in his advice to the Premier, which was often turned down, Brackenbury was faithful in implementing C.R.'s instructions.

'Exactly at eleven in the morning, Brackenbury would walk into C.R.'s office, take instructions and have them carried out.'[47] On his part, C.R. did not think it below his dignity to take a few steps to the Chief Secretary's room if he had something to discuss.

Shortly before Brackenbury retired in the middle of 1938, C.R. tried to obtain the acting Governorship of Orissa for him, but Erskine informed C.R. that the Viceroy disapproved of the idea. 'It is rather unfair to Brackenbury and a mistake,' C.R. commented.[48]

The Cabinet gave Brackenbury a farewell party; at C.R.'s instance, the Governor had the Brackenburys stay in Government House for a few days after they had wound up their house; and, to Erskine's surprise, C.R. said that the government would bear part of the cost of a reserved compartment that took the Brackenburys to Bombay.

In June 1938, All India Radio opened a station in Madras. In an inaugural talk, C.R. explained the radio to his unseen audience. As was his style, he painted pictures with words:

> You can [now] hear a joke cracked in London and laugh in response here . . . The air carries sound like a bullock cart; the Akash — the sky and ether — carries it across enormous distances like a steamship or train. (*The Hindu*, 16.6.38)

The Premier added, however, that 'the braying of distant donkeys is not much better than of neighbourhood donkeys.'

Prakasam presented a Bill to safeguard the rights of peasants and tenant-farmers, the fruit of an eighteen-month effort by a committee he had chaired. Congress MLAs gave Prakasam an ovation; landlords and European members opposed the Bill as expropriatory. Langley said it had been begotten in envy, conceived in hatred and delivered in malice.

The idea of compensating zamindars at market prices was firmly rejected by C.R.:

> In the other hemisphere, they once had very valuable properties. Slaves they had. Was compensation paid when slavery was abolished?

Krishnamachari made the valid observation that the Bill gave no benefits to the actual tiller. 'While [the reforms] destroy the zamindar, they bring no relief to the worker,' he said. Conceding the point, C.R. said: 'We may have other duties to cultivators . . . and to everybody else; but to each in its own time.'[49]

Seeking to transfer resources from the zamindar to the tenant-peasant though not to the landless labourer, the Bill was radical for its time. The Raj conveyed word that it stood little chance of receiving assent.

Fort St. George and the Assembly did not use up all of C.R. On evenings he was likely to go to a friend — perhaps to T.K. Chidambaranatha Mudaliar (T.K.C.), the literary critic and Kamban scholar, with whom he would discuss the Ramayana or the Tamil language — or to mount a platform and talk on any one of a wide assortment of topics.

The Raj's chief guardians, Zetland and Linlithgow, both of them Scots, were, in Zetland's phrase, 'enormously tickled' on hearing that C.R. — 'the leading protagonist in the cause of teetotalism' (Zetland) — had accepted an invitation to the St. Andrew's Dinner of the Caledonian Society of Madras. They were aware, as Linlithgow put it, 'that perfect sobriety on such occasions is not always observed.'

Happily, the Caledonians stayed sober, and the Premier was in merry form. He referred to the Scottish words on the menu — 'the funny spelling mistakes' — asked, 'Why do you not correct the proofs?' and added:

> I was a little pleased, let me confess, to hear what was said in dispraise of the Englishman and in praise of the Scot. We would like at least to imagine that you are quarrelling among yourselves. (Laughter) . . . But your island is too small for you to quarrel, and your people too great to commit that mistake. (Cheers)

> I have nothing to complain, as Prime Minister, with regard to the manner in which I have been served by you who still thought it worthwhile to carry on here in spite of the horrible changes that have taken place, and the more horrible changes that may take place.[50]

This period of Congress's compact with the Raj saw nervousness among Muslims in Hindu-majority provinces. Pointing to the mostly Hindu Congress Ministers, the Muslim League, led single-mindedly by Jinnah, told the Muslim public that white rule was being followed by Hindu rule. The explanation of Congress that it was an Indian and not a Hindu body, offered with sincerity and repeated from a thousand platforms, could not convince the bulk of the Muslim qaum.

Despite sedulous efforts, C.R. was unable to convince Madras's Muslim MLAs that the Hindi introduced in 125 schools had nothing to do with Hinduism. He argued that it was not a Sanskrit but a Persian word, that it merely meant the language of Hind, and that in any case his Ministry preferred the term Hindustani which, according to the Encyclopaedia Britannica, had 'an opulent vocabulary of words understood everywhere by both Mussulmans and Hindus.'

He had no effect on Jinnah, who 'complained bitterly' to the Mahatma that the Hindi pushed by the Madras Ministry was a burden on the Muslims.[51] The League leader's bigger grouse, however, made in relation to all the Congress Ministries, was that Muslims were losing out in the scramble for government jobs. A committee set up by the League, headed by the ruler of Pirpur, formally made the charge; a Congress offer to have it examined by the Chief Justice of India, Sir Maurice Gwyer, was rejected by the League.

A volley of figures unloosed in the Assembly by C.R. demolished the charge. Out of a total of 85,352 government jobs in the province, Muslims, he said, held 12,525, or 14.7 percent, as against a 6 to 7 per cent share in population. In eighteen months of Congress rule, the provincial Public Service Commission had selected 261 Muslim officers compared with 168 in the preceding eighteen months.

Some other Muslim percentages in Madras were: High Court judges, 7; district judges, 15 1/2; Madras city judges, 35; deputy superintendents of police, 18; police inspectors, 19; sub-inspectors, 14; constables, 22.

During the War, the Viceroy asked for a study of the Congress Ministries' record on minorities. The report on Madras, drawn up largely by British officers, gave the C.R. Ministry, in the words of Peter Crombie, its coordinator, 'a remarkably clean bill.'[52]

Early in the legislature's life, a Member asked for 'two Harijans in the cabinet.' 'There are two already,' C.R. at once replied, 'Muniswami Pillai and me.' Combining conviction for his people with a disarming gentleness, Pillai was a fine representative. Out of the House of 215, thirty were Harijans; separate Harijan electorates, withdrawn because of the Gandhi fast of 1932 and the subsequent pact between caste Hindus and Harijans, would have resulted only in 18 Harijan members.

In August 1938, when M.C. Rajah, one of the South's leading Harijan figures, moved a Bill for removing the social disabilities of Harijans, C.R. gave it the Ministry's backing. As his Bill was being passed, Rajah said that C.R. had helped draft it some years earlier. It made discrimination in jobs, wells, public conveniences, roads, transport, schools and colleges an offence.

In its first eighteen months, the C.R. administration took in 55 Harijans in first-grade government jobs, as against 25 in the previous year and a half. Out of 907 constables appointed between July 1937 and August 1939, 137 were from the scheduled castes, an impressive proportion for the time.

For years it had been C.R.'s ambition to open the great temples of the South to the Harijan. Power enabled him to realize it in large measure. But his path to the goal was neither smooth nor straight: opponents tried to impede him, and he himself chose a winding route.

To begin with, in January 1938, he promised Rajah support for a measure that would give worshippers the right by majority vote to open a temple to Harijans; this again was a piece of legislation that C.R. had helped draft in 1933. Later C.R. turned cautious and decided that the measure should apply only to the district of Malabar.

Why the caution? Perhaps C.R. did not want the guns of orthodoxy booming at him when he faced steady fire over Hindi. Why Malabar? This was chosen because it was adjacent, and in C.R.'s phrase 'first cousin,' to Travancore,[53] where by a proclamation the young Maharaja had already opened public temples to Harijans.

At this compromise, Rajah declared, 'I have been deceived'.[54] However, he declared his support for the Malabar Temple Entry Bill, which was passed despite strong criticism in September 1938.

An event in Madura sparked C.R. to do more. A majority of the trustees and priests of the famed Meenakshi temple declared that they wanted to let the Harijans in but feared proceedings for 'offence to religious sentiment.' C.R. promised them protective legislation 'in eight days' if they took the lead. On 8 July 1939 C.R.'s old friend Vaidyanatha Iyer took a group of Harijans to the temple; the authorities allowed them in.

Receiving the news in Madras, C.R. was 'beside himself with delight'; he did not sleep that night (*The Hindu*, 10.7.39). Others reacted differently to the Madura explosion. A criminal case was initiated against the temple's executive officer, and a purification ceremony was demanded.

On 11 July a draft of a Temple Entry Indemnity Bill was

published, followed six days later by an ordinance incorporating its features. The ordinance and the Bill indemnified temple officials who had opened or might open temples with the permission of government.

By this time Tanjore had thrown open all its 90 temples. The Courtallam temple had also fallen. However, a pandit at Srirangam, the renowned Vaishnava temple, told the Vaishnavite Premier that there was 'a rub': 'the shastras do not permit [temple entry].' C.R. replied that the shastras were 'like the infinite ocean from which . . . one can draw pearls and coral as well as mire and shark.'[55]

With its unconcealed signal to temple officials to be bold, the indemnity measure was fiercely criticized. Krishnamachari likened it to Ghazni's temple violations in a distant era, and predicted bloodshed. 'The blood will be on your head,' he told the Premier. C.R.'s reply was that there was 'no use my being a Minister if I cannot protect the people who brought this about.'[56]

Tirupati did not open its doors, but ancient barriers all over the province were collapsing, and there was no bloodshed. And while some leaders of the Depressed Classes pointed out that economic and political power mattered more than temples, many in the communities excluded for centuries witnessed' history, and triumph, before their eyes.

A duel over the indemnity law took place in the second chamber between the Premier and V.S. Srinivasa Sastri, who was an acknowledged master of the art of oratory. Said Sastri:

Are there not thousands and thousands who are not criminals, who are not hereditary oppressors, who honestly believe that certain exclusions have a proper sanction? Is a year or two too long to bring them over to our side?

If Madura was an epic act, let it remain an epic. Why protect them from the results of the action which they took knowingly? . . . Nothing will be lost if this Bill is stayed and a straight-forward Bill for open entry into the temples were brought forward.

Interrupting, C.R. asked if Sastri was in favour of a simple law declaring the temples open. The Premier added: 'Was that his advice? May I pause for a reply?'

Sastri: My answer will be long, sir.

C.R.: If the answer is to be long, then I presume, sir, that it is an argument and not an advice . . .

Sastri: I have not brought out this Bill; I am here only in the position of a critic; if circumstances lay it upon me ever to take up this question, I will not adopt this indirect backdoor method.

C.R.: Sir, he has still not said, 'Follow the other method.'

'Sastri's speech,' commented C.R., 'was one of extraordinary perfection. But having said that, having appreciated it in full measure, I must say that it was all too much like a lady's umbrella — a silken umbrella, perfect in form, in beautiful symmetry, full of colour and beauty — which gave no protection against sun or wind or rain.[57]'

The 1939 metaphor of the lady's umbrella was a talking point in Madras even in the early eighties.

It was time again for Congress to choose a President. Subhas Bose sought re-election — we saw that his predecessor, Jawaharlal, had had two successive terms. But it was plain that Bose differed from the Mahatma on some basic and immediate issues. Unlike Gandhi, Bose thought that the country was ripe for mass disobedience against the British, and his estimate of the ominous European scene varied substantially from Gandhi's.

Bose rejecting Gandhi's advice to withdraw, and Azad declining Gandhi's advice to stand against Bose, the Mahatma endorsed the candidacy of Pattabhi Sitaramayya, whose name had been proposed by the Andhra Congress. Before the voting, Bose argued that a Congress President should function not like a constitutional monarch, the position thus far, but as a Prime Minister; and he repeated an allegation that the old guard was ready, contrary to Congress directives, to compromise with the Raj over an all-India federation.

Bose won over Pattabhi by 1,580 votes to 1,375, and Gandhi

said he had been defeated. Yet, as Bose put it himself, 'a large majority of Congressmen who dislike[d] the high command did not want to give up Mahatma Gandhi' (*The Hindu*, 7.5.39). With Congress unprepared to reject Gandhi, and Bose unwilling to be a mere chairman, there was a stalemate at Tripuri, on the banks of the Narmada, where Congress met in March 1939 for its annual session.

Subhas was ill and incapacitated at Tripuri and Gandhi absent — he was in Rajkot, fasting over what he saw as a breach of promise by the Rajkot ruler. C.R., who went to Tripuri, did not like Bose's victory or his radicalism; and he was perturbed by Bose's presidential address — read out by Subhas's brother Sarat — which called for an ultimatum to the Raj.

C.R.'s response to the stalemate was to back a resolution that regretted the aspersions cast upon the old guard — the latter were 'hurt to the quick,' Nehru said[58] — and asked Bose 'to appoint the Working Committee in accordance with the wishes of Mahatma Gandhi.'

The drafting of this resolution, which was moved by Pant, the U.P. Premier, probably owed much to C.R.[59] Seconding it, C.R. spoke with a directness that delighted traditionalist ranks and drew waverers to their side. Despite the tempers of Tripuri, he was heard in complete silence:

> There are two boats on the river. One is an old boat but a big boat, piloted by Mahatma Gandhi. Another man has a new boat, attractively painted and beflagged. Mahatma Gandhi is a tried boatman who can safely transport you. If you get into the other boat, which I know is leaky, all will go down, and the river Narmada is indeed deep.

> We have tried Mahatma Gandhi for 20 years — to our satisfaction. What he says he means. He promises the minimum but performs the maximum.

> Do not think, 'We will get into the new boat for a while and then again get back into the old boat.' You may not survive to get back to the old boat for, as I said, the new boat is leaky.[60]

The resolution was passed. The parable of the boatman was

acclaimed. But Bengal did not forget C.R.'s remarks against her favourite son. Nine years later, shouts of 'Leaky boat! Leaky boat!' were hurled at C.R. when he arrived in Calcutta as Governor of West Bengal.

Implementing the Tripuri directive was more than what Bose was prepared to consider. He resigned the Presidentship. A little later he left Congress altogether. But his honour was intact; and in his future lay daring deeds and a nation's love.

At a meeting in Calcutta, the AICC asked Rajendra Prasad to fill the place vacated by Subhas. The occasion, presided over by Sarojini Naidu, was a stormy one, Bose's supporters alleging that Prasad's election was unconstitutional. When it was over, C.R. said to the harried chairperson: 'Sarojini, yours has been a Mrs Herculean performance.'[61]

12

Hitler

1939

The first quarter of 1939 saw conflicts between C.R. and the Raj. C.R. objected when the Raj wished to deploy the Madras police to quell riots in some of Orissa's princely states. Then the Raj objected when C.R. desired to transfer and censure a Collector, Alan Crombie, following an incident of firing in a jute mill in his district, Vizag. Also, C.R. sought a reduction in salaries protected by the Raj's special laws. Finally, he asked to be consulted in the appointment of High Court judges.

The Raj yielded wholly on the first point and partially on the second. C.R. had asked if Erskine subscribed to the view that 'neither the Prime Minister nor the Minister in charge of services nor the Minister in charge of the department concerned, nor all the Ministers together' could shift or censure an officer.[1]

Though C.R.'s Ministry often assigned officers to new duties, transferring an ICS officer as a mark of disfavour was a different matter altogether. In the end the Ministry was allowed to move Crombie to Bellary and to ask the Federal Public Service Commission to inquire into Crombie's role in the firing, but a public censure was not permitted. (Five months later, the Commission exonerated Crombie.)

On the remaining points the Raj gave nothing away, and C.R. pondered resigning. Not dipping into handsome earnings when he had touched lower salaries seemed unfair to him. As for appointments to the High Court, he wrote to the Governor (2.2.39):

I am certain that when the Secretary of State or the Governor-General consults Your Excellency in regard to such matters, your Prime Minister has an inherent right to be taken into confidence and to be consulted . . . The question has assumed a very serious shape.[2]

Describing a meeting where he told the Ministers that the Raj would not yield over salaries or the High Court, Erskine observed that one of the Ministers who

would never, if he could help it, under any circumstances, demit office, no matter what point of principle was involved, and who has had quite sufficient political experience to recognise a crisis when he sees one, [became] exceedingly perturbed. His face went a nasty dark-green colour and at one period of the discussion his teeth even began to chatter . . .

The idea of the Ministry's resignation was dropped. C.R. discussed with his colleagues the alternative of his resigning alone, leaving 'one of them to step into his shoes,' but they dissuaded him.[3]

To what he saw as the exploitation and intensification of racial and caste divisions, C.R. reacted memorably in the Assembly:

With due deference to Sir Pannirselvam, I say that we . . . will land ourselves in utter hopeless retrogression if we go on in this manner . . .

This agitation about Hindustani . . . has been converted into a regular propaganda which creates communal hatred. Is it good for anybody? Is it only this government that is to reap the results of this communal hatred? . . . Has an earthquake converted Tamil India into an island, separated from the rest of India?

When England has forgotten centuries ago the difference between Norman and Saxon and Celt, when we have the standing example of America before us, we are saying this is a dark man, this is a fair man; this is an Aryan, that is a Dravidian; this is a Scythian, that is a Mongolian and that is a Jew.[4]

When the Ministry was assailed for not trying to break the Raj-devised constitution, C.R. replied:

> The Hon'ble Member who spoke about this subject does not
> know the technique of breaking the constitution . . . Just as
> we grow without knowing we have grown, just as no man
> knows when he cast off his childhood or boyhood or his
> middle age, constitutions do not know when they have been
> broken . . .

An objection that his Ministry had not carried out a threat to resign was answered with unkind humour:

> It may be, sometimes, that... it looks almost that we are going
> to resign and other people get themselves ready to take our
> places. But [then] we get unpacked and other people have to
> go disappointed, and we are still in harness.

In reply to criticism of his new taxes, he said:

> I do not remember having told any group of people or any
> audience that we will reduce taxes all round. But we did say
> that the rural population would have less tax . . . It is easy
> enough to condemn the sales tax, the property tax, the
> entertainments tax and the petrol tax and to say that we won't
> have any taxes whatsoever. But it is not good for the country.[5]

He was, thus, a teaching parliamentarian as well as a trenchant and merciless one. The Mahatma, for one, observed that C.R.'s 'ability as a parliamentarian among Congressmen' was 'unsurpassed' (*Harijan*, 10.9.38).

By the summer of 1939 war seemed likely in Europe. The Raj said it would amend the Government of India Act to enable the centre to declare an emergency and, during an emergency, to override or take over provincial governments. Objecting emphatically, C.R. termed the measure 'a grave inroad into the field and status of provinces' and voiced the fear of an emergency declaration well before a war.[6] Despite such protests, the amendment became law.

On 1 September Hitler's armies invaded Poland. Two days

later, within hours of Britain's declaration of war, the Viceroy proclaimed India a belligerent state. He did this on his own, without consulting either the Central Assembly or the easily identifiable leaders of Indian opinion.

A year earlier, when war seemed possible, Patel had told Lumley, the Governor of Bombay, that Congress leaders 'would expect to be consulted . . . and invited to approve participation in the war.' Lumley had passed the word to Zetland, who, in turn, informed the British Cabinet.[7]

In 1938, C.R. had asked for a meeting regarding the possible war between the Viceroy and Gandhi. The day before Hitler attacked Poland, C.R. revived the proposal; Erskine conveyed it to the Viceroy. Thus the Raj had looked at, and rejected, the idea of sounding out Congress or Gandhi before declaring India's belligerency.

Even so, the Mahatma told Linlithgow that he regarded the war with 'a British heart.' He could not commit Congress, Gandhi added, but personally he was for Congress giving unconditional though nonviolent support to the Raj. Congressmen seemed divided. While many sympathized with the anti-British stand of Bose, who labelled the War imperialist, C.R., leading the moderates, could contemplate Congress giving 'wholehearted support to Britain in the fight against gangsterism personified.'[8]

He did not mind if this conflicted with the creed of nonviolence; though vital, in C.R.'s view, to the Indian struggle for freedom, nonviolence could not be the norm for all battles. In return, Britain, should announce a time-table for Dominion Status for India: as an earnest gesture of progress towards Dominion Status, some Congressmen should be taken into the Central Government in New Delhi.

Equidistant from C.R. and Subhas was Nehru, named chairman of Congress's War sub-committee, comprising Patel and Azad himself. While declaring opposition to Nazism, Nehru said that Indians 'will not participate [in the War] as slaves' (*The Hindu*, 18.9.39). At his instance, the Working Committee asked Britain to spell out her aims in the War and their application to India; the response would determine Congress's stand.

While Congress waited for the Raj's reply, C.R.'s police arrested all German males in the Presidency and handed them to the Raj's military. Anti-aircraft guns were installed in Madras city; the harbour was guarded, the Marina seafront blacked out.

Some Congressmen in the South — Bose's followers — made anti-War speeches. B.W. Day of the ICS, serving in Madras, would later recall that C.R. was 'strongly opposed to this sort of thing and in principle prepared to take action, but there was always something that prevented his sanctioning a prosecution.'[9] Without a Congress-Raj settlement, it was not easy for C.R. to prosecute critics of Britain's War.

At the end of September C.R. told the Press that 'Congress was negotiating with the British government in regard to the political status of India' (*The Hindu*, 30.9.39). Early in October, Gandhi, Prasad, Congress's Acting President, Nehru and Patel talked with Linlithgow; also invited by the Viceroy were Jinnah and the Princes, Ambedkar and the Hindu Mahasabha.

Some days later C.R., in his words, had 'full, free, frank and cordial' talks with the Viceroy in New Delhi. The Premier asked for 'a number of Congress leaders to be appointed to the Viceroy's Executive Council,' but Linlithgow was cool.[10]

Stopping in Wardha on his way back to Madras, C.R. spent two hours with Gandhi, discussing, among other matters, what he might do if he gave up office. Desai thought that C.R. would write on the Upanishads or learn Hindustani himself as 'expiation' for imprisoning anti-Hindustani agitators, but the Premier told him that he would probably teach, using the medium of handicraft![11]

On 17 October the Viceroy spoke. India, he said, would have constitutional talks, not freedom, at the end of the War; for the duration of the War, Indians could sit on a largely decorative consultative committee. In the declaration, Linlithgow referred also to 'the conflicting interests and claims' of Indian groups. In a letter to his King the Viceroy justified and described his divide-and-rule exercise:

As soon as I realised that I was to be subjected to heavy and sustained pressure designed to force from us major political concessions as the price of Congress's cooperation in the war effort, I summoned representatives of all the more important interests and communities in India, including the Chancellor of the Chamber of Princes and Mr Jinnah, . . . and interviewed them one by one, . . . a heavy and trying task but well worth the trouble.

[The declaration] does not give to Congress what they are asking for, which is an understanding by Your Majesty's Government that India will be given political independence at the conclusion of the war . . .

[The declaration] has made plain the fact that we cannot concede to Congress the validity of that party's claim to speak for the whole of India.[12]

C.R. termed the Viceroy's statement 'deeply disappointing.' He felt that 'a great and unique occasion' had been 'simply thrown away' (*The Hindu*, 18.10.39). Subhas saw in the statement the 'strongest justification' of his stand. Gandhi said it was stone instead of bread and also divide-and-rule.

When C.R. protested to Erskine, the Governor — so he reported in a letter to Linlithgow — charged that Congress 'had made a bad psychological mistake in attempting to use England's difficulties as a lever to bargain for an immediate political advance at the centre.' Apparently, the Premier was also told 'quite plainly' that 'the British people were the last nation in the world who would submit to blackmail in time of war.'[13]

Does blackmail go with sympathy? The Mahatma's concern for the British was expressed several times: seeing it the Viceroy, according to his son and biographer, Lord Glendevon, was 'deeply moved.'[14] About Hitler, Gandhi had said: 'It almost seems that Hitler knows no God but brute force and will listen to nothing else' (*The Hindu*, 5.9.39).

The Raj was well aware also of C.R.'s feelings. As Erskine had written to the Viceroy two months before the War started, 'He himself (C.R.) wanted us to win any possible war against the Totalitarian countries.'[15] Subhas, true, spoke another language, but he was no longer in the inner ring of Congress; in August, in fact, he had been barred for three years from any elective post in Congress because of his defiance of directives.

If Congress's sympathies were clearly with the Allies, its political demands were not conceived after the declaration of War. At virtually every legislative session, Congress Premiers, including C.R., had asked for constitutional advance at the centre; party resolutions had invariably done the same.

When, following the start of the War, Congress reiterated these demands, the Raj's custodians reacted not with surprise but with relief at the prospect of a termination of the Raj-Congress understanding and the departure of Congress Ministries.

On 16 September, Erskine forwarded to Linlithgow C.R.'s plea that the Viceroy should see Gandhi and Nehru. The Governor added, however: 'Personally I think we should not enter into any bargain for if Congress do go out it will be their funeral and not ours.'[16]

For Erskine and many others in the Raj, disputes among Indians were a blessing: they required the Raj's continuance. Erskine's feelings about Indian independence came across in a phrase he used while writing to Linlithgow at the end of 1939: 'If, by bad management of our affairs, we were ever forced to leave India . . .'

That Linlithgow's views were not very different is suggested by his assurance to the King, quoted earlier, that Congress was being denied any 'understanding . . . that India will be given independence at the conclusion of the war.'

Its demands rejected, Congress had to choose between losing power in the provinces and losing prestige at the grassroots, where Indian freedom seemed to matter more than the War in Europe. It was not a difficult decision. The War and its emergency provisions were reducing Ministers to the status of the Raj's civil servants. If they did not arrest any Congressmen criticizing the War, the Governor, it was clear, would have them arrested anyway.

The Congress Working Committee decided that the Ministries should go. According to V.P. Menon — whose drafting and administrative skills were used by the Raj and later by the government of free India and who chronicled the transfer of power — the resignation of eight Congress Ministries helped create 'a conviction among the British that the Hindus were their irreconcilable enemies' and paved the way for partition.[17]

Before the resignation, Akbar Hydari, ICS, had privately remarked that his British colleagues were happy that the Congress Ministries were likely to be asked to go. When this word was conveyed to Nehru, the latter exploded. 'It is none of Hydari's business,' said Nehru, 'what we should decide in the Working Committee. I am going to pull out all the Ministries.'[18]

The Congress withdrawal gave Jinnah a large opening. In celebration he announced a Deliverance Day. In the period that followed, the Muslim League gained in strength. Yet Congress could not have sustained a wartime partnership with the Raj without some progress towards Indian liberty. It would have been savaged as a toady party.

The Working Committee resolution asking the Ministries to resign was, in Gandhi's words, 'studiedly moderate.' It left open the door for negotiations with the Raj.

E.V.R., the Justice Party and M.C. Rajah declared their unequivocal support for the War. But the public in Madras seemed solidly with C.R. Held at this juncture, district board elections across the Presidency went resoundingly in Congress's favour.

On 25 October C.R. spoke engagingly to students of Queen Mary's College for Women. The next day he moved a resolution in the Assembly calling upon his Ministry to resign.

The opposition criticized scathingly. The Congress did not speak for all India, said the Kumararajah. Langley attacked the summoning of the House 'merely for registering the fiat of a caucus sitting behind closed doors in Wardha.' Pannirselvam claimed that Congress did not represent Muslims, Christians or the Scheduled Castes. In any case, he said, 'I have no inclination to be troubled with India. I care for my own country — and that is the Dravida Land.'

The League MLAs were equally critical, but two independent Muslims acknowledged C.R.'s justice during his tenure, and another independent, G. Krishna Rao, said that the Ministry had protected minorities and should not go. Krishnamachari quoted the remark of Zetland, the Secretary of State, that the Madras Ministry had shown 'grit and ability to rule.'

'Thank God we have not done worse than we have,' said C.R. in his reply, which moved beyond modesty to become a classic farewell to power as well as a text for Congress's response to Hitler's war against India's rulers. Several passages deserve reproduction:

> We have tried to be just. We have tried to be careful. We have tried to set aside partisan claims of all kinds. So far as our own conscience goes, our work has been satisfactory.
>
> What the Muslim League says is that the minorities can only be protected by the standing army of a foreign government . . . Do I not know Mr Jinnah? Do I not know the innermost ambition of his heart that India should be free? But . . . to say, 'Let England be always here,' is a terrible conclusion to which this Assembly cannot possibly be a party.
>
> Honourable Members of the Opposition, one after another, stated, 'Congress does not represent the people of the whole of India. This all-inclusive claim should be rejected.' I say, why reject it? Cannot one man speak on behalf of India if he speaks rightly and truly? . . .
>
> The British are a democratically governed people. But they are an imperialist people . . . They do not want any other people to rule over them, but the Secretary of State is to govern India. One man is to govern India.
>
> Mr Langley . . . appealed to our sense of right, a very proper thing to do. He said, 'This war is a good war. Mahatmaji has said so'. . . . But one step more is wanted, that is, we should join.
>
> Has [America] joined the war? No. 'Cash and carry'—that is their formula . . . A great people, who went to civil war for the sake of the liberation of the slaves, . . . a people with a very keen sense of duty — did these people join the War? . . .
>
> Do we say anything so bad as 'cash and carry'? No. We say, 'Let us go not at the end of a leash but as a free people.'
>
> In the statements with which England went to war, it was stated that the world should be free; . . . that they are attacking Germany . . . because they wanted to defend liberty against aggression. Naturally, the people of India began to ask

themselves, 'Is this liberty only for Europe, for the small peoples of Europe, or is it also for the large and ancient people who have been in this land for thousands of years and who have been in friendship with Britain?'

We could have had swaraj in the palm of our hand if the Muslim League had played the game. If it be necessary, we could even have fought afterwards among ourselves. If we had asked for that which belongs to India together, we could have got it.

Sir, . . . We go away. We cannot confer any further benefits on the people of this country through this Assembly and through the Government. [Let] all Members say that the people of India should govern themselves in a democratic manner.

I am too wise a politician to imagine that my advocacy will prevail. Still, every man should make his attempt . . . At least a few Members of the Opposition will vote with me, I think.

The British had questioned, said C.R., India's fitness for freedom. Assuming India had weaknesses, what was England's wish? Accusing England of not declaring 'your own desire in the matter,' C.R. went on to quote from 'the greatest of the plays of the greatest of poets,' *Lear:*

The eldest daughter said to the king, 'I love you more than words can wield the matter; dearer than eyesight, space and liberty.' Lear was pleased and said, 'Take this vast portion of my kingdom.' The next girl said she loved him even more; she also got an ample share.

But the third said, 'I love you as I should, neither more nor less. I cannot give away all my love to you. I have got to keep a portion of it for my future husband.' Lear got angry . . .

Congress cannot give all its love to Britain. It must reserve that which is India's share.

Was it reasonable to expect Britain to give India freedom at a time like this?

Let me pause and ask, Sir, could there have been a more favourable occasion? The whole country (Britain) is moved, to a man . . . England has been asked, all the men, women and children, to think about fundamentals. It is the most appropriate time for thinking about India also.

Admitting that Congress could be asked, 'Is Hitler better? Are you not helping him?' C.R. said:

It is a very difficult question to answer. But you (Britain) are responsible. You have made India noncooperate.

Referring to the new measures his Ministry had plannned, including 'a law laying down anew the relationship between the Zamindars and the tenants,' and the 'many things which yet remain to be done,' he said:

The house was bedecked. The bride was to come in. But no, we say suddenly. The pandal is to be pulled down. The festivity is to be postponed.[19]

Muthiah Chettiar called it 'a very eloquent' address. Pannirselvam said it was 'one of the most marvellous speeches I have ever been privileged to listen to.' Krishnamachari thought it the Premier's best performance in the House.[20] Yet it added only a handful of opposition votes to Congress's large majority.

On 30 October C.R. resigned. Section 93 was invoked, and Erskine commenced his long-hoped-for rule with the help of advisers.

Though resignation was, to C.R., right and necessary, the fact was that Hitler had ruined his show, and the Raj's rigidity prevented its salvage. Day, who went to C.R. 'on the day the Ministry resigned . . . to collect the despatch box keys from him,' found him 'very angry and bitterly disappointed . . . at being diverted' from the 'vast amount of work waiting to be done, which he was able and willling to do.'[21] However, a reporter saw the Premier cheerfully signing certificates for his drivers, clerks and peons, and noticed that C.R.'s table was clear, with files and the despatch box gone (*The Hindu*, 31.10.39).

As Premier and administrator, C.R. had his defects. Early in their relationship, Erskine noticed an element of unrealism when C.R. exhorted Indian members of the Raj's services to forgo a slice of their pay. The appeal was rejected, and C.R. learned not to be starry-eyed. There was some justice, secondly, in a comment by the writer C.R. Srinivasan that C.R. 'should take a longer view of things' and 'relieve himself from routine work' (*The Hindu*, 24.1.38).

With his itchy pen, C.R. gave more attention than a Premier should to the correcting of drafts, though the process did not take much of his time; and Srinivasa Sastri for one felt that C.R. accepted unnecessary speaking engagments: 'He must pour out his mind on every occasion, great and small.'[22]

A tendency to act impulsively was another weakness. An emotion or a brainwave could dictate his position, as happened over Hindi. Also, he encroached on the roles of his Cabinet colleagues, answering questions addressed to them in the legislature, or taking over some of their work. Proceedings of the Assembly sometimes give the impression that the portfolios of education, prohibition and agriculture — assigned, we know, to others — were also his.

The Premier's office, where the Cabinet conferred, was referred to by some Ministers as C.R.'s classroom. The line between supervision and takeover was inevitably thin — we saw earlier that C.R. had admitted to the Mahatma that it was in his nature to mind others' portfolios.

This weakness was an extension of C.R.'s gifted mind. As Krishnamachari would say, C.R. 'thought at least three steps ahead of anyone else.'[23] Knowing that his answers would be more effective, C.R. had no hesitation in rising in a colleague's place. While his centrality brightened Assembly proceedings and stabilized the secretariat, it reduced the opportunities his colleagues had to learn, grow or shine.

C.R. 'honestly believes,' Pannirselvam said during a debate over Hindi, 'that what he has set his mind upon is the will of the country,' and Krishnamachari spoke of the Premier's 'overpowering personality.'[24] Controlling others was far from his desire, but he could be obstinate. 'Rajaji will not take advice, though he willl listen to you with the utmost courtesy,' said Sastri at the time.[25]

Refusing to incorporate a conscience clause in his Hindustani policy or to consign Section 7 to limbo, he lost ways of weakening the agitation against him. His contempt for escape-doors was not always wise.

Believing that it was vanity to pay attention to one's image, he took no steps to prevent some avoidable misunderstandings. Thus, many in the Telugu region continued to think erroneously that he was against a separate Andhra; and some radicals retained a sense that he was overgenerous with the British and unduly attached to their procedures. Jawaharlal, for instance, expressed an opinion that the Presidency's administration was 'perilously like the old Government.'[26]

When he made the remark, Nehru could not have known that some, though not all, of the British officials thought that C.R.'s blind spot was his inability in any circumstances to condone the use of force. According to Day, C.R. was 'sometimes induced to go some way towards exonerating the police, but never the whole way.'[27] Congress radicals and the Raj's officials were bound to differ over law and order; C.R. differed from both.

As for his strengths, we have already noted his capacity for work, incorruptibility, intellectual brilliance, debating skill and vigilance over public spending. He was also a firm leader. In Day's words: 'The Prime Minister was emphatically the head of the administration. None of us could have any doubts about that.'[28]

If C.R. sought to assert the autonomy of the Congress vis-a-vis the Raj, he did the same for the province vis-a-vis New Delhi, and his Ministry vis-a-vis the Congress or any supposed trend of other Congress Ministries. We saw his lack of enthusiasm for conferences of Congress Premiers convened by the party president. When he was asked in the Assembly, 'Do you know that the (Congress-run) C.P. Government has repealed the Criminal Law Amendment Act?' he coolly replied: 'The question should be put to the C.P. Assembly.'[29]

F.W.A. Morris, chosen to implement the sales tax law, noticed other qualities: 'absolute courtesy, patience and friendliness' towards civil servants, an 'ability to listen to a complicated exposition of intricate details, seldom if ever asking for a repetition of a point,' and the communication straightaway of 'a clear and unambiguous decision.'[30]

He was helped, too, by a healthy unconcern regarding his Ministry's life and by his awareness that it would go out the moment a serious Congress-Raj breach occurred. As he told the Assembly in 1938, he was 'ready to retire the next morning if necessary.'[31]

If his administration was firm, it was also ready to learn. Thus, acceptance of the Horwill report was followed at once by a detailed statement, unusual by the standards of a later era, in which the government admitted inadequacies in its methods of riot-control, regretted that tear gas had not been used in Chirala, conceded that if the union leader had been sent for in time tempers might have subsided, and spelt out new guidelines for its officers (*The Hindu*, 19.4.38).

Again, the inflexibility that some noted in him was not accompanied by intolerance. He asked Congress MLAs to be brief when they spoke in the Assembly and to hear out attacks on the Ministry. Muthiah Chettiar, the Opposition leader, would recall, 'Though [C.R.] had a comfortable majority, . . . he welcomed the criticisms of the opposition and gave them a patient hearing.'[32]

Racially, too, as over politics and the Hindu-Muslim question, C.R. revealed a refreshing freedom from narrowness. Asked in May 1939 why a European had been appointed Presidency Magistrate, C.R. replied that he was 'the most suitable person.' 'Government deprecate,' the Premier added, 'reference to the race of the officer in this or any other case.'[33]

Despite his thin frame, dark glasses, austere bearing and zeal for causes like prohibition, C.R. possessed human qualities to which officials responded. He saw and made jokes. He forgot the not-so-distant past of prison-going. He put himself in the shoes of the officials he was with, whether they were veterans or trainees. They found him winningly modest as well as strong.

After his first encounter with C.R. in a small district town, J.F. Saunders was 'definitely a C.R. Fan,' as he would afterwards recall. He was 'graceful' and 'courteous' to Morris, 'a very lovable character' to Day, and an object of 'respect and affection' to Indian ICS officers like Abbas Khaleeli, who later served in Pakistan, and P.A. Menon, a future ambassador to Germany.[34]

Jack Munro's response has been referred to earlier. Peter Crombie, who first met the Premier as Revenue Divisional Officer, Malappuram, would recall:

> Although he was already over an hour late on a very heavy official tour, he insisted on receiving me immediately and having half-an-hour's private chat not only on the welfare of the people of the area (who were largely Moplah) but also my own reactions to the life of a young I.C.S. officer in the country . . . No wonder we loved to serve under him.[35]

It is unlikely that the Mahatma knew in any detail of the impact C.R. had made on officials. But he had assessed that 'like a satyagrahi' C.R. was 'winning victories without bluster, without wrangling but by conversion, by carrying conviction' (*Harijan*, 10.9.38). C.R. himself once said in the Assembly: 'I am a satyagrahi, using the weapon of nonviolence even inside the government.'[36]

Hostile, at this juncture, to the 1935 Act and unenthused by the Rajaji Ministry, Jawaharlal would, in time, alter his assessment of both. Shortly after independence, he told the Tory leader, R.A. Butler, that the Act 'proved to be the organic connecting-link between the old and the new.'[37] And about the C.R. Ministry he wrote in 1941: 'It might be said that the Madras Government did more during its brief career than any other provincial government.'[38]

Krishnamachari would describe the C.R. administration as 'a model provincial government.'[39] Recalling C.R.'s 1937-9 performance, K. Kamaraj, an MLA at the time, Chief Minister from 1954 to 1962, and later, as Congress President, largely responsible for the choice of two Prime Ministers of India, would speak of C.R. as 'the greatest Chief Minister' the southern province had had.[40]

13

Cogitation
1939-41

Though beginning to lean on a stick while walking, C.R. was fit at 61 and now had leisure for things he could not do as Premier. He worked on a new edition of his commentary on the Upanishads and resumed spinning. The peons returned to Fort St. George. The car was surrendered.

There was an immediate need to cut expenses. Though the Assembly had not been dissolved and C.R. was entitled to an MLA's emoluments, he had forsaken these. His capital consisted of what had remained of the Salem earnings and a bit saved out of the Premier's salary. Interest on this, a monthly rent of Rs 75 from the Salem house, and royalties, as yet meagre, from his writings made up a small income that just about met the needs of C.R.'s household.

On 25 December he wrote to Jack Munro: 'This is Christmas day and I swear by the Christ you and I worship under different names that I do not desire any harm but wish all good luck to every British man, woman and child.' In April the following year when C.F. Andrews died, C.R. remarked, 'There was no truer friend of India, no more religious soul' *(The Hindu,* 5.4.40).

The resignation of Congress Ministries notwithstanding, Gandhi and the Raj both professed anxiety for an agreement. To Congressmen, one test of the Raj's sincerity was its attitude towards the policies of the resigning ministries.

Some Governors seemed to pass the test. The UP Governor, for instance, said that he regarded himself as a trustee for the Ministry that had resigned; and in the Central Provinces the Governor announced that he would extend prohibition to three new districts.

But not Erskine, who desired real power. 'Given a free hand,' he wrote to Linlithgow, 'I could run a highly popular government.' He found the UP Governor's statement 'astonishing' and the step in the Central Provinces (C.P.) objectionable. 'I do not in any way consider myself,' he informed the Viceroy, 'as a trustee for my late Ministry.'

Within a week of C.R.'s resignation, Erskine wrote to Linlithgow of wanting 'immediately to issue a Government order making Hindi optional rather than compulsory in schools.' Not keen to supply Congress a grievance, Linlithgow asked Erskine to obtain C.R.'s agreement first.

On C.R. telling Erskine that he would regard the change as 'a declaration of war' and seeking the extension of prohibition to 'six more non-littoral districts,' the Governor asked Linlithgow if he was to govern the Presidency 'by the kind permission of C.R.' Describing C.R. as 'a very cunning Madrasi Brahmin,' Erskine persisted with his demand over Hindi. In March 1940, just before the Governor's term of office ended, he obtained clearance from Zetland and Linlithgow.[1]

The rebuff had to be pocketed by C.R., who knew that the Presidency could not be mobilized for defending compulsory Hindi. The conflict did not prevent C.R. from penning Erskine a letter of farewell on handmade 'Gandhi' paper:

> May you both have a safe return home . . . A Brahmin's blessings may have some potency still! May your enemies be confounded into goodness, and may your people and we ever remain friends . . . Au revoir.[2]

In London, the ambitious Erskine called on Zetland and told the Secretary of State that 'he hoped in any ministerial reshuffle . . . to take over' from him. As Zetland put it in a letter to Linlithgow, 'so blatant a frontal attack' seemed to be 'a little lacking in delicacy.'[3]

Erskine won a by-election in Brighton and entered the House of Commons but, scarcely a favourite of Churchill, who assumed the Premiership in 1940, he was not taken into the Cabinet. Later in 1940, he made remarks that suggested that he had forgotten his wrangle with C.R. His former Premier, Erskine said, was 'a remarkable man' and 'an admirable head of a ministry,' compromises with whom had 'enabled the administration to be carried on with the minimum of friction.' Erskine added that the Congress Ministry had been superior in performance to its Justice predecessor (*The Hindu*, 10.10.40).

His successor as Governor of Madras was another Scotsman, Arthur Hope. Three months after his arrival, he and C.R. met in Ooty. 'It was supposed to be a secret meeting,' said Hope to the Viceroy, 'but the whole of Ooty knew about it that afternoon and the whole of Madras Presidency next day.' Added Hope:

> To my surprise at 1.30 when I asked him to stay for lunch, he said he would be delighted to do so and sat next to me, and talked without ceasing, but only drank some lemonade.[4]

By this time, Congress had made up its mind to offer a restrained defiance under Gandhi's direction. The idea was to compel Britain's attention without embarrassing her during the War. The decision was taken at a session in Ramgarh in Bihar, presided over by Abul Kalam Azad. Defending the decision, C.R., who was included in the Working Committee, said that while Congress still stood for a settlement, it could not accept the paramountcy of one side and the dependency of the other (*The Hindu*, 2.3.40).

A new sound, electrifying to some and troubling to others, was heard at this time: 'Pakistan!' In January 1940, the Muslim League president, Muhammad Ali Jinnah said that Hindus and Muslims were not only distinct, they were two nations. And in March the League passed a resolution in Lahore that only the creation of sovereign, Muslim-majority territories would be acceptable to Muslims.

Addressing the Raj as well as Congress, the League hinted support for the War effort if its Pakistan demand was accepted in principle, and announced unremitting opposition to any Congress-Raj agreement that did not concede Pakistan.

Aghast and dismayed, C.R. saw in the slogan 'the sign of a diseased mentality.' He accused Jinnah of wanting to 'take India into the condition of the Balkan states.' A sovereign Muslim state carved out of India was 'hardly the remedy for the minority problem.' And had not the Mahatma said that Muslims were as likely as Hindus to govern a free India? C.R. was reminded of 'the old story when one of the two claimant mothers was quite willing to divide the baby while the other claimant proved her case by agreeing to hand over the baby.'

Perhaps, speculated C.R., what Jinnah really wanted was 'fuller amplitude for the Muslim provinces' and an assurance that they would not be overborne by a Hindu-controlled centre. This 'laudable desire' was attainable without 'cutting up India.'

However, if the League insisted on 'puncturing the tyre and stopping the progress' of the Indian car, then Congress would have to fight both the Raj and the League (*The Hindu*, 4.1., 23.2. & 26.3.40).

Gandhi spoke similarly. On his part Jinnah claimed that Hindus and Muslims 'neither intermarried nor interdined.' Their customs, literatures, epics and heroes were different: 'very often the hero of one is a foe of the other.' Added Jinnah:

> It is amazing that men like Mr Gandhi and Mr Rajagopalacharya should talk about the Lahore resolution in such terms as 'vivisection of India' and 'cutting up the baby into two halves.' . . . Where is the country which is being divided?[5]

If disobedience against the Raj was called for, what shape should it take? While Gandhi cogitated, Hitler launched his blitzkrieg. Norway and Denmark, Holland and Belgium, even France collapsed before the Nazi tanks. Replacing Chamberlain as Prime Minister, Churchill faced long odds.

C.R. felt it 'almost impossible to turn from the international scene to our own problems.' Yet Indians could 'not serve civilization by forgetting our rights. We cannot help the Allies by agreeing to be a subject people.'

He thought, too, that a deal could be struck. Britain might want to get as an ally 'a free India when she has lost France' (*The Hindu*, 9.6.40). True, Britain was tapping even an unreconciled India for soldiers, supplies and space, but would she not offer Indians a solid share in the governance of India in order to obtain their enthusiastic partnership?

Believing that Britain might do this, C.R. persuaded Congress, for the first time in twenty years, to disobey the Mahatma. In a resolution, the Congress Working Committee said that Congress would prosecute the War as an ally if Britain declared that India would be free at its end, and if an all-party national government was formed in India right away.

In Gandhi's view, the resolution conflicted with nonviolence and misread the Raj's mind. A three-hour talk with Linlithgow at the end of June had reinforced his assessment that Britain was not about to act handsomely by India, and he had smelt a Raj-League understanding to foil Congress.

Ignoring the Mahatma's advice, the Working Committee agreed with C.R. Some of its members thought that the fall of Paris, which occurred some days after Gandhi's parleys with the Viceroy, was a new inducement for Britain to settle with Congress. Others yielded to C.R.'s persuasive skill. He won converts, conceded Gandhi, because of his 'persistency, courage, skill and considerateness towards opponents' (*The Hindu*, 9.7.40).

Azad, the President, was one of the first to back C.R., but, as the Mahatma put it, 'Sardar Patel was his biggest prize.' Jawaharlal voted against C.R., as did Ghaffar Khan, the latter resigning from the Working Committee because it rejected Gandhi's view.

Subhas Bose, who had no qualms about embarrassing Britain, was arrested in early July. Also detained was the youthful Congress Socialist, Jayaprakash Narayan. From jail Jayaprakash exhorted Nehru:

> Rajaji has stabbed us in the back. It was a great relief to know that you . . . opposed the infamous thing. But is that enough? . . . You should resign your seat on the Working Committee. After a settlement, i.e. if it comes about, you should leave the

Congress and form another political organisation. Vallabhbhai
and Rajaji have not hesitated to break with Gandhiji. Will you
hesitate to fulfil your obvious historic task?[26]

At the end of July 1940, C.R. triumphed again, this time with
the AICC, which was meeting in Poona. Pointing out that
Gandhi had recruited soldiers for World War I, C.R. argued that
nonviolence, while necessary in the fight against the Raj, might
not work against Hitler. Congress had never claimed that a free
India would do without any army. They could not 'fly off from
reality': there was nothing wrong or inconsistent in telling
Britain that 'if she did what they want, they would be prepared
to give India's help,' moral as well as military.

'How long will you wait for the British response?' Nehru
asked. 'We have to trust our opponent to do the right thing,'
replied C.R., but he agreed that 'this offer cannot be holding the
field indefinitely' (*The Hindu*, 29.7.40). Despite Jayaprakash's
call, Nehru changed his stand and voted for C.R.'s resolution.
By 95 votes to 47, the AICC endorsed it.

'Quietly and without raising his voice,' Nehru was soon to
write, referring to C.R.'s success, 'he would argue for his
viewpoint and gradually undermine the mental defences of those
who disagreed with him.'[7]

Though C.R. maintained that Gandhi 'continued to be the
leader,' the latter's views had been cast aside. The Mahatma
claimed, however, that 'Rajaji and the Sardar will again be with
me.' He would prove right; the breach would be shortlived. All
the same, it disclosed significant differences. Said Gandhi:

I differ fundamentally from [Rajaji] . . . [Not that] I am afraid
of power . . . but since this office question cropped up, I saw
that our thoughts were in different directions.

As Premier, C.R. had seen the value of even limited power. If
the British did 'liquidate the Executive Council and install a
national government in full control at the centre,' Congress
would have a unique opportunity to do good. The Mahatma, on
the other hand, thought that 'while some day or the other we
will have to take office,' the time was not opportune.
Congressmen needed to realize that the masses were in a state

of 'smouldering discontent' towards the British (*The Hindu*, 9.6., 5.8. & 14.8.40).

It was obvious that if a settlement with the Raj led to a national government, C.R. would have a key position in it. Thus, referring to persons to whom the Raj might have to offer power at the centre, Gandhi wrote in September: 'One day it may be Rajaji, another day it may be Jawaharlal' (*Harijan*, 22.9.40).

But C.R.'s, and Congress's, terms were clear. 'Mere expansion of the Viceroy's Executive Council would satisfy none,' said C.R. (*The Hindu*, 2.7.40). In practice if not in law, the Viceregal veto had to go.

If the prospect of power elicited Congress's 'Poona Offer,' as it came to be known, that offer also owed something to the sympathy for the Allies harboured by men like C.R. Yet he did not think that a Congress-Raj agreement was very likely.

Though, as C.R. put it, 'British businessmen [in India] had realised the gravity of the situation and appealed to the government to come to terms with the Congress,' (*The Hindu*, 1.7.40) the views of the senior ICS Britons, the men advising the Viceroy and the Secretary of State, were, in C.R.'s opinion, reactionary and out of date.

'I am afraid a curse of bad diplomacy and wrong judgement is operating on Britain,' C.R. had said on 22 July (*The Hindu*, 23.7.40). In a letter to G.A. Natesan, written between the Working Committee and AICC meetings, he seemed to indicate the probability of a clash with the Raj:

> I am a reasonable man, a practical-minded fellow, a conservative, a lover of peace and one who dislikes gambling on poor people's lives. But I cannot give in to Britain's arrogance. I have gone to the point that Honour can take us, and I cannot surrender any further, and am prepared for the worst thereafter.[8]

Early in August, through a Viceregal statement, Britain responded to the Congress. If the Raj, Congress, the League and the Princes reached an agreement, a certain number of politicians would be included in an expanded Viceroy's Council. But the Viceregal veto would not be shelved. At the end of the War, a body set up 'with the least possible delay,' would 'devise the framework of a new Constitution.'

Failing, thus, to promise independence, the statement however assured Muslims and other minority 'elements in India's national life' that Britain would never allow 'their coercion into submission' to a majority government (*The Hindu*, 7.8.40).

'I am angry with [the statement],' C.R. said at a public meeting, adding, 'I want you also to feel angry.' He thought the Raj's reply to the Poona Offer had 'justified Ulsterism' (*The Hindu*, 12 & 13.8.40). Finding C.R. 'completely disillusioned and disappointed,' Nehru thought that since C.R. had 'taken the lead' in attempting to come to terms with Britain — 'even at the risk of parting with Gandhiji' — the failure 'was felt by him probably more than by any other person.'[9]

Two months after the Viceroy's response, Jawaharlal, unable to get over C.R.'s success in influencing the Congress, referred — in an epilogue in his autobiography — to Rajaji's 'brilliant intellect and penetrating power of analysis' as 'a tremendous asset to our cause.'[10] And Hope, the Governor of Madras, recommended to the Viceroy the early 'shutting up' of C.R., adding, 'He is obviously angling for the Gandhi succession and is in fact leading Congress throughout India.'[11]

To show that Congress was at least as anxious as the British about the position of Muslims, C.R. now addressed a proposal, via a reporter of London's *Herald*, to the Raj and the League:

> Let me make a sporting offer. If HMG will agree to a provisional national government being formed at once, I undertake to persuade my colleagues in the Congress to agree to the Muslim League being invited to nominate a Prime Minister and let him form the national government as he would consider best (*The Hindu*, 23.8.40).

Though a Muslim leader, the Raja of Mahmudabad, objected that the League-led cabinet envisaged by C.R. would be dependent on the Hindu majority of the central legislature. *Star of India*, a Muslim paper of Bengal, found C.R.'s proposal 'electrifying' (*The Hindu*, 29.8.40). The Raj, however, refused to discuss it, and Leopold Amery, Zetland's successor as Secretary of State, told the Commons that 'no new approach to the Indian question would be considered' (*The Hindu*, 6.9.40).

Satyagraha was now unavoidable. 'If we do not exercise our capacity for a struggle now,' C.R. said, 'our spirits will die' (*The Hindu*, 17.9.40). As Gandhi had predicted, C.R. was back with him, and so was Patel.

But what sort of satyagraha would they perform? Gandhi came up with an answer. Carefully selected individuals, including C.R., Nehru, Patel and Azad, would recite the unlawful slogan, 'It is wrong to help the British war effort with men or money.' Anything more would hurt the Allies; anything less would suggest acceptance by India of her subject status.

In addition, Gandhi thought of a fast but gave up the idea after C.R. demanded to know 'why and to what purpose.'[12]

As the first satyagrahi, the Mahatma chose Vinoba Bhave, then in his early forties. After Gandhi's death, Bhave would found the land gift movement, Bhoodan. Bhave repeated the simple protest framed by the Mahatma and was arrested for sedition. Jawaharlal was arrested next. Patel followed.

Before C.R.'s turn came, he said, 'When the dust and din . . . dies down, the world will wonder why Britain behaved in this manner towards a people who were prepared to forget all past wrongs and claimed only their birthright' (*The Hindu*, 18.11.40).

On 30 November, in letters addressed to half a dozen persons including Muthiah Chettiar, the leader of the opposition in the Madras Assembly, and Abdul Hamid Khan, the leader of the League MLAs, C.R. used the Gandhi-prescribed sentence and justified it:

> The British Goverment have ordered India to be in the War without asking her legislature. Other parts of the British Commonwealth were allowed the choice of remaining neutral . . . . Taxes rejected by the Legislative Assembly are being imposed by the fiat of the Viceroy . . .

> It is wrong therefore to help the British war effort with men or money. A copy of this letter is being sent to the authorities so that they may proceed against me if they desire.

Ten minutes before 10.00 a.m. on 3 December, Assistant Commissioner of Police Yusuf Ali, accompanied by other officers and men, arrived at the Bazlulla Road house. A smiling C.R. said, 'I am ready' and bid family members, friends and a crowd farewell.

Abbas Ali, chief Presidency magistrate, tried C.R. immediately. 'Did you write the letters?' he was asked. C.R. answered, as *The Hindu* was to put it, 'in a firm tone amidst pindrop silence,' 'Yes.'

Ali: 'Do you suffer from low blood pressure?'

C.R.: 'I do not wish to submit myself to a medical examination.'

Ali: 'I feel it my duty to sentence the accused. One year.'

Then, in a quavering voice, Ali quoted Arjuna's famous confession — 'My body trembles, my breath stops, my bow slips from my hands' — and expressed the hope that as a student of the Gita C.R. would understand a magistrate's duty. After he had apologized to Ali, 'I am sorry I have caused you a certain amount of embarrassment,' C.R. was taken to a place he knew well, Vellore Central Jail.[13]

In deference to the Gandhian code, no Congressman bothered the Raj with disobedience during the Christmas season. However, by the summer of 1941, nearly 15,000 had been arrested. Intentionally moderate, the campaign did not go beyond dramatizing the urge for freedom.

Transferred within days to Trichy jail, C.R. found that he was being locked up each night. Interviews were infrequent and brief — twenty minutes was the limit. Intelligence men heard each conversation. A letter arrived from Gandhi:

> I know you don't need a letter from me. Letters are meaningless when hearts can speak to each other. I know you are doing your duty there as we are trying to do ours outside. Do keep well and complete your Hindi learning.[14]

C.R. devoted a few spells to Hindustani in the Urdu script, studied the Ramayanas of Valmiki, Kamban and Tulsidas, and shared his insights. As one of the Trichy 'family' would later recall:

> Soon after breakfast every morning a group of us read Valmiki's Ramayana . . . C.R. would sit in an easy chair, with about 15 to 20 of us sitting on a carpet spread on the floor in front of him.[15]

C.R. also held classes on the Gita, the Kural and Shakespeare, and attended a course on Carnatic music conducted by a fellow-prisoner, K. Varadachari. Other jailmates would afterwards recall that C.R. 'explained some of the situations [in a couple of the Shakespearean tragedies] in a masterly manner,' 'carefully took 1 1/2 ounces of rice for his meal,' was 'continuously involved in study' and 'spent his time busily but with ease and joy.'[16]

From Edinburgh, Professor Tait had sent a volume of *Scott's Journal*. Mindful of Tait's illness, C.R. asked Narasimhan, who received the fortnightly letter that C.R. was allowed to send, to add to a note of thanks the hope that the professor was 'safe and going strong in some good and well-protected place.'[17]

It was noticed by the Trichy 'family' that when C.R.'s brother Srinivasachar, who was the manager of P. Subbaroyan's farm, visited the jail to see Subbaroyan, the former Premier denied himself a bonus interview with his brother.[18]

Kripalani, the Congress General Secretary, whom Gandhi had exempted from the satyagraha, was allowed to meet C.R. in Trichy. The prisoner told Kripalani that he wished to see greater numbers filling the Raj's jails. But the Mahatma had ruled out mass disobedience.

Months went by in study — and thought. C.R. wondered — unthinkable idea! — whether Congress should not concede what he had only some months earlier dismissed as 'diseased', the Muslim League's demand for Pakistan. Alternatively, should not Congress abandon disobedience, which in any case was petering out, and make a fresh offer to the Raj?

Modest-sized hope flickered for a moment. Kasturi Srinivasan, editor of *The Hindu*, came to Trichy Jail and showed C.R. a message that Sikander Hyat Khan, the Unionist Premier of the Punjab, wanted to send to Amery, the Secretary of State, with whom Sikander had cordial relations. It suggested a way for Amery to conciliate both Congress and the League.

If C.R. approved of the draft, said Srinivasan, Sikander would send it to Amery. C.R. said it was acceptable. Srinivasan conveyed C.R.'s reaction to Sikander, but the initiative was aborted by British civil servants close to the Punjab Premier.

Learning of the C.R.-Srinivasan interview, and its purpose of narrowing the gap between Congress and the League, Linlithgow reproached Hope, the Madras Governor, for having allowed it:

> Perhaps you would let me know whether Srinivasan was allowed to see Rajagopalachariar alone or whether anyone was present. I do not want to go too far in the direction of facilitating formulations of policy or of tactics . . .[19]

After the Srinivasan interview, politicians or intermediaries were no longer permitted to meet C.R., who wondered and waited and sought to enrich his mind and spirit. Outside, Hitler had attacked the Soviet Union. Tagore had died. And some days before C.R.'s term was to end, Doraiswami, 25, and Rajagopal, 22, sons of his brother Srinivasachar, died of typhoid. Both the boys had been brilliant, winning gold medals.

On 6 October 1941, his term over, C.R. was released.

14

Rebellion

1941-44

With shrewd suspicion, the Mahatma wrote to C.R., 'All eyes are on you including mine!' C.R. had indeed come up with fresh ideas. After consoling his shattered brother, he showed up in Sevagram. However, Gandhi was cool to C.R.'s proposal of another offer to the British.

Holding that Britain was unlikely to respond positively, the Mahatma also found it difficult to support the Congress's involvement in the War. A month later he and C.R. met again, and talked for over five days. This time Vallabhbhai also joined in the discussion. Like C.R., Patel had just come out of jail. Patel declared himself wholly with the Mahatma.

Released, along with Azad, on 4 December, Nehru wrote in his diary, 'I am afraid C.R. is going to be troublesome.' Jawaharlal added that he was glad that 'Bapu is firm as a rock.'[1] However, C.R. enlisted the Maulana's support and sought that of the rank-and-file.

His hands were strengthened after 7 December, when Japan attacked Pearl Harbor and commenced its sweep across the Pacific, and the USA joined the Allies as a belligerent. Making public his differences with Gandhi, C.R. said in a convocation address at Lucknow University (*The Hindu*, 14.12.41):

I have worked with Gandhiji these 22 years and feel a just pride of having helped him to develop and put into action his

principles and methods. Many are the ties that bind me to
him. It is not a pleasure to discover a difference and recognise
it as leading to a parting of ways . . .

We keep our face turned steadily in the direction of ahimsa
but cannot make the mistake of killing the principle itself by
opposing it to commonsense or reality. The defence of India
is a case to be treated as an exception.

Meeting in Bardoli towards the end of December, the Congress
Working Committee adopted C.R.'s line, recognized 'the new
world situation,' and offered cooperation to the Allies if India's
freedom was declared.

Sensing his colleagues' mood, Gandhi did not press his
views. C.R. wrote about him to Devadas (1.1.42):

He is wonderfully good to me. But what wonder really? He
was ever that. Well, events have taken an unexpected turn.
Still, nothing may come out of it. What even then? I have
done the right thing and have the satisfaction of having done
it against heavy odds.[2]

Meeting at Wardha to consider the Working Committee's
resolution, Gandhi urged the AICC not to disown its leaders,
his own views notwithstanding. Added the Mahatma:

That nothing is to be expected from the Government is
probably too true. Only the resolution puts the Congress
right with the expectant world . . . It is no longer open to the
Government to say that the Congress has banged the door to
negotiation on the impossible ground of nonviolence. (*Harijan*,
25.1.42)

If Gandhi's words helped C.R. at the AICC, C.R.'s 75-minute
speech, delivered 'amidst repeated applause' also helped. In this
speech C.R. answered Patel and Prasad, who had dissented from
his proposal, and Nehru, who had said that C.R.'s was 'a
primrose path' (*The Hindu*, 18.1.42). Others had asked if it was
wise to invite Japan's antagonism, and some suggested that C.R.
was hunting for office and betraying the Mahatma; Simon Peter
and the cock were mentioned.

Pointing out that Indian soldiers enlisted by the Raj were
already in combat against Japan, C.R. added:

Are you going to tell Japan that the Indian soldiers were forcibly taken out of India and made to fight? Our cooperation is available if the British do the right thing.

Supposing the central government is placed in my hands, then I would take it. But if the Madras government is given to me without control of the centre, I would not touch it . . . If I am a hunter, please credit me with being a big game hunter (*The Hindu*, 18.1.42).

The Bardoli line was endorsed at Wardha, where, in a significant move, Gandhi designated Jawaharlal as his successor. Fifteen years earlier, he had spoken of C.R. as his successor. Now, at Wardha, Gandhi said:

Pandit Jawaharlal and I have had differences from the moment we became co-workers, yet I have said for some years and say it now that not Rajaji, not Sardar Vallabhbhai, but Jawaharlal will be my successor.[3]

Had C.R. paid for advocating a rejection of the Mahatma's stand, and for having referred, in Lucknow, to 'a parting of the ways'? Was Jawaharlal being rewarded for his attachment to Gandhi? He had said at Wardha that Congress was the Mahatma's 'creation and child and nothing can break the bond,' and Gandhi had responded by noting that Nehru's 'love for and confidence in me peep out of every sentence referring to me' (*Harijan*, 25.1.42).

We know, however, that C.R.'s personal attachment to Gandhi was as deep as Nehru's. The truth was that Nehru's popularity was wider than C.R.'s; in particular, he attracted the youth and the Left in a measure that C.R. could not match.

Again, his lack of faith in negotiations with the British was more in accord with the public's mood than C.R.'s willingness to keep trying. 'As a preliminary,' C.R. said in a speech at about this time, 'I shall trust the Britisher more than he (Nehru) does.'[4] Moreover, having failed to master Hindi, C.R. was not in a position to achieve a rapport with the vast North Indian masses. Gandhi realized that the nation as a whole was more likely to turn to Nehru than to C.R.

Finally, Gandhi recognized a philosophical bond, in the broadest sense of the term, between himself and Nehru. 'I know this,' the Mahatma said, 'that when I am gone, he (Nehru) will speak my language' (*Harijan*, 25.1.42).

The philosophical ties between Gandhi and C.R. were more obvious; C.R. was independent and sharp, he had courage, his wit was arresting, as was his integrity, and he drew fair crowds. But he lacked Nehru's charisma. Desiring a successor who would be a magnet as well as a kin in thought, the Mahatma picked Jawaharlal.

If C.R. felt cheated or hurt by Gandhi's pronouncement, he did not show it. In any case, Japan and its advance were now his chief concern. Hong Kong, the Philippines and Malaya fell; Indonesia and Thailand accepted Japan's overlordship; on 15 February, the citadel of Singapore surrendered, and British troops were on the run in Burma. Soon, it seemed, the attackers would be on Indian soil, probably in South India. Detesting the notion of an exchange of masters, C.R. spent the first three months of 1942 in an impassioned, ceaseless bid to prepare a defence against Japan, while continuing to demand freedom from the British.

The C.R. of this period comes across as a patriot on fire, not only willing but eager to be a War leader and convinced that he could be one if the Raj and Congress came to terms — if the Raj yielded the substance of freedom. His speeches are numerous, the crowds huge, the cheers loud and prolonged.

Madras, 21.1.42: Today the battle-fronts include bazaars, the houses of civilians, plantations, fields and factories. Is it good, in such a situation, that there should be division between government and soldiers on the one hand . . . and tremendously popular organisations like the Congress and the Muslim League on the other, over whom such illustrious persons as Mahatma Gandhi and Quaid-e-Azam Jinnah preside?

I do not want to surrender to the Japanese. Why should I? I am not carried away by mere hatred [of the British].

Madras, 23.1.42: We want now and at once a government of the nation, in charge of everything. This is the way to turn on the switch in India and make the 400 million lamps glow.

You will have to tell me how many are prepared to join the army, the navy, the workshops, the civil defence . . .

If . . . Britain fails to do her duty . . . [there] must be voluntary government throughout the country.

The Premier of Britain is dogged, calm, stubborn, and we must take our hats off to him for that. But he does not seem to have imagination . . . His friends have not the courage to stand up to him; they are frightened when they see his bull-dog mouth and cigar.

Madura, 29.1.42: While Mr Churchill is asking for a vote of confidence in Parliament, I will ask you if you repose confidence in me. (*The vast audience raises hands.*)

Hospet, 6.2.42: Because we are tired of our present rulers, let us not make the mistake of welcoming rulers who will be ten times worse.

Virudhunagar, 9.3.42: If we resist, the Japansese will find themselves without food after a few days.

Tirunelveli, 10.3.42: There are a few morbid-minded persons who are imagining that I am anxious to become a Minister once again, and that is why I am engaged in this propaganda . . . In modern war, even Ministers would be bombed, and these morbid-minded people may feel some satisfaction in that . . .

Whenever the people of India demand freedom, they are told that there is a quarrel between Hindus and Muslims . . . It seems as though the British should rule wherever there is a mixed population by some chance.[5]

What the Raj thought of C.R.'s campaign is best conveyed by Governor Hope's words to the Viceroy (22.3.42):

Rajagopalachari has been touring a great deal and has done good in telling the people that India has nothing to gain from the Japanese. On the other hand, his attitude that Britain can no longer defend India and that if 'freedom' were granted the

nation would miraculously be able to defend itself is causing a
lot of harm.[6]

While, as we have seen, C.R. significantly spoke of Gandhi and
Jinnah in the same breath, he also blamed the League leader for
taking 'an impossible stand.' Thereupon Jinnah challenged C.R.
to present a concrete offer:

> If Mr Rajagopalachari will define some basis, some common
> ground, and then find the Muslim League taking an impossible
> attitude, it may lie in his mouth to accuse me (*The Hindu*,
> 23.2.42).

Churchill had disliked and resisted pressures from Roosevelt
and Chiang Kai-Shek for moves towards an Indian solution, but
the fall of Rangoon on 8 March forced his hand. On 11 March
he announced that his Cabinet colleague Sir Stafford Cripps was
taking new proposals to India.

At first sight the proposals he brought were not without
appeal. They offered full Dominion Status after the War, with
the right of secession from the Commonwealth; a constituent
assembly whose members would be elected by provincial
legislatures or nominated by the princes; and, immediately, a
national government composed of representatives of the leading
political parties.

However, provinces wishing to stay out of the projected
dominion could do so when the time came. Included to obtain
Jinnah's acceptance, this clause seemed to open the door to
Balkanization. Although Congress's leaders disliked this provision
as well as the right given to the princes to nominate delegates
to the constituent assembly, they did not, Gandhi excepted,
make a major issue of either.

Their objection lay elsewhere. Azad, the President, accused
Cripps of going back on his word after first indicating that the
new government would function like a cabinet and not be
subject to the Viceroy's veto. Concurring with Azad's charge,
Linlithgow would tell Wavell: 'Cripps did not play straight over
the question of the Viceroy's veto and Cabinet responsibility
and did make some offer to Congress.'[7]

Congress objected, moreover, to the provision that defence would, in substance, remain the charge of the British Commander-in-Chief.

For a moment it looked as if a compromise worked out by a group that included Cripps, C.R. and Colonel Louis Johnson, Roosevelt's emissary in India, transferring some, though not all, crucial subjects to an Indian defence minister, would overcome the 'defence' hurdle. However, resenting American interference, Churchill cabled Cripps that he would accept no arrangement regarding defence that did not have the full agreement, directly communicated to him, of Linlithgow and Wavell, the C-in-C. The latter two made it clear that they did not approve of the Cripps-C.R.-Johnson formula, and the Cripps mission collapsed.

C.R.'s first reaction had been to suggest acceptance of the Cripps proposals, but, as Prasad would later recall, C.R.'s opinion changed 'when it became clear that the Viceroy was not willing to relax his special powers.'[8] Explaining the breakdown of the talks, C.R. told the Press:

> We were proceeding all along under an impression that . . . the Governor-General would accept the advice of the Ministers, and that the only reservation was the authority of the C-in-C and of the British War Cabinet . . . We were aghast when we were told that all the new members of the government would only function like the present Executive Council members.[9]

> At the present moment, defence is practically the whole of government . . . If defence is to be strictly reserved [in British hands], the popular attitude of apathy if not hostility towards the British cannot be transformed (*The Hindu*, 6.4.42).

As a last ploy, Johnson proposed to the White House that Nehru and C.R. be flown to America to talk with Roosevelt, but, chary of annoying Churchill further, the American President asked Johnson to drop the move.

In April, while Cripps was still in India, Japanese bombs were dropped on two of the South's coastal towns, Coconada and Vizag. The Raj ordered the evacuation of several coastal habitations. The seeming imminence of a Japanese attack on South India and the failure of the Cripps mission combined to trigger new ideas in C.R.'s mind.

On 15 April he asked America and Britain to 'place at our disposal at once the crudest weapons in the line of small arms,' (*The Hindu*, 16.4.42). Eight days later, modifying his analysis of the failure of the Cripps initiative, he said, 'I cannot tell you who is to blame' (*The Hindu*, 24.8.42).

Those in the Congress who disliked the British and looked forward to deliverance by an Asian power now formed one pole. C.R. led the opposite pole by pointing to the Japanese menace as India's primary concern. Taking on two adversaries, Britain and the Muslim League, had proved frustrating. Now the Japanese had opened a third and by far the most dangerous front. As C.R. saw it, Congress now had no choice except to settle with the League and with the Raj.

His perception of the threat to South India from the Japanese prompted him to reach another decision: he would attempt to form a government in Madras. The hunter of big game was now ready to settle for a smaller, provincial prize — and eager to take on the Japanese. If necessary, he would conciliate the Raj and the League.

However, embittered towards Britain after the parleys with Cripps, the Working Committee was no longer likely to be persuaded by C.R. Aware of his growing isolation in the Committee, C.R. reached yet another crucial decision: Congress in the South should be ready to act on its own.

After meeting C.R. on 18 April, Hope informed the Viceroy that he had found the former Premier 'very changed in his outlook' and 'quite helpful over the War.' C.R. indicated his willingness to 'come back at the head of a coalition government' which would include the 'Justice party, the Muslim League (if allowed by Jinnah), Christians, Scheduled Classes and even one European.'

'What if Congress refuses you permission to lead a coalition ministry?' asked Hope. 'I will be prepared to break away and run an independent show down here,' replied C.R.[10]

At C.R.'s instance, the Madras Congress Legislature Party

(MCLP) passed two resolutions that were to lead to a fierce controversy and, ultimately, to his resignation from the Congress. By the first, the MCLP recommended to the AICC that it should concede the League's claim for the separation of 'certain areas,' and thus secure the League's support for 'a national administration at this hour of peril.'

By the second resolution, the MCLP sought the AICC's permission for including the League in a popular government in Madras that would prepare South Indians to face any Japanese attack (*The Hindu*, 25.4.42).

Across India, Congressmen seemed outraged by the suggestion that Congress should concede separation and knock on the doors of the League and the Raj. Azad said he was 'greatly astonished' by the MCLP resolutions. (*The Hindu*, 27.4.42). Nehru termed C.R.'s move 'undesirable' and 'extraordinary' (*The Hindu*, 28.4.42). Patel was furious. The Mahatma was frankly critical and also understanding:

> I am wholly opposed to him (C.R.). But I hold that Rajaji has acted in a wholly constitutional manner. I am a lover of personal freedom and free expression of views however embarrassing they might be . . . He was hasty in pronouncing his opinion on vital things before he had consulted his colleagues, but who can help being hasty in these times, especially if he thinks he has something precious to give?[11]

When, following the MCLP meeting, C.R. arrived in Allahabad for an AICC session, black flags were waved at him by workers of the Hindu Mahasabha. Azad told him that before sponsoring his MCLP resolutions he should have discussed their far-reaching contents with his national colleagues. C.R. agreed with Azad, expressed regret, and resigned from the Working Committee. The Viceroy informed the King that C.R. had 'left the working committee to conduct a campaign in favour of wholehearted participation in the war.'[12]

Early in May the AICC met.

C.R.: 'Let us dare. Let us give to [the Muslims] what they are asking. They will themselves say they do not want it if you . . . throw it on the table.'

A voice: 'Do all [Muslims] want it or only the Muslim League?'

C.R.: 'It has been difficult to dislodge the League from its position of control and influence with large masses of Muslims.'

Nehru: 'No!'

C.R. (to Nehru): 'Produce a communal settlement and I will go down on my knees before you' (*The Hindu*, 3.5.42).

Pointing out that the Working Committee had said, in its reply to the Cripps offer, that Congress could not think in terms of 'compelling people of a territorial unit to remain in the Indian Union against their declared and established will,' C.R. claimed that the MCLP resolutions conceded nothing more.

He was cordially cheered at the end of his speech, but the Congress was in no mood to endorse separation. In *The Hindu's* phrase, Nehru 'spiritedly' opposed C.R. So did many others. A C.R. motion in defence of the MCLP step was defeated 120 to 15.

With a large, impulsive, and, as Gandhi noted, hasty gesture, C.R. had sought the League's cooperation for an anti-Japan Hindu-Muslim front in the South. In the process he lost his Congress base. After Allahabad, the Congress MLAs of Madras began to desert him. Eventually, only seven were to stand by him; all hope of 'an independent show' run by C.R. vanished.

A passionate lover of seemingly lost causes, C.R. took the question of separation to the public. Repeating C.R.'s argument, Mian Iftikharuddin, president of the Punjab Congress, said that C.R.'s was 'actually the most effective unity of India move, not a Pakistan move' (*The Hindu*, 11.5.42). Three members of the League working committee, Khaliquzzaman of the U.P., Nazimuddin of Bengal, and Nawab Mohammed Ismail of Bihar, welcomed C.R.'s initiative, as did a number of Muslim journals.

The Communists hailed his anti-Japanese stand as well as his espousal of minority rights. From Bangalore Navaratna Rama Rao notified his personal support. The pro-Congress masses were not converted, but C.R. obtained a large hearing. Srinivasa Sastri, opposed to the Pakistan idea, heard C.R. at Salem and wrote to a friend:

> C.R. had a triumph yesterday. An audience of 20,000 listened for an hour-and-a-half without the slightest disturbance . . . We can't deny Rajaji great prestige and popularity.[13]

A Madura meeting he addressed was 'one of the biggest held in the city,' but angry critics shouted at him. 'If I am to be afraid of you,' C.R. told them, 'how am I to face Japanese aggressors if they come?' *The Hindu* reported (22.5.42):

> A missile was thrown at Rajaji. He jumped into the crowd of hostile demonstrators and declared, 'You want to attack me? Come on, here I am.'

To large numbers in the South, Rajaji and the Congress had for years been synonymous terms, and C.R. was the Mahatma's voice. To hear C.R. dissenting from Gandhi and from Congress shocked and baffled them. In the end the great bulk of the South's Congress supporters gave Rajaji their respect but not their obedience.

Gandhi, too, had been reflecting, and the solution he came up with was the ultimate one: the British should leave. Congress should ask the British to Quit India, and organize mass action if they did not. As Gandhi saw it, their unwillingness to part with power, preparedness to divide India, which the Cripps package had revealed, and withdrawal from Malaya, Singapore and Burma, had earned the British the hatred of India. 'Orderly British withdrawal' would 'turn the hatred into affection,' he claimed.

The thought of Quit India was electrifying to many Indians, but C.R. objected, and a public debate between Gandhi and C.R. ensued. 'There is no reality,' C.R. declared, 'in the fond expectation that Britain will leave the country in simple response to a Congress slogan' (*The Hindu*, 16.6.42). In a letter to Gandhi, C.R. argued that Britain 'cannot add to her crimes the crowning offence of leaving the country in chaos to become a certain prey to foreign ambition.'[14]

Gandhi replied that with the launching of Quit India, 'the whole of India's mind would be turned away from Japan.' 'Today,' he added, 'it is not.' C.R., on his part, saw a Congress-League understanding as the golden key. Once that occurred, 'the next day's post would bring the charter of freedom' (*The Hindu*, 16.5.42).

While conceding that it was 'a noble thing to strive for Hindu-Muslim unity, equally noble to strive to ward off the

Japanese intrusion,' Gandhi called C.R.'s plan 'wholly unnatural' (*The Hindu*, 31.5.42).

After a letter (3.6.42) in which Gandhi said to C.R., 'No more wordy warfare with you by me in the Press,' the two met in Wardha for long talks, but differences remained. Gandhi wrote to him:

> Mahadev was telling me how sad you were over my obstinacy in not appreciating what was so plain to you . . . But I am built that way. Once an idea takes possession of me I can't easily get rid of the possession. I suppose you are of the same build. Therefore there seems to be no escape but to suffer each other's limitations! (5.7.42)

By questioning Quit India and expressing openness regarding Pakistan, C.R. was inviting hostility. At a meeting in Bombay's Napoo Hall, a tar-filled paper ball hurled at him amidst shouts of 'Rajaji Murdabad!' and 'Akhand Hindustan Zindabad!' hit him on the temple: his face and shawl were smeared. For several minutes, until the noise died down, C.R. stood 'with utter unconcern.' Then, in a slow, measured tone, he said:

> Friends, let me first of all congratulate the young man who threw tar at me with such perfect aim. He and I disagree. But India needs determined men like him to beat back the imminent Japanese invasion and to win and retain freedom.[15]

Jinnah noted that C.R. was no longer 'talking of Pakistan as vivisecting India or cutting the cow or baby into two' (*The Hindu*, 31.5.42). However, a resolution commending C.R.'s approach was defeated 32 to 24 in the League's U.P. committee. The Communists backed C.R., and he defended the removal of the Raj's ban on them. They were opposed to Quit India: the Soviet Union was Britain's ally.

Old lieutenants such as Santhanam, Sadasivam, publisher of the weekly, *Kalki*, and its editor, Krishnamurti, supported C.R.; featuring C.R.'s arguments, *Kalki* was brought out twice a week for a spell. But C.R. was increasingly angering mainstream Congressmen.

In July, K.Kamaraj, the thirty-nine-year-old president of the Tamil Nadu Congress Committee, asked C.R., in some ways the father of the provincial Congress, to show cause why action should not be taken against him for attacking Congress resolutions.

Nehru charged that C.R. was 'splitting the Congress over Pakistan.'[16] Patel, chairing the Congress Parliamentary Board, who in 1937 had persuaded C.R. to assume the Premiership of Madras and had been one with C.R. from 1919, was angrier. In a message sent via Gandhi, he sought C.R.'s resignation from the Assembly. Gandhi advised a further step:

> It will be most becoming for you to sever your connection with the Congress and then carry on your campaign with all the zeal and ability you are capable of.[17]

Though rejecting the charge that he was working against Congress, and contending that members could not be 'totally debarred from persuading Congressmen to alter their opinions,' C.R. left Congress. A letter from him to Kamaraj acknowledged 'the value of discipline as well as the need for liberty of thought' and stated that he was resigning 'in order to be absolutely free to carry on my campaign' (*The Hindu*, 10.7.42).

He resigned, too, from the Assembly. The MCLP met again and cancelled the resolutions it had passed at C.R.'s instance.

As for Quit India, first the Working Committee and then the AICC, which met in Bombay on 7 and 8 August, endorsed it. Misgivings had been expressed by Azad and by Nehru, who was anxious about the defence of China and Russia, but the two fell in after sensing the Mahatma's fire and the grassroots support for Quit India.

If Britain withdrew, said Congress, a provisional government 'formed by the cooperation of the principal parties' would allow Allied troops to be stationed in India — a significant concession from Gandhi that made it easier for Nehru to support Quit India. If Britain rejected the Quit India call, 'a mass struggle on nonviolent lines on the widest possible scale' would be launched 'under the leadership of Gandhiji.' If leaders were put behind bars and Congress committees prevented from functioning, then 'every man and woman . . . must be his own guide.'

Resignation had not subdued C.R. He saw the Mahatma again, called on Jinnah who had charged that Quit India was aimed at coercing the British to sanction a Hindu raj, and reported back to Gandhi. On the eve of Quit India, making a fresh effort to bridge the Gandhi-Jinnah divide, C.R. cabled the Mahatma:

> Feel you should ignore Jinnah's allegations and definitely offer him such quota of provisional government as he wants and ask him to nominate his men. This along with your names on behalf of Congress will rationalise your demand of Britain and force acceptance of proposals.

Replied Gandhi: 'Every effort has been and will be made in the direction indicated by you though not identical.'[18]

Two days later, the AICC sanctioned the Quit India struggle. Gandhi said he would launch it after talks he hoped to have with the Viceroy. But the Raj's wartime regime, ready with its plans of arrests, bans and reprisals, took no chances. By dawn on 9 August, Gandhi and other leaders had been put away. And Congress was banned.

India exploded in reaction. A few pockets declared themselves free. Factories were brought to a halt. Demonstrators streamed out of bazaars, factories, villages and colleges, condemning the arrests. Often they were fired at: six hundred were killed in the first few days of the August Movement, as it came to be called.

Nonviolence was not uniformly observed in this open rebellion, the gravest threat to British rule since the 1857 Rising. False reports of the Mahatma's approval of violence 'for this struggle' encouraged acts of destruction. Trains were derailed, telephone and telegraph wires cut, police stations and post offices burnt down. From the other side, the Raj's forces fired in scores of places on unarmed crowds and, on several hundred occasions, freely used the lathi.

Though incidents continued for months, by the end of August the back of the rebellion was broken. The House of Commons was informed that over a thousand had been killed by the end of November; the actual figure was doubtless higher. About a hundred thousand nationalists were jailed, many of them for the duration of the War.

The banishment of the Mahatma and the Working Committee had emptied the national stage; part of it was filled by C.R. His first public reaction to the arrests was a lament: 'My words have fallen on deaf ears, both of my colleagues and of the British government' (*The Hindu*, 11.8.42). Four days later he made a sharp comment on the violence that was occurring: 'If any people think that they are helping Gandhiji by these ruinous activities, they are deluding themselves and bringing cruel discredit on him' (*The Hindu*, 15.8.42).

The Mahatma, and C.R., suffered a serious blow, a week after Gandhi's arrest, in the sudden death of Mahadev Desai, who had been detained, with the Mahatma and Kasturba, in the Poona house of the Aga Khan.

Some members of the Ashram he had started in Tiruchengode left in order to join the Quit India campaign. C.R. was hurt but it was clear that his task now was not to defend himself in his controversy with the Mahatma or Congress: it was to defend Congress, despite all his differences with it, and to keep the Gandhian flag flying.

Thus he refuted Amery, the Secretary of State, who, accusing Congress of having tried to seize power through a coup 'after the manner of modern dictators,' had added that Indian soldiers attached to the Allies would be demoralized if Congress shared in the governance of India. Terming the coup charge a 'black falsehood' and declaring that crushing Congress was 'a psychological impossibility,' C.R. neatly turned the tables on the question of the Indian soldiers:

Will the British Government agree to abide by the free verdict of the fighting forces in India? We will gladly agree to abide by it (*The Hindu*, 23.10.42).

His eager, restless mind produced a new scheme: Let the Viceroy induct into his Council some Congress leaders, including a few of the jailed, and a larger number of the League's nominees, with the War Cabinet in London retaining the right to prosecute the War from India. Jinnah, with whom C.R. canvassed the idea, was non-committal but the League's paper, *Dawn*, sounded positive.

In Britain the former Chief Secretary of Madras, C.R.'s

friend Brackenbury, wrote to *The Times* welcoming the scheme, and a British committee which included some MPs asked the Secretary of State to facilitate a visit by C.R. to the UK. But the Raj was in no frame of mind to let recent rebels enter the government or even to let C.R. enter Britain. The Viceroy, moreover, refused to allow C.R. to meet Gandhi in prison.

Calling on Linlithgow in November, C.R. had suggested that Gandhi was likely now to be readier for a compromise and could be expected, if C.R. was permitted to meet him, to authorize C.R. to condemn the violence that had taken place. Despite a fifty-minute talk, the Viceroy turned down C.R.'s request.

The Raj's calculations are revealed in a letter that Linlithgow wrote to Hope. A Gandhi-C.R. meeting, the Viceroy said, would have an 'instantaneous depressing effect on all non-Congress elements.'[19] The public explanation for the refusal was that the Mahatma was 'under restraint for revolutionary activities' and had not apologized for 'the bloodshed he had provoked' (*The Hindu*, 14.11.42).

Even *The Statesman*, British-owned, regretted the decision. It added: 'True, being a big man, [C.R.] asked for a big thing . . . Would harm have been done?' (14.11.42)

Gandhi forced the Raj's hands. Repeated government charges, circulated in India and abroad, especially in America, that the Mahatma had condoned if not plotted the August violence, and insinuations that he was secretly working for the Japanese, drew from Gandhi a demand for proof or clearance from the Viceroy.

Linlithgow refusing to oblige him, Gandhi resorted to his distinctive weapon, the fast. He did not wish to die, said Gandhi, but he would combat the injustice done against him by not eating for 21 days.

The fast commenced on 10 February 1943. At one point it looked as if he would die of the ordeal, and three Members of Linlithgow's Council, H.P. Mody, M.S. Aney and N.R. Sircar, resigned when their plea for Gandhi's release was not heeded by the Viceroy.

Some of Gandhi's family were allowed to visit him. As a relative, C.R. too was able to call on Gandhi. For four days from the seventeenth day of the fast, by which time the crisis had passed, C.R. saw him daily.

From Gandhi, C.R. obtained a complete disapproval of sabotage and violence. C.R. learnt, too, that in a letter to the Viceroy written soon after his arrest Gandhi had deprecated the deeds of violence, while disclaiming responsibility for them. (Though this letter had reached Linlithgow well before C.R. saw him in November, the Viceroy, in his remarks to C.R., had 'deplored the absence of any condemnation of these [violent] happenings on Gandhiji's part, though he had newspapers.'[20])

The Mahatma and C.R. talked 'both seriously and lightly,' the latter informed the Press (*The Hindu*, 4.3.43). On Gandhi's request, C.R. provided an interpretation of Francis Thompson's *Hound of Heaven*. But C.R. also presented to Gandhi, first verbally and then in writing, a formula for a Congress-League agreement. Gandhji said he could assent to it.

This was the much-discussed, much-reviled and prophetic Rajaji formula. It required the League to cooperate with Congress in the formation of a provisional national government if, on its part, Congress agreed to abide by a plebiscite on the question of Pakistan. As to when and where the plebiscite should take place, C.R.'s formula said that it should be held *after* a transfer of power from Britain — in *contiguous Muslim-majority districts* in the North-West and East of India. In the event of separation, mutual agreements for safeguarding defence, commerce, communications and for other essential purposes would be entered into.

In April 1943, a month after his meeting with Gandhi, C.R. met Jinnah. Without revealing the formula or Gandhi's acceptance of it, C.R. indicated to Jinnah that Gandhi was flexible over Pakistan, whereupon Jinnah declared via *Dawn*, which reached Gandhi in his detention camp, that he was open to an initiative from Gandhi. The Mahatma responded by sending a letter to Jinnah proposing a meeting, but the Raj would not forward the letter.

Three different wars were being fought at this time: Britain against the Axis powers; Congress against the British; the League against Congress. None of the parties felt that its war could be postponed. In the drama of these three great and simultaneous clashes, the C.R.-Gandhi and C.R.-Congress dispute of 1942 formed an intriguing sub-plot.

If this 1942 sub-plot had been resolved differently — if Congress then had agreed to make to Jinnah the offer that C.R. had in mind — would the course of the main drama have been affected? Would there have been a Congress-League accord? If so, would the British have yielded the substance of freedom, rendering Quit India needless?

Hindsight tells us that the probability of Jinnah agreeing in 1942 to the plebiscite that C.R. had in mind was not large; we will see that such a plebiscite was later rejected by Jinnah. There is no indication, moreover, that the British would have conceded a joint Congress-League demand; in turning down such a demand, the Raj might even have cited the disadvantages to India of partition.

Finally, C.R.'s tactics reduced such chances as existed in 1942 of Congress adopting his proposal. To overcome the virtually sacred notion of Indian indivisibility, C.R. needed the assistance of his Working Committee colleagues. By springing his Madras resolutions, he alienated their sympathy. Shortly after being hopelessly outvoted at the Allahabad AICC, he claimed that his views on the Pakistan demand had been 'known to my colleagues for some time' (*The Hindu*, 5.5.42). They knew he was reflecting but not that he intended to act; the headlines regarding his resolutions shocked them.

There was thus an inevitability about the failure of C.R.'s 1942 initiative; the sub-plot and the drama had to run their courses. All the same, his bold, independent and characteristically impulsive stand was useful. It obliged a proud and powerful Congress to face what it would rather have wished away, the roadblock set up by the League.

Phillips, Johnson's successor as Roosevelt's personal representative in India, called on C.R. in Madras and afterwards drew a picture:

Rajagopalachari, one of the few real statesmen in India, greeted me with a warmth which touched me deeply. He led me into a room almost bare of furniture. A chair had been provided for me beside the mattress on which he seated himself. On the whitewashed walls there was only one picture, that of Gandhi.[21]

With the Raj in control and his colleagues and the Mahatma in prison, C.R. waited, despaired, and every now and again pushed at Britain's closed doors to see if they would yield. Occasionally he would seek refreshment at the waterfalls of Courtallam, where T.K. Chidambaram, the literary critic, was his host.

He met Aruna Asaf Ali and some others who were underground. In ways different from his, they too were striving to maintain nationalist morale.

A drought of major proportions hit Kerala and the Rayalaseema districts, and a great famine devastated Bengal, showing the Raj in poor light. But the danger from Japan was receding, even if it never disappeared. It looked as if she had been halted east of India. The change in the fortunes of war tended to confirm the British in the wisdom of their India policy. 'Let us face it,' C.R. said in September, 'India is the weaker party' (*The Hindu*, 24.9.43).

As 1944 opened, Wavell, successor to Linlithgow as Viceroy, talked with C.R. in Madras. In response to a question from the latter, Wavell 'frankly and off the record' said that he 'would not accept a "National Government" with so many nominees of Congress and so many of Muslim League, who took their orders from outside.'[22]

In February it became clear that C.R.'s Pakistan views had not changed. He told a public meeting (*The Hindu*, 29.2.44):

Remaining together might mean treachery, separation could mean peace. You can of course tie a cat and a dog together, drag them along the road and say, 'What perfect unity!' The way to real unity, however, was to say, 'Go if you want. Come back if you want. Remain if you want.'

That month Kasturba died in detention, her head resting in Gandhi's lap. C.R. had respected Kasturba from the moment he first heard of her part in her husband's South African battles.

Over the years affection had softened esteem, and Lakshmi's marriage with Devadas had brought closeness. To Devadas he wrote:

> Ba was born to be a queen and she attained that status through a toilsome part. Let us reserve our emotion for the living (*The Hindu*, 28.2.44).

In April 1944, C.R. felt that the moment had arrived for revealing to Jinnah the Mahatma's acceptance of his Pakistan scheme. Calling on the League leader in Delhi, C.R. produced his surprise. 'Gandhiji is willing,' he said, 'if the League and Congress fight together now for a national government — to ask Congress to accept Pakistan. Here is the formula he agrees to.'

As Jinnah studied the piece of paper, C.R. waited for a positive reaction from him. It never came. Jinnah saw at once that C.R.'s Pakistan was smaller than what League spokesmen had been claiming (Jinnah himself had never described its boundaries), and also that it was linked to a plebiscite and a treaty of separation.

'Your scheme does not satisfy me,' Jinnah told C.R. After their talk, G.D. Birla asked C.R., 'How did your meeting go?' 'Jinnah is too old,' replied C.R.[23]

Early in May, following word that Gandhi was seriously ill with malaria and dysentery, C.R. attacked the Raj for continuing to detain the Mahatma. He did not know that the decision to release Gandhi had already been taken. The gates opened on 6 May and Gandhi was let out.

15

'Moth-eaten'

1944-46

Gandhi convalesced on the Juhu sands outside Bombay. Not everyone wished him a speedy recovery. An entry in the diary of Wavell, the Viceroy, reads: 'Winston sent me a peevish telegram to ask why Gandhi hadn't died yet!'[1].

Eight weeks after the release, Gandhi and C.R. met in Poona where the Mahatma unexpectedly attended a meeting of a women's welfare body named after Kasturba. C.R. was there as a trustee. Playing a characteristic role, C.R. talked Gandhi out of his idea of asking Wavell to reintern him.

By this time Gandhi had announced that he was willing to meet the Viceroy for a settlement. From Poona, at the Mahatma's instance, C.R. accompanied him to the hill town of Panchgani, where they learnt that Wavell had turned down a meeting with Gandhi. The Mahatma's response was to explore a settlement through a letter. He proposed a national government responsible to the Central Assembly to be matched by Congress's full cooperation with the war effort. Wavell answered that the proposal was not acceptable, not even as a basis for discussion.

There was another party to be dealt with. To Jinnah C.R. wired a message from Panchgani: he was releasing his formula to the Press and wanted to know if Jinnah would object to an announcement of his having rejected it. Jinnah wired back that it was wrong to say that he had rejected the scheme. If Gandhi dealt with him direct, he would refer the formula to the League.

On 17 July Gandhi wrote to Jinnah suggesting a meeting and urging the League leader not to 'regard me as an enemy of Islam or of Indian Muslims.' Jinnah replied proposing a meeting in his house, 10 Mount Pleasant Road, in Bombay, but at the end of July he described the C.R. formula as 'a parody and a negation' of the League's Pakistan resolution and intended 'to torpedo' it. Jinnah added that C.R. was offering 'a maimed, mutilated and moth-eaten Pakistan.'[2]

But Gandhi was prepared to strive for Jinnah's conversion. Fourteen times, between 9 and 27 September, the two spoke to each other tête-à-tête and recorded their conversations in a series of letters that contained more than 15,000 words. Photographs in the Press showed the two leaders smiling. Many in the land prayed. The Viceroy, on his part, felt 'sure that the G-J meeting will result in a demand for the release of the working committee.'[3] During the period of the talks, C.R. stayed with Gandhi in another Mount Pleasant Road residence, Birla House. The Mahatma gave his friend daily reports.

But the talks failed. The Pakistan that Gandhi was prepared to recommend to the Congress, based essentially on the C.R. Formula, was termed wholly unsatisfactory by Jinnah, who offered four objections. Firstly, this Pakistan was too small — leaving out the Muslim-minority districts of the Punjab and Bengal, it was only 'a husk.' Secondly, it was not totally delinked from India. Jinnah felt that the treaty of separation included in the Formula, or, as Gandhi put it, 'the bonds of alliance between Hindustan and Pakistan,' would abridge Pakistan's sovereignty.[4] Thirdly, the Pakistan of the C.R.-Gandhi conception was to come after independence — 'as soon as possible after India is free,' the Mahatma had said to Jinnah, whereas Jinnah wanted Pakistan before the British left and under British auspices. He did not trust a Congress-ruled India to implement a promise of division. Finally, this Pakistan was subject to a plebiscite, and one, moreover, where non-Muslims too would vote.

Gandhi did not yield on any of these points. As he saw it, every argument for the separation from India of Muslim-majority areas supported the separation from Pakistan of areas where non-Muslims were in a majority. Again, said Gandhi, while both he and Rajaji conceded self-determination 'without the slightest hesitation,' 'utterly independent sovereignty, so that there is nothing in common between the two,' seemed to him 'an impossible proposition.'[5]

Where Jinnah saw two nations, one Muslim and the other Hindu, and wanted this 'fact' shown on the map, Gandhi could countenance nothing more than agreed separation between brothers. Since only Indians, and not the power ruling over them, could decide whether they stayed together or separated, independence had to precede separation. In C.R.'s unemotional view, however, it was 'idle to imagine any material difference arising out of the order in which the two events, withdrawal of British domination and partition, take place.[6]'

On all the other points C.R. agreed with Gandhi. Thus he held that a plebiscite of all adults was a legitimate preliminary to separation; to deny a vote to some was 'inconsistent with all modern notions of constitution-making.'[7] And he reminded the League that its Pakistan resolution of 1940 claimed 'contiguous . . . areas in which the Muslims are numerically in a majority' — not all of Bengal and the Punjab.

'Jinnah's contempt for your formula and his contempt for you is staggering,' Gandhi said to C.R. during the course of the talks[8] In part at least, Jinnah's dislike stemmed from the tendency of newspapers reporting the talks to associate C.R. with Gandhi and Jinnah. As far as the League leader was concerned, no third person qualified for mention in relation to the negotiations.

Gandhi had written to Jinnah, after the talks:

> Our conversations have come about as a result of your correspondence with Rajaji in July last over his formula . . . and my own letter to you suggesting a meeting between you and me.

Jinnah replied

> It is entirely incorrect and has no foundation in fact for you to say that our conversations have come about as a result of

> my correspondence with Rajaji in July last over his formula . . .
> It is entirely in response to your letter of July 17, 1944.[9]

Three years after the Bombay talks, Jinnah would obtain what Gandhi and C.R. were unprepared to offer — an 'utterly independent sovereignty' — and he obtained it *24 hours* before Britain's departure from the rest of the subcontinent. Nevertheless, the area of the Pakistan he secured was almost exactly the one offered by Gandhi and C.R. and dismissed by him as moth-eaten. It is tempting to speculate that if he had accepted this solution in 1944, the subcontinent might have had a peaceful separation rather than the 1947 Partition of killings and migrations. Questioning the wisdom of Jinnah's 1944 rejection, the League leader Khaliquzzaman would observe in 1961, 'The right of self-determination by Muslim votes alone . . . formed a demand without parallel in world history.'[10]

What emerged from the talks? One, a clearer understanding of what Jinnah wanted. Gandhi had asked him to give 'in writing what precisely you want me to put my signature to.' Though Jinnah refused to do this, his demands were revealed by the Gandhi-Jinnah conversations and correspondence. Two, an increase in Jinnah's prestige. The fact that the Mahatma had sought the talks and then gone fourteen times to the League leader's house added to Jinnah's following, already vast, among India's Muslims.

Congress leaders in jail reacted adversely to word reaching them of Gandhi's bid with Jinnah. In *India Wins Freedom* (1959), Azad would claim that he had told Working Committee colleagues detained with him at Ahmednagar Fort that 'Gandhiji was making a great mistake.'

But the Mahatma was unrepentant. To strive to meet Jinnah halfway was, in his view, a duty. He had intended to meet the League leader before his 1942 arrest, then tried to make contact from behind bars, and, finally, fulfilled his wish. After the breakdown he said: 'We have parted as friends. These days have not been wasted.'[11]

There was no sign either that C.R. regretted the approach to Jinnah. But to Devadas he wrote (30.11.44):

My own conviction is that there can be no agreement with Jinnah under present conditions.[12]

For many in Congress, it was not a new thought.

For much of the second half of 1944, C.R. gave Gandhi company — in Panchgani, during the Bombay talks, and in Sevagram.

Many disapproved of Gandhi's talks with Jinnah, and blamed Rajaji for them; some considered C.R. a dangerous influence on the Mahatma. A conversation in Sevagram between Gandhi, who was experimenting at this juncture with a salt-free diet, and C.R., who was about to leave for the South, shows the amusement that this attitude brought to a relationship that was always merry:

C.R.: I may be able to return by the 30th.

G.: I shall look out for you.

C.R.: If you so desire.

G.: What is the meaning of 'looking out for you'?

C.R.: One looks out for dangers, too, sometimes.

G.: (laughing) You may put it that way. I want that danger. I have to compare notes about several things.

C.R.: I hope both of us will have forgotten all our notes by then.

G.: Then we shall laugh together and fatten.

C.R.: But how can you fatten if you don't eat salt?

G.: I have lived without salt for years in South Africa. Here I interrupted the rule but have now reverted to it.

C.R.: When people have to do without salt in their diet, they are likely to lick their walls and eat clay, like children, to satisfy their natural craving for salt.

G.: The walls will be cleaner! This is the beginning of the laugh to which we will abandon ourselves when you return.[13]

Resenting C.R.'s stand over Pakistan, elements from the Hindu

Mahasabha tried unsuccessfully to block an address he had been invited to deliver at Nagpur University. In his speech, C.R. said:

> Let me ask those who apprehend evil from my address: is your case so weak that it can be endangered by a speech of mine? . . . Or is it your view that these graduates . . . are yet so poor of understanding that they cannot safely stand a single assault on my part?

> And what is this heresy I am guilty of? I stand for a solution of the Muslim issue . . . It is not dishonour or submission to tyranny to allow the majorities in any area to be in more than subordinate charge of those areas, which is the offer we made to Mr Jinnah and with which he is not satisfied.[14]

In C.R.'s view, Gandhi having made his attempt with Jinnah, the ball was now in the British court. As C.R. put it, 'A move on (*by the British*) and a threat to stragglers (*the League*) that they will be left behind are the conditions necessary to create the will to agree.'[15]

Wavell's cogitations also suggested a British move. In October 1944, his Viceroyalty a year old, he informed Churchill of his assessment that the 'present Government of India cannot continue indefinitely or even for long' and that 'British soldiers [would not] wish to stay [in India] in large numbers after the war to hold the country down.' Arguing that 'the failure of the Gandhi-Jinnah talks has created a favourable moment for a move by His Majesty's Government,' Wavell sought Churchill's approval for an effort for

> a provisional political Government . . . within the present constitution, coupled with an earnest but not necessarily simultaneous attempt to devise means to reach a constitutional settlement.[16]

After Churchill had sat on the proposal for five months, Wavell confronted him in London in the spring of 1945. As the Viceroy would record, Churchill 'launched into a long jeremiad about India . . . for about 40 minutes' and seemed to advocate 'partition into Pakistan, Hindustan and Princestan etc.'[17] Finally, however, Wavell extracted HMG's clearance for the initiative he had in mind. By this time the War in Europe had ended, though fighting continued in the Pacific, and fresh British elections were announced.

Returning to India, Wavell declared in the middle of June that the Congress Working Committee members were being freed and that he would invite Indian leaders to Simla for talks about a new Executive Council 'more representative of organised public opinion' and composed, apart from the Viceroy and the C-in-C, entirely of Indians. Wavell expressed the hope that if there was agreement on a new Council, provincial ministries that had resigned in 1939 would resume office.

Those invited to Simla included the Mahatma, Jinnah, Azad, the Congress President, all provincial Premiers and also those, including C.R., who had resigned their Premierships in 1939. Hope was in the air again — and joy over the release of Azad, Nehru, Patel and their colleagues after three years in detention.

Wavell, urging the Congress leaders not to harbour undue fears regarding the Viceregal veto, proposed a Council with an equal number of Muslims and caste Hindus, the latter drawn from Congress as well as outside Congress, plus a Hindu from the Scheduled Castes, and possibly one or two representatives of other minorities.

Gandhi and the Congress accepted the proposal. As C.R. would put it, 'For the first time in Congress history, [its] leaders had thrown their whole weight into a British plan.'[18]

Wavell wanted one of the Muslim seats to go to a non-League Muslim, possibly a member of the pro-War Unionist party which was in office in the Punjab. However, Jinnah insisted on the right to nominate all the Muslim members and made an additional demand. In Wavell's words, the League leader

> refused even to discuss names unless he could be given the absolute right to select all Muslims and some guarantee that any decisions which the Muslims opposed in Council could only be passed by a two-thirds majority — a kind of communal

veto. I said that these conditions were entirely unacceptable and the interview ended.[19]

The Raj now — in the summer of 1945 — had two choices: to go ahead with the Congress, keeping vacant some seats for Jinnah to fill if he changed his mind; or to abandon the project of a new Council. Several Governors advised Wavell to take the first course, but that would have meant a Congress-dominated Council, to which both the Viceroy and Churchill were opposed.

As Wavell would admit (in a 1946 letter to the King), what the Congress-led 1942 movement had done to the war effort when he was Commander-in-Chief in India was a memory 'he could never rid his mind of.'[20] Had the Raj gone ahead with Congress, Jinnah, who well knew, as C.R. had indicated, that 'stragglers' risked being 'left behind,' would perhaps have come in line.

In the event, Wavell pronounced the Simla talks a failure and dismissed the leaders. The result was a rise in Jinnah's prestige among the Muslims of India, and a crucial shift of ground in the Punjab from Khizr Hyat Khan, the Unionist Premier, to the League.

While in Simla, C.R. emerged unharmed from an assault by a Hindu extremist with a lathi. The way in which the talks ended dismayed him. He had arrived on the hill with expectancy — in Wavell's words, he was 'the only [Indian] invitee' to have sent 'a cordial and unequivocal acceptance.'[21] After the failure, C.R. asserted that if the Viceroy's 'purpose in summoning the conference' was 'only to get Mr Jinnah to agree . . . we could have told Lord Wavell that it would be a waste of energy.'[22]

A similar comment was, however, made about C.R.'s approaches to Jinnah by some of his Congress colleagues. Wavell recorded in his journal: 'I am told that Rajagopalachariar got properly told off by the Working Committee apparently for having instigated Gandhi to the discussions with Jinnah last autumn.'[23]

In August 1945 atom bombs were dropped on Hiroshima and Nagasaki and Japan surrendered. Shortly after word came that

Subhas Bose, who was guiding the Indian National Army (INA) with Japanese help, had been killed in an air crash. For some years now, he and C.R. had represented two opposing poles in Congress. To Subhas's older brother Sarat, who was still in detention, C.R. wrote expressing

> admiration for your brother who has now attained everlasting life, released from the bondage against which his soul rebelled. Subhas knew his mind and had the courage to go along the path his reason dictated to him.[24]

Soon after the dismal end of the Simla talks, Labour registered a landslide victory in Britain. The new government summoned Wavell home and authorized him to announce that elections to India's central and provincial legislatures, long postponed owing to the War, would be held at the end of the year or early in 1946.

These elections were vigorously contested. Not because the legislatures yet had adequate powers — they did not — but because the elections seemed likely to influence the succession to the Raj.

C.R. was willing to enter the Madras Assembly again. Despite his 1942 resignation, he had seen himself as a Congressman at the Simla conference. In August 1945, following a letter from C.R., Azad readmitted him into the organization. Others too championed C.R.

While claiming that 'nobody regrets C.R.'s attitude during the last three-four years more than myself,'[25] Patel was determined to enlist C.R.'s skills. His hope was that C.R. would enter the Central Assembly and lead Congress there, but he discovered that C.R.'s 'mind was in the province.'[26]

But what was the mind of the province? C.R.'s Premiership in 1937-9 had been unchallenged and indeed brilliant, but his subsequent positions over Quit India and Pakistan had isolated him. Men like the Mahatma, Azad and Patel were ready to forget the past and restore the southern province's leadership to C.R., but Congress workers returning from two or three years in prison were not.

Yet, it was hard to find an alternative to C.R. Prakasam's popularity was confined to the Telugu districts. Satyamurti was dead. Kamaraj, president of the TNCC, had the advantage of a Quit India imprisonment but was largely unknown in Andhra. Inside and outside the Presidency, a move to draft C.R. gathered momentum.

As in 1937, Patel, who was retained as chairman of Congress's Parliamentary Board (CPB), played a key role. It was decided that C.R. would again contest from the graduates' constituency, and that three of his nominees plus five of Kamaraj's, including Kamaraj himself, would select Congress candidates in the Tamil districts, subject to the CPB's approval.

However, friction marked the C.R.-Kamaraj relationship, and a majority of the candidates selected were opponents of C.R. Still, C.R. might have completed the exercise but for a charge revolving around a visit the Mahatma had made to the South. Though planned well before Congress leaders were released or elections thought of, the visit was portrayed as part of C.R.'s strategy for installing himself as Premier. Throwing in the towel, he wrote to Gandhi (21.2.46):

> I haven't the strength to fight any longer. I bore much all these days. I struggled hard to work without minding the calumniators but I give it up now . . . I must yield to the longing of my heart not to be misunderstood.[27]

The sudden gesture shocked C.R.'s friends, but it was not out of character. He had abruptly left the field in 1923 after being accused of ambition. In 1936 he had resigned his offices in Congress because a close friend, T.S.S. Rajan, had violated party discipline. These gestures of a sensitive and impulsive individual to whom public life was fascinating but expendable hurt C.R.'s credibility as a political leader. Patel's reaction was candid:

> This is what I was afraid of all the time. You do not know how unjust and unfair you are to others. After all this trouble, you want now to let us down! How can anybody support you if you were to act like this? You do not even consult us, but that has always been your way of life (22.4.46).[28]

C.R. did not contest. But the story had not ended. As expected, Congress obtained a large majority, 165 seats out of 205, but there was no consensus regarding a leader. When Prakasam, Kamaraj and Madhava Menon — heads, respectively, of Congress's committees in Andhra, Tamil Nadu and Malabar — sought the Congress High Command's advice, the latter suggested C.R.'s name but clarified that its opinion was not binding.

By 148 votes to 38, the Congress MLAs of Madras rejected the High Command's advice. Then they split ranks. In a contest between Prakasam and Muthuranga Mudaliar, who was backed by Kamaraj, the Telugu leader won by 82 votes to 69, the rest, mostly C.R. supporters, remaining neutral.

16

Freedom!

1946-47

The 1945-6 elections showed that India had been polarized. Congress won almost every general seat in the central and provincial legislatures and the League virtually every Muslim seat, except in the NWFP, where the Congress-backed Redshirts led by the Khan brothers were victorious. Eight provincial ministries were formed by the Congress, which also obtained a share in governing the Punjab. There, despite an overwhelming success in Muslim seats, the League did not win a majority in the Assembly. In Bengal and Sind the League headed coalition ministries.

In February and March 1946, Britain's Labour government made unprecedented declarations. First, it announced a Cabinet Mission to India for working out India's political future, comprising three Ministers: Lord Pethick-Lawrence, Secretary of State for India, Sir Stafford Cripps, President of the Board of Trade, and A.V. Alexander, First Lord of the Admiralty. Next, Premier Attlee said in the House of Commons that if India wished she could choose to have independence.

An exuberant C.R. exclaimed: 'Swaraj will be a fact within six months or at the most two years' (*Hindustan Times*, 18.3.46).

The Cabinet Mission arrived in New Delhi on 24 March. Pethick-Lawrence, who led the 'three wise men,' was a pacifist who sympathized with Indian aspirations. The brilliant Cripps, the Mission's dominant personality, was confident in what

Wavell called his 'ability to make both black and white appear a neutral and acceptable grey.' Alexander was socialistic at home but, in Wavell's words again, 'in reality an imperialist, disliking any idea of leaving India.'[1] As Viceroy, Wavell joined the British negotiating team as its fourth member.

Azad and Nehru negotiated on Congress's behalf, but C.R. also argued the Congress case during a three-hour talk he had with the Mission. After the meeting Pethick-Lawrence told Wavell that C.R. was 'the biggest man in Indian politics.'[2]

In his first discussion with the Mission, the Mahatma suggested the C.R. Formula as a compromise. The Mission offered Jinnah the 'truncated' Pakistan of this Formula and clarified that it could be entirely sovereign. But the League leader turned it down.

The Mission then sought Jinnah's reaction to a loose Indian Union and autonomy within it for the large Pakistan that Jinnah seemed to want — the whole of the Punjab, Sind, Baluchistan, the NWFP, the whole of Bengal and Assam. Without saying anything that might be construed as approval, Jinnah seemed ready to accept this, but he indicated also that his group of provinces would claim the right to secede after five years.

In negotiations with the Mission, Congress made it plain that it would deny Jinnah this route to a Greater Pakistan. The principle of a group or groups within India was, however, accepted by Congress. While the League wanted all the Muslim-majority provinces plus Assam joined together in a 'Muslim' grouping, Congress sought a right for provinces such as Assam, the NWFP, Sind and Baluchistan to stay out of a 'Muslim' group in the first place, and another right to leave after joining.

The Mission's 'solution' was presented in its clever and deliberately inconsistent scheme of 16 May, designed to satisfy both Congress and the League both.

Para 15 of the Declaration of 16 May read: 'Provinces *should be free* to form groups with executives and legislatures, and each group *could* determine the provincial subjects to be taken in common.' This indication of *optional* grouping was however contradicted by Para 19, which laid down that representatives chosen by the newly-elected provincial assemblies — to form, ostensibly, a single Constituent Assembly for India as a whole — '*shall*', after a joint preliminary session, meet separately in three Sections, virtually as three separate Constituent Assemblies.

Representatives from all Hindu-majority provinces except Assam were to meet in 'Section A' and settle a constitution for their group as well as for the provinces in the group; representatives from the Muslim provinces in the northwest of India would meet in 'Section B' and frame a constitution for their group and its provinces; meeting in 'Section C,' representatives from Bengal and Assam, including the northeastern areas, would do likewise.

This meant that the fate of the NWFP, which had just elected a pro-Congress government and in effect rejected Pakistan, and of the Sikhs of the Punjab, would be decided by the Muslim majority in Section B; and that the Muslims of Bengal, forming a majority in Section C, would control Assam.

A sub-clause in Para 19 no doubt said that *a new* provincial legislature elected under a constitution so framed could leave its group. However, Sections B and C seemed capable of preventing a province's exit — by, for instance, laying down that 'no unit can opt out except by a two-third majority.'[3] The NWFP and Assam could thus be compelled by their Sections to remain in a 'Pakistan' group against their will.

The League 'accepted' the 16 May plan but, reiterating its 'unalterable goal of a complete sovereign Pakistan,' made it clear that its assent was qualified. Congress took time to decide. Assamese leaders sent strong protests, and the Mahatma said he could not agree to Assam being overwhelmed. ('There is no other way of fitting Assam in anywhere except in Pakistan,' Jinnah, in contrast, had said in April.[4])

Ever ready with a solution, and eager for a settlement, C.R. proposed acceptance of 16 May, inclusive of Para 19, with the proviso that no provincial constitution drawn up by a Group would be valid until approved by the province or by the Union Constituent Assembly. To a majority of Congressmen, however, Para 15 was fair — provinces could form groups — but Para 19 was unacceptable — provinces should not be compelled.

Their hands were forced by another British statement, that of 16 June, regarding an Interim Government. On this question, too, Congress and the League had clashed, the latter insisting on the right to select all Muslim Ministers. Congress was willing to keep out its Muslim President, Azad, against whom Jinnah seemed allergic, and proposed Zakir Hussain, as a single non-League Muslim, but Jinnah attacked Hussain as a quisling.

Yielding to Jinnah in their 16 June statement, the three Ministers and Wavell invited to the Council six Congressmen — Nehru, Patel, C.R., Prasad, Jagjivan Ram and Hare Krushna Mahtab — five from the League, and three others — Baldev Singh, a Sikh, N.P. Engineer, a Parsi, and John Matthai, a Christian — but no non-League Muslim.

Though, for a while, C.R. and Patel favoured acceptance — confident of the support of Singh, Engineer and Matthai, they pictured a 9-to-5 majority over the League in the Council —, the two changed their minds after *The Statesman* published letters exchanged between Wavell and Jinnah. In this correspondence the League leader was given three assurances: Congress could not substitute a Muslim for one of the six Congressmen invited; Jinnah would be consulted by the Viceroy if a question of substituting Singh, Engineer or Matthai arose; and the Council could not decide a communal question by simple majority vote.

After this it was impossible for C.R. or Patel to recommend acceptance of 16 June. Cripps and Pethick-Lawrence, however, drew Patel's attention to Clause 8 of the statement, which indicated that Congress and the League would be free to propose alternative names for their quota of Council seats, *if they were 'willing to accept the statement of May 16.'*

On 23 June, Patel, C.R., Nehru, Azad and Prasad met together, examined the opportunity offered by Clause 8 — an opportunity also available, they knew, to the League — and decided to grasp the power now within their reach.[5]

Two days later, Gandhi advised the Working Committee against accepting 16 May or 16 June. Silence greeted Gandhi's opinion. He asked if he could leave; his followers remained silent; Gandhi left. The Working Committee decided to reject 16 June but accept 16 May, with its own 'interpretation of some of the provisions of the Statement' — of Para 19, in particular.

As soon as it was known that Congress had rejected 16 June but accepted 16 May, the League, which had already consented to 16 May, informed the Viceroy that it was agreeing also to 16 June. But the possibility of a League-dominated Council had slipped out of Jinnah's hands. Congress was back in the running, and Jinnah was furious.

With some justification, he accused Congress of insincerity and Cripps and Pethick-Lawrence of collusion with it. In Congress's view, which also had some basis, Wavell's leanings were towards the League; and Congress underlined the fact that while 'accepting' 16 May, the League had reaffirmed its Pakistan goal.

Gandhi commented that Jinnah, 'a great Indian and the recognised leader of a great organisation' should not have been dealt with 'in a legalistic manner'[6]; but he chose not to stand in the way of his lieutenants — C.R., Vallabhbhai, Jawaharlal, Prasad and the rest — who wanted to secure the power they had smelt.

Congress was invited to send its names for the Council. A League-led government, to which at least three Indians out of four were opposed, was forestalled; yet this success had been achieved through Congress's deliberately equivocal acceptance of 16 May — a response virtually forced, it must be said, by the plan's contradictory language.

On returning to London, Cripps claimed before the House of Commons that the Mission had been 'purposely vague.'[7] Through ambiguity it hoped to secure the signatures of Congress and the League both. The League was allowed to feel that it could obtain both a large 'Pakistan' area and, before long, independence for it; and Congress that it could both concede and prevent a Muslim grouping within India.

The outcome was an escalation of hatred.

In the summer of 1946, while the Cabinet Mission was in India, Congress selected a new President. At Gandhi's instance, Jawaharlal succeeded Azad. Most provincial Congress committees had preferred Patel, but Nehru's younger age, wider popularity, international standing, and greater acceptability to the Left and to India's Muslims influenced Gandhi's choice. Vallabhbhai withdrew when the Mahatma gave the word. It was a re-enactment of the 1929 story.

This intervention by Gandhi in April 1946 was his last decisive act in Congress affairs. After 25 June, when the Working Committee silently allowed him to leave, Gandhi functioned as one who had yielded the reins. He would continue, if asked, to counsel them, but the lieutenants — principally Nehru, Patel, C.R., Prasad and Azad — had taken over.

After Nehru formally named C.R. to the Working Committee — he had served as a regular invitee for some time now —, Subbaroyan referred to Congress's acceptance of the grouping of Muslim provinces and said publicly that 'what Rajaji said in 1942 has proved right in 1946' (*Hindustan Times*, 11.7.46).

Nehru was offended. In a private letter to Subbaroyan, of which he sent a copy to C.R. with the covering remark, 'I hope you will understand,' Jawaharlal said that Congress 'functioned today in continuation of the policy of 1942' and that 'if in the future a conflict arises between this policy and what used to be Rajaji's policy in 1942, it will be difficult for Rajaji and me to be in the same executive.'[8]

Yet Nehru made no public contradiction. He could not have comfortably done so, for in a 'Note for Congressmen' he sent out four months earlier Nehru was willing to concede 'some kind of separation' — though defence and foreign affairs 'were obviously common subjects' — and a 'division of the Punjab and Bengal' — almost the Rajaji Formula of 1944.[9]

The truth was that Jawaharlal so hated the idea of Pakistan that he tended to deny Congress's, and his own, concessions towards it, including the acceptance of grouping. Four days before shooting off the letter to Subbaroyan, he had in fact declared that grouping would probably never come to fruition, and that the Constituent Assembly would have the power to alter the Mission plan.

Jinnah exploded. First he demanded that the British dismiss Congress's acceptance and, in view of the League's 'genuine' acceptance, invite him to form a government. Next, when there was no sign that the British would do what he wanted, he had the League rescind its acceptance. The British, he charged in the middle of July 1946, had surrendered to the 'fascist, caste Hindu Congress.' At last, said Jinnah, 'bidding goodbye to constitutional

methods,' the League would — on 16 August — launch Direct
Action to achieve Pakistan. He described Direct Action as a
pistol, comparable in his view to Britain's pistol of authority
and Congress's pistol of mass struggle.

The League's withdrawal from 16 May deprived it of the
right of inclusion in a new government. Alienated, in any case,
by Jinnah's threat, the Raj invited Nehru to bring a Congress
team into an Interim Government. Though Ministers would
technically be subject to the Viceregal veto, Wavell assured them
of 'the greatest possible freedom in the exercise of the day-to-day
administration of the country.'[10]

Nehru had wanted an explicit promise on the veto but C.R.
and Patel were satisfied, and the Working Committee authorized
Nehru to accept the Viceroy's invitation. Not to do so, C.R.
argued in a letter to Patel, would invite the charge of 'funking
responsibililty' when Jinnah had 'declared civil war.'[11]

Direct Action Day proved frightening. Bengal's League
Ministry, led by H.S. Suhrawardy, had declared it a public
holiday. There was murder, arson, rape and looting while the
police watched. For two days Hindus were at the receiving end.
Retaliation followed. About 5,000 were killed and 15,000 injured
in five days of rioting. On 21 August, Patel wrote to C.R.:

> This will be a good lesson for the League, because I hear that
> the proportion of Muslims who have suffered death is much
> larger.[12]

C.R.'s remedy was the dismissal of Suhrawardy and the Bengal
Governor's direct rule. Burrows, the Governor, had in any case
told Wavell that 'Suhrawardy had forfeited everyone's
confidence.'[13]

But the Viceroy's response to the Great Calcutta Killing
was different. Summoning Gandhi and Nehru, he demanded
their signatures to an acceptance of compulsory grouping. Gandhi
called his language 'minatory' and Nehru said Congress could
not yield. Though rebuffed, Wavell lacked grounds for rescinding
the invitation to Congress; instead he resolved to bring the
League also into the Interim Government.

This was C.R.'s wish too. 'There will be no rejoicing until
the League also shares responsibility,' he said before he was
sworn in — nine days after his colleagues — as a Minister in the

Interim Government. It would be the first job in the North for C.R., now almost 68.

The Ministry — formally still described as the Viceroy's Executive Council — also included Nehru, who though designated Vice-President functioned as a de facto Premier, Patel, Prasad, Asaf Ali, Sarat Bose and Jagjivan Ram from Congress, two independent Muslims, Shafaat Ahmed Khan and Syed Ali Zaheer, and — to represent, respectively, Sikhs, Christians and Parsis — Baldev Singh, John Matthai and C.H. Bhabha.

Nehru, who kept External Affairs, and Patel, the Home Minister, inaugurated with this Interim Government the efficient, often uneasy and at times tense duumvirate that governed India from the summer of 1946 to the end of 1950. They offered Finance to C.R., who however asked for a lighter burden. He got the portfolio of Industry and Civil Supplies. In his journal the Viceroy wrote that C.R. would 'obviously be a considerable addition to the debating and administrative strength' of the cabinet.[14]

Technically, these former rebels against the Raj were now Ministers under the Viceroy, and so appointed, on HMG's recommendation, by the King himself. In fact, however, they owed their seats of power to the lead of another man. On three successive days C.R. called on Gandhi, who was staying in one of Delhi's sweepers' settlements. His lieutenants moved into the Raj's abodes.

The house that C.R. was allotted was the first on Clive Road, named after one of the Raj's founders. A stone's throw from the Viceroy's House, it was a comfortable dwelling with a garden. Namagiri and Narasimhan accompanied C.R. into it.

Patel had invited C.R. to move into his house on Aurangzeb Road. Both were widowers needing for the first time to live in Delhi. A shared house might offer practical advantages. But C.R. declined the offer. He could not afford to be seen as belonging to the Sardar's 'camp.' Over the years he had been closer to Patel than to Nehru, but the latter two now needed a neutral colleague.

Yet C.R.'s rapport at this juncture with Patel is noteworthy. 'There are many things to talk to you,' Patel had written at the end of August. He wanted C.R. to 'think out . . . the plan that we may have to follow on the first sitting of the Constituent

Assembly' and help 'evolve a rough scheme of the provincial constitution and also of the Union Constitution that we may like to push through.'

On another occasion Patel wrote: 'We will have to discuss . . . the election of the next President as a sequel to the expected resignation of Pandit Nehru [and] about allocation of portfolios also . . . You must be here at that time without fail.'

C.R. had proposed to Patel the inclusion in the Cabinet of Ghaffar Khan, whom he called 'a sturdy and straight representative of the NWFP.' When Patel learned of the delay in C.R.'s arrival in Delhi, he wrote: 'New intricate problems and difficulties arise every day and we have to face them without your help or advice. The sooner you come the better.'

On his part, C.R. acknowledged, in a letter to Patel, the latter's role in Congress's acceptance of 16 May: 'The violence of Mr Jinnah's chagrin is the measure of the wisdom of our decision at a critical moment. It is all due to your firm and thoughtful stand.'[15] Sadly, the violence of the months that followed would call into question this unqualified praise of Congress's decision of 25 July.

Thus far C.R. had not had a close teamwork with Jawaharlal. He was yet to feel a temperamental or philosophical kinship with Nehru. Now, however, the relationship between them had a chance to grow.

Three days after C.R. was sworn in, the dark-green Plymouth assigned to C.R. was shot at while it turned into Curzon Road (now Kasturba Gandhi Marg) from Connaught Circus. Fortunately C.R. was not in the car, having alighted some minutes earlier and climbed up to his daughter Lakshmi's second-floor flat on Connaught Circus. The bullet, fired from the rear, pierced the hood of the boot. The assailant was not identified.

'If you want to see Jinnah, I cannot prevent you.'[16] This was Nehru's response to the Viceroy when, on 11 September, Wavell told him of his intention to invite the League into the Interim Government. Jinnah told the Viceroy that the League would come in but not commit itself to 16 May, the Constituent

Assembly or a Union. Wavell did not object: if Congress could come in without accepting compulsory grouping, why fetter the League?

This time — at last — the Viceroy disallowed a League veto on a Congress Muslim in the Council. Jinnah's reply to this was to include a (Hindu) Scheduled Caste leader from Bengal, J.N. Mandal, among his nominees. The League leader kept himself out: he would not function under Nehru.

One Congress Minister, Sarat Bose, and two independent Muslims, Ali Zaheer and Shafaat Ahmed Khan, were dropped to make room for the League's nominees, who numbered five as against the six from Congress that remained.

Wavell pressed the Congress to let the League have the Home portfolio, but Patel made it plain that he would rather resign than give up Home. As a solution, Finance, held by Matthai, was offered to the League. C.R., who said that Matthai could have Industry instead, found himself as Education Minister.

The League's team, led by Liaqat Ali Khan, who took the Finance portfolio, acted from the start as a parallel government, ignoring Nehru's status as the Council's Vice-President. The 'coalition government' was openly a house at war. Ispahani, Jinnah's 'personal envoy' in America, said at the end of October: 'The League's participation . . . only means that the struggle for Pakistan will now be carried on within as well as without the Government.'[17]

Invited by HMG to London, Nehru, Jinnah and Liaqat defended their conflicting interpretations of the 16 May document there. Thereafter, on 6 December, a Cabinet Declaration pronounced in the League's favour: provinces *had* to join their Groups and abide by the constitutions that Groups made for them.

However, Jinnah was still not willing to accept 16 May or join the Constituent Assembly. As a result, Congress demanded the League's ouster from the Interim Government. The deadlock was complete. And passions were fierce.

On 20 February 1947, HMG made a historic move. Attlee announced that Britain would 'transfer power . . . by a date not later than June 1948' to 'some form of Central Government . . . or in some areas to the existing Provincial Governments' or in other 'reasonable' ways. As for the princely states, the Raj's Paramountcy would end with the transfer of power; the successor government(s) could not automatically claim it. The Premier added that Wavell would leave and be succeeded by Lord Louis Mountbatten.

As Gandhi pointed out in a letter to Nehru, the Declaration afforded scope for 'Pakistan for those provinces or portions which may want it.'[18] In London, Churchill denounced the 'shameful flight' and 'premature, hurried scuttle' he saw in the Declaration, but the House of Commons backed Attlee.

If Britain seemed ready to contemplate India's independence and partition, Congress's will to resist partition was weakening. If the deadlocked Cabinet was an indication of what was in store in a united India, was the latter worth fighting for? C.R., Patel or Nehru could not propose an appointment or a transfer without encountering a demand from the League that the Viceroy should decide.

Three days *before* the Attlee announcement, Patel told Wavell that he was 'quite prepared to let the Muslims have the Western Punjab and Sind and NWFP if they wished to join, and Eastern Bengal.'[19]

HMG's word that independence might in some cases go to provinces ignited a struggle for their control. Already running Bengal and Sind and able to count on Baluchistan, the League mounted a campaign to obtain the Punjab and the NWFP as well, and to bring down Assam's Congress Ministry.

Targeted as a stooge of Islam's enemies, Khizr Hyat Khan resigned the Punjab Premiership on 2 March. The next day, the Governor asked the Khan of Mamdot of the League to form a new Ministry, whereupon the leader of the Sikhs, Master Tara Singh, exhorted Sikh youths to act.

Different private armies now took to arms. Killings began, Mamdot was dismissed, and the Governor took over, but within days at least a thousand had been killed in riots in Rawalpindi and elsewhere in the Punjab.

On 8 March the Congress Working Committee, inclusive of

C.R., Nehru and Patel, met in New Delhi and proposed — without inviting or consulting Gandhi, who was in Bihar — the partition of the Punjab. In effect, Congress was conceding Smaller Pakistan.

Wavell left India on 23 March. A man of few words, he did not like the idea of a divided India, but his greater dislike of Congress ascendancy made him sympathetic towards the League. Yet C.R. was prepared to acknowledge, in a farewell letter, the 'justice, firmness, patience and ability' with which the retiring Viceroy had 'worked for an honourable settlement.'[20] Wavell's Journal shows that his talks with C.R. often went past politics to history and literature.

Cripps had considered coming out as Wavell's successor. His wife Isobel, stopping in New Delhi in December on her way home from a visit to China, asked C.R. for his advice. Replying frankly that Nehru continued to lack confidence in Cripps, C.R. discouraged the idea.[21]

The Crippses accepted the advice — and persuaded the Mountbattens to succeed the Wavells. A General was followed by a handsome, well-connected Admiral with enormous natural abilities as a diplomat.

Since HMG had fixed the June 1948 deadline and given Mountbatten plenipotentiary powers, Indian politicians took care not to offend him. Mountbatten realized, too, that by then Congress would not resist partition. Patel and Nehru were frank with him about their disillusionment with the 'coalition' Government. On 11 April C.R. told him that 'a unified India could not be imposed by force' and that attempts to do so 'could lead to civil war.' But he asked for a provision for reunion if partition was decided upon, and for some common arrangements — C.R. had not forgotten his Formula!

This was a line that Jinnah had steadfastly opposed, and even Nehru and Patel now wanted a swift, clean, total cut. As for Gandhi, he made one final, unexpected move to preserve Indian unity.

Arriving in Delhi from Bihar, he proposed to Mountbatten and the Congress Working Committee that Jinnah be invited to form a government for India as a whole. We saw that C.R. had made an identical 'sporting offer' in February 1940. But now, along with the rest of the Working Committee, he opposed the idea. In a terse entry in an engagements diary, C.R. wrote on 13 April: 'Gandhiji's ill-conceived plan of solving the present difficulties' was 'objected to by everybody and scotched.'[22]

We know from a letter from the Mahatma to Mountbatten that one Working Committee member, Ghaffar Khan, did support the plan. The rest, including C.R., thought that Jinnah no longer merited the offer. Gandhi's last throw was in vain.

The Mountbatten Plan now took shape. It laid down that India, the Punjab and Bengal would be divided. Both India and Pakistan would be Dominions. The princely states would have the right to join either Dominion or stay out: HMG's Paramountcy would end. Congress realized that accepting Dominon Status would increase New Delhi's leverage with potentially troublesome princely states, and elicit the goodwill of the British officials, civil and military, still serving in India. Through Kripalani, who had succeeded Nehru as President, the Working Committee assented to the Plan.

Jinnah was hardly enthusiastic about a truncated Pakistan but nodded his acceptance after Mountbatten told him that 'the only alternative was to keep India completely united.'[23] On the night of 3 June, Nehru on behalf of Congress, Jinnah for the League and Baldev Singh for the Sikhs aired their acceptance on the radio. On 15 August India would be free and divided.

When the AICC met in the middle of June, Gandhi asked for an endorsement of the Working Committee's decision. His lieutenants — Nehru, Patel, C.R., Prasad, Azad, Kripalani, Pant and others — had not heeded him but he was not going to defy them: apart from the fact he had built much into them and shared their struggle for thirty years, he did not see a team that could replace them.

In his speech before the AICC, Nehru said that the Mountbatten Plan had been anticipated by what Rajaji had proposed in 1942-44. Patel said that the Plan would give them '70 to 80 percent' of India, after the 'removal of a poisoned limb.' By 157 votes to 29, 32 remaining neutral, the AICC ratified acceptance. C.R. did not speak to the AICC, but in an article for the *Hindustan Times* (22.6.46) he claimed:

We offered this to Mr Jinnah three years ago. We have not
agreed to anything which Gandhiji had not freely offered to
Mr Jinnah then. 'Why then has Mr Jinnah agreed [now]?' ...
Let us drop all this analysis ... There is no other part of the
world where four hundred million are furnished with a single
democratic state.

Though the Mountbatten Plan was not quite the Rajaji Formula
under another name — unlike the Formula, the Plan envisaged
no formal bonds between India and Pakistan —, Khaliquzzaman,
the League leader, would ask in 1961 why the Formula was
turned down if 'it was the intention of Mr Jinnah to agree to
a truncated Pakistan.'[24]

More than territory was being split. The division of the
country's civil servants, defence forces, institutes, records and a
variety of assets and liabilities had to be worked out. It was a
prodigious task, largely accomplished by officials, but politicians
too played a helpful part. Along with Patel and Prasad, C.R. was
a member of the Partition Council formed for the purpose:
Jinnah, Liaqat and Nishtar sat opposite.

Problems of succession and partition claiming priority, the
ministerial work of C.R. and his colleagues inevitably suffered.
In C.R.'s case, the position was made more difficult by changes
in his portfolio. After shifting from Industry to Education when
the League came in, he reverted to Industry and Supplies when
Asaf Ali was sent as Ambassador to the USA and Azad,
replacing Ali, desired Education.

Within days of assuming office, C.R. called upon scientists
working for the government and civil servants not to 'subordinate
themselves to the whims and fancies of politicians, however
illustrious they may be' (*Hindustan Times*, 18.9.46). Dharma
Vira, then a young official and later Governor of West Bengal,
would recall:

With his pleasant, paternalistic manners he put me at ease ...
He encouraged his officers to express their views fearlessly and
if he did not agree with them he did not try to coerce or
browbeat them but convinced them through discussion and
reasoning.[25]

Most Britons in the Indian administration were now leaving.
C.R. tried without success to convince a few that 'there would
still be a career' for them in India. W.G. Lamarque, a district
officer in the South during the Rajaji Ministry and now a deputy
secretary in New Delhi, was one of them:

> I had a long talk with my Minister C. Rajagopalachari, wisest
> and kindliest of Indian statesmen. He strongly advised me to
> stay . . . I replied with complete honesty that if it was just a
> question of continuing to work for him, I would readily stay,
> but that one day there would arise a new king, which knew
> not Joseph, and then my future would be uncertain.[26]

Education was in C.R.'s care for just over two months: he had
no time to do much for it. He hoped that schools might
'introduce song and dance' into children's lives (*Hindustan
Times*, 10.1.47) and felt that university education in Indian
languages was quite feasible. To his Clive Road neighbour, the
civil servant B.K. Nehru, who had pleaded for high-quality
schools for talented children, C.R. replied:

> You want, young man, a new Brahminism. This country will
> not take it. It wants equality, not excellence.[27]

As Minister of Supplies, he held charge of controls over the
distribution of some commodities, necessitated by the War. He
disliked them. While conceding that controls did not 'convert
an orthodox democracy into a Communist or Nazi state,' he felt
that giving to some 'the exclusive right of dealing in certain
articles' was 'a monopoly system' and 'merely another form of
patronage.' It was a view he would stress forcefully — and in
opposition to Nehru — in the sixties.

He thought foreign capital needed regulation but 'a total
ban could not be accepted,' for 'narrow nationalism' was out of
date. Nationalization was 'not practicable at the present time';
if carried out later, 'compensation will go along with it.'[28]

Besides Industry, C.R. was responsible for Science and
Technology. Anticipating future innovations, C.R. argued for
adopting a decimal system, the metre instead of the yard, and
the kilogram rather than the pound. Money was sanctioned for
six national laboratories; the Indian Standards Institute was

launched; and a Board of Atomic Research was formed, with Homi Bhabha as chairman. But C.R. disavowed any attempt towards an atomic bomb.

The opening signature in the Book of Members of the Constituent Assembly is that of C.R., who was elected to the body by the Madras Assembly. But the ministerial offices he held and the positions he occupied later prevented any substantial role by C.R. in the Constituent Assembly's deliberations.

In the Central Assembly, which he faced as a Minister, he was helped by his clear voice. 'Mr Rajagopalachari has the best microphone voice on the Government benches,' observed the *Hindustan Times* on 13.4.47, adding, 'He particularly shines in answering supplementaries.'

Invitations to inaugurate a conference or deliver a talk poured in at a great rate. C.R. accepted many of them. His enjoyment of speaking — and capacity to give pleasure and illuminate — was undiminished.

In December 1946 there was a blow. His second son Ramaswami, a doctor, died in a Madras hospital at the age of 43. Namagiri heard her father sobbing in the bathroom after he had received the news. The death of Ramaswami, of whom he was very fond, added to C.R.'s responsibilities. Along with her five children, his widow Thangam joined Namagiri and Narasimhan as part of C.R.'s household.

In childlike phrases C.R. gave expression to his thrill on the day of freedom (*Hindustan Times*, 15.8.47):

> The independence of India is a settled fact! I have seen it with my own eyes! I wish I were young again.

His dream, first dreamt unshaped in the nineties of the previous century, was being fulfilled. Vindication made C.R.'s joy doubly sweet — the 1947 transfer of power seemed based on his 1942 proposals, which at that time had been termed traitorous. To his old friend Rama Rao, C.R. wrote (8.6.47):

A great incubus is off India's chest. Yet it is what I asked them to do . . . I find a mischievous pleasure in watching and enjoying my colleagues' studied silence on the subject. Vanity all over.

As 15 August approached, joy was overlaid with terrible pain and fear in many Indians and soon-to-be Pakistanis. Millions were uprooted, and a great many — Hindus, Muslims and Sikhs — were slain.

With the League's Ministers leaving for Pakistan, the Cabinet had to be formed afresh. Also, many British Governors were returning home and needed to be replaced. Nehru and Patel made most of the selections, seeking Gandhi's advice at times but also often consulting C.R.

On 30 July 1947 Patel and C.R. were discussing the importance of Bengal, which needed a new Governor, and recalling the Great Calcutta Killing of August 1946, when, unexpectedly, the Sardar said to C.R.: 'You should handle Bengal. You are one of the few who can.'[29] Patel also said that Nehru and the Mahatma agreed with him, and that West Bengal's Chief Minister, Prafulla Chandra Ghosh, wanted C.R. in Calcutta.

So he was being eased out of Delhi! Governors in free India would have little power. But C.R. did not argue or protest. He agreed. A week later the papers announced a revival of disturbances in Calcutta. Ten were killed and 85 injured on 7 August.

At a farewell occasion in New Delhi, Pattabhi Sitaramayya, who was to become Congress President the following year, said:

Let me make a prophecy. When Members of the Lower House have to elect the President of the Indian Republic, I have no doubt that the legislature's choice will be that of C.R.

Replied C.R.:

I do not know what job I am going to do, or what work is expected of me. But harmony and peace in West Bengal has to be restored (*Hindustan Times*, 14.8.47).

One of those who saw C.R. off at the airport on 14 August was N.V. Gadgil, who had been named to the new Cabinet. He has recalled:

> Rajaji took me aside and said, 'Your main task in the Cabinet will be to see that the two important persons (Nehru and Patel) do not fall out.'[30]

17

Calcutta
1947-48

The appointment of C.R. as Governor of West Bengal was not welcomed by all. Subhas Bose's brother Sarat, who had moved away from the Congress after being dropped from the Interim Government, reminded Bengal that C.R. had opposed her favourite sons, Chittaranjan Das and Subhas.

Nonetheless, 'a large crowd that surged round the plane' greeted C.R. on his arrival on 14 August. There were cheers at several places along the route to Government House, but at Sham Bazar a group of young men displayed placards that asked C.R. to 'Go Back' and shouted 'Leaky Boat!' as his car drove past. They were throwing at him the phrase he had employed in the 1939 debate over Subhas's Presidentship of the Congress.

Until midnight C.R. was the retiring Governor, Burrows' guest in Government House; from midnight until Burrows' departure at dawn, the latter would be C.R.'s guest.

Fireworks lit the night sky. The curfew which for nearly a year had emptied Calcutta's streets in the later hours was completely ignored. From trucks, cars, taxis, bicycles and tramcars came shouts, hoots or bells of joy. Steamboats turned on their sirens. Students took out a torchlight procession. As dawn broke, a huge throng pressed against the gates of Government House. Soon the gates were flung open and the masses flooded in.

Thirty seconds before 8.00 a.m. C.R. mounted a pavilion that had been set up on the lawns. At the first boom of a 17-gun salute fired from Fort William, he unfurled the national flag. This triggered, as *The Statesman* put it, 'a wild outburst of joy which swept Government House and its environs for hours together.'

At least 200,000 people swarmed into Government House, many pushing their way into its halls and rooms, handling the portraits and dancing on the sofas. C.R. instructed that all were. to be allowed in. The revellers greeted British officers who responded with ringing cries of 'Jai Hind!' As C.R. appeared on a window, lusty shouts of '*Rajaji-ki-jai*' went up.

But the reality of Partition stabbed rejoicing hearts. Addressing the West Bengal Assembly on 15 August, C.R. expressed the fond hope that the bars of division would 'ere long melt away' and that 'the two free States will come together once again into a wise and lasting union.'[1]

From 9 August the Mahatma had been in Calcutta. He had intended to go to Noakhali in what was now East Pakistan, but, importuned by the city's Muslims, had stayed on in Calcutta — in Hydari Manzil, a dilapidated Muslim house in the Hindu-majority locality of Beliaghata. Also living in that house, at Gandhi's instance, was Suhrawardy, whose Premiership of Bengal had ended with the province's partition — he had been replaced by Ghosh in West Bengal and Nazimuddin in East Bengal.

Aided by the efforts of Gandhi and Suhrawardy, peace had returned to Calcutta by 15 August. The next day C.R. called on the Mahatma — their first meeting in free India. C.R. took Gandhi's hands in his and held them, neither saying a word.

Then they talked of possible violence and refugees — and also of how the Mahatma could not possibly live in the sort of house that C.R. tenanted. Suhrawardy, who had joined the meeting, said, 'Gandhiji likes to live with the people. He has no fascination for palaces.'

'That's why he was put in the Aga Khan's palace,' said C.R. The Mahatma laughed. The Governor's military secretary noted that after ninety minutes the two old friends simultaneously picked up their large pocket-watches, consulted them, looked at each other, and parted.[2]

In the Punjab, killings were turning gladness to dust. Mercifully, Calcutta seemed to remain peaceful. Towards the end of August, Mountbatten wrote to C.R.: 'You and Gandhiji have achieved miracles in Calcutta.'[3]

Luckily for C.R., Chief Minister Ghosh and his colleagues wanted C.R. to play more than a Governor's merely constitutional role. The Governor was asked to preside over some Cabinet meetings, and the Chief Secretary and other Secretaries called regularly on him with files. These practices no longer obtained in other provinces, and Governors elsewhere who sought similar privileges were told by Patel, the Union Home Minister, that a voluntary decision of the West Bengal Cabinet had conferred exceptional privileges on C.R.

Having been commissioned by Nehru, Patel and the Mahatma to keep the communal peace in West Bengal, C.R. asked military and police chiefs to report regularly to him, advised them and helped ensure support for them. Thus he wrote to Mountbatten: 'I hope you will not draw away any more troops from here. Calcutta is doing well so far, but there are mischief-makers with illicit arms.'[4] Ghosh, a bachelor with a reputation for integrity and an admirer of C.R. from the 1922 Gaya days, did not mind the Governor's activism.

To regard Calcutta's Government House as home required effort. With C.R. were Namagiri and Narasimhan, Thangam and her five children. Yet a full month after moving in he wrote to Burrows: 'I am still trying to familiarise myself with your late residence.'[5] To Colonel Chatterjee, his military secretary and surgeon, C.R. complained about the size of his bedroom: 'It is not convenient for a man of my eyesight to grope about in the darkness in search of a distant switch.'[6]

It was not a home designed to encourage self-reliance. Skilled servants seemed needed at every turn: to shut the massive windows, bring down the huge velvet curtains, remove the heavy embrodiered bedcovers, work the geysers . . . The number of attendants bothered C.R., who wrote to Devadas: 'I feel like living in a cage here with people all round peeping through the bars.'[7]

Some Gandhians wanted to convert the House at once into a hospital or handicraft centre. Calcutta's National Library needed more space; on its behalf some looked covetously at Government House. Cool to the proposals, C.R. pointed out that the question concerned not Calcutta alone but also Government House in New Delhi and Governor's residences in all provincial capitals; it called for thought, not hasty gestures.

Yet the Governor of West Bengal had two additional houses: one in Darjeeling, and another in Barrackpore, twenty miles west of Calcutta on the banks of the Hooghly. At C.R.'s instance, the Barrackpore establishment was handed over to the police.

A Governor's life had its compensations. One childhood ambition he fulfilled was a ride in the engine of a train — the Governor's special train.

On three issues, C.R.'s personal convictions seemed to conflict with what was apparently expected of a Governor. All his life, in line with his ancestors, he had been a vegetarian. His children and grandchildren had followed the tradition. Meat had never been served or cooked under his roof — in Salem, in the Ashram, in Madras, or at 1 Clive Road, New Delhi. Would he allow it now for his guests at Government House? Overcoming a feeling that meat at their table would constitute too drastic an innovation for his family and himself, C.R. gave guests a choice of vegetarian and non-vegetarian food.

But he would not serve alcoholic drinks. Whether foreign or Indian, distinguished, common or radical, his guests had to be teetotal in his presence. 'You see, my house is dry,' C.R. would explain. There were, however, a few occasions when C.R. allowed his staff to assist particularly 'needy' house guests — in their rooms.

Racing was the third issue. In the past, C.R. had opposed it as a form of gambling. But when the British and Indian representatives of the Calcutta Turf pressed that the Governor's Cup should continue and that he should present it himself, C.R. yielded. He was in part influenced by his desire to retain the confidence of the British mercantile community in Calcutta, which ran the Turf.

The Press publicized C.R.'s presentation of the Cup. From

Poona, the Gandhian, Valji Desai, wrote protesting that Rajaji was 'making our independence ugly' by lending his prestige to racing. Though C.R. argued that 'the presentation of a prize to the owner or trainer of a horse which wins' was like giving medals to 'boys who come first in a university examination,' he was not really sure of his stand. 'I may be even wrong with regard to horses,' he said to Desai.[8]

While C.R. relied upon the deterrent effect of soldiers to maintain communal peace, he also strove to spread a philosophy of non-retaliation. To Liaqat Ali Khan, now Premier of Pakistan, who in a letter to C.R. had deplored 'the situation in East Punjab,' C.R. wrote of 'the vanity of retaliation and the worthlessness of hatred.' He sent a similar text to Baldev Singh, who had underlined the West Punjab killings. 'Retaliation,' C.R. said, would 'only mean a steady increase in difficulties.'[9]

He praised Bengal's Press for displaying restraint, which, C.R. conceded, was never easy: 'A man is usually fonder of his opinion than even of his child.' When one of Calcutta's Muslim newspapers, *Morning News*, wrote a constructive leader, the Governor sent the editor a warm note: 'It gave me great pleasure to read your editorial. This is to express my appreciation.'

In a speech to Calcutta's Muslim Chamber of Commerce, C.R. made a personal pledge:

> Whatever may be my defects or lapses, let me assure you that I shall never disfigure my life with any deliberate acts of injustice to any community whatsoever.[10]

Within three weeks of Independence, however, Calcutta saw a setback, and Gandhi responded with a fast. Several Muslims had been slain in the city, and an angry crowd of Hindus had hurled abuse, a brick and a lathi at him. The Mahatma was accused of overlooking what Hindus had suffered.

The brick and the lathi missed him, but Gandhi declared that until sanity returned to Calcutta he would eat or drink nothing save water — with, if necessary, some drops of sour lime juice to counter nausea.

For three hours C.R. argued with the Mahatma against the fast. When Gandhi said he wished to be 'wholly in God's hands,' C.R. asked, 'Why the provision then about sour lime?' The Mahatma said he would do without it.[11] In the end C.R. found himself with a familiar task — persuading the public to create conditions for Gandhi to break his fast.

'This time,' C.R. said, 'we can throw the blame on no outside or foreign government if his precious life ebbs away.' Calcutta, he pleaded, should send Gandhi 'with the laurel of victory round his aged brow' to the Punjab, which needed him (*The Statesman*, 2.9.47).

Addressing policemen, soldiers and officials, the Governor, who shuttled between disturbed areas and enforcers of the law, said:

> It is your sacred duty to protect the person, property, and the honour of everyone. You should strike down the offender even though he belongs to your own community. If you betray any communal partiality, it will break even my stony heart, not to speak of him who is crucifying himself for our sake in Beliaghata (*The Statesman*, 5.9.47).

Five hundred policemen in North Calcutta, including some British and Anglo-Indian officers, fasted for 24 hours in sympathy with Gandhi, while remaining on duty. On the evening of 5 September, C.R., Chief Minister Ghosh, Kripalani, the Congress President, and Suhrawardy told Gandhi that peace had returned. Brought by Ram Manohar Lohia, the Socialist leader, five young men entered Gandhi's room, confessed their complicity and surrendered arms.

Two Bengali leaders of the Hindu Mahasabha, a Muslim, a Punjabi Hindu and a Sikh signed an undertaking that C.R. dictated. At 9.15 p.m. that evening, Gandhi broke his fast, drinking from a glass of lime juice offered by Suhrawardy.

In C.R.'s evaluation, nothing that Gandhi had achieved, 'not even independence,' was 'so truly wonderful as his victory over evil in Calcuta.' Gandhi had 'been the successful one-man Boundary Force in Bengal, when forces numbering 50,000 have failed elsewhere' (*The Statesman*, 6.9.47).

Obtaining his laurel, Gandhi left for Delhi en route to the Punjab, where communal killings had reached fiendish proportions.

C.R. felt that 'India has gone back three centuries to reach independence.'[12] In a letter to C.R., Nehru wrote from Delhi:

> There is indecency abroad. All grace, pity and standards of behaviour have vanished. The best of us are affected by this prevailing mania . . . There is something elemental about this phenomenon, something in the nature of a Greek tragedy . . . Many people criticise me. We are living in a war atmosphere and the only thing permitted . . . is to curse the enemy and to cover up one's own errors and sins . . . Fortunately for us Gandhiji has been here like a tower of light and a rock of strength. (9.10.47)

Moved by Nehru's spirit, C.R. returned encouragement and a tribute:

> I agree with every word of what you have written . . . You are great and are doing your best. Be courageous and do not yield to that against which your inner spirit protests . . . Is it not wonderful that Gandhiji has been spared for us all during this great crisis? (18.10.47)

A distant event now affected C.R.'s fortunes. The heir to the British throne, Princess Elizabeth, was getting married to Philip, nephew to Mountbatten. The latter was attending the London wedding, and an acting Governor-General was required in New Delhi. Mountbatten, Nehru and Patel discussed possible candidates, and it became 'absolutely clear' — Mountbatten would afterwards recall — 'that the only possible choice was Rajaji.' By stature if not by seniority, he was the most eminent among the Governors. The Mahatma was consulted; his reaction to C.R.'s name 'was entirely favourable.'[13] After C.R.'s agreement was obtained, it was announced that he would function as Governor-General from 10 to 24 November.

Accompanied by Namagiri, C.R. arrived in Delhi on 9 November by an IAF Dakota. At ten the next morning he was sworn in by the Chief Justice of the Federal Court, Hiralal

Kania. In the evening he called on Gandhi, who was living as the guest of Ghanshyamdas Birla at Birla House, his Punjab visit put off because of Delhi's troubled state.

During the two-week tenure, Ministers, diplomats, politicians and officials called on C.R. As acting head of state, he launched the Constituent Assembly's first session as the provisional Parliament.

On the evening of 20 November C.R. threw a party to mark the royal wedding that was taking place in London. This was a splendid affair, with Nehru, Patel, the rest of the Cabinet, and the diplomatic corps present, and the Ballroom decorated with the Union Jack and the Tricolour.

But the high point had come earlier that afternoon — when Gandhi called on C.R. at Government House. Over the years the Mahatma had visited Government House often enough — to sign his pact with Irwin and talk with Linlithgow, Wavell and Mountbatten. But this was the first and last occasion when an Indian head of state was receiving him.

C.R. had wanted to welcome his old chief, and relation, in his latest temporary home, and Gandhi too was curious to see how his independent-minded disciple looked in his role as a successor in the line of Warren Hastings. When C.R. called on him at noon on the 20th, the Mahatma asked if he could drop in at Government House to see Sarojini Naidu, the UP Governor, who was convalescing there, and then spend some minutes with the Governor-General.

C.R.: 'Of course. When?'

G.: 'At 2.30 p.m. today?' The Governor-General showered the Mahatma with rose petals when he turned up with his entourage at the South Court entrance. The two spent half-an-hour with Mrs Naidu and then walked to a drawing room where they sat on a sofa and chatted for another thirty minutes.

C.R.: 'Will you try an idli?'

G.: 'Idli? In Gujarat the sambandhi offers sweets.'[14]

C.R. was with the Mahatma seven times during his sixteen-day spell in Delhi. The final meeting, lasting an hour, took place just before C.R. left on 26 November for Calcutta, where he uttered prophetic sentences:

I saw Gandhiji just before I got into the plane . . . He is sad beyond words. It is not an exaggeration to say that in his own way he is suffering as Christ suffered on the eve of the great tragedy recorded in the Gospels (*Amrita Bazar Patrika*, 29.11.47).

On 13. January Gandhi started yet another fast. His aim, the Mahatma said, was communal peace in Delhi and justice for minorities in India and Pakistan. C.R., who had protested against every fast thus far by Gandhi, did not argue against this one. Asking for prayers in temples, mosques, churches and synagogues throughout Bengal, he added:

The only sane man today is Gandhi. I have wrangled with Gandhiji on similar occasions in the past. But this time I confess I am not inclined to wrangle (*The Statesman*, 15.1.48).

On the fourth day of Gandhi's fast, C.R., wearing a turban to respect Sikh custom, spoke at a Calcutta gurdwara:

Gandhiji has become insolvent because he has taken upon himself all the debts of our people. Today he has gone to a great banker, God, in order to repay the money (*The Statesman*, 17.1.48).

Leaders and citizens in Delhi met Gandhi's conditions, as did the Indian Cabinet. He ended the fast on 18 January. 'Death draws back,' wrote *The Statesman*. 'No longer creeps it closer, hourly, to a great man, frail and aged.'

Writing to the Mahatma, a relieved C.R. said: 'I was speaking to you without speaking.' Replied Gandhi (21.1.48): 'Of course you were right in speaking to me through your silence . . . From calm I have entered storm . . . I observe you have lighted upon the fittest job for you.' The Mahatma had written his last letter to C.R.

C.R. was about to enter his car for a function in Calcutta when Singaravelu, an ADC, shouted that the Press Trust of India (PTI) had just phoned to say that Gandhi had been assassinated.

Mountbatten confirmed the news over the phone. To PTI C.R. offered three sentences:

> We have been robbed of our greatest possession by a senseless lunatic. May God help India in this hour of her greatest distress. May all hatred, all suspicion end with this sacrifice of our dearest leader.

His plane for Delhi the next morning was delayed several hours by fog. By the time it touched down, most of Delhi was at Rajghat. Tears flooded down C.R.'s face as he embraced his daughter Lakshmi — the Mahatma's daughter-in-law —, who met him at the airport. By the time C.R. reached Rajghat, flames had enveloped Gandhi's body. Around the flames C.R. met Nehru, Vallabhbhai, Azad and Sarojini Naidu, comrades bereaved like him. As he was to recall subsequently, 'We could do nothing but clasp one another in our arms and weep.'

Carrying an earthenware pot which contained a portion of Gandhi's ashes, C.R. returned to Calcutta on 4 February. On the ride from the airport to Government House he 'held on lovingly to the urn.' On his instructions the ashes were kept near his study and guarded over the next eight days by a relay of sentries.[15]

During C.R.'s absence, a letter from Pyarelal, Gandhi's secretary, had arrived. Posted in Delhi on 29 January, it said, 'Bapu is O.K. in every respect.' On 5 February C.R. made one of his most memorable speeches:

> Mahatmaji was very dear to me, but I do not grieve for him. No man can find a death so glorious. He was walking to join and lead a prayer . . . He was a few minutes late and so he was walking fast . . . How many of you would not like to die when running to pray?

> Mahatmaji did not die in bed, he did not call for hot water or doctor or nurses. He did not die mumbling incoherent words in sickness, unable to identify the relatives and friends around him. He died standing, not even sitting down. The man who did him to death emptied a bullet into his belly and two into his chest, so that the pain lasted only one moment. He made up for his lost five minutes by going straightaway to his Ram.

He was a friend and lover of all the men and women he met. Indeed he was like Krishna and Krishna died when a hunter's arrow pierced and sucked his life away. So also our Krishna has died.

On 12 February, standing on a barge in the sacred Ganga at Barrackpore, C.R. emptied the urn into the river. Watched by a million men and women gathered on the embankment or filling countless steam launches, motor boats and country craft, C.R. seemed to sway perilously; Chatterjee and Singaravelu held him. 'The ashes were pulling me,' C.R. later said.[16]

The Gandhi-C.R. relationship is one of the romances of the freedom movement. With the exaggeration that is often a symptom of love, C.R. would claim that he had 'admired and loved [Gandhi] throughout twenty-eight rich years of intimate joint labour as never man admired and loved another' (*Harijan*, 30.1.49). It was a love that could overcome the pang of a sharp difference and the guilt of a disloyalty. With the Mahatma's going a part of C.R.'s life had ended. On the night of 12 February, C.R. spoke over the radio:

So it is all over! The world feels so empty! Dreadfully empty! Devotion made us see Bapu in the ashes. But the solemn wisdom of our ancestors called us to consign the ashes to the elements . . .

Do not demand love. Begin to love and you will be loved. This is the law and no statute can alter it. If we do not follow the law, and let the law die with the teacher, we shall indeed become accomplices to the murderer. But if we follow the law with our hearts, [Bapu] will live in us and through us.[17]

Patel, the Home Minister, and Premier Nehru were criticized for not protecting Gandhi's life. C.R. powerfully defended them:

Have there not been scores of occasions when he was in the greatest of danger during these 40 years, in South Africa and India? Did the Government of India protect his life? During the last few years did not the greatest anger and highest passion develop like a storm, and did he not live? Did the

Government of India protect him? Is it not idiotic to blame the Government of India because God has taken him away?[18]

The physician-politician, Dr Bidhan Chandra Roy, had replaced Ghosh as Chief Minister in January. With Roy's installation, C.R.'s 'special' role ended and secretaries stopped bringing files to him: Bengal had fallen in line with the rest of the country. The communal troubles that had necessitated an exceptional role from C.R. were over, and in any case Roy, surer than Ghosh of his political base, did not feel that he needed to lean on the Governor.

A Governor in Calcutta can feel the pulse of some of India's neighbours. The Nepalese Premier, Sir Padma Shumshere Rana, called on C.R., and the Burmese Foreign Minister, U Tin Tut, was C.R.'s house-guest more than once, as was Khwaja Nazimuddin, Premier of East Pakistan.

Also in the stream of guests and callers at Calcutta's Government House were Eamon de Valera, President of Eire, M. Visvesvaraya, Mysore's modernizer, C.V. Raman, the Nobel laureate, and the Mountbattens.

In a speech after the dinner given by C.R. in his honour, Mountbatten recalled that his engagement to Edwina had taken place in India — in 1922 in Room 13 of the Viceregal Lodge in Simla. Replying, C.R. said, 'I asked myself where I was at that time. The answer was, in Room 65 — of Vellore Jail.'[19]

Almost every speech by C.R. had quotable phrases — wise, pithy, epigrammatic and original.

To girls in a school: 'Do not depend on powder and rouge, depend upon your laughter. It will improve your beauty and character.'

To Anglo-Indians: 'In a sense every modernized Indian is an Anglo-Indian. If you speak Bengali with the proper intonation, Bengalis would hug you.'

On the communal killings, to students of Calcutta University: 'May the blood that flowed from Gandhiji's wounds and the tears that flowed from the eyes of the women of India serve to lay the curse of 1947, and may the grisly tragedy of that year sleep in history.'

On Vande Mataram versus Jana Gana Mana as the national anthem (his own preference was for the former, the song that had spelt freedom when he was young): 'If Rabindranath and Bankimchandra had come down here today, they would have shaken hands, but disciples are more fanatical than gurus.'

On Partition: 'By reason of the partition of the province there is a great deal of loss, but there is also some profit. You cannot get a Hindu-majority government for Bengal except by partition. If you do not want partition you must have the courage to accept a government run by the Muslim majority.'

And there were the parables: 'Those claiming special rights as they had made sacrifices for freedom are like cooks who say that they have sweated near the fire and will therefore eat all the food themselves. The dishes of independence are for the enjoyment of everybody.'

On American-Soviet relations, in the presence of Henry Grady, the US ambassador: 'Let us hope that the caustic soda of Russia and the oil of America will one day mix and give the world the soap she requires.'

On being addressed as Dr Rajagopalachari: 'Some universities have been good enough to confer on me *honoris causa* degrees . . . A mother has the liberty to call her child a good boy. But that does not mean that others should also call him a good boy. Please address me as Mr or Shri Rajagopalachari.'[20]

Driving down to a soccer game on the Maidan (the roars of its crowds were heard in his study), he asked Chatterjee, 'Do they play football or bootball here?'[21] He was alluding to the players' transition from bare feet to shoes.

On 1 April a courier brought a letter from Nehru:

> You know that Lord Mountbatten is leaving his office about the 22nd June. We have to find a successor for him, and inevitably our eyes turn to you . . . I hope you will agree. Your presence in Delhi will be a great help to all of us, and especially to me. (30.3.48)

It was obvious that the name of C.R. would occur to anyone thinking of a replacement for Mountbatten (who, it was known, wanted to rejoin the Admiralty), if not as the only name, then as one on a short list. Rajendra Prasad, President of the Constituent Assembly, and Sarojini Naidu, Governor of the UP, were also possible successors. Still, while C.R. was doubtless delighted by the invitation, it did not astonish him. To Jawaharlal he wrote:

> It is very pleasant to be told . . . that my presence at Delhi will be of great help to you all. The proposal has been threatening to come for some time past . . . I should like to have a few days to think it over.

C.R. added that it had often occurred to him to return to Madras, 'which you know I intensely love,' as 'a private citizen and be of some help as an elder.' (2.4.48)

Nehru pressed. Making explicit what he had implied in the first letter, he said that Patel and he were united in their desire to have him. And on 11 April he wrote:

> I am waiting for your reply . . . We want you here to help us in many ways. The burden on some of us is more than we can carry.

'The language of your communications leaves me no room to resist,' C.R. replied (15.4.48). Thanking Jawaharlal 'for the honour' and 'for the confidence,' he added, 'I hope I shall be of some help in spite of my misgivings.'

Behind C.R.'s misgivings were several factors. One, simply, was his modesty. While he was ready, in a sense, for anything, it had never been his belief that nature or destiny had constructed him for the country's highest office. Secondly, a Governor-General's position had considerable responsibility but not much power. Thirdly, Nehru and Patel were likely on occasion to have conflicting expectations of him.

What overrode the doubts, apart from the distinction of what had been offered, was the plea that he was needed. Confirming Nehru's word, Patel wrote: 'You would be of great help to us . . . After Bapu's death it is all the more essential that the remnant of his circle should pull its weight together and the counsels of each should be available to all.' Though confessing to Patel his 'serious doubts,' C.R. added that he did not mind 'being compelled to undergo the ordeal of Government House in New Delhi' if 'I can be of any use to you and Jawaharlalji' (4.5.48).

In perspective, of course, the idea that he would become free India's first Indian head and, simultaneously, a successor in the line of Governors-General was more than startling to C.R. He smiled at fate's latest turn. 'It is very funny,' he wrote in answer to a congratulatory letter, 'how I have been knocked about from place to place without my wanting it.'[22]

The replacement of a dashing young white Admiral by a bald old teetotaller with a stick and a stoop, a brown face and an affinity with Gandhi made news the world over. *The Times* of London thought that C.R. would 'carry on the work of his old friend Mahatma Gandhi.' 'There is nobody in India today,' observed *The Statesman*, 'who seems so directly heir to Mahatma Gandhi's wisdom as the first Indian Governor-General-to-be.'

Some commentators suggested that Hindu-Muslim and India-Pakistan relations stood to gain by his choice. The *Hindusthan Standard* said that 'men of all communities find it easy to repose their trust in him,' and *The Times* wrote of 'the respect he enjoys in Pakistan as well as in India.' 'People in Pakistan,' said the *Pakistan Times*, 'will welcome Rajaji's appointment because in C.R. India will have a shrewd, level-headed and non-communal leader.'

Kingsley Martin wrote in the *New Statesman*: 'Over a wide field he is the wisest and most level-headed person in India.' The *Louisville Courier-Journal* thought that C.R.'s 'humility, kindliness and generosity' might help 'offset the excess sophistication of the world of power.' The *News Chronicle* decided that 'the world will be a better place for his presence in one of the seats of power.'

London's *Daily Express* predicted that there would be 'no more cocktail parties' at New Delhi's Government House and the *Daily Graphic*, also of London, termed C.R. 'a violent prohibitionist.' Sub-editors, the world over, struggled with the spelling and length of C.R.'s name and were grateful for the initials and for 'Rajaji.'

Jinnah cabled his 'warm congratulations' and Prime Minister Liaqat Ali wrote them out by hand. Letters came from those who had been with C.R. in school or college. One was from Abdul Rahim, 'a citizen of Hosur, a schoolmate, not a classmate, Your Excellency, in the old tiled building which exists even today.' In his reply, C.R. welcomed 'a loving voice from the old days when I was less known and more happy.'

Ex-Governor Erskine and British officers who had served under C.R. in Madras sent enthusiastic letters. City councils all across the South passed resolutions of happiness. Opponents of 1946 joined in praise. C.R. was described as 'the greatest Indian administrator' and as having the 'keenest vision and greatest foresight.'

An old friend, T.S.S. Rajan, once again a member of the Madras Cabinet, wrote to C.R. that 'as the foremost Indian living today' he deserved the honour. And from Bangalore Rama Rao wrote: 'You will, God grant, live in history by the side of your immortal friend, the Mahatma.' Patiently C.R. answered the large congratulatory mail.[23]

With his ten-month term, commenced when the odds were not favourable, C.R. had succeeded in winning Bengal's affection. His talks and parables had gone down well. He was not a Nehru or a Subhas with the crowds, but numerous intelligent audiences had taken to him. His accessibility and the tidy simplicity shown in his manner and dress left a mark, and his intellect and frankness impressed the bhadralok.

His role over communal relations was widely admired. *Amrita Bazar Patrika* wrote (6.5.48): 'Rajaji's initiative in the maintenance of communal peace will long be remembered by the people here.' According to the Muslim-owned *Morning News* (5.5.48), C.R.'s 'earnest moving appeals . . . finally stirred the conscience that had sunk to its lowest depths.'

As unabashed a Hindu as he was a defender of Muslim rights, not hesitating to refer to 'our ancient wisdom,' C.R. also appealed to Bengal's conservative elements, who took note of C.R.'s regard for Bengal's past. This regard was disclosed when C.R. eagerly glimpsed, from a train window, the birthplace of

Bankim, and when he stood, quite moved, in Ramakrishna's room. Of Ramakrishna he said, 'He was the Upanishads and the Bhagavad Gita in flesh and blood.'

The *Patrika* made the valid criticism that C.R. spoke more of 'the rose of Bengal's cultural happiness' and less of 'the thorns of many material unhappinesses.' Yet C.R. had touched the Bengali heart, including the heart of Sarat Bose. 'Rajaji has been a good Governor,' Bose told Prafulla Ghosh.[24]

Observers noted that C.R. had become what he had not been since his 1942 deviation from the Congress line — popular. Visiting Calcutta with Mountbatten, the latter's press attaché, Alan Campbell-Johnson, wrote of Rajaji, 'His popularity today is good to see.'[25] 'Rajagopalachari Go Back!' was not heard again after his first day in Calcutta. 'The wise Rajaji' increasingly became Bengal's appellation, until the time came for his departure, when the *Patrika* headlined its editorial, 'Our Rajaji.'

Bengal's attitude greatly moved C.R. In sweeping yet heartfelt sentences he gave expression to his feelings. Referring to 'the honey that I found in Bengal,' he said:

> Truly I say that barring the period of childhood, these ten months amidst the people of Bengal have been the happiest period of my life. All the travail and dreariness of years were forgotten in the affection I found here, in me for the men and women of this place, and in them for me.[26]

Doubtless contributing to the contentment he felt were the peace, security and comfort of a Governor's life. Though he rebelled against aspects of these, the fact remained that for the first time in nearly thirty years his and — much more importantly — his family's wants were fully met, and he was saved from involvement in political controversy.

Before leaving Calcutta, C.R. made two pronouncements on a Governor-General's role:

> He will have to cultivate good feelings between party and party, class and class, between Ministers who govern . . . and the [political] minorities who are governed, between Ministers on the one hand and the permanent servants on the other.[27]

The second remark pertained to the Governor-General's power, to which someone had referred, to take over the State in an emergency:

> May God save me from such an emergency, which would mean a serious calamity. I would ask you not to think on these lines.[28]

At a farewell occasion, he said:

> Please see how, without any great effort, I have succeeded in conquering the hearts of the people assembled here. Copy me, do not praise me. I have done nothing for the poor people of Calcutta or Bengal. But they have appreciated my feelings towards them.[29]

The Government House staff gave him a pair of sandals. 'I shall value it more than a silver casket or a gold trinket,' C.R. said. 'It will not be necessary for me to find a place to keep your present. I will wear it.' The Governor said he felt that the staff he was leaving behind was 'a large family connected by blood with me,' and added, 'Whenever you do any wrong, think that I am near you to see it.'[30]

18

Palace

1948-50

From the end of 1929, New Delhi's Government House had been home and headquarters to the men ruling India on the King-Emperor's behalf — the Lords Irwin, Willingdon, Linlithgow, Wavell, and Mountbatten. The great Edwin Lutyens had chosen the House's location. He designed this five-acre building of red and white sandstone and marble of many hues which had a mile and a half of corridors and 340 rooms. The Mughal Gardens, spread over 15 ½ acres and including the sunken Purdah Bagh, were positioned to capture the setting sun. In the Durbar Hall, the Banquet Hall and the Ball Room, the jewels, coronets and tiaras of many Indian princes and of five Viceroys and Vicereines had glittered under crystal chandeliers.

Now this was going to be the home of one whose father had once known, and prized, a monthly salary of five rupees, and who himself had once toyed with the idea of using bullets and the bomb for ending British rule. That rule had ended, but India was a Dominion and C.R. would enter Government House as the King's representative!

It was an irony that flowed over from fable to real life. C.R. imagined himself 'shaking hands with Warren Hastings across the ages and saying, "You were the first and I am the last" ' (*The Statesman*, 9.6.48).

A drizzle that ended a scorching spell in Delhi greeted

C.R.'s plane from Calcutta. Mountbatten, Nehru, Vallabhbhai and other Ministers and the military chiefs (who were all British still) were at the airport. In complete silence C.R. took a salute. Accompanied by Jawaharlal, C.R. rode to Government House, where picturesque bodyguards flanked a red carpet laid along the grand staircase leading to the Durbar Hall.

In the evening the Mountbattens gave their last reception, an immense affair with nearly 6,000 guests. Most wanted to meet C.R., who commented later: 'I saw many new faces but they seemed to know me for ages. I met people who volunteered to assist me in whatever way they could and I got plenty of advice gratis.'[1]

At night Mountbatten and he had a tête-à-tête. The two agreed with each other that Pakistan's eastern wing might secede in 25 years or so. (When Bangladesh became independent in 1972, the accurate joint prognostication was publicly recalled by Mountbatten).

The next day, 21 June, C.R. was installed in the brightly lit Durbar Hall as India's head. His white khadi contrasted well with the red of the throne, and the new Governor-General's blue standard, containing three Asoka lions atop a circular C., and an R within the C, was displayed beside the national flag.

In a brief address, C.R. noted that for the first time a son of the soil had been 'entrusted with the honour and duty of the Head of State.' He praised Mountbatten for his energy, asked to be judged himself by standards 'suitable for one inexperienced in arms or diplomacy,' and prayed that he would 'steer clear of error' (*Hindustan Times*, 22.6.48).

After the ceremony he gave a reception in the Long Room; the Prime Minister called on him, as did the Agent-General of Hyderabad, which the Nizam was trying to turn into an independent state; the Mountbattens left that day and there was a banquet by C.R. at night; he was launched.

He had to get to know and prune his new possessions. Two houses on the Governor-General's grounds, in the past residences for senior members of the staff, became homes of Ministers; the

Prime Minister's secretariat and the archaeological museum were found additional space in Government House; a forest near Dehra Dun where the Viceroy and his guests used to hunt privately was turned into a sanctuary; the Governor-General's band was wound up; and corn and vegetables were sown on the estate.

Occasionally, C.R. swung a tennis racket on one of the House's grass courts, his shawl tied round the dhoti as a belt; though he never stepped into the estate's pool, he had some sessions at the billiard table; and he shocked some by rifle-shooting at the range where his bodyguard practised. After asking the commandant 'to feed the weapon and make it live,' he 'held the rifle like an expert' and fired four times. In Chatterjee's opinion, the Governor-General's performance, 'taking all factors into account, was creditable.'[2]

Shankar, the cartoonist, sketched several amusing attires for the new Governor-General's consideration, and Louis Fischer also joked with C.R. about the latter discarding khadi and 'donning a military uniform with gold epaulettes.'[3]

He saw a great variety: masses at his 15 August reception; petitioners and memorialists; friends of his youth; comrades of his 1930 salt march; rulers of other lands and politicians of his own; Governors of provinces and diplomats posted to Delhi. K.P.S. Menon, foreign secretary at the time, recorded:

> All the heads of missions were . . . almost overcome by Rajaji's charm. This was the more surprising because his predecessor and his wife were known as perfect charmers . . . Rajaji almost eclipsed them in the quality of grace.

> The contrast between him and his diplomatic guests was startling. They would be dressed up in uniform, with gold braids, medals and decorations; and he would be in his dhoti and shirt, spotlessly white and clean. Rajaji, as it were, stripped the diplomatic guests of their uniform and saw right through them, without causing them the slightest embarrassment . . . And they responded warmly. They felt they were . . . in the presence of . . . a nice, wise old man who had somehow strayed onto the Governor-General's throne.[4]

Once when addressed as 'Your Excellency' by Novikov, the Soviet ambassador, C.R. responded, with mischief in his eyes,

'But I thought you in Russia had discontinued the use of all titles.' 'Yes, Your Excellency,' the diplomat replied, 'but that was at the start of the revolution. Then we realized it was a mistake.' 'What?' C.R. innocently exclaimed. 'The start of the revolution was a mistake?' Even the Russian could not repress a smile.[5]

At a tea-party on the central lawn, when C.R. looked up to see a flight of green parrots sweeping across the sky, a guest asked whether the birds lived close by. C.R.'s reply was recorded by Chatterjee:

> I am not sure of their address, but every morning they fly towards Palam, and return about this time. See their punctualilty, the precision of flight formation, the speed, manoeuvrability in the air, and the obedience to the leader . . . These birds never collide or crash . . . But you should see them descending on a maize field. They bring themselves to a sudden halt and park themselves softly on the plants, almost hugging the mature corns.

The eloquence was formidable, and the guest asked the Governor-General if he was a birdwatcher. 'I am a manwatcher,' replied C.R., 'but they come to my cornfields and my routine coincides with theirs.'[6]

To encourage resourcefulness against the grain shortage, C.R. had some of his acreage converted into cornfields. Some feared that the beautiful lawns and gardens were being disfigured. The anxiety was ill-informed: the House's gardens were at a safe distance from its fine crop of corn. C.R.'s feelings for his grounds' flowers are preserved in a letter he wrote to Rama Rao at the end of March 1949:

> The garden is dying. The best part of the spring and the dappled glory of the flower beds is gone. I never before possessed this wealth of flowers but now that I had it for a time I feel sad when I see the little things fade and wither before their harsh father the sun.

Manga had been dead for 33 years. She who had been spared C.R.'s prison-going had also missed his entry into the palace. There was only one small group photograph in which she could be seen. C.R. had her face lifted out and enlarged. The young woman of 26 — he was old and would grow much older but Manga would always be young — joined him on the first floor of Government House, looking at Namagiri from a wall of the bedroom of the Viceroy and the Vicereine.

C.R. had asked his daughter — the House's hostess — to take that chamber. Across a corridor was the bedroom he chose for himself — a small room used earlier by the Vicereine's lady-in-waiting. Rajaji had two portraits put up in it, one of Ramakrishna and the other of the Mahatma.

He picked up classics from the House's library, consulted journals, loved to study maps, enjoyed spotting errors of language. In between interviews he was apt to open an encyclopaedia. Week by week he would send *Country Life*, inherited from his predecessors, to British friends living in India. 'It has interesting articles about birds,' he said once to Horace Alexander, the Quaker, 'and every number has the portrait of a beautiful young lady for the frontispiece. It is none the worse for that.'[7]

Theoretically, Britain had given the rulers of the Indian princely states freedom to join India or Pakistan or claim independence, but Mountbatten had warned them that the last option was not realistic. Even so the Nizam of Hyderabad, ruling the biggest of all the princely states, sought independence. Shortly before the British left the subcontinent, he had tried in vain to enlist their help in acquiring Goa from the Portuguese: he desired access to the sea.

Hindus in Hyderabad, who comprised the great majority, became restive both at the Nizam's unwillingness to join India and at his encouragement of the Razakars, militant Muslims aiming at a sovereign, Muslim-ruled state.

From the day he assumed office, C.R. tried to help resolve the question diplomatically, using as a channel an old friend, Sir Mirza Ismail, who had been the Nizam's Dewan or Premier. Recalling that as chancellor of Osmania University the Nizam had conferred a doctorate on him in 1944, C.R. offered, in a message to the Nizam, 'to do all in my power to help a peaceful settlement.' On his part the Nizam had requested C.R.'s 'personal contribution' to make matters easier.

In New Delhi's view, wholly shared by C.R., peace was dependent on a ban on the Razakars and the presence in Hyderabad of some Indian troops. In courteous but firm language, C.R. put forth these demands to the Nizam, adding the promise that 'in any political solution Your Exalted Highness's prestige and position will be safeguarded.'

Turning down the suggestion for banning the Razakars, the Nizam also said that 'allowing Indian troops to remain in my territory is out of the question.'[8] A version of what happened thereafter has been provided by V.P. Menon, secretary in the States Ministry at the time:

> The Governments of the neighbouring provinces were much concerned . . . about the activities of the Razakars and the refugees who were leaving the state . . . The States Ministry pressed their view that we should occupy Hyderabad and put a stop to the chaos there.

> The Prime Minister was strongly opposed, and he was very critical of the attitude of the States Ministry. Sardar left the meeting in the middle. The same afternoon the Governor-General, C. Rajagopalachari, called a meeting in his room of the Prime Minister, Sardar Patel and myself. It was then decided that we should occupy Hyderabad.[9]

A letter from C.R. conveyed a thinly disguised ultimatum: inaction by the Nizam would 'force the Government of India to act on their own initiative.' The message was repeated in a telegram signed by C.R., sent on 12 September: 'I still hope Your Exalted Highness will not disregard my advice.'

Shortly before dawn the next morning, Indian soldiers crossed Hyderabad's boundaries. In four days the Nizam surrendered, banned the Razakars, welcomed the troops and pleaded with C.R. for honourable treatment. By this time the Nizam had lost several hundred Razakars and state soldiers; the Indian army lost ten men.

The Nizam was told that he could remain Hyderabad's constitutional head and retain most of his privileges, but executive rule would be in the hands of a military governor until the time was ripe for an elected set-up.

If the swift completion of the movement gratified C.R., he was equally pleased by the communal peace that prevailed all over India during the action. To him the latter was 'a second miracle,' comparable to what the Mahatma had achieved in Calcutta a year earlier. At a thanksgiving service at Jama Masjid, where over 20,000 were present, C.R. spoke frankly about 'the gangsters in Hyderabad' who had 'forced the Nizam' into folly (*Hindustan Times*, 27.9.48).

C.R.'s active role over Hyderabad, exceeding the scope of a constitutional head of state, was a product of the peculiar Nehru-Patel-C.R. relationship. C.R.'s views, and not just his signature, mattered to Jawaharlal and Vallabhbhai. Moreover, disagreement between the two sometimes necessitated intervention by C.R., who was trusted by both. The Hyderabad episode was probably one of the things Patel had in mind when a few months later he said about C.R.:

> He knows how a constitutional Governor-General has to behave and he knows how to keep within limits and yet how to break the limits (*Hindustan Times*, 23.2.49).

Meanwhile the man C.R. had tried hard and for long to conciliate, the Quaid-i-Azam, had died in Karachi, following a heart attack. To his sister Fatima, a loyal presence always at Jinnah's side, C.R. wrote:

> Dear Sister, My deepest sympathy and the sympathy of all my people and my Government to you and your people (*Hindustan Times*, 13.9.48).

Coveting 'first-hand knowledge of every shade of opinion,' including of those unable to 'afford a pilgrimage to Delhi,'[10] he travelled as often as possible. If visiting a familiar place, he ran the risk, in his words, of inviting the anger of friends 'because I have not shaken hands with them, or gone to their homes, or looked at them and smiled.'

However, from a car in Bangalore he recognized, in a knot of onlookers, 'Lame' Rajan who had cooked for him three decades earlier in Salem. After thrusting a hundred-rupee note into the cook's hand, C.R. had him driven home in an official car. And when Guruswami the cobbler rushed at the Governor-General's car in Madras and security men caught hold of him, Rajaji said, 'Don't meddle with him. He makes fine chappals.'[11]

Gandhi's death was on many minds, and everywhere C.R. was asked to open a college or hospital in the Mahatma's name or to unveil a Gandhi portrait or statue. He found it hard to do the latter: his grief was fresh and the likenesses were seldom good. But Gandhi was one of his incessant themes.

> He was like a rocket which went up in a blaze and disappeared in the sky. It did not come down to die. It died at its highest illumination . . . Let us try as far as we can to keep his memory not in marble or plaster or bronze but in the tissue of our hearts.[12]

He had not lost his skill with images. English was 'the airline all over India,' providing 'immediate means of communication at higher levels.' Correcting the educational system was 'like trying to repair a railway train while it is in motion.' It was not possible to 'close all schools and think quietly for a year.'[13]

Walking with the Governor-General in Simla, T.V. Parasuram from the Press Trust of India observed, 'Isn't Simla beautiful?' 'Yes,' agreed C.R., adding, 'Have you seen Ooty?'[14] He was not going to lose his pride in the South.

Repeatedly he claimed ordinariness for himself, and drew attention to his lack of powers. For example:

> I have no powers. All the powers I exercise are exercised strictly on the advice of Ministers. I stand before you . . . as an unworthy symbol of a great thing . . . Nobody taught me how to behave if I should be made Governor-General.

Close to the humility in C.R.'s blood was his Hinduism:

> There is no country which can be governed more easily than India. You have only to appeal to tradition . . . I am not the Governor-General. Sri Ram is . . . Thank you for your address to me. I shall place it at Ram's feet.[15]

He offered his view on the springs of great art:

> Could any man on earth conceive the dance of Siva if he did
> not see God behind all the diversities in this world? Could
> anyone paint the Ajanta frescoes if he did not believe with all
> the strength of his soul in love and compassion? Could anyone
> have given us the Taj unless he loved as greatly as Shahjahan
> did? (*Hindustan Times*, 7.11.48)

Was the Governor-General's salary of Rs 20,000 a month
consistent with the norms C.R. and the Congress had espoused
over the years? Nehru explained to the AICC that taxes removed
Rs 13,000 from the salary and that out of the remaining Rs 7,000
'the Governor-General had to meet certain necessary expenses,
whether he liked it or not.' All the same, as Nehru informed the
AICC, C.R. felt that the Rs 20,000 figure was too high. The
Cabinet decided that from January 1949 he should get Rs 5,500
a month tax-free, which was the salary the draft Constitution
had fixed for the President of the contemplated Republic.[16]

Jawaharlal, Vallabhbhai and C.R. constituted an impressive
trio, yet some foreign observers wondered whether Indian
democracy would last. Attlee, the British Premier, who had
visited India in 1928, wrote to Nehru in March 1949:

> At the moment with statesmen such as yourself, Sardar Patel
> and Rajagopalachari in the leading positions, the danger of
> dictatorship may be remote, but it might arise in a great
> subcontinent like India.[17]

To C.R., the key to India's future lay in a healthy relationship
between Nehru and Patel. In a letter in October 1948 for the
birthday of Vallabhbhai, who had striven successfully for the
integration into India of the princely states, C.R. wrote:

> Birthdays do not count with you and me and one day is as
> good as another. Yet . . . I congratulate you most sincerely.
> Many dear colleagues have passed away, and our beloved
> leader who was our fountain of love and inspiration was
> snatched away from us.
>
> You have borne a great burden with courage and ability and
> by the grace of God with pre-eminent success. Our Prime

> Minister is the beloved of this land. Who can resist his
> sincerety of purpose? . . . You and he can and will overcome
> all difficulties.[18]

Should the Constitution that was being prepared enshrine the
pledges given to the princes when they acceded their states to
the Indian Union? And what should the Constitution say about
compensation to landowners for lands acquired by the State?
These were two of the issues on which Nehru and Patel, unable
to agree with each other, sought C.R.'s views.

The Governor-General was evidently in favour of 'a general
guarantee in the Constitution that all assurances given in
connection with the integration of states' would be 'binding.'[19]
On the second question, while C.R. agreed with Nehru that the
State could not 'pay up full value before setting right anything
that is found to be a curse,'[20] he tried to evolve a compromise
acceptable to Patel.[21]

Nehru and Azad, the Education Minister, wanted an inquiry
into the affairs of Benares Hindu University; Patel was opposed.
C.R. gave his clear support to the latter, saying that while a
study of a group of universities might be in order, it would be
wrong to single out one for a probe.

If vacancies arose for posts of Governors or High Court
judges, or action towards a justice involved in irregularities had
to be decided upon, Nehru and Patel consulted the Governor-
General. An indication of how C.R. saw the role of a Governor-
General, and of Governors, can be had from accounts in
newspapers of a conference of Governors held in May 1949.

Chairing, and commanding, the conference, C.R. lists the
agenda, invites the Prime Minister and the Deputy Prime
Minister to speak, tells the Governors that reporters would
'soon leave and then there will be a frank discussion,' and adds:

> You should not imagine that you are just figureheads and can
> do nothing . . . Our Prime Minister and Deputy Prime
> Minister do not hold that view. They want you to develop
> your influence for good.[22]

Mercy petitions had to be finally disposed of by him. While the
views of the Prime Minister and the Home Minister carried

weight, Nehru was anxious that on this question the head of
state should have personal discretion. C.R.'s philosophy regarding
the death sentence was spelled out in a confidential letter to a
few friends:

> There are certain situations where the taking of life offers
> itself as a solution to people in distress and difficulty . . . If the
> only sanction is a term of imprisonment, the urge to kill will
> have its way. . . To retain the death penalty in the statute
> book and to give large powers to the judges to give an
> alternative sentence even in cases of proved murder in cold
> blood seems to be the only proper thing to do.[23]

The parents of Nathuram Godse, the Mahatma's assassin, and
the wife of Narayan Apte, sentenced to death along with Godse,
pleaded with the Governor-General for a waiver of the sentence.
They were joined by a few Gandhians and by two of the
Mahatma's sons, Ramdas and Manilal, who argued that Gandhi
would have advocated mercy. Nehru and Patel, however, were
at one with the Governor-General when the latter turned down
the petitions. C.R. said that he saw the assassination as 'the
wickedest act of modern times.'[24]

When differences arose between C.R. and Nehru or Patel,
they were generally settled by frank talk or by airing any
emotional bruises. Once when C.R. complained to Vallabhbhai
about the tone of a letter from him, Patel replied:

> I am sorry if my letter gave you any impression of lack of
> courtesy. I am sure you will agree that I would not even be the
> last person to be guilty of any act of discourtesy to you
> personally or to the high and distinguished office which you
> hold.[25]

Nehru's tendency, as C.R. would later put it, 'to propose
plebiscites for every problem,' once provoked the Governor-
General into writing, a satirical doggerel. After smiling at his
product, C.R. tore it up.[26]

To sign assent when he did not agree was not pleasing for
C.R.; at times he would enter next to his signature the words,
'Against conscience.' Neither was it pleasing for Nehru or Patel
when the Governor-General requested the Cabinet to reconsider

a decision. Occasions of these two kinds were rare, however, and made bearable by the comradeship, indeed the affection, in C.R.'s relationships with Jawaharlal and Vallabhbhai.

The ending of the year stirred memories. On 31 December he wrote to the widow of his old teacher, Tait, saying, 'I cannot let 1948 pass without letting you know how much I owe your husband.'[27] In January Rama Rao came as his house guest: did they recall their first meeting as boys in a miserable eating house in Chickpet, Bangalore? Lady Mountbatten and her daughter Pamela were among the others who visited and stayed under his roof.

Namagiri was coping well as hostess. Guests found her well-informed and observant. But when Latin diplomats invited by her father kissed her hand, Namagiri would seize the first chance to get at some soap and water!

Some of his visitors were bright. After informing a journalist that he had no hobby like 'kennel-keeping, hunting, yachting or painting,' C.R. added, 'Although I once belonged to the bar . . . I do not even possess one in the House.' 'Ah,' said the journalist, 'there is a big bar between the two bars.' But C.R. would not be topped. 'Barring the fact,' he retorted at once, 'that both are often linked with big men.'[28]

Once in a while there was time to write an article. He reviewed Bernard Shaw's *Sixteen Self-Sketches* for the *Hindustan Times* (19.6.49) and offered a fresh angle on Shaw: 'Kindliness is his strongest point . . . Dislike is a put-on for the sake of his pet passion, the desire for unusualness.'

An important old friend — and old foe — E.V.R. the Periyar spent two hours with C.R. on one of the latter's southern visits, wanting advice: should he or should he not marry a woman forty-odd years his junior? The wedding took place and was one of the reasons for a split in E.V.R.'s Dravida Kazhagam. Some of C.R.'s critics in the South accused him of encouraging the marriage in order to discredit and divide the Dravida movement, but Philip Spratt seems to have conveyed the truth in his *DMK in Power*, published when C.R. and E.V.R. were both living:

The fact is that [the Periyar] consulted Rajaji (despite politics they have remained good friends), and Mr Rajagopalachari, a good Victorian, replied that as the lady's name has been compromised, it was his duty to marry her.[29]

More speeches and broadcasts. There were witty ones, like the talk to the newly-formed All-India Music Society:

There are no people as quarrelsome as the artists. They are very good in their own art but when they step out a bit they become inharmonious ... You have called your society an All-India Music Society ... At Oxford they do not call themselves the All-England University. Cambridge is not the All-World University. Take Harvard. They do not call themselves All-American (New Delhi 19.6.49).

At times, he was utterly candid, as in his talk to leaders of different tribal groups in Shillong:

Unless all of you are linked to a strong government like that of India, it is not safe. The very customs which you wish to preserve will be blown away in a storm ... China threatens Tibet and Burma is divided, whereas India is established and can defend you and your families (27.12.49).

Occasionally, to the dislike of Cabinet Ministers, he would propose a radical reform, as he did in Bombay (8.8.49):

I venture to suggest to crusaders of compulsory primary education whether we cannot be content with three days in the week for schooling. Our schools ... could then take two sets of children in the week. Give the childen a chance during the other four days to work with their parents. [In the villages] the homes are homes as well as trade schools, and the parents are masters as well to whom the children [can be] apprenticed.

He could invest a formal occasion with lively wisdom. At the opening of the National Physical Laboratory in New Delhi he said:

It would be wonderful if research could help us to develop a strain of rice that has shed its wasteful habit of wallowing neck-deep in water. Yet ... the biggest discoveries ... come by accident.

True to feminine type, the goddess of science rejects the direct
mercenary approach and prefers to be gracious by her own
choice and only when you approach her for her own sake.[30]

From 26 January 1950 — so the Constituent Assembly had
decided — India would be a Republic and need a President to
replace the Governor-General. He would be elected, in this first
instance, by the Constituent Assembly.

It had seemed clear that the Assembly would be guided by
the wishes of Nehru and Patel. In June 1949 their wishes, as yet
unannounced, were that C.R. should continue as head of state.
True, the name of Rajendra Prasad, who had presided over the
Constituent Assembly, had been mentioned; true, moreover,
that when Patel and C.R. hinted to Prasad that a statement from
him scotching rumours that he was interested in the post would
be helpful, he confined himself to declaring that 'there can be
no question of any rivalry between Rajaji and myself for any
post or honour.'[31]

Still, it looked likely that the Congress members
predominating in the Assembly would carry out a joint
recommendation by Jawaharlal and Patel in C.R.'s favour. By
the end of September, however, it was clear that there would
not be a joint proposal, that Prasad was interested in the
position, and that a majority in the party preferred Prasad.

While eager to install Rajaji, Nehru overestimated his
capacity to succeed. He also committed two tactical blunders.
The first was to send a letter to Prasad indicating a preference
for C.R. and requesting Prasad to propose C.R.'s name. Sent
without consulting Patel, the letter only made Prasad keener on
the Presidentship.

Nehru's second mistake was to move — against Patel's
advice — a resolution proposing C.R.'s name at a meeting of the
Congress Parliamentary Party. He was leaving for the United
States and wanted the question settled before his departure.
When several speakers opposed the resolution, Jawaharlal looked
for help from Patel, who, however, merely proposed that the
question be deferred until the end of Nehru's American trip.

Returning from America, Nehru offered Prasad the

chairmanship of the Planning Commission that was envisaged. When Prasad did not bite this bait, Jawaharlal wrote to him of the need for the 'five of us, you, Rajaji, Vallabhbhai, Maulana and myself,' to tackle together the deterioration that had assailed Congress — 'the cracking up, with great rapidity, of the noble structure that Bapu built,' as Nehru put it — and threw a hint about Prasad taking up the Congress Presidentship. Finally, he said:

> It is patent that there are only two persons who might be chosen as President of the Republic — yourself and Rajaji. There is no other. One of the two, it seems to me, should take the initiative of declaring that he will not stand . . . Rajaji himself was anxious to retire to his village and the only consideration for him was whether his colleagues and his duty demanded something else. He would gladly issue a statement about retiring himself, if his colleagues so desired.[32]

However, not only was Prasad unwilling to retire, Patel by this time was definite that he should not. Not that he preferred Prasad to C.R. Morarji Desai and Ghanshyamdas Birla, both of whom enjoyed Patel's confidence, have recalled that Vallabhbhai felt that C.R. would be as good a President as Prasad.[33] Nor did Vallabhbhai swallow the line that Nehru wanted C.R. 'as a prop against his deputy Prime Minister.' According to Dwarka Prasad Mishra, another of Patel's close friends, Vallabhbhai 'believed that once elected as President C.R. would not blindly support Nehru disregarding national interests.'[34]

Patel changed his attitude when he saw the feeling in the party and also a chance to bring Nehru down a peg. His only worry now was about Prasad backing out at the last minute. To him he sent the message, *'Agar dulha palki chhod kar bhag na jaye to shadi nakki.'* ('Provided the bridegroom does not desert the palanquin, the marriage is assured.') However, as Mishra recalls, 'the bridegroom was firmly sitting in the palanquin and the marriage party need not have been anxious.' Prasad was ready, in fact, to be 'harder than a diamond.'[35]

He informed Nehru that a withdrawal by him would be interpreted as 'dictation' and 'a betrayal.'[36] The ball was now in the court of C.R., who promptly announced his retirement.

Why was the party not keen on C.R., whose success as Governor-General had been unquestioned? That he came from outside the Hindi belt and was not fluent in the language were perhaps factors. 'The protagonists of Hindi favour Rajendra Babu,' Nehru told Patel.[37] But the biggest reason was C.R.'s 1942 role.

Most Members of the Constituent Assembly had taken part in Quit India. Prasad had gone to prison with them while C.R. was proposing accommodation with the British and the League. If one of the two had to be the first President, they would choose Prasad, unless Nehru and Patel jointly urged them to the contrary.

C.R. did not try to charm the Members the way he had charmed the diplomats. He enjoyed high office but a patient and tactful effort to keep it was beyond him. Nor was it in him to ask for Patel's favour, though one word to Patel, with whom C.R. had personal and ideological links of long standing, might have fetched him the Presidentship.

Patel would die in less than a year and in ten years C.R. and Nehru would be engaged in sharp political conflict. Yet C.R. was never to express, in public or private, deliberately or absent-mindedly, to strangers or confidants, bitterness at Nehru or Patel for not being chosen President. Was it that C.R. concealed his true feeling with remarkable success? It is more likely that he had philosophy enough to smile both at his entry into Government House and his exit from it.

Whether or not C.R. was sorry, Nehru definitely was. His wish had been denied, his pride hurt. Now he spent as much time as he could in C.R.'s company. It was impossible for C.R. to think of blaming someone who looked as downcast as Jawaharlal. C.R.'s not holding a grudge against Vallabhbhai is more interesting, and perhaps explained by his knowledge that Patel threw his weight behind Prasad only after Nehru's haste and over-confidence had botched the exercise. After C.R. had announced his retirement, Patel evidently said to him: 'Jawaharlal has spoilt everything. I wanted to do it tactfully. He has rushed the matter.' 'Why are you offering me an explanation?' C.R. replied. 'I am not keen on the office.'[38] And though it appeared to C.R. that Prasad wanted the honour ('I could see in Rajendra Prasad's mind hesitation and even perhaps desire,' he wrote to Rama Rao), he had the wisdom not to blame or judge his old colleague from Bihar.

To the Mountbattens, C.R. wrote on New Year's Eve:

> The desire for a change in personnel when there will be such a great formal change in the Constitution is natural and has rightly overridden other considerations. Of course I am also glad to be relieved at the top of the tide and not left on the beach by a receding wave. I go without any diminution in the affection and trust with which my dear colleagues sweetened the days of my ripe years.[39]

The same day he also wrote to Rama Rao, who had sent a characteristic letter. 'Is there,' asked C.R., 'any prize or crown greater than the intimate approval of a dear and tried friend?'

The final two months had their quota of tours: he did Gauhati and Shillong, Cuttack and Puri, Hyderabad and Vizag, and repeated Madras and Bangalore. When the wish was expressed in Madras that he should continue as head of state, he cited his age — 71 — and asked, 'Do you still think that I should pull the bullock-cart?' (*Hindustan Times*, 18.12.49)

The strenuous business of winding up — parting letters to Governors, Rajpramukhs, the miltary chiefs, the Chief Justice, Cabinet Ministers, a fearsome series of farewells, packing, planning the transfer of Thangam's children to schools in the South, and so on — was now added to the chores of a Head of State.

Letters and messages were pouring in, offering farewell, tribute and evaluation. Chief Justice Kania said he had found C.R. 'appreciating the other man's point of view and treating his view as also put forth for the benefit of the country.' Admiral Parry, the British C-in-C of the Indian Navy, thought that 'the true wisdom of the undying civilisation of India was represented in Government House.' The *Hindustan Times* gave expression to a common note: 'Though Rajaji has more than earned his rest, it is doubtful whether he will be allowed to enjoy his retirement in peace' (25.1.50).

At an informal Government House lunch, C.R. posted the President-elect, who would take office on 26 January, with some aspects of life in the House. The 24th was packed with protocol and emotion. President Sukarno and his wife arrived in the morning and had to be met at the airport. Jawaharlal, his sister Vijayalakshmi and daughter Indira came to lunch. In the afternoon C.R. was At Home to the House's employees. They gave him a farewell address in Hindi, English, Tamil and Bengali. C.R. told them that 'many Muslims, many Hindus, and many Sikhs' would always be working together in the House and that he was leaving them 'in the care of a good successor'(*Hindustan Times*, 25.1.50).

As he walked over to his study, he found on his desk a gift from his Ministers: a crystal Buddha and a silver plate bearing the Ministers' names. An accompanying letter from Jawaharlal quoted a Cabinet resolution that referred to the Governor-General's help to them and stated, 'He has not only enhanced the prestige of India but further endeared himself to his own people.' Sitting alone in the study, C.R. was overcome. As he was to say later that night at a banquet given by Nehru, 'All my mother came into my eyes.' Said Jawaharlal at the banquet:

It is rather odd to think of Warren Hastings and you in the same line of succession . . . You made people feel that . . . it made not the slightest difference to you whether you lived in the Viceregal Palace or in a little village in Salem district . . .

Because I was often troubled in mind and spirit I came to you and sought your advice and I always found it very helpful. And so when the time comes for you to go away from here there is a feeling of a slight emptiness in me.

In his reply C.R. said:

Sometimes the truth comes upon us with overpowering conviction. Now I realise that the greatest joy in life is to give up a thing and go. What greater reward can I have than the feeling which you heard expressed by the Prime Minister?

I therefore go, my friend Mr Prime Minister, with very great joy in my mind. The only thing which worries me is the feeling that I perhaps leave some of you with a sense of relative loneliness. I wish I could go and also remain here but that is not possible . . .

The Prime Minister and his first colleague, the Deputy Prime Minister, together make a possession which makes India rich in every sense of the term. The former commands universal love, the latter universal confidence. Not a tear need be shed for anyone going as long as these two stand four square against the hard winds to which our country may be exposed.

Addressing the ambassadors who were present, C.R. said:

The Prime Minister says I have done very well and many of you, my dear friends of the diplomatic corps, have been saying the same thing, before me at any rate — I do not know what you have said in my absence. What is the secret? I am a simple fellow. I do not hate anybody (*Hindustan Times*, 26.1.50).

On the 25th there was a broadcast to the nation:

I feel deeply thankful for the affection showered on me by all sections of the people, which alone enabled me to bear the burden of an office to the duties and conventions of which I have been an utter stranger (*Hindustan Times*, 26.1.50).

The Durbar Hall, 26 January. Rising from his throne, C.R. announced, 'in clear and distinct tones,' the birth of the Republic. Then he asked the President-elect to move over to the throne. While Prasad did so, C.R., older by five years, patted a blessing on his shoulder. Then Prasad was sworn in.

Nehru decided that pageantry should mark C.R.'s departure for Madras. There was a guard of honour beside the great steps, a drive in a six-horse coach to the House's front gates, and a ride in an open car to the airport, where C.R. received a combined guard of honour from the Army, the Navy and the Air Force.

Just before walking to his place, he embraced Prasad and with almost trembling fingers placed round the President's neck a garland of homespun cotton thread hued in the colours of the national flag. Jawaharlal escorted C.R. and Namagiri into the twin-engined Air Force Dakota.

Up rose the plane. Below, after some moments, lay what now was Rashtrapati Bhavan, with North Block and South

Block looking like its extended arms. There was India Gate and the Old Fort. Buildings and roads soon shrank and gave way to little rectangles, where specks — the faithful peasants — slowly moved on the good earth. Mood matched panorama, and C.R. penned in the plane a letter to Prasad:

> My dear Rajen Babu, My thought goes back naturally to you all whom I have left behind. There is an almighty, kindly and vigilant Power that has evolved this beautiful and great world out of the primordial substance.

> May that Power bless you and our dear country and the men and women entrusted to your charge and that of your colleagues! . . . I go out with joy in my heart at the beautiful manner in which the little changeover has taken place. There was nothing to mar the beauty of it. God bless you all. Yours affectionately, C.R.

A postscript to the letter said: 'Please show this to Jawaharlal and Vallabhbhai. I am not writing separately to them.'[40] It would have been natural to write to Jawaharlal, who had been responsible for the grandeur of the send-off. But to write to the President was proper: C.R. was not as complete a stranger to 'the duties and conventions' of high office as he had claimed in his broadcast.

19

'Matchstick'

1950-51

The Bazlulla Road house needed an extra room before it could take in C.R., Namagiri, Narasimhan, Thangam and her five children. While that was being added C.R. stayed in a bare house in Adyar that Lakshmi had just acquired. To Rama Rao C.R. wrote:

> I am leading an interesting and disabled existence without secretaries, ADCs and staff . . . For years now I have lived without touching stamps or coins or having to think and plan for my private existence . . . Till now I was, though Governor-General, a Sanyasi free from cares. Now it is difficult and housekeeping is not pleasant.

He felt the heat — there was no air-conditioner in Adyar or at Bazlulla Road, when he returned there — and had trouble with his eyes. 'Black wandering spots hover before my eyes . . . It is a race that cataract runs with the better known friend that pays court to old men!' he wrote to Rama Rao.[1]

The pension of Rs 1000 a month to which, as a former head of state, he was deemed entitled, began to arrive, and there were' moments when it looked as if he had retired. In a letter to Rama Rao, he said:

> The desire to take up work that haunts the mind of old' warriors on their retirement from ther long labours should be

resisted as severely as a desire to marry again and look after a young girl (20.3.50).

This was a reaction to Rama Rao's wish for a fresh assignment, but C.R. was also addressing himself, for Nehru had urged him to return to Delhi. As what? There was speculation when C.R. was seen boarding a plane for Delhi at the end of April. 'Are you becoming the Vice-Chancellor of Delhi University, sir?' he was asked at the airport. 'I would prefer the Vice-Chancellorship of Madras University,' C.R. replied (*Hindustan Times*, 28.4.50).

Nehru wanted C.R. in the Cabinet, believing, no doubt, that this would strengthen him vis-a-vis Patel. But when, as he had to, Jawaharlal spoke of his wish to Patel, the latter at once remarked that C.R. would make an excellent Foreign Minister — a hit at Jawaharlal, who held the External Affairs portfolio and was possessive of it.

In the event, Jawaharlal offered C.R. Finance, with the alternative of the chairmanship of the Planning Commission. Either would be too strenuous, C.R. thought; finally, Nehru, Vallabhbhai and he agreed that he would assist as Minister without Portfolio, 'a kind of fifth wheel,' as C.R. put it in a letter to Rama Rao (19.5.50).

Not exactly an instance of 'severely and firmly resisting' a new assignment! That Nehru and Patel both wanted him sufficed for C.R., who was not conscious of any loss of dignity in joining a Cabinet that had very recently been subordinate to him.

But it took him eighty days, including some spent recuperating in Ooty, before he joined duty in Delhi. C.R. and Namagiri flew to a welcome at the airport by both Nehru and Patel. Nehru drove with them to Lakshmi's flat in Connaught Circus. On 15 July Prasad swore C.R. in, and a few days later Namagiri and he moved to their latest address at 1 York Place. Many years later, Lal Bahadur Shastri would live as Prime Minister in this house with a large garden.

Nehru asked C.R. to head the Cabinet's Economic Affairs Committee, hitherto chaired by the Finance Minister, Chintaman Deshmukh. The latter would recall:

> Rajaji would come to the meeting of the Committee, ... take
> the chair, and turning to me would say, 'Now, Mr Deshmukh,
> please conduct the meeting.' I thought that was very gracious
> on his part.[2]

Jawaharlal himself presided over the External Affairs Committee, which also included Patel, C.R. and Gopalaswami Iyengar. An account of a discussion in this Committee on the future of Goa, then under Portuguese rule, has been provided by K.P.S. Menon, who was present as an official. According to Menon, C.R. opposed a proposal for curbs on travel by Goans to India and on remittances to Goa.

Goans were 'our brethren,' C.R. evidently said; hurting them would hurt 'ourselves.' At this Patel proposed 'going in' and taking over Goa. 'It is two hours' work,' he said. According to Menon, 'Nehru objected to this suggestion strongly; it would amount to an invasion and India would lose her reputation for nonviolence.' C.R. backed Nehru and the proposal was dropped — for the time being.[3]

But on Tibet, attacked by Peking at the end of October 1950, C.R. and Patel were on one side and Nehru on the other. Nehru regretted the Chinese action but spoke of Peking being motivated by fears of American acts against the Red regime. On the other hand, Patel publicly denounced the action.

Though there was no public statement by C.R., at Cabinet meetings he advocated a firmer Indian response. 'Rajaji was then in the Cabinet and he opposed Nehru's Tibet policy,' recalls N.V. Gadgil, who was also in the Cabinet.[4] K.P.S. Menon, Foreign Secretary at the time, describes how C.R. 'sent for me for a talk on Tibet . . . and argued forcibly that we should not recognize Chinese sovereignty or even suzerainty over Tibet.'[5] In a letter on the subject to Nehru, C.R. was frank:

> May God help us from drifting to be just a satellite of China!
> I feel hurt whenever Panikkar (India's ambassador to Peking)
> tells us with extreme satisfaction that China is very friendly to
> us and has no territorial ambitions. We do not want any
> patrons now, do we? (1.12.50)

A different facet of the C.R.-Nehru relationship emerges from an account of another meeting of the Foreign Affairs Committee.

B.N. Chakravarty, an official present, recollects the outcome of a discussion that had found C.R. and Nehru on opposite sides:

> The Prime Minister said, 'You see, Rajaji, the majority is with me.' Rajaji grinned and said, 'Yes, Jawaharlal, the majority is with you but logic is with me.' The Prime Minister laughed and despite the majority support accepted Rajaji's views.[6]

Files do not cascade towards a Minister without Portfolio and C.R. was not pinned to his desk. He saw a Test match against a Commonwealth eleven and conferred fruitlessly over Kashmir with Liaqat Ali, who made a visit to Delhi. The English version of his Mahabharata was published, and he delivered three lectures on the Gita. 'The Gita,' he said, 'is like a railway guide. You should travel with its help, not commit it to memory' (*Hindustan Times*, 21.11.50).

He found time, too, to answer letters from strangers asking for advice on personal problems. But he saw as his main task the maintenance of the Nehru-Patel relationship, which was now under heavy strain. 'Nehru would come to the house with a long face,' recalls Namagiri, referring to this period. 'Anna would ask me to get coffee and the two of them would talk alone.'[7] Often the subject was Vallabhbhai. And on his visits to Patel, who was no longer in good health, C.R. would hear complaints about Jawaharlal.

The question of a new Congress President almost led to a rupture. Purushottam Das Tandon of the UP, with his striking bearded face and a richly-deserved reputation for independence and integrity, offered himself for the post, as he had done a year earlier, when Pattabhi Sitaramayya of the Telugu country had defeated him in the balloting.

Patel backed Tandon. Nehru thought him old-fashioned and too much of a Hindu and did not conceal his views. Also, he may have felt threatened by a Patel-Tandon combination.

Searching for a way of securing Tandon's withdrawal, Nehru asked C.R. if he would accept the party post, but C.R. was not willing. In the event, Tandon was opposed by J.B. Kripalani, who received Nehru's support.

On the morning of 26 August, when it was clear that Tandon was winning, a deeply hurt Jawaharlal told C.R. that he would leave both Congress and the Government. Predictably, C.R. asked Nehru not to overreact. Later in the day Jawaharlal wrote to C.R.:

> I think most Congressmen know how I feel . . . If, in spite of this, Tandon is supported and encouraged and elected, that seems to be the clearest of indications that Tandon's election is concerned more important than my presence in the Government or the Congress . . . I shall consult you of course before I take any step (26.8.50).

Not having asked the party to choose between Tandon and himself, Nehru could not — C.R. pointed out — accuse Congress of withdrawing confidence from him. Patel's reaction was that Nehru was bluffing. 'If he wants to resign, let him.' Following Tandon's triumph, this was Patel's attitude, conveyed to C.R.

C.R. could not agree with Patel. If Nehru's pride forced him to resign, every Congress unit in the country, from the national executive down to each village committee, would split. Moreover, Nehru was the country's most popular figure, whereas Patel was too ill to run the government.

Namagiri recalls that C.R. hardly slept that night of 26-27 August. 'He was greatly agitated. Next morning early he went to the drawing room, phoned Sardar and told him: "You alone cannot do it. Don't try to get rid of him. What are you going to do without him? You are sick." '[8]

C.R. succeeded. Both Nehru and Patel backed away from the edge of a precipice. It was still a wounded Nehru who had another letter hand-delivered to C.R. on 27 August, but not one talking of resigning:

> If on a major issue, to which I attach importance, my colleagues go against me, then there is something wrong somewhere . . . I suppose I am not big enough for the job . . . I am a kind of a show window for the outside world and to some extent for people in India, but I am supposed to keep to my place and not interfere too much in the real business of life.

On his part Patel wrote to C.R. (27.8.50) that he wanted 'to be able to relieve Jawaharlal of his mental distress,' but a new hurdle was Tandon's unwillingness to include Nehru's friend Rafi Ahmed Kidwai in his Working Committee. Nehru declared that if Kidwai was kept out of the executive, he himself would stay out.

To prevent the proclamation of a major rift, a frantic C.R. called on Patel, who now was quite unwell, tried to involve the far-removed Mountbattens, and, accompanied by Maulana Azad, even requested President Prasad to persuade Tandon to yield! The President asked his staff to contact Tandon but changed his mind before they got through.

In a public statement, C.R. said that India needed 'the continued guidance' of both Nehru and Patel and added:

> Some of us who have pulled together all these 35 years must do so to the end of our active lives (*Hindustan Times*, 23.9.50).

Undaunted by an infructuous three-hour meeting in which Nehru, Patel, Tandon, Azad and he participated, C.R. wrote a letter urging Tandon to accept Kidwai:

> Here is the last and only hurdle for a historic settlement. May I entreat you to swallow the poison? You can do it and indeed be all the stronger for it (28.9.50).

If Nehru kept himself out, added C.R., he too would have to stay out and return to Madras. Courteously but firmly Tandon sent the ball back to C.R.:

> My hope still is that Jawaharlalji will join the Working Committee without insisting as a condition precedent that any particular person should be taken on it. Your persuasion will, I feel, help (8.10.50).

By this time Patel had made an unexpected gesture. Speaking at Indore on 2 October, he said:

> Our leader is Jawaharlal Nehru. Bapu appointed him as his successor in his lifetime . . . It is the duty of all Bapu's soldiers to carry out Bapu's request . . . I am not a disloyal soldier (*Hindustan Times*, 3.10.50).

A stirred C.R. wrote to Patel:

> Even in the printed report your Indore speech was touching.
> In the actual spoken word it must have been so greatly
> moving. You have done all one can do. If even this does not
> satisfy people's suspicions, what can man do! (5.10.50)

But Nehru was not really satisfied. His confidence, however,
had returned. He wrote to C.R. (10.10.50):

> I have written a letter to Purushottam Das Tandon on
> 'Culture.' I am enclosing a copy of it for you, as you might
> be amused.

The reply was crisp:

> Tandonji will surely be puzzled at the contents as well as the
> timing of your letter on 'culture.' Why this now when the
> only question is, 'Will you be a member of his Working
> Committee?' (11.10.50)

Nehru, however, seemed adamant. He wrote to C.R. (13.10.50):

> You will forgive me for not abiding by your advice in this
> matter.

And Patel thought the breach had come. Writing to C.R. he said
(13.10.50):

> It is painful to prolong this process of mental torture and we
> must end it now as I see no hope . . . I have gone to the
> farthest extent . . . but I see that it is all no good and we can
> only leave it to God. Thanks for the trouble you have taken.

Aided and abetted by C.R. and Azad, the fates helped. After
three marathon meetings on Sunday, 15 October, Tandon
announced that twenty persons had agreed to join his Working
Committee. Nehru, he said, was one of them, as was C.R.,
though Kidwai had been excluded.

Telegrams congratulated C.R. for his mediatory role, but he
knew that the reconciliation was qualified and half-hearted. And
very soon there was reason for real worry. To Rama Rao he
wrote:

> Sardar Patel is very ill . . . He is unable to go to Parliament
> or leave his house.

On 12 December Patel had to be flown to Bombay for treatment. C.R. saw him off at the airport, as did Prasad and Nehru. Three days later Patel died. Jawaharlal and C.R. flew together to Bombay for the funeral where, as Vallabhbhai's oldest friend, C.R. made the oration, tears rolling down his shrunken cheeks. They had been very close, personally and ideologically. And Patel's death had removed the only brake on Nehru.

Nehru told C.R. that he would have to take up Home, and C.R. knew it. No one else could step into Patel's chappals, but C.R. nursed no illusions about being another Sardar. Health and luck permitting, he might manage to retain the confidence of the services and keep an eye on the provinces. But there was no question of his balancing Nehru's weight and influence.

Though he became number two in the Cabinet and, when Nehru was away, chaired its meetings and officiated at functions for visiting heads of government, he was not styled Deputy Prime Minister. That designation seemed to die with Patel.[9]

True to character, C.R. proved a conservative Home Minister. The Communists had launched a violent movement in Hyderabad's Telengana districts, and C.R. went all out to suppress it. According to B.N. Mullick, head of intelligence at the time, 'We were ordered to end it and there were to be no excuses. The Prime Minister favoured a less severe approach but Rajaji carried the day. In the end we were able to report to him that the movement had been broken.'[10]

A crucial weapon in the Telengana operation was the Preventive Detention Act, which Patel had brought in. Piloting a Bill to extend its operation by a year, C.R. was unsparing in his attack on secrecy and violence. The Communist technique, he charged, was to lure men by the prospect of sacrifice and danger, drive them into 'complete criminal outlawry' and hold them by blackmail. 'Any officer found guilty of misusing his powers under the Act would be regarded as an enemy of the state,' C.R. promised. But the Act would be used against violent persons, blackmarketers and 'those who continually incite communal passions' (*Hindustan Times*, 10 & 20.2.51).

Did he remember his leaflet of May 1919, issued against the

Rowlatt Act, where he had promised opposition to any law 'to suspect and imprison without trial even if the government is democratic and purely Indian'?

The first amendment to the Constitution, qualifying the rights to property and free speech, was made while C.R. was Home Minister and with his effective defence in Parliament. In the government's view, the amendment was called for to safeguard land reform legislation and to check incitement to violence. It also enabled C.R., towards the close of his term, to move and push through his controversial Press Bill.

The Raj's instrument for controlling the Press, the 1931 Press Act, was still on the statute book but would not have survived a challenge under the new Constitution. With the first amendment a regulatory law became possible. C.R.'s Press Bill empowered the government to obtain, by court order, security from an impeached publisher or journalist. The accused could insist on a jury of journalists or public men and had the right of appeal to a High Court.

C.R. claimed that he would not have thought of his Bill if a Press Council, capable of 'inducing all sections of the Press to conform to known standards,' was in place. Limited to two years, the law, he said, would be repealed earlier if the profession created its own supervisory body. After a long and strenuous debate, the Bill was passed in October 1951. According to Chalapati Rau, founder of the Indian Federation of Working Journalists and friend of Nehru:

> Rajaji was shrewd over the Press Bill. When I expressed my reservations to Nehru, he asked me to meet Rajaji. 'Please bring as many colleagues with you as you want,' Rajaji said to me when I sought an appointment. The interview presented no difficulty to Rajaji, for my colleagues freely contradicted one another.[11]

With C.R.'s backing, an official of Britain's MI6 was invited to India. Thereafter — despite some coolness from Nehru — senior intelligence men from India attended secret courses in Britain.[12]

As Home Minister, C.R. denied passports to a few who had been invited to the Soviet Union or China. One or two successfully appealed against C.R.'s decision to Nehru, but there was at least one instance, that of R.K. Karanjia, editor of *Blitz*, where C.R. allowed a passport though informed in writing by S. Dutt, the Foreign Secretary, that Nehru 'does not like at all the idea of Karanjia's going to China.' C.R. took the view that Karanjia 'is fully in possession of his own mind and will and is not likely to be affected for better or worse in Peking.'[13]

Mullick, the intelligence director, suggested prevention of a visit to India planned by Rajni Palme Dutt, the Communist leader — 'Indian by name but a British citizen,' as Mullick described him. C.R. ruled that Dutt should be allowed to land but desired that 'a friendly member should ask a question in Parliament on the subject.' In his answer, C.R. 'would expose the real aims of Palme Dutt and the Communist Party.'[14]

In another decision, C.R. held that while 'it would be undesirable . . . to let government servants engage themselves in RSS programmes,' young men should not be kept out of the administration 'merely on the ground that they have previously taken part in RSS activities . . . in school or college or immediately thereafter.' The elucidation was passed on to all chief secretaries and chief commissioners.[15]

The Home Minister was expected to promote Hindi, which the Constitution had termed the national language, but, doubtless recalling the storm raised in 1937-9 when he had made Hindi a compulsory subject in southern schools, C.R. said:

> Let me respectfully warn Hindi lovers not to depend upon the
> coercion of a numerical majority of an ill-knit population . . .
> It will lead to disintegration and hostility rather than unity
> (*Hindustan Times*, 28.12.50).

Zapu Phizo having begun an independence movement in the Naga Hills in the Northeast, Bishnuram Medhi, the Assam Chief Minister, informed C.R. of his plans to 'strengthen the district administration' to counter the movement. C.R.'s reply to Medhi, a copy of which also went to Assam's Governor, offered another perspective:

> The Constitution contains provisions designed to confer a
> wide degree of regional autonomy for these tribals. It seems to
> me also necessary that we should appoint as many of the hill

people as possible both in superior and inferior posts, ignoring conventional standards.[16]

Civil servants again noted his evident resolve that friends or relations should not profit from his being where he was. When a letter came charging that a Delhi-based official whose family he had known intimately was corrupt, C.R. minuted:

> CID must keep watch on his movements . . . If he is found guilty on enquiry he must be tried for the offence and dismissed, if necessary.[17]

Mullick, the intelligence chief, would later recall C.R.'s functioning as Home Minister:

> Rajaji never asked me to carry out a single wrong decision . . . He gave clear and straight answers and left nothing in doubt — and never sought to escape responsibility for a mistake. Even Patel took political considerations into account, but Rajaji never. The party did not like this attitude of his. He was more at home with officials than with the party.[18]

H.V.R. Iengar, the Home Secretary, would describe C.R.'s style:

> One of the first things I did as soon as he took charge was to send him a note about the activities of the Communist Party of India, in those days the main preoccupation of the Home Minister . . . Rajaji sent for me a few days later and started what looked like a cross-examination . . . I began to wonder whether Rajaji himself was a member of the Communist Party!

> I became exhausted and began to feel I was an ignoramus. Then Rajaji smiled. It was for him partly an intellectual exercise and partly an attempt to probe my own study . . .

> I took to him a case of a Bengali police officer of Assam who had been subjected to disciplinary proceedings . . . I thought it was a routine matter which would be disposed of in a couple of minutes. Again I was subjected to a rigorous cross-examination.

> How was I certain that the officer making the inquiry was

fair-minded? . . . Was I aware of the tension in Assam between Bengali and Assamese officers? Then Rajaji closed the matter by saying that he agreed with my recommendation.[19]

It was a style that Mullick, too, would remember:

Once I saw a note by Rajaji disagreeing with the department's recommendation and then, later on in the file, his signature endorsing our proposal. 'How have you agreed?' I asked him. He smiled and said: 'It was not all one-sided, as all of you made it out to be. In my note I pointed out the other side. But when both sides are considered, your recommendation is correct. Where is the contradiction?'[20]

More at home with officials than with party people, C.R. was not interested in expanding his political base, for which the Home Ministership would have been an ideal asset. The lawns and front rooms of 1 York Place were free of lobbying politicians, and his evenings, too, could be devoted to the Home Ministry's files.

A unanimous vote of the Madras Assembly had made C.R. a member of the Upper House of Parliament. Though, as we have seen, he had to initiate some unpleasant measures in Parliament, his flair enabled him to win support, and opponents acknowledged his effectiveness. Thus Deshbandhu Gupta, a Member from Delhi and editor of the Urdu daily *Tej*, who with Ramnath Goenka of the *Indian Express* kept up a steady attack on the Press Bill, said when it was approved: 'The passage of the Bill is a personal triumph for the Home Minister' (*Hindustan Times*, 8.10.51).

He turned interruptions to good account. When Shyama Prasad Mookerjee, who had left the government early in 1950, said in the middle of a Rajaji argument, 'Please remember you have ceased being a lawyer,' C.R. replied, 'But I have not ceased being reasonable.'[21] On another occasion, C.R. was referring to the problems of centrally-administered territories when Thakur Lal Singh of Bhopal, one of the areas involved, interrupted, 'It is because they are kept under your thumb.' 'No, sir,' said C.R.

at once, 'we are keeping them in our lap' (*Hindustan Times*, 27.5.51).

The record of the Press Bill debate contains the following exchange:

> *C.R.*: At an early stage of the debate, an hon'ble member was pleased, in his dislike of me, to find a bad name to give me and called me Chanakya.
>
> *H.V. Kamath*: It is not a bad name at all.
>
> *C.R.*: Now Chanakya, some call him Vishnu Gupta, historians call him Kautilya, is a great name.
>
> *Kamath*: An honoured name.
>
> *C.R.*: The intention of the hon'ble member was not to honour me. It was only my luck that a good name occurred to him, for which I thank the goodess of accidents. (*Loud thumping*)[22]

Goenka accused C.R. of harbouring a dictatorial mind. Replied C.R.:

> I must tell Mr Goenka that democracy does not mean constant hunger for popularity or the constant fear of unpopularity . . . Let no one mistake the battle between right and wrong, which must be fought in one's breast, as a battle for dictatorship (*Hindustan Times*, 4.10.51).

At the final sitting on the Press Bill, C.R. said:

> There is nothing wrong in this Bill. There is nothing of which I am ashamed. On the contrary, I am proud, for it is the first time in the history of the Press laws that a system of judicial trial has been introduced and the Government made a common complainant.[23]

Shortly before the vote on the Bill, Gupta complained that the Press gallery was empty. C.R. pounced on him: 'Shouldn't the Press have freedom in this matter also?' (*Hindustan Times*, 7.10.51).

In the assessment of Durga Das, who as a journalist had been covering the legislature in New Delhi since the 1920s, C.R.'s performance over the Press Bill 'excelled in advocacy any ever known in the annals of the Central Legislature' (*Hindustan Times*, 18.9.51).

Correctness, courtesy and thoughtfulness marked Jawaharlal's conduct towards C.R. He had gone to the airport to welcome C.R. when the latter came to talk about joining the Cabinet and again when he came to join. Off and on he would send across to C.R. some fruit, a book, or clippings from a foreign journal.

> *Nehru to C.R., 18.5.51*: Perhaps the enclosed two articles by G.D.H. Cole in the *New Statesman* might interest you.

In his reply C.R. summarized Cole's points, reacted to them, and added: 'You can see that I can think and write as vaguely as G.D.H. Cole' (19.5.51).

While he appreciated Nehru's cultured attitude, Patel's death had modified their relationship. Nehru's need for an ally or reconciler in his dealings with Patel had vanished. His visits to C.R.'s residence virtually stopped. There is no indication that his regard for C.R. had diminished, but there was no need any more to trouble C.R. at 1 York Place.

N.V. Gadgil, a member of the Cabinet at this time, thought that after Patel's death Nehru 'began to think of himself as omniscient.'[24] But it was more in the scene, and less in Nehru, that the change had occurred. The counterweight, Patel, had gone.

Yet C.R. found it hard to accept the change. He who had given comradeship as well as combat to Nehru's father Motilal was unable to swallow a line-up where Jawaharlal was the Leader and others, including himself, followers.

Whether because of the sin of pride or the virtue of self-respect, life in the Nehru cabinet lost its charm for C.R. There were some differences, too. The two disagreed, for instance, on what the Gandhi samadhi at Rajghat should look like. H.V.R. Iengar, Home Secretary at the time, who saw official papers that passed between C.R. and Nehru, sensed that 'all was not well between the two.' Nehru would 'alter Rajaji's drafts even when nothing material or substantial was involved.'[25]

However, over Nehru's differences with Prasad, which began to surface at this juncture, C.R. backed Jawaharlal. Expressing misgivings regarding the Hindu Code Bill that Parliament was considering, Prasad indicated to Nehru that he might withhold assent to it, a threat he did not in the end carry out. C.R. supported the Bill and, more important, agreed with Nehru that the President had to go by the Cabinet's advice, even if such a direction was not explicit in the Constitution.

The eminent lawyer, Alladi Krishnaswami Iyer, and the Attorney General were asked to give their opinions; a letter that C.R. wrote to Nehru regarding the opinions reveals the closeness of their consultation on this question:

> I am returning Alladi's very good note. I agree with you that it should be sent to the President along with the Attorney General's note. Please remember when sending the note to the President to delete the words I have marked on page 6 and also to send in some form or other the portion marked by me in [Alladi's] covering letter to you (9.10.51).

Evidently it was Nehru's attitude towards Congress President Tandon that troubled C.R. the most. When Tandon did not heed Nehru's counsel for action against some Punjab Congressmen, Jawaharlal told Tandon he would resign from the Parliamentary Board. Informing C.R. of his decision, Nehru said that he had 'weighed all the consequences' (9.6.51). Offended that Jawaharlal had neither consulted him nor informed him ahead of time, C.R. wrote:

> I have your letter telling me about your having written to Tandonji [of] your desire to resign from the Parliamentary Board. I see nothing but misfortune for the country in the line you are taking . . . You should tell me now when you will release me from Government. I think my usefulness is over. (9.6.51).

Nehru did not press his resignation but soon another conflict arose. Kidwai and Ajit Prasad Jain, Ministers in the Nehru government and old opponents of Tandon, left the Congress to join the new Krishak Mazdoor Praja Party started by Acharya Kripalani. Kidwai left the government as well but Jain did not.

When Tandon urged Jain's removal, and the Congress executive in UP — the state to which Nehru, Tandon, Kidwai and Jain all belonged — joined in the demand, Nehru not only refused; he resigned from the Working Committee and the Parliamentary Board.

Informed by Nehru of his resignations from Congress's apex bodies, C.R. wrote back:

> I do not understand this. You should relieve me before you do all this and confuse and destroy the Congress. Please do not go mad (7.8.51).

Tandon resigned the Presidentship, and Congress bodies across the nation passed resolutions asking Nehru to fill the vacated chair. Just a year earlier Nehru had said to Tandon that 'it would be improper' for him to preside over Congress 'so long as I remain Prime Minister' (8.8.50). Now, however, Nehru was willing to be persuaded and the party was willing to persuade.

Early in September 1951, Nehru was elected President, his name proposed by Govind Ballabh Pant, the U.P. Chief Minister. Invited by Jawaharlal to join his Working Committee, C.R. declined.

C.R.'s departure from Delhi seemed also linked to the elections that had been announced. The free vote was what C.R. had fought the British for; now he loathed the compromise with big money and vote-banks that elections seemed to entail. He found ticket-hungry Congressmen caught in 'a fatal ecstasy,' reminding him of 'the lepideptora [that] fly into the burning flame to die.'[26]

Nehru suggested that he stay until April the following year, when the new Parliament would be constituted, but C.R. replied that 'an inner voice' was compelling him to leave at the earliest. His decision was announced, but the published reasons, age and fatigue, did not disclose the whole truth.

The deeper reality — his unhappiness and bitterness — is revealed in a letter he sent at this juncture to Mountbatten, who had proposed that C.R. should help Nehru by serving, even for a short while, as High Commissioner in London:

> You and Edwina are so intensely interested in Jawaharlal

Nehru that, may I say, you have no eyes to see or mind to think about any others. Rajaji is just a match-stick to light the cigarette... You throw the match-stick into the ash-tray without a thought after it has served the purpose...

I am so tired and so hungering for rest, you can't guess it...

My career is truly remarkable in its zigzag. Cabinet Minister, Governor without power, Governor-General when the constitution was to be wound up, Minister without Portfolio, Home Minister and parliamentary work, and now the proposition is Acting High Commissioner in the U.K.! Finally I must one day cheerfully accept a senior clerk's place somewhere and raise that job to its proper importance (8.10.51).

Across the border, Premier Liaqat Ali was assassinated. In a letter to Ghulam Mohammed, who became Pakistan's Governor-General in a reshuffle, C.R. wrote:

It is difficult to predict what is in store for us all. But if we three — yourself, Nazimuddin Saheb (the new Premier) and myself as private gentlemen — fail to recreate lasting wisdom and love between our two peoples, I should pass out in sadness (24.10.51).

Learning of C.R.'s decision to retire, Rama Rao wrote a moving letter from Bangalore. He had not failed C.R. in half a century of friendship. Neither had C.R. ever let Rama Rao down. Aware of Rama Rao's hunger for affection, C.R. tried to assuage it with letters and assurances. At the same time, with Rama Rao as perhaps with no one else, C.R. was himself, saying what came to mind.

C.R. to Rama Rao, commenting on a newspaper picture sent by the latter of a doubtful holy man in the company of President Prasad, 9.3.50: I managed to keep exploiters at a good distance but poor Rajen Babu can't do it.

C.R. to Rama Rao, 1.12.50: Papa (C.R.'s daughter Namagiri) is excelling herself in her devotion, vigilant care and diligence. God indeed and everyone round about me have been so kind to me. I know what an unworthy soul I am. I am just unburdening myself.

Rama Rao to C.R., on 'Patel's death, 16.12.50: So far as I know — you will say I don't know much — there is only one man who can complete [Patel's] work.

Rama Rao to C.R., 23.5.51: Here is something from Winston Churchill's 'The Second World War': 'I had recourse to a method of life which I found greatly extended my daily capacity for work. I always went to bed at least for one hour as early as possible in the afternoon.'

C.R. to Rama Rao, 24.5.51: Am I as great as Winston Churchill because I too go to bed for one hour as early as possible in the afternoon and feel refreshed by the blessed oblivion?

Rama Rao to C.R, 1.6.51: You are both of you great, and you both sleep in the afternoon, but I have seen a number of people free from all suspicions of greatness enjoy the 'blessedness of oblivion' between, before and after meals . . . In fact they are awake only *during* them.

At a farewell meeting, C.R. said that henceforth 'my prayers, not my brains, will help' Nehru and his colleagues. Gracious as always, Jawaharlal gave a lunch for C.R. Prasad was present. Both were at Willingdon airport, as were Azad and other Ministers and diplomats, when on 1 November 1951 C.R. left for Madras. There citizens and rulers made the journey to Meenambakkam to welcome back the South's tired, proud son. He was 73.

20

'Downfall'

1951-54

Back in his Bazlulla Road home, C.R. savoured the success of his Mahabharata — both the Tamil and English versions were sold out and reprints were in the pipeline. Jawaharlal wrote that 'Delhi seems to be somewhat different without you. I feel rather lonely now' (22.11.51).

On his part C.R. was by no means clear about his own future. A suggestion (made by Rama Rao) that he should write his memoirs did not appeal to him. Apart from a horror of self-centred autobiographies, C.R. did not feel that all he had was his past.

True, he had hungered for a break and was enjoying it. He read a lot, including Robert Louis Stevenson's *Thrillers*. 'You must have read these pieces long ago,' he wrote to Rama Rao. 'They were reserved for my second childhood.' He enjoyed, too, an English translation of an old Tamil story of his own, saying to the translator: 'I read it now in a state of complete non-remembrance of the story I wrote. I think — though I say it — it is a good story.'[1]

And he agreed when Krishnamurti, editor of *Kalki*, proposed that he create, week by week, a version of the Ramayana for the journal. Yet he had not turned his back on the world — he had not, for one thing, resigned his seat in Parliament. When a newspaper reported that he 'desired to live like a sanyasi,' C.R.

issued a prompt disclaimer: 'I hope people will not take it that I made this claim or used this phrase.' Intrigued by the disclaimer, a Bombay commentator wrote, 'One wonders in what office he may turn up next'(*Times of India*, 28.12.51).

It was a shrewd observation, but the writer who made it must have been as startled as everyone else when, three months later, C.R. was sworn in as the Chief Minister of Madras!

How did it happen? Led to the hustings by the charismatic Nehru, Congress did very well everywhere except in the South. Trickling in from early January to mid-February 1952, the final results from Madras gave the Congress only 152 out of 375 seats. The Chief Minister, Kumaraswami Raja, and five of his cabinet had lost. The Communists won 61 seats, nine small parties found representation, and there were 63 successful independents.

Congress's debacle was most pronounced in Malabar, where it won only 4 out of 29 seats, and the Telugu country, where its tally was 43 out of 143. In the Tamil area it won 96 out of 190 (Narasimhan won the Krishnagiri Lok Sabha seat) and in South Kanara 9 out of 11. Reasons for the failure were soon supplied: a foodgrains crisis; loss of touch with the masses; Communist skill in playing on discontent; and the Andhra following of T. Prakasam, Chief Minister in 1946-7 and now a key figure in the Kripalani party.

Though he had lost his own seat, Prakasam claimed the support, not proved, of a front of 166 MLAs, including the Communists and independents. Unable to choose between Prakasam's claim and TNCC chief Kamaraj's assertion that 'only the Congress is going to rule,' the Governor, Maharaja Krishnakumarsinhji of Bhavnagar, whose retirement was due, referred the question to the President.

The Congress High Command, conferring in February and again in March, did not know what advice to give Nehru, who did not know what to advise the President, who was thus unable to send any word to the Governor. But by this time some in Madras felt they had found the answer: the South's son who had done big things in the past and was now not doing much. Though he was 73, if with his prestige he formed a ministry, it would survive. Most of the smaller parties and independents would support it.

The solution occurred almost simultaneously to several: to Raja, who as the 'caretaker' though defeated Chief Minister could play an important card or two; to Ramnath Goenka, the newspaper proprietor who had fought C.R. over the Press Bill and, earlier, had striven to deny C.R. the new Republic's Presidency; to C. Subramaniam, one of the successful Congress candidates, A.N. Sivaraman, editor of *Dinamani*, and others.

Most Congressmen saw C.R.'s appointment as the way out. If he was drafted, their link with power could continue. If not, there would be President's rule, if not Red rule. On 13 March *The Hindu* reported that Subramaniam as well as Congress's local committee at Virudhunagar had appealed to C.R. to take up the leadership. It was the signal for a flood of resolutions and telegrams.

The draft-C.R. forces received the enthusiastic backing of the Maharaja's successor in the Governor's seat, Sri Prakasa, who had just ended a term as a Minister at the centre. As Sri Prakasa would soon write (12.4.52) to President Prasad, 'After endless parleys, everybody came to one and only one solution — that the only person who could save the situation was Rajaji.'[2]

But would C.R. agree? When Goenka and Sivaraman called on him to probe his mind, he suggested President's rule and prayers to providence. But they as well as Subramaniam and Pattabhirama Rao, a newly-elected Telugu MLA, who also called on C.R., surmised that he was open to the idea. However, visitors asking the direct question were told that he was too tired. On 24 March Kamaraj and Sanjiva Reddy, the APCC chief, informed Nehru that 'attempts to persuade Rajaji' had been 'unsuccessful.' Reporting this, *The Hindu* added that Nehru expressed 'regret.'

Meanwhile C.R. had taken off for Courtallam, the watering resort. He was terribly torn. The proposition was exciting — it brought the scent of poetic justice. For C.R. remembered, though no longer with bitterness, that Madras had rejected him six years earlier. Perhaps, he grinned under a Courtallam waterfall while contemplating Kamaraj's inability to stop the run now towards him. And no doubt he recalled how enjoyable the 1937-9 Premiership of Madras had felt.

Yes, he liked to run Madras. Moreover, power was pursuing him, rather than the other way round. Yet there was another side. Was it dignified for a former Governor-General to become a Chief Minister? Also, he would be acutely embarrassed if he showed willingness but Nehru was cool — so far Jawaharlal had not voiced support for the move to draft him. Again, Kamaraj, whose backing was crucial, had not yet come to him.

Finally, and about this C.R. was perfectly clear, there was no question of his contesting a by-election. He had kept out of the Lok Sabha fray — in part at least out of disgust at the role of money in elections — and would not now ask to be voted to the Assembly. Though we have no direct evidence of it, another factor may have been an unwillingness in C.R., a Brahmin in an increasingly anti-Brahmin climate, to risk caste confrontation as well as possible defeat.

In any case, Raja, Goenka, Subramaniam and company had been hard at work. On 29 March C.R. was back in Madras. That day the Congress Legislature Party unanimously resolved to request C.R. to lead it, and a delegation led by Raja that included Kamaraj and Reddy carried the resolution to C.R.'s first-floor room on Bazlulla Road.

'You must save the province,' said Raja. 'You can stay on,' C.R. said to Raja.[3] This, earlier, had been Kamaraj's proposal too. The idea was that Raja would be elected leader and later returned in a by-election, the procedure adopted in Bombay over Morarji Desai, who also had narrowly lost his seat but was wanted as Chief Minister by the party.

'No, Rajaji,' said Raja without hesitation. 'I have come to request you to take the place.' 'At this rate,' said Rajaji, 'if Salem is in trouble you will ask me to become the municipal chairman.' Then he pleaded his age, asked to be spared — and enquired if they had Nehru's consent.

On 30 March *The Hindu* quoted Raja as saying that C.R. 'was still of the same mind and pleads inability, mainly for reasons of health.' Raja added, however, that he, Kamaraj and Reddy would continue their efforts to persuade Rajaji. Since C.R. had deflected the ball towards Jawaharlal, it was to him now that the Madras party sent a deputation: Subramaniam and Mrs Soundaram Ramachandran.

Calling on Nehru on the morning of 30 March, they presented the MLP resolution. Nehru made three points. One, he would not himself advise either the Madras party or Rajaji. Two, he would abide by the decision of the Madras party. Finally, if Rajaji agreed to take the lead, he should get himself elected as soon as possible to the lower house in Madras. Jawaharlal also sent, via the deputation, letters to Rajaji and Kumaraswami Raja. To C.R. he wrote:

> I had remained aloof for two reasons. One was that I did not feel justified in pressing you to undertake this heavy burden . . . The second reason was that I wanted the Madras Party to decide completely by itself . . . For my part I naturally accept it.[4]

On 31 March C.R. told Raja and Subramaniam that he was willing, but he also told them, as well as everyone else in Madras, that he was 'absolutely definite that he would in no circumstances stand for election' — to quote from Governor Sri Prakasa's letters of 1.4.52 to Prasad and Nehru in Delhi.

Now the Constitution was flexible enough to permit such obduracy: a member of the Upper House could function as Chief Minister. However, in his note to Raja, Nehru had written: 'It must be understood of course that early steps will have to be taken for Rajaji's election to the Madras Assembly.'[5]

To install C.R. on his terms would amount to flouting Nehru's wish, but the alternative was to lose C.R. and, with him, every chance of a Congress government. Raja and the Congress leaders of Madras chose the first course and, with Governor Sri Prakasa's full cooperation, proceeded at once to swear C.R. in as Chief Minister, before Nehru could come to know of C.R.'s inflexible condition.

A candid letter sent by Sri Prakasa to President Prasad on 1.4.52 described what happened in Madras:

> Yesterday was a day of great goings and comings; of tense moments of anxiety; of much hard thinking and heart searching as to what was right and ought to be done. I met the Chief Minister twice and Rajaji also was good enough to come and talk to me fully . . . I must not worry you with details; but

late in the afternoon the clouds, luckily for all, cleared, and it was agreed:

(i) that I should nominate Rajaji to the upper house, and in order that the matter may not look too obvious, I should nominate two or three other people along with him; (ii) that after this, the Congress party in the assembly should unanimously elect Rajaji as their leader . . . The programme as detailed above went through to schedule . . .[6]

C.R. was nominated under a constitutional clause that enabled a Governor, when advised by a Chief Minister, to send to the Upper House persons 'having special knowledge in such matters as literature, science, art and social service.' No doubt C.R. qualified under both literature and social service, but the clause was not quite conceived for accommodating a Chief Minister-to-be who thought poorly of elections. The spirit of the Constitution had been violated.

Even apart from that, was it proper for C.R. to accept the Chief Ministership? When the possibility was first raised, 'Kalki' Krishnamurti likened it in his weekly to Ramana Maharshi becoming chairman of the Tiruvannamalai municipality. Reading a mistaken story that C.R. had rejected the pressure, Dr T.S.S. Rajan, C.R.'s old friend and ministerial colleague in the late thirties, wrote to him, 'You have saved your self-respect.'[7] 'We had put Rajaji at the level of Delhi, not at Madras level,' the leader of the opposition in Madras, Tenneti Viswanatham, would soon say.[8]

In a defensive phrase in a letter to Nehru (4.4.52), C.R. referred to 'the notion that all work is equally noble.' Some, of course, admired the audacity of the 73-year-old C.R., including, predictably, Rama Rao, who wrote to his friend (1.4.52):

Only an overpowering call of duty could justify this sacrifice . . . I remember Ruskin somewhere lauds the heroism of the tired guardian of the temple who leans half-fainting on his sword but springs up like fire to meet a menace.

But the doubts did not disappear. The day after he was sworn in, C.R. himself said, 'In my private journal I would call this my downfall' (*The Hindu*, 2.4.52). We do not know whether he was referring to his acceptance of the leadership, or to the nomination, or to both. In a brave defence of the nomination in the Assembly, C.R. said:

> Did not the framers of the Constitution imagine that there would be circumstances when a man not elected would have to be called in for the good of society?[9]

'Rajaji should seek an early opportunity to get himself elected to the popular House,' wrote *The Hindu* (2.4.52). C.R. was unmoved. With himself C.R. may have argued that he was entitled to set his own terms for a job that was being pushed on him. Also, had he not opposed elections 'on principle'? But should such an opponent enter an elected body?

The haste with which C.R. was nominated and chosen leader, and the obvious decision to present everybody, including Nehru, with a fait accompli, also left an unpleasant taste. Yet, given C.R.'s firm stand regarding a by-election, the exclusion of Nehru, and therefore speed, was essential. Raja and Sri Prakasa calculated that while Nehru was not likely to agree to C.R.'s terms ahead of time, he would hesitate to disturb an arrangement once it had been made.

The judgement was vindicated. Though put out for some days by Sri Prakasa's word that Chief Minister Rajaji would not contest a by-election, Nehru was soon engaged in friendly correspondence with C.R. about the latter's Ministry. C.R. told Nehru:

> I am struggling to find a team who may inspire confidence. The field is very limited and poor (4.4.52).

The tricky exercise took C.R. nine days during which he allowed few to know his mind. Then he acted with finality. Producing a list of 15 including himself, he declared that 'all appointments are closed' (*The Hindu*, 11.4.52). Many of the chosen learnt of their luck from newspapers or on the radio. On 10 April they were sworn in.

Apart from Manickavelu Naicker, head of the Commonweal Party, which had 6 MLAs, the rest were Congressmen. C.R. was keen to have the eminent and independent educator, Lakshmanaswami Mudaliar, as number two. It was an astute thought. The presence of Mudaliar, esteemed both in anti-Brahmin and Brahmin circles, would have weakened the opposition that C.R. was bound to receive from the former, but Mudaliar declined.

The support of all groups except the Communists was invited by C.R., and he even issued a public welcome to Prakasam. The latter spurned it but a number of independents and the smaller parties responded, even though, barring the case of Manickavelu Naicker, office had not been offered. C.R.'s majority was obvious from the day the Assembly first met, and the vote of confidence that followed went 200 to 151 in C.R.'s favour.

Shrewdly and mercilessly, C.R. played on the unexpressed yet very real fear of the Communists harboured by many of the MLAs sitting with them on the opposition benches. In his first Assembly speech he said:

> I am here to save my country from the traps and the dangers of the Communist party. (*Applause*). That is my policy from A to Z. I am placing my cards on the table. I am your enemy number one, and may I say you are my enemy number one. This is my policy.

> And what is the Communist policy? Every difficulty, every discontent, every complaint must be taken up, expanded, exaggerated, repeated, added to, rolled on and made to grow like a snowball . . .

The public's chief concern was food. Lengthening ration-shop queues and soaring open-market prices of rice had played an important part in Congress's electoral setback. Asked by a reporter, 'Will there be an increase in the food ration?' the Chief Minister replied, 'You must pray for rain' (*The Hindu*, 11.4.52).

He repeated the advice in a broadcast.

In the Assembly there were taunts. 'The Congress is relieved that Rajaji is at the helm, and Rajaji is relieved that God is at the helm,' said a Communist member. Asking if the scoffers had better methods of inducing rain, C.R. added, 'No irony, no sarcasm or ridicule, no cocksureness of upstartist knowledge can shake me from my faith in God.'

Fortunately for C.R. and the people of the South, rain

arrived; almost unbelievably, it arrived in early May. The waters came pouring down, emboldening C.R. to move in a direction towards which the long queues for rice had often nudged him: decontrol.

Convinced that there were stocks in the countryside, and confident now that they would soon be replenished, he decided, a month after taking office, to remove the controls on the distribution and price of rice.

Rafi Ahmed Kidwai, the new Food Minister in Delhi, agreeing, C.R. announced decontrol. Within days grain started to flow and the queues disappeared. At least for a year C.R.'s decontrol was such a success that even the Communists did not oppose it.

Another popular measure was an ordinance, later replaced by an Act, that aided small tenants and farm labourers in Tanjore district, the granary of the Tamil country. Following clashes between landlords and tenants, many evictions had been ordered in the area. The new law prohibited evictions, enabled restoration if eviction had taken place, and put up the labourers' wages.

The province's handloom weavers, feeding some five million mouths, were also given some relief, and C.R. strove hard but unsuccessfully to reserve all weaving of coloured saris and bordered dhotis for them. His Assembly voted unanimously for the proposal, but the Centre disallowed it.

His rule, in short, was going down very well. The crowds he was attracting were large, and there were unfounded stories that taking advantage of his obvious popularity C.R. would go in for a snap election.

Disarmingly C.R. had said, 'I was in a different world, with the characters of the Ramayana, and I have forgotten everything about the legislature here' (*The Hindu*, 2.4.52). But MLAs found that his skills were intact, as when there was a demand to know what C.R. had written to Nehru about the formation of a new Andhra state.

C.R.: It is a confidential letter.

Viswanatham: Under what provision of the law is the correspondence treated as confidential.

C.R.: These are letters from one gentleman to another and gentlemen's correspondence is always private.[10]

Having to face his strong personality, his ministerial colleagues did not initiate much. 'He will be the Member, the rest of you numbers,' Kamaraj had warned Pattabhirama Rao, one of the younger Ministers.[11] Obeying C.R.'s instructions, the Ministers kept the corridors of Fort St. George clear of partymen, which meant that officials 'felt free to do their duty according to their lights,' as one of them, M.V. Subramaniam, would put it. Subramaniam would add that 'the administration was toned up to a level that has not been reached before or after, since independence.'[12]

C.R.'s industry made a mockery of his earlier talk of fatigue. 'On an average,' he told the Assembly, 'I see 100 files a day. Each has a problem, a tragedy or a history behind it.'[13] His candour, too, was striking. Thus a radio appeal for a public loan would start as follows: 'Very poor people, please switch off, this appeal is not intended for you'![14] It was not dull working under a Chief Minister like this, who also produced memorable phrases at will. For example, a few weeks after saying how he viewed the Communists, he told the Assembly: 'Let me now name my enemy number two — the Public Works Department.'[15]

Yet what impressed officials did not carry the party. While conscious that it owed its current fortune to C.R., Congress nonetheless disliked some of his utterances, as when he said to a huge beach audience that the shrinkage in Congress's strength was 'good for democracy' and proved 'the South's intelligence,' and added: 'I have been called to sweep away the cobwebs and clean the drains of the houses of Congress' (*The Hindu*, 2.4.52).

In any case, he could not really clean Congress without controlling it. Lacking the stamina and patience for party management, he spurned all suggestions that he take over the TNCC. Kamaraj, who had left the TNCC presidentship following the electoral setback, soon resumed the charge.

It was time to carve out Andhra, the battlecry of all the Telugu MLAs before and after the elections. Those in the opposition spoke only in Telugu, which C.R. understood and in which he occasionally replied. Unlike the Mahatma, who saw practical worth in linguistic provinces, C.R. thought they would impede national intercourse and economic advance. Nehru and, before his death, Patel were of a similar mind, but the virtually unanimous Telugu sentiment could not be denied. After Potti Sriramulu died fasting for a separate Andhra, New Delhi yielded.

'The sooner it is put through, the better,' C.R. advised Nehru in December 1952.[16] Simultaneously, he said that Madras city, where Tamils greatly outnumbered Telugus, could not go to Andhra. Yet proximity, old links and their reading of history had persuaded many Telugus that the city had to go with Andhra. Or, argued Prakasam, who had formed an action council over the issue, the city should be turned into a joint capital or a union territory.

Opposing the demand, C.R. was not willing even to see Madras as Andhra's temporary capital. Admitting that many Telugus would call him 'ungenerous, hard and partisan,' he claimed he was saving the future from disputes.[17] At the same time he put his foot down against a Tamil demand for Tirupati. That his remote ancestor Nallan Chakravarti had lived in the temple city was immaterial, as was an old Tamil text referring to Tirupati as the northern boundary of the Tamil country. Only numbers mattered, and in Tirupati these were clearly in Andhra's favour.

To escape from charges of partiality, C.R. proposed, to Nehru and Sri Prakasa, that he should resign as Chief Minister and President's rule for the province should follow, enabling officials to partition it. But there was little question of Nehru accepting such a suggestion; as for Sri Prakasa, he simply said to C.R., 'If you go, I hope you will please allow me also to go.'[18]

Happily, mistrust was forgotten by the time the state formally split on 1 October 1953. In the Assembly Tamil MLAs offered Andhra their good wishes, and Telugu MLAs, their battle won, spoke in English. 'We shall feel the pain of it when there is nobody to give us trouble,' said C.R., adding that he would particularly miss the 'young and bright faces' of the Andhra Communists with whom he had crossed swords.[19]

The Communists received a jolt. Deserting their company, Prakasam became Andhra's first Chief Minister — through Congress support. It was a development that C.R. had publicly and privately espoused.[20] When Prakasam went to C.R.'s home to share his joy, C.R. did not allow his visitor, six years' older than him, to climb the Bazlulla Road steps. The two talked in Prakasam's car. C.R. expressed his gladness, and the eyes of the lion of Andhra were wet.[21]

The 'tired old man' was putting to shame his ministerial colleagues, some of whom were half his age, sailing unflinchingly into the sea of files at Fort St. George, facing questions and debates in the two houses, touring a district a month, and keeping up a daily schedule of correspondence, visitors, talks and functions. But he never ceased reminding himself of his age and fragility. In an engagements diary he would note, 'Ill for the last three days,' 'The hernia has burst on the left also,' and so forth. After calling on C.R. in the autumn of 1952, the American author Louis Fischer wrote to him:

> May I now gently chide you? You told me yesterday that you were a frail boy and had always been frail, and yet you have managed to live with your frailty to 73. So why can't you continue to be frail and live on and on . . .[22]

Almost daily he found diversion in books — amazingly, his eyes were cooperating. Police officials anxious about a likely riot and desirous of instructions would visit Bazlulla Road in the morning and find the Chief Minister 'lounging in an easy chair, reading.'[23] And C.R. would spend minutes on chores that were perfectly needless and perfectly charming. Thus he would pen author R.K. Narayan a note:

> Sometimes good luck brings about a combination of time and mood and I read one of your contributions in the *Hindu*. And then I am bewitched by the talent and sparkle of it and a joy overwhelms me . . .[24]

Or he would read Thornton Wilder's *The Bridge of San Luis Rey* twice over, finding it 'wonderfully good' — and then inform the publishers of misprints he had noticed. Or, spotting an archaic phrase in a government order ('His Excellency the Governor is *pleased* to declare Madras city a cholera-affected area'), he would instruct a change. Or he would advise *The Hindu* on how Tamil vowels should be spelt in English, or propose ingenious and indeed sensible reforms for the Hindi script to Govind Ballabh Pant, the UP Chief Minister, who had merely wanted C.R. to bless a conference on script reform.

Callers included Aneurin Bevan, Edwina Mountbatten, Eisenhower's Democratic opponent Adlai Stevenson, and the US Vice-President, Richard Nixon. For Nixon, the encounter with Rajaji was 'the most memorable' of a trip on which he 'met scores of Presidents and princes and Prime Ministers.'[25] However, according to Henry Ramsey, the American Consul General in Madras at the time, C.R. himself was 'not highly impressed' with Nixon.[26]

If some interesting faces appeared before him, others were, simply, disappearing. Rama Rao reminded him that at their age milestones were tombstones. Erskine, his 1937-9 Governor, Muniswami Pillai, one of C.R.'s staunchest Harijan allies, Gopalaswami Iyengar, who had been his colleague in the Delhi Cabinet, and two close Muslim friends, Asaf Ali and Shafique-ur-Rahman, died. Thirty years earlier, Rahman had been C.R.'s companion in Vellore Jail. C.R. recalled him as a 'saint in the disguise of a citizen.'[27]

T.S.S. Rajan, friend of forty years, died in Trichy. Earlier, C.R. had secretly taken an overnight train to see the ailing Rajan and flown back to Madras in time for the day's work. And T. Vijiaraghachariar — T.V. — whom he had met at the turn of the century in Salem, went. C.R.'s 1953 engagements diary contains the following jottings:

Feb. 21: T.V. very ill and suffering. *Feb. 28*: T.V. passed away last night and I got the information this morning. My heart is made of stone and I don't weep.

Apart from hearing sad news, C.R. was having to do unpleasant things. Madras city's tramway had to be closed. Rebelling police constables had to be rounded up and some dismissed. Requests of intimate friends had to be turned down. A.V. Raman, close since Salem days, sought a grant for completing an English-Tamil dictionary, a project that C.R. had encouraged over the years. Now, however, he was unwilling to extend governmental help. Raman's son would recall that 'a curt official communication rejecting the request hurt my father deeply.'[28]

When Rama Rao asked for an introduction to Morarji Desai, Bombay's Chief Minister, C.R. first gave the following note (14.2.53): 'My dear Morarji, Sri Navaratna Rama Rao is an old classmate and lifelong friend who just wishes to pay his respects to you . . . He is the best English scholar I know of in India and a very dear friend.' Soon, however, C.R. asked his friend why he wished to meet Morarji. Admitting that he had had a business interest in mind, Rama Rao returned C.R.'s introduction.

Rising levels of water in the province's reservoirs and of money in its coffers would fill C.R.'s heart with satisfaction. 'The rains have been ample and the districts are thoroughly under cultivation,' he noted in his diary. 'Not an inch left out' (27.11.53). Likewise, 'The loan has been heavily oversubscribed. Nine crores for five crores' (23.7.53).

His spirits were fed, too, as his jottings testify, by the warmth and size of the crowds he drew on his tours. Thus (about Madura), 'Deeply touched by what I saw.' 'At Trichy. Enormous big public meeting.'

With audiences in a hall he was as much of a hit as ever. To Presidency College students he said: 'Education does not consist in carrying a very heavy load of knowledge in your head. Will you call a donkey which carries a heavy load of clothes on its back a well-dressed one?'[29] While in a car together, Narasimhan asked his father how he found his similes. Replied C.R.:

My difficulty is not in finding but in choosing and rejecting. Everything is a simile — this car, the trees, the crows, the lamp-post . . .[30]

His random 1953 jottings, consisting of up to six sentences put down every few days, reveal his interests and opinions, and at times some inner experiences.

> 17.6.53: What a dream I had last night. It is now more than 12 hours after I got up from it. But the pain and terror still continue . . . I was in abject want and I begged for Rs 5 from people I did not know and I was disappointed. I have lost my way, missed my train and all that on numerous nights. But this is the first experience of this kind.

> 9.7.53: Enjoying Cicero. More his letters than his superbly eloquent essays . . . Letters show politics of Rome 2000 years ago as of today.

> 10.8.53: Saw Gemini Vasan's picture *Avvaiyar*. T.K. Shanmugam's play is a hundred times superior to this picture . . . A lot of stock scenes of thunder, lightning and storm, of water flowing and elephants trooping and cardboard fortresses falling . . . The music is execrable!

> 25.11.53: Went to Thorapalli. What a ruin and what squalor! The river and the old tamarind trees were the only things that remained to bring forth the old days to mind. It was melancholy altogether to go to this place which was so dear in my childhood . . . What poverty all over and all round! This is India indeed after 70 years.

But reawakened memories fought the disappointment, and to cousin Singaramma — daughter of uncle Ramaswami Iyengar — who was living in 'the old, old house,' C.R. spoke of their grandmother Rangamma:

> Rangamma's father gave this house to her. Don't sell it. I want to be cremated here near the river.

Some Thorapalli villagers said to him: 'You have achieved so much, but why have you done nothing for Thorapalli?' Replied the village's greatest son: 'A man earns and gives his earnings to his wife, who feeds all the guests first. Only if anything is left can she eat.'

The separation of Andhra meant the end of C.R.'s indispensability. In the residuary province, Congress MLAs constituted a majority and were capable of ruling without C.R.'s help. He wanted to resign and, as we have seen, said so to Nehru, who, however, stamped out the idea. 'I am sorry I cannot think of releasing you,' Jawaharlal wrote (12.2.53). It was Nehru's assessment — as one of his Ministers, Mahavir Tyagi, had informed C.R. — that 'Rajaji has saved Madras for us.'[31]

Though C.R. stayed on, he seems to have sensed risk in not resigning. In his diary he wrote (14.2.53):

> What shall I do with Jawaharlal Nehru? Whatever I might do he will not get irritated or release me. His affection and his patience have indeed become a trouble. He insists on crucifying me.

But C.R. was nursing the crucifixion-wish himself. It was manifested in his brilliantly-conceived, and suicidal, scheme for educational reform, introduced just before Andhra's separation.

The Constitution had said that all children should enter primary school. In Madras only 47.8 per cent were enrolled — figures elsewhere were no better — and three out of five of these were likely to leave school before putting in the prescribed five years.

C.R. decided that he could attack the problem by reducing a child's time in primary school from five to three hours a day. Teachers and buildings would serve twice in a day — and therefore, in theory at least, twice the number of pupils. In addition, schoolchildren would spend the two hours gifted to them in learning creative skills from parents, relations and neighbours.

With this single, simple, sweeping stroke, C.R. hoped to double the literacy rate at the elementary level and, simultaneously, impart creative skills to the pupil's hands. Contemplated for long and advocated by him while he was Governor-General, the reform was influenced by his own childhood. As he told the Madras Assembly:

> When I was a little boy, I had to walk one mile to go to the primary school, go there early in the morning, come back for the midday meal, have a hurried meal and run to reach there in time, and then come back in the evening . . . I hated the six-hour school.[32]

Forty-six years earlier, in an article in Patna's *Hindustan Review* (June 1907), C.R. had described village teachers as 'angry ill-educated' men given to 'hammering down the human curiosity' of the child. Not diminishing with time, this distrust of teachers was accompanied in C.R. by a romantic view of rural artisans. As Governor-General he had said:

> The food is grown, the cloth is woven, the sheep are shorn, the shoes are stitched, the scavenging is done, the cartwheels and the ploughs are built and repaired because, thank God, the respective castes are still there, and the homes are trade schools as well, and the parents are masters as well, to whom the children are automatically apprenticed.[33]

Now, as Chief Minister, he was in a position to translate the vision. He argued:

> It is a mistake to imagine that the school is within the walls. The whole village is the school. The village polytechnic is there, every branch of it: the dhobi, the wheelwright, the cobbler.[34]

As C.R. saw it, children would 'observe' rural skills in the first three years and learn them (from the community) in the remaining two. But this learning would not be compulsory, and girls would stay at home, unless their parents desired the contrary. The government reckoned that out of 32,000 primary schools in the province, over 21,000 had children only from 'occupational' families who would 'automatically' impart a creative outlook to their wards. The less than 11,000 schools left would tap craftsmen and farmers in their villages.

In other words, the 'polytechnic' part of C.R.'s reform would be the village's responsibility. No 'experts' were to be recruited, and to begin with at any rate no financial provision was made for the outdoor programme. C.R.'s claim that the reform would correct the Indian bias against manual work was thus based primarily on wishful expectation. Another weakness stemmed from C.R.'s haste — he had the scheme launched in June 1953, before obtaining the Assembly's sanction.

However, it was the scheme's seeming validation of the caste system that invited the fiercest opposition. The reform was

attacked as a Brahmin's device to condemn boys of lower castes
to their father's occupations. Wanting to preserve and disseminate
the skills of the countryside, C.R. was accused, with devastating
effect, of seeking to preserve the caste system, indeed to perpetuate
higher-caste domination.

Where a nostalgic, romantic C.R. saw relief and smiles on
the faces of Tamil boys, and dexterity coming to their hands, the
fathers of some of the boys saw malice in C.R.'s heart. They
were encouraged to do this by the fiery, bearded E.V.R., who
had been a thorn to C.R.'s first ministry and who now stumped
the Tamil districts, warning the Dravidas against the machinations
of Rajaji, the Aryan whose forefathers had descended down the
Khyber Pass to subjugate the sons of the soil.

To K.M. Panikkar, ambassador in Cairo, who had praised
a talk by C.R. on Hinduism, he wrote (16.7.53):

> I am doomed to the purgatory of a caste-hatred-ridden state
> like Madras. But alas I still love the southern country and its
> people. What is one to do?

Though M.V. Krishna Rao held the education portfolio, the
reform was C.R.'s idea and burden. C. Subramaniam took
charge of education after Krishna Rao left with the other
Andhra MLAs, but the scheme remained the Rajaji scheme. It
had defenders. Zakir Husain, the educator who would become
the President of India, approved of it. The Central Advisory
Board of Education welcomed it. The state of Bihar considered
adopting it and asked for details.

But where it mattered, in Madras, resistance was strong and
growing. At the end of July 1953, just before the departure of
the Andhra MLAs, there was ambiguous voting. A motion for
dropping the scheme was defeated by the Speaker's casting vote,
but another motion for staying the reform and referring it to a
committee was passed 139 to 137.

How was the Ministry to stay the reform without dropping
it? 'The scheme is stayed where it was was on the date on which
the Assembly adopted the resolution,' said Subramaniam.[35] It
would not, in other words, be extended to towns or the small
percentage of rural schools still teaching for five hours a day.
Opposition MLAs called it 'a wonderful interpretation.'[36]

C.R. would have invited less hostility had his defence of the scheme been confined to the adequacy and advantages of a shortened schoolday. But he got carried away by the potential he saw in 'the village polytechnic,' and made a gift to E.V.R. and others of the issue of caste. Some of the reform's opponents defied laws and courted arrest. Among them was C.N. Annadurai, who had broken with E.V.R. to form the Dravida Munnetra Kazhagam (DMK).

The flow of sentiment was unmistakable. 'My education policy has stood in the way of my general political popularity,' C.R. admitted in the Assembly (24.12.53). But he was not going to yield. 'I have left this undone all these years and feel I should attempt it at least now,' he said.[37] At the end of the year he claimed that in the district of Madura, scene of sustained agitation against the scheme, admissions had gone up by 40 per cent.[38] And with some truth he maintained that but for his reform 'people outside would not have taken very much interest in education.'[39]

But the tide of hostility repulsed all arguments. Remarkably, however, C.R.'s personal relationship with E.V.R. survived. After a public occasion attended by both, C.R. noted in his diary (20.12.53): 'E.V.R. and I had prophets' meeting. Big gathering greatly happy at our being together.'

The politician profiting from the creation of Andhra was Kamaraj. Congress's Tamil MLAs, a majority, as we have seen, in the truncated house, owed their tickets to him. Gaining, too, from the unpopularity of Rajaji's education scheme, Kamaraj probed C.R. in September 1953 about a change in leadership. C.R. had suspected his intentions for a while. His 4 May jotting was:

> It happens I am reading Julius Caesar III. Kamaraj is stabbing Caesar I fear just the same way. God forgive him.

Now, in September, C.R. issued a public reply to the private challenge. Let the legislature party meet, he said in a statement, 'and see if it wants a new leader. From Delhi Nehru sent word that there was no occasion for such a exercise, and Kamaraj backed away very fast.

However, in November, Varadarajulu Naidu, who had announced his readiness for the chief ministership before C.R. was drafted — and whom C.R. had defended in the celebrated 1919 sedition case — asked for a change in leadership and claimed the backing of 39 other Congress MLAs. Nehru said that Naidu's action was 'highly improper,' but the revolt revealed the current. A short sentence from C.R., 'I suspend the education scheme in view of lack of support,' would have arrested the flow. But C.R. was, well, C.R. All Kamaraj had to do was wait.

By the beginning of 1954, C.R. was fully 75. As always there were interesting engagements: meetings with men like Louis St. Laurent, the Canadian Prime Minister, or the scientist Julian Huxley. Or with Soviet artistes performing a ballet. To Nikolai Bespalov, the deputy minister leading the troupe, C.R. remarked with calculated indiscretion, 'I may say, music takes us near God' (*The Hindu*, 20.2.54).

As Chief Minister he ensured a Gandhi memorial of the kind he wanted in Madras city — a simple, open, attractive place for communion with God. C.R. would explain that it was while hastening to pray that Gandhi had died. At his suggestion Sri Prakasa and the Government of India agreed that the memorial should occupy a portion of the Governor's estate in Guindy. The only building Rajaji ever 'built' — he laid down its concept, raised funds for it from citizens and personally approved the stone-carvers — the Gandhi Mandapam of Guindy can be seen as an expression in stone of C.R.'s sentiment for the Mahatma.

In February, Subramaniam found it necessary to scotch speculation that C.R. would 'become Congress President, or rejoin the Nehru Cabinet, or retire' (*The Hindu*, 10.2.54). An opposition MLA, Antony Pillai, said in the Assembly that 'the very people who hailed Rajaji's leadership two years ago as a godsend' now wanted him to go, and a colleague of Pillai's, Jivanandan, observed, 'Rajaji speaks like a weary man' (*The Hindu*, 7.3.54).

But the most ominous words came from a former Chief Minister, O.P. Ramaswami Reddiar. Addressing C.R. in the Madras Council, Reddiar said: 'Please give up the scheme without any more ado. It is a new handle to the blackshirts (*E.V.R.'s followers*). Persistence will only sound the death-knell of our party' (*Indian Express*, 10.3.54).

C.R. now fired his final round of ammunition. Answering Reddiar, he said: 'It is wrong to give up the scheme . . . Look at the animal world. Anything that turns its face forward carries the day. That which turns its back loses the battle' (*Indian Express*, 11.3.54). And Subramaniam declared that with the reform attendance was increasing — and that in June the scheme might be extended to towns.

There was an uproar, and a meeting of the Congress MLAs was fixed for 24 March. Nature, too, was speaking — C.R. was attacked by bronchial pneumonia. Aware that he had to go, he offered his head in exchange for the scheme's continuance. But Kamaraj was too astute to accept the deal. Calling at Bazlulla Road on 23 March, he said, 'You stay, Rajaji, but please suspend the scheme.' 'My staying is now impossible,' replied C.R. Once it was clear that C.R. would resign, Kamaraj offered a sop: the scheme would not be immediately dropped. Together they decided to put off the party meeting.

On 25 March the papers referred to free talk of C.R. wanting to quit. Later that morning a 'weak and pale' Rajaji, absent from the house for a dozen days, slowly walked to the Assembly floor and delivered a five-minute statement 'in a calm and clear tone.' It was 'heard in pin-drop silence.'

> Ever since I fell ill this time, I have beeen thinking of relieving myself. I do wish to be relieved and I must make the best arrangement possible (*Indian Express*, 26.3.54).

He did not touch on the education scheme or indeed on anything other than his fatigue, but there was some bitterness in his remark about 'an undue, almost indecent desire for an event to happen' — a reference to the stories in the morning's papers. Later in the day he met the Governor, his ministerial colleagues and the Congress MLAs, and claimed that 'Congress will vote as a party' in support of his scheme. For a month the scheme was not touched. In May it was dropped.

Once more his Tamil country had rejected C.R. Kamaraj was proposed for the post of leader by Varadarajulu Naidu. In the election, C.R. presiding, Kamaraj received 93 votes as against the 41 that went to Subramaniam, who had offered himself at Rajaji's instance. C.R. announced the result, and Kamaraj was 'profusely garlanded and lustily cheered' (*The Hindu*, 31.3.54). Wisely, he retained most of the Rajaji team, including Subramaniam. On 13 April C.R. was formally released of his charge.

He had not consulted Jawaharlal over his decision to resign. Neither did Nehru, who knew of C.R.'s intention a week before it was publicized, make any move to prevent his departure. C.R. had thus begun, run and ended his show without involving Nehru. It had been an exercise in independence. In fact, it was because he relished independence that he much preferred the Madras job, with all the poison over caste it seemed to attract, to a comfortable post *under* another in New Delhi.

They had written to each other frequently and not always on 'business.' Thus C.R. would want to know more about the man Vijayalakshmi's daughter Rita was marrying. Nehru would reply (26.8.53): 'Avatar Krishna Dar is a . . . quiet and rather shy young man. He comes from a Kashmiri Brahmin family. And so, rather accidentally, we are reverting to our community in this marriage of Rita.' Or C.R. would send 'blessings and good wishes' on Nehru's birthday.

Visiting Madras shortly after C.R.'s resignation, Nehru spoke of C.R. in generous terms. In response, C.R. wrote (19.4.54):

I have no words to pay you back even in slight measure for the affectionate and most gracious terms in which you referred to this sole remnant of a bygone generation.

But there were differences. C.R. had discussed a few of them, at the end of 1952, with Louis Fischer, Gandhi's biographer. C.R. apparently expressed the hope that with time Nehru would change some of his views. After the talk, Fischer wrote to C.R. (18.9.52):

I believe that some straight talk to the power that is would do a lot of good, for I doubt whether time cures certain diseases . . . You are the one man who, after your achievement in the state, could appeal to his mind.

P. Ramamurti, the Communist MLA who became the opposition leader in Madras after the separation of Andhra, thought that Nehru's reluctance to come to C.R.'s aid over the education scheme produced 'a sharp bitterness' in the latter,[40] but this view is not easily corroborated.

What is certain is that C.R. had done his best to push himself off his chair. He would rather yield his head than his idea; and he would persist with the latter even when there was no hope of success. He knew he had run into a wall but claimed there was danger in turning back. In a letter to Asoka Mehta, a future member of the Indian Cabinet, he spoke, to Mehta's distress, of 'moving forward more or less blindly.'[41]

There was some truth, therefore, in what he had himself written to Rama Rao shortly after the tide had begun to turn against him (17.8.53):

I am having my share of trials and tests. I am not entitled to any pity, for it is all of my own making.

A stubborn crucifixion-wish was not, however, the only feature of his Chief Ministership. He had given his province fiscal health. Just before C.R. took over, Chintaman Deshmukh, the Union Finance Minister, had said to Sri Prakasa that if things did not improve in Madras he would 'ask the Reserve Bank to decline to honour your cheques.'[42] Now the state had, in the Governor's words, 'very good finances.'[43]

Also, as the *Indian Express* put it (14.4.54), 'the tone both of public life and official administration improved.' A judge of the High Court would say, 'There was never even a semblance of any attempt to interfere with the administratrion of justice during Rajaji's regime.'[44]

Others noted, as in 1937-9, his attentiveness, courtesy, and good humour towards the opposition benches. After the resignation was announced, Lakshmanaswami Mudaliar, opposition leader in the Council, said of C.R.: 'No one has greater parliamentary gifts . . . and no one has maintained the traditions of parliamentary life to the extent to which he has. No one has given to the whole house the dignity and the status that he has' (*The Hindu*, 31.3.54).

In the view of the *Indian Express* (1.4.54), by pre-empting in 1952 a Communist role in the government, C.R. had 'retrieved a situation that bordered on anarchy.' The newspaper was repeating an assessment made earlier by Govind Ballabh Pant, the UP Chief Minister. In a letter to C.R. (3.9.53), Pant had said: 'Madras was on the brink of a precipice and has been luckily saved by you.'

But we know there was another side—above all, his refusal to get himself elected.

21

Wolves
1954-8

With Rajaji's exit, Sri Prakasa became Chief Minister. He now made what C.R. termed 'a most kind personal proposal.' Whatever it was — perhaps an offer to recommend to Nehru a new position for C.R. —, the proposal was turned down. 'I hope you will fully and freely acquit me of pride,' C.R. wrote to the Governor (23.4.54).

He publicly referred to Kamaraj's 'good sense and firmness' (*The Hindu*, 20.4.54) — perhaps hoping that the new Chief Minister would retain the education reform. When the scheme was given up, C.R. expressed his regret in restrained language: 'It did not have a fair trial . . . I had planned to find finances for the out-of-school portion of the scheme.'[1]

Many had written praising his latest term in office and lamenting his departure. In a characteristic public statement, he asked them not to expect replies. 'I have no help with writing or typing work,' he explained, adding, 'I cannot spare the energy to assist those with problems' (*Indian Express*, 24.4.54). Clarifying, in an interview, that he was not 'retiring from public life,' he revealed lack of foresight when he added, 'I might even consider myself a life member of the Congress high command' (*The Hindu*, 20.4.54).

Antibiotics clearing his lungs, he had plunged into the Ramayana rendering that he had put off in favour of the Chief

Ministership. The Ramayana took him over, exercising his intellect, refreshing his spirit, cooling his resentment. Week by week he retold the tale in *Kalki*; in July the *Sunday Standard* started serializing it in English. He loved the labour and the public loved his direct, heartfelt pieces. But C.R. could not forgive the hero his ultimate hardness towards Sita. At the end of 18 months' toil, he wrote to Rama Rao, who had assisted with the English version:

> Yesterday I finished the last chapter of the Tamil series of
> Valmiki and sent Rama back to Ayodhya after his disgraceful
> performance on the battlefield with Sita (20.10.55).

The English series continued for another year. Then, as a paperback, C.R.'s Ramayana, along with his earlier Mahabharata, achieved virtually unmatched sales.

On 15 August it was announced that C.R. would be the first recipient of free India's highest award, the Bharat Ratna. It was, at bottom, Nehru's decision, though President Prasad made the actual presentation on 26 January 1955. C.R. was moved and delighted. 'I cannot pretend not to find pleasure in the token of affection received from friends and colleagues,' he wrote (21.8.54) to V.T. Krishnamachari, who had grown up not far from him and at the same time, and was now deputy chairman of the Planning Commission.

To many the Bharat Ratna seemed a hint that despite his disclaimer he had in fact retired. He certainly read like one who had, returning again and again to Shakespeare, coping with *Paradises Lost and Regained*, re-reading Samuel Johnson, and finding Jack London's *White Fang*, to which Rama Rao had introduced him, 'a deep book.' Once (24.3.50) he had written to Rama Rao, 'I always felt it was a bad thing to read books and be absorbed in that pleasure.' Now the sin was being daily committed.

Apart from books there were the journals sent by their owners or by embassies and consulates. Now, with time on his hands, he could do justice to them.

He tried to compose verses, often on the atom bomb, which was worrying him more and more. Coming across a set in

Bhavan's Journal, Rama Rao wrote to C.R.: 'Your talent for English versification is a pleasant surprise for me.' C.R. also put into English verse a long chapter from the Ramayana of Kamban, the Tulsidas of the South — a respectable, moving rendering.

Most evenings he would go to the house of his friend for forty years, A.V. Raman, the ex-engineer and scholar whose dictionary scheme he had refused to finance when he had been Chief Minister. Though confined to his room, Raman had immense vitality, and C.R. enjoyed his frankness.

Leaves were falling, would always fall. T.K. Chidambaram Mudaliar had died early in 1954. At the end of the year, Krishnamurti, the editor of *Kalki*, suddenly went. He had helped with *Vimochanam* during the faith-filled Ashram days in the twenties, and remained close ever since. Through *Kalki*, he carried C.R.'s thoughts and works to the Tamil country.

C.R.'s reputation had travelled far, and many a visitor to Madras hoped to enter a meeting with Rajaji in his or her diary. A young American applying for an interview wrote to C.R.:

> Mr Casey (the Australian Foreign Minister at the time), who is a very close friend of my mother's, urged her to tell me to drop you a note because — I hope I am not telling tales out of school — 'you are the wisest man in India.'[2]

C.R. would put off some and meet others. In the view of Henry Ramsey, the American Consul-General in Madras from 1953 to 1957, C.R. 'had an uncanny ability to choose to meet only with the more interesting ones.'[3] C.R. liked the Ramseys, turned up often at their home, prescribed medicines for them and, in an unusual gesture, went to Central Station to see them off when they left Madras.

A couple like the Ramseys evoked his warmth, but America did not. Her refusal to put to sleep her 'new monsters,' as C.R. called the nuclear weapons, was depressing and embittering him. At the end of 1954 he had sent a 1300-word letter on the subject to the *New York Times*, which published it in full. In it C.R.

advocated what some Americans and Europeans would campaign for a quarter-century later, a unilateral abjuring of the nuclear bomb:

> Let either America or Russia begin . . . Indeed she who committed the mistake first is duty bound to begin now; not as a penalty, but as a noble privilege. I believe that America can do it. She is morally big enough . . . We speak the truth irrespective of others not doing it; we are kind and honourable irrespective of the conduct of others. Let each not wait for the other.

Did he really think that America's leaders would listen to this appeal sent, as he put it, 'from an obscure corner of this busy world'? We do not know. But he was being egged on by his depths. The anxiety was old. Though more opposed to Japan's war aims than any other Congress leader, he had attacked the nuclear flattening of Hiroshima and Nagasaki. 'Let us hope that oblivion will rest on this latest invention,' he had said at the time.[4]

Now, his mind free to rove, read and worry as it had not been for twenty years, he felt he must sound an alarm — and keep sounding it.

The battle against the Bomb became, and stayed, a passion; but at this stage it also reflected C.R.'s search for a new role. Rich books, banter with visitors and with grandchildren, the imminent prospect of great-grandchildren jostling on his yet-firm knees, letting mellow wisdom, his own as well as that of the Epics, percolate to a still-ardent public — these gave him pleasure, even thrilled him at times, but did not satisfy his whole being.

He turned 76, then 77, and then 78. An old dog was growing older. Perhaps, one of these days, it would be found crumpled and lifeless on the floor. It was easily ill or tired, often long-faced and seeming very ancient, the back unshapely and weak, the legs burdened and deliberate in movement. Mind you, it was still capable of tricks. Given an audience of young intelligent dogs, its face would brighten, the limbs would find energy, and with a frisk or a bounce it would arouse admiration.

But that was nothing compared to when grandpa dog smelt a wolf! Suddenly it was taut, gleaming and agile, the guide of the neighbourhood pack — the dog that had found its role.

To be wise, even to be sparklingly wise, was not good enough for C.R. as he journeyed past his late seventies. He needed wolves.

Would a juicy bone have been similarly transforming? If sent for by Jawaharlal to collaborate in the running of India, would C.R. have found satisfaction? No bone was offered. Had C.R. asked for one he would have got it. 'If I had written to Mr Nehru and said I had a nostalgia for Delhi, he would certainly have invited me to return,' C.R. would say in 1959.[5]

He was too proud to ask. Also, his experience in 1951 had told him that Nehru, while liking C.R. as an adviser or a showpiece on call, did not really want a partner. On his part Nehru did not invite him because he may have felt that a 75-year-old should in fact retire, or feared that a C.R. at his elbow would cramp his style.

C.R.'s buoyancy would thus depend largely on wolves. The Bomb was one of them. It seemed to restore muscle to his spirits. In letters and statements to the Press, and in conversation with men like Ramsey, he would castigate America, but not the Soviet Union, and reject the doctrine of deterrence. 'God help the next generation! I am ashamed of my century,' C.R. told Ramsey (23.12.54).

He argued that in atomic warfare the Soviet Union's ruthlessness would give her an advantage. American rulers would hesitate, but not the Kremlin. America, and the world, would therefore be safer in a world without atomic weapons. American initiative could lead to such a world. Weaker in nuclear weapons (even if more callous), the Soviets would agree to their banishment.

But what if the Soviets secretly retained their nuclear weapons? Even if they did not, would not their great superiority in conventional weapons enable them to rule the world? 'Despite hours devoted to the subject,' Ramsey would say later, 'neither side persuaded the other.'[6]

Not all his Indian public agreed with C.R.'s campaign. That

his 'tearing and tempestuous' propaganda was beamed only at atomic weapons, not at war in general, was one criticism; another was that he was interfering in America's right to decide her defence. Going ahead regardless, C.R. also embarrassed Nehru somewhat by saying that if America did not renounce the Bomb, India should renounce American aid.

Then, at the end of 1955, he had the chance to focus on the Soviet Union. Bulganin and Krushchev, Russia's joint rulers at the time, were visiting India and coming to Madras. Just before their arrival in the city, word came of the detonation in the Soviet Union of 'the biggest bomb ever.'

C.R.'s comment that Russia and America were polluting the world's atmosphere was in the papers the day Bulganin and Krushchev landed in Madras. Bulganin, the Soviet Premier, had been assigned Raj Bhavan's 'Rajaji Suite.' Seated next to him at a banquet, Rajaji first told Bulganin that Krushchev and he had been 'absolutely wrong' in their assertion that slave labour had built India's ancient monuments.

Then he asked Bulganin if Russia would forsake the Bomb unilaterally. To this the Premier replied in the negative. But to the question whether he would agree unreservedly to a joint renunciation and its supervision, Bulganin's answer was, yes.

With Krushchev C.R. had two conversations. One took place at a cultural evening while Chandralekha danced. and Vasanthakumari sang. Krushchev confirmed what his colleague had said, and as directly.[7]

Though people might disagree on how to chain it, the Bomb was unmistakably a wolf. But when C.R. cried in 1956 that Hindi or, to be precise, its imposition on the South, was a danger, some of his friends in the North were dismayed. And Congressmen in the South thought he was embarrassing them: his strictures on Hindi sounded a little like the line of the DMK, now Congress's chief southern foe.

The obdurate enforcer of Hindi in the late thirties still

stood for that language being made 'part of everybody's education,' but he assailed the idea of Hindi soon becoming India's sole official language.

He had, in fact, cautioned against such a policy when he was Home Minister, and he was sure it would not work. It would make no sense if the Central Government gave Madras residents Hindi passport forms or Hindi telephone bills. Likewise, letters in Hindi from a government department in New Delhi, Lucknow or Patna to counterparts in Madras, Trivandrum or Shillong would be unintelligible. English, argued C.R., would be a better *official* language and would not spell discrimination against the South or other non-Hindi regions, whereas Hindi would. 'The Centre ought to declare,' said C.R., 'that English would remain the official medium.' If it did not, the South would protest — and lose interest in the oneness of India.

Riots over provincial boundaries had disturbed several parts of India. To C.R. they were a foretaste of the consequences of imposing Hindi. He had not liked the new boundaries decided upon. Maharashtra, he thought, had 'been given a raw deal'[8] — there was an unwillingness, which was later overcome, to let Bombay city be included in it.

And he was sad that the Malayalam and Kannada districts of Madras would be detached, as the Telugu districts had been. Its mix of languages and cultures had been the strength of Madras, and C.R. feared that the province, 'once so big and important and progressive will hereafter grow narrow-minded and intensely anti-culture.'[9]

His solution, entirely ignored, was for a single southern state of all the Telugu, Tamil, Kannada and Malayalam areas, a large Dakshina Pradesh that would 'retain the political significance of the South' (*Indian Express*, 27.11.55).

To many, C.R.'s words seemed harsh, even threatening. Prasad, for example, wrote in his diary that C.R.'s words were 'couched in the minatory terms of Jinnah.'[10] Another angle disturbed Devadas. 'Have you given up,' he asked C.R., 'the direct method of discussion with Jawaharlalji and others?'[11]

But C.R. was not without a case. He mobilized support for it all over the Tamil country, and in Calcutta and Hyderabad.

His arguments were not easily answered. Eventually, early in 1958, first the Congress and then the Central Government announced that English would continue as the official language, though Hindi should also be used side by side and 'should ultimately' become the official medium. The date of Hindi's enthronement was left to the future.

C.R. was not wholly satisfied, but a significant victory had been achieved, and it owed much to his role.

After warning of the Bomb and before spotting Hindi, C.R. had barked at another 'wolf' — the BCG vaccine against tuberculosis. On this occasion he did not quite retain the supporters attracted by his first shouts. His stand was that neither the usefulness nor the safety of the vaccine had really been established, and that the government's programme of mass inoculation was diverting resources from nutrition and public health.

The health department claimed that C.R.'s attack was based on old and discredited fears, and that some of the scientists he had been citing against the vaccine had changed their opinion. The cases where the vaccine had allegedly caused harm seemed to wilt under scrutiny.

A.B. Shetty, Madras's Health Minister, said that C.R.'s strictures had resulted in 'a progressive fall' in the numbers coming forward for vaccination. 'Why don't you convince Rajaji?' asked an opposition legislator, Swayamprakasam, adding, 'The controversy is confusing the public.' Replied Shetty: 'The member may make that attempt. I wish him all success' (*Indian Express*, 20.8.55).

No one convinced C.R.; six years later he would again write of his fear; but he was less insistent.

Falling leaves . . . Prakasam died in 1957. 'There is not a home today in Andhra that does not mourn,' said C.R. (*Swarajya*, 1.6.57). Two months later Devadas passed away in Bombay. On hearing the news, C.R. took the night plane. At the stop in

Nagpur he sobbed uncontrollably when he saw Devadas's 20-year-old son Ramchandra, his grandson, who was flying to Bombay from Delhi.

'A jewel of a boy had a jewel of a girl and it is all smashed,' he wrote to Rama Rao (21.8.57). For almost 40 years, ever since, as an 18-year-old, Devadas came to the South to teach Hindi, he and C.R. had been devoted to each other; and the loss to Lakshmi really hurt. Three years earlier, in a letter to Ramsey, he had described his feelings for her: 'My daughter lost her mother before she could know or remember and I had to bring her up entirely. So I am rather fond of her!' To Devadas's 12-year-old son Gopu he wrote:

> You should not let yourself go sad. Appa is not in his body
> but lives in your memory. He has acquired in your memory
> a fine and beautiful body like that of a god. And remember
> many others have faced the death of their fathers and grown
> up.

Then, in February 1958, A.V. Raman died. To Rama Rao, C.R. wrote (11.2.58): 'Indignation incarnate was he and a very good man. His wife seizes my hand to wipe her tears.'

Other loved leaves, young ones, had been grafted elsewhere. Granddaughters Janaki, Tara and Indira were married between 1956 and 1958. After Janaki's marriage he wrote to Rama Rao (11.9.56): 'The girl cried and took leave of me last night . . . I could not sleep well . . . Yet I pretend to follow the doctrine of detachment.'

Tara's husband, a Bengali agronomist, was thus described by C.R. to Rama Rao: 'Cultured, well-behaved, brainy, tallish, healthy, well-shaped and not bad in the face' (10.3.57).

From July 1956, C.R., who had been communicating his thoughts through *Kalki* in Tamil, had a new platform, the English weekly *Swarajya*. Every week now he could tell a wider audience what bothered him. *Swarajya's* editor and owner, Khasa Subba Rao, in the past a frequent C.R. critic, offered him this conduit.

T. Sadasivam, publisher of *Kalki*, who for a while now had placed himself wholly at C.R.'s disposal, said he would ensure *Swarajya's* viability.

In his opening piece in *Swarajya*, C.R. quoted Socrates — 'I am a sort of gadfly' — and added: 'The need is great for a gadfly weekly which can close down any time and start again any day without serious loss, and which is governed by a sense of truth and public welfare and does not look for mass popularity' (14.7.56).

Within a few months Egypt was attacked by England, France and Israel over a dispute about the Suez Canal. 'We must part now,' was the heading of C.R.'s piece on the subject: he felt that India had to quit the Commonwealth. Over Hungary, into which Soviet troops moved, he seemed somewhat less agitated, though he admitted that it was 'the scene of great wrongs.'

C.R.'s British friends, most of them openly critical of their government's action, which was soon to miscarry, were upset by the sharpness of C.R.'s attitude. 'Don't leave us,' Pethick-Lawrence wrote in a typical letter. 'Help us to rescue our country' (6.11.56). But C.R. was unmoved. His British friends need not have worried too much. C.R. had no influence now over Nehru, who had no intention of quitting the Commonwealth.

On the eve of the 1957 Indian elections, C.R., who had allowed his membership of Congress to lapse, declared in *Swarajya* that he would vote 'for a person of reliable character' (26.1.57). In the past he had always said, 'Vote Congress.' Except in Kerala, where the Communists were successful, Congress won everywhere, including in Madras, where Kamaraj was Chief Minister once more. Congress's triumphs included Narasimhan's re-election to Parliament.

But C.R. was not abandoning the literary world. He went through *The Portable Johnson and Boswell*, edited by Louis Kronenberger, with a toothcomb. Below the editor's criticism of Johnson's ponderousness and polysyllables, C.R. wrote, 'I agree with Johnson wherever Kronenberger presumes to differ.' And against Johnson's famous revision of his first reaction to a play, 'It has not wit enough to keep it sweet,' into 'It has not vitality enough to preserve it from putrefaction,' C.R. entered this marginal comment:

Anglo-Saxon simplicity of words does not necessarily make for clarity. The second Johnsonian form is really clearer.

On a margin of Trollope's *The Prime Minister*, he scribbled: 'Mr Trollope, you do not know when your story is finished.' And when Monica Felton said to him, 'You must have read Marx at one time,' he replied, 'Never,' grinned, and added, 'Not a word.'

On another occasion he said to the Englishwoman, 'During the last few weeks I have been reading the novels of Jane Austen.' *Felton*: 'Which?' *C.R.*: 'All of them. *Northanger Abbey* was the last . . . There must be at least three hundred and thirty varieties of female characters, and Jane Austen understood nearly all of them.'[12]

As he approached and passed his eightieth birthday, he read Lamb, Thackeray, Tolstoy, *The Book of Daniel*, and *The Iliad*. Output matched input: articles in *Swarajya* and *Kalki*, statements to the Press, letters, talks, outpourings on global wrongs, national errors, individual habits . . .

Flashes of gaiety apart, he did not exude the steady optimism that some religious men possess and others simulate; he seemed, at times, to worship the God of Anxiety; worry frequently sat on his face and frustration showed in his voice; but in the late fifties — his late seventies and early eighties — he remained true to Gandhi's 1939 remark: 'Rajaji is one of the most God-minded men I know.' The Almighty, accordingly, featured regularly in *Swarajya*, *Kalki*, and his talks.

In politics, however, the old man was shifting. In August 1957 he wrote:

A strong opposition is essential for the health of democratic government . . . Since the Congress party has swung to the Left, what is wanted is a strong and articulate Right (*Swarajya*, 17.8.57).

Agreeing, many told C.R. that he was the one to lead a Right party. His answer was a variation of 'Impossible — a dilapidated old fogey like me?'

The Bomb was never forgotten. And when, in 1957, it was announced that Britain would explode a device on Christmas

Island in the Pacific, C.R. declared that India should protest by leaving the Commonwealth. Nehru again disagreed.

When Sputnik was launched, C.R. said to Monica Felton, 'Now that the Russians have sent up their toy moon, nobody could accuse them of weakness . . . if they said they would stop making the Bomb.' 'Why don't you write to Krushchev and say so?' Felton asked. C.R. replied, 'What would be the use? They would hardly listen to . . .' Felton interrupted, 'an old fogey like you.'

Rajaji laughed, and when Monica repeated her advice, he said no in a tone that was 'definite, beyond argument.' But he wrote to Krushchev all the same. The answers C.R. received were long, full of propaganda and aided by flattery: at times a Delhi-based Soviet diplomat would bring to Bazlulla Road a Krushchev letter in Russian, with an English translation.

Still, a point came in 1958 when the Soviet Union did unilaterally suspend its tests. 'I am very glad Krushchev took your advice,' Felton said rather coldly to C.R. Imre Nagy of Hungary had been executed by this time, and Felton, a left-leaning idealist, had turned very anti-Krushchev.

'My advice!' C.R. laughed sarcastically. However, he added, 'But I suppose I had a certain responsibility.'[13] He was overjoyed. Earlier he had wondered whether 'amoral Russia' might not prove 'more Christian' than the 'Christian' West.[14] Now he wrote, 'Russia has taken a Gandhian initiative' (*Swarajya*, 19.5.58).

Soon, Soviet tests were resumed, on the ground that the West had not responded in kind. Criticized by the *Indian Express* for having shared an anti-Bomb platform with E.M.S. Namboodiripad, Kerala's Communist Chief Minister, and reminded of his 1952 remark that Communists were his enemy number one, C.R. replied: 'I am far too interested in the stopping of test explosions to be misled by such arguments' (*Indian Express*, 26.6.58).

To the skilled eye, ear and pen of Monica Felton are owed a number of vivid glimpses of C.R. in the late fifties, which she incorporated in her *I Meet Rajaji*. Visiting India in 1956, Felton, an Englishwoman with a lame leg, who had written a novel and a travelogue, decided to get to know C.R. — she had heard adulatory as well as 'contrary opinions' about him, listened to a tape in which he had spoken on Suez, and been struck by his words and 'cool, slow voice.' Of their first meeting, in December 1956, she would recall:

> His voice was young and exquisitely precise . . . He treated the English language gently, as if he loved it. He was not omniscient and self-absorbed, as the old and the famous generally are. His curiosity was fresh and searching . . . He questioned me about my life and I was astonished to find myself telling him things that I had never told to anyone.

Four weeks later, calling on C.R. in Delhi, where he was giving a talk, his 'look of unalterable sadness' underneath 'the great bare dome of his head' filled Monica with 'pity for this aged man,' but Rajaji surprised and nettled her by pitying her. They were meeting on the second floor, and C.R. asked her, 'Surely you didn't walk up all those stairs with that lame leg?'

C.R. presented her the ornate, but also functional, walking-stick that Rama Rao had given him when he became Governor-General. Over the next several years, based in Madras as a freelance writer and would-be Rajaji biographer, Monica often called on him. Illness and the chores of each day put off the biography, but she brought out *I Meet Rajaji* and also a book on Sister Subbalakshmi. In 1970, her main aim unrealized, she died in Madras.

Yet *I Meet Rajaji* is an invaluable and lively record. His probing at the first meeting had revealed Felton's agnosticism. At their third meeting, looking straight at her, he asked, 'Why don't you believe?'

Some months later Monica spoke of her frustration over the biography.

C.R.: 'Why don't you give it up?'

Felton: 'It is what I came here to do.'

C.R.: 'Yes, and now it has become an attachment. When people form an attachment to an idea, they stick to it beyond reason . . . That is why our religion places so much emphasis on the need to maintain a detached attitude.'

It was quite an exhortation, but when Monica retorted,

'And do you practise what you preach?' all C.R. could do was grin. The grinning C.R. appears again and again in the Felton portrayal — as does, less frequently, the melancholy Rajaji. 'I saw,' writes Felton, 'that his look of age was like a mask. With a grin it slipped off and he was ageless.'

Felton discovered, too, that on occasion he could be forgetful — or untrue. Once he had said to her:

I believe that humanity has lost its chance. The fun is over . . .
I think God has had enough of us. I think he is going to spray the whole world with DDT.

Some weeks later Monica said to him, 'I have been thinking about what you said to me about God and DDT.'
C.R.: 'What did I say?' Felton reminded him.
C.R.: 'I could not have said that.'
Felton: 'You did. I wrote it down.'
C.R.: 'Long afterwards. Your memory misled you.' 'No,' insisted Monica, 'I wrote it the same day.' Finally C.R. admitted that Felton might have been right.

At eighty his phrase-making was not bad. During a discussion with Felton and Khasa on the Gandhi assassination, he said:

Some people think that if the guard had been adequate Gandhiji would not have been killed. Others think that it was destined that he should die at that particular time, that it was the right time for him to die, the fulfilment of a pre-destined propriety.

Noticing that Felton had pulled out her notebook, Khasa said to Rajaji: 'She is writing down what you said.' C.R. grinned: 'She is collecting English phrases, that's why.' Turning to Felton, the self-professed agnostic, he added: 'But the phrase is not quite right. It should be "the fulfilment of an evolutionary must." '

In 1959, their bond having lasted 67 years, C.R. wrote to Rama Rao, 'I hope the miracle of our love on earth will be given as long a lease of life as in His decree it is good for us.' Their closeness is revealed in the kind of letters they exchanged.

Rama Rao to C.R., 13.9.54: Would you read — for me — once more Shakespeare's sonnet, 'When to the sessions of sweet silent thought'? Milton — it was some feat [your] reading Paradise Lost through. I for one found that mass of gold too heavy.

C.R. to Rama Rao, 13.11.54: Have you read Johnson's Preface to his Dictionary in full original? I have not read a nobler piece of writing . . . Parts bring tears to the eyes . . .

C.R. to Rama Rao who, following C.R.'s advice that India should leave the Commonwealth, had asked, 'Why ever did you join?' 27.11.56: The theory was that we must preserve [any] 'areas of peace' and the Commonwealth was such a one. My own impression is that our international caste led us to it. We knew England best and it was a good club to be in.

C.R. to Rama Rao, 27.11.56: Never let a cold keep you long in its clutches. And don't for God's sake precede me. It is not good protocol.

C.R. to Rama Rao, 2.3.58: You asked if Maulana (*Azad, who had just died*) deserved all that is being said of him. He was a good type — broadminded, scholarly and gracious and one who had a kind of hold on the Prime Minister due to much association and a common dialect and a pro-Muslim complex in the latter. He liked me and I liked him.

Rama Rao to C.R., 11.9.58: Reading Lamb from cover to cover must have been as grim a triumph of the will as the traversing of Paradise Lost and ditto Regained, great and beautiful as the Himalayas and about as easy to conquer.

Rama Rao to C.R., following a 'Swarajya' article by the latter on meat, alcohol and smoking, 13.9.58: Aren't you, by implication, rather hard on people whose habits are not yours? I don't agree either with an indiscriminate sanctification of discipline . . . Mere abstinence from what gives pleasure is a very dilute suicide — that is all.

At the end of 1958, Madeleine Slade, or Mirabehn, who had joined the Mahatma in 1925, sent C.R. a typescript of her memoirs, which she said were likely to be published in the winter of 1960-1. C.R. wrote back: 'God bless you — angel pure — I bless you on behalf of Bapu as well as of myself . . . It is a most interesting human story. [But] winter of 1960-61 is far in God's horizon for me.'[15]

22

Swatantra

1958-62

In 1959, the elderly watchdog became a greyhound! Ignoring ailments and shaking off inhibitions, Rajaji, 80, decided to challenge Jawaharlal, who seemed to embody power, fame and vitality, with a new political party.

Events and his own analysis propelled C.R. Congress, he felt, was steadily corrupting. Though committing themselves, in 1955, to 'a socialistic pattern' and, later, to plain 'socialism,' its members seemed to be getting richer rather than more caring. In 1956 C.R. had publicly asked: 'Congressmen look so well off. Have they taken up new avocations and earned money? Then how have they made money?' (*Indian Express*, 28.5.56)

'Anyhow, somehow,' was his answer at the time. Now, three years later, he replaced it with a phrase that would become central to Indian political debate for the rest of the century. It was the 'permit-licence-quota' raj, he said, that was fattening Congressmen. The socialistic pattern, where the state controlled, 'permitted' and farmed out business, was enriching Congressmen, officials and favoured businessmen — and harassing the rest.

A realization began to stir in him that if he wished to oppose state control of business he would have to oppose Congress itself. While he was thus cogitating, Congress came out with a new agricultural policy. It had three prongs:

government takeover of the grain trade; ceilings on land holdings; and cooperative cultivation of land. Aired in 1958, the guidelines were confirmed by Congress at its Nagpur session in January 1959.

To C.R. this policy represented a wolf that needed immediate chaining, and he barked at once and loudly. 'Violent Socialism,' 'Retreat from Gandhism' and 'Why I Show the Red Flag' were some of his articles assailing the new policy in *Swarajya*, the *Hindustan Times* and the *Indian Express*.

Bureaucrats, he argued, would make incompetent traders. Land ceilings would be unconstitutional and would dry up the flow of grain into towns. And rural industrialization, the soundest route to more jobs, would suffer if the bigger farmers were squeezed out.

In the ceiling proposal C.R. saw greed for votes and exploitation of jealousy, not sympathy for the landless. Calling it 'a child of sadism' (*The Hindu*, 6.1.59), he warned: 'The egalitarians are hovering over the land like eagles' (*Swarajya*, 27.12.58).

He was scathing about the joint ownership and farming that Jawaharlal and some of his advisers were presenting as an answer to the fragmentation of India's cropland. Common cultivation, he said, was 'not an idea born of experience or thought' and had only been tried in countries 'where personal liberty is absent and forced labour is commandeered' (*The Hindu*, 6.1.59). In advocating it, Congress was 'borrowing from the Communist his brush and paint' (*Indian Express*, 19.1.59).

Peasants were most efficient when they farmed their own land; 'an unwilling people yoked to the law' would grow the minimum. In sum, joint cultivation would be 'as bad for the farm as polygamy is for the family' (*Swarajya*, 17.12.58 & 14.2.59).

In the middle of 1958, referring to 'the gradual collapse of independent thinking' in Congress, he had asked: 'Has socialism been adopted only as parrots learn to speak' (*Swarajya*, 10.5.58). The manner in which Congress accepted the new agricultural policy seemed to confirm his worst fears. After a sharp rebuke from Nehru, critics of joint farming and ceilings had meekly voted for the new policy — only six hands were raised in opposition.

Calling Nehru, for the first time, 'the Congress dictator,' C.R. also said: 'The single brain-activity of the people who meet in Congress is to find out what is in Jawaharlal's mind and to anticipate it. The slightest attempt at dissent meets with stern disapproval and is nipped in the bud' (*Swarajya*, 17.1. & 28.2.59).

Suddenly, at this juncture, Indira Gandhi, Jawaharlal's daughter, was named party president. Her talents were yet a secret, and she had had no experience of party work. Several of Nehru's colleagues were offended by the choice but said nothing. C.R. felt outraged.

Two years earlier, he had spoken somewhat academically of the role a Right party could perform. Now, perceiving a threat of joint farming and the collapse of independence in Congress, he called for a Conservative Party of India:

> Men do not feel any inclination to become wage-slaves, and peasants are least inclined . . . A wide public is waiting to give support to an opposition formed on a sound basis, because the people have realised that one-footed democracy is no good and is not distinguishable from coercion and totalitarianism (*The Hindu*, 6.1.59).

For a year or so, he had been urged to lead an initiative against Congress socialism by men like Minoo Masani, the former socialist and now an independent MP, P.K. Deo, the Maharaja of Kalahandi in Orissa, Murarji Vaidya of the Forum of Free Enterprise and Janakinandan Singh, leader of a group of breakaway Congressmen in Bihar. So far C.R.'s reply was that he was 'too old, too long a Congressman and too close to Nehru personally to consider an active re-entry into politics.'[1]

After Nagpur, the pressure was stronger. C.R. deflected it, first, towards Jayaprakash Narayan. Though a socialist himself, J.P. had spoken of the need for a conservative party and for opposing Congress. Inscribing his best wishes, J.P. tossed the ball back to C.R. This time C.R. threw it towards Chintaman Deshmukh, who had resigned a few years earlier from Nehru's

Cabinet, and whose talent and integrity C.R. esteemed:

> You are aware that for a considerable time now I have been
> convinced of the need for an opposition party and that it
> should be a conservative party whatever name it may adopt.
>
> Everyone who agreed with me, looking for a good leader,
> could find none and ended with asking me to do it, which I
> have been saying is impossible. [Then] there was a flash and I
> saw at once who it must be. 'Here is the man,' I said to
> myself. 'Deshmukh fits it to a tee . . .'
>
> If you agree to place youself at the head of this movement, it
> will be my duty to get young and do all in my power to make
> it a success. (15.4.59)[2]

Though touched, Deshmukh pleaded inability. Simultaneously,
with Deshmukh's reply came Nehru's first comment on C.R.'s
criticisms. At a public meeting in Madras, Jawharlal referred to
his 'affection and respect' for Rajaji, and then said, 'May I
perhaps venture to say one word to him with great respect; and
that is, a litle charity in his thinking may sometimes not be out
of place.'[3]

In the middle of May 1959, Monica Felton said to C.R.:

> I have been thinking that if I were the mother of you and the
> Prime Minister, I would bang your two heads together and tell
> you to stop arguing and run things together. Each of you has
> qualities that the other has not. You would make a superb
> combination.
>
> *C.R.*: It is too late. Our Prime Minister has arrived at a point
> at which it is impossible for him to change his views. And I
> have reached a detachment which makes it out of the question
> that I should ever return to public affairs.[4]

Two weeks after uttering these categorical words, C.R. addressed
a Bangalore meeting convened by M.A. Sreenivasan of the
Forum of Free Enterprise, where, speaking just before him,
Masani had assailed Congress in scathing terms.

'Mr Masani is a parliamentarian,' C.R. began, 'and he
cannot use strong words. I am free to do so.' He went on to
accuse Nehru of megalomania, and the hall exploded with

applause. Next morning, on 30 May, Rajaji told Masani that the time had come to start the new party.

On 4 June, the day's engagements listed in the Madras papers included a meeting of the All India Agriculturists' Federation (AIAF) to be addressed by Masani in the evening. When Monica Felton met C.R. in the forenoon, he told her that though Masani was 'the real speaker,' he too would be saying something, and that she would be welcome 'if you have nothing better to do.' 'Nothing in his manner or tone [suggested] that the occasion was of the slightest importance.'

After the conversation with Felton, C.R. went to Woodlands Hotel to confer with Masani, N.G. Ranga, the Andhra MP and AIAF leader (he had protested against Congress's land policy by resigning his post of secretary of the Congress parliamentary party), V.P. Menon, who had been a close aide of Vallabhbhai Patel, and several others.

At this get-together twenty-one principles for a new party were agreed upon, including equal opportunity for all Indians, anti-statism and encouragement of thrift and individual initiative — but a suitable name seemed to elude the 'midwives.' Rajaji suggested the Conservative party, but Ranga preferred an Agrarian party and Masani a Liberal, Centre or Democratic one.

J.P. was in Madras on that day, and C.R. made another attempt to enlist him as the new party's first president. Though declining the offer, J.P. expressed his goodwill.

In the evening, those gathered at Vivekananda College to hear Masani were happily surprised to see Rajaji and J.P. too step on to the dais. What Rajaji said was a greater surprise.

'This morning,' he said, 'a new political party was formed.' Stunned for a moment, the audience then gave a terrific round of applause. Continued C.R., 'And the name of the party is' — and it was the turn of Masani, Ranga and the other midwives to be surprised — 'Swatantra Party!' He had settled on the name while being driven to the meeting! This time the loud applause was instantaneous.

'I had never seen Rajaji more radiant,' wrote Monica Felton. Following the declaration, she added,

He was no longer the frail old man I had met when I first
came to Madras. His eyes were brilliant. His skin was like
gold, and the fringe of hair around the back of his head was
not silky, like the hair of an old man, but wiry and strong,
with the dense gleam of aluminium.

Half-disconcerted (thinking of the biography she hoped to write)
and half-delighted, Monica asked C.R.: 'Do you think you are
going to succeed in your enterprise?' Rajaji laughed and said, 'It
will be all right if I can live to be a hundred.'[5]

Ranga was the Swatantra Party's first president and Masani soon
became general secretary, but it was clear that C.R. had agreed
to lead the party. His clash with Nehru was now formalized.
Yet theirs was a strange confrontation. 'We are positive friends
and love each other,'[6] he had said after Jawaharlal charged him
with a total lack of charity and a year earlier he had written:

> Some dear people have the jitters because Rajaji and Nehru are
> quarrelling . . . Yes, I have differed and have spoken harsh
> language for the sake of clarity. But can't friends differ and
> yet continue to love one another? (*Swarajya*, 3.5.58)

On his part Jawaharlal would continue to speak of his 'respect
and affection' for C.R., but the two did not talk their differences
over. Perhaps each waited for the other to make the first move;
perhaps, too, each thought the other to be unbudgable. It was
C.R.'s further belief that only the pressure of public opinion
would affect Nehru.

He had expressed this belief in a letter to Nehru after the
latter had publicly lamented (*Indian Express*, 19.3.58) C.R.'s
'cold war' on the language issue. Claiming that 'ten years ago,
as an integral part of our freedom,' he had 'pledged' himself to
the 'duty to warn you as elder brother,' C.R. added (21.3.58):

> I am aware of your love . . . I assure you my affection for you
> is unchanged. But I have found in recent times that my advice
> carries no weight with you . . . I see that you are moved only
> by 'public opinion' — indeed often moved by public pressure
> against your own conviction . . . Hence this what you call
> 'cold war.'

C.R.'s warmth for Nehru withstood the launching of Swatantra. A small framed picture of himself with Nehru that for years stood on a shelf near his bed remained where it was — it would stay undisturbed until his death.

Some critics quipped that the elder statesman had become an aged iconoclast, while others lamented C.R.'s loss of detachment. A more serious question was whether he could not have fought Nehru from within Congress. Yet Congress seemed inhospitable to a dissenter, the more so after Nehru told partymen opposed to his land policy: 'If you do not agree with us, you can get out of the party.'[7]

Thereafter, Ranga had left Congress and another critic, Charan Singh, had resigned from the UP cabinet. On his part C.R. had too much pride and too little patience for a long-term exercise of converting humiliating defeats in successive Congress meetings into ultimate victory.

To some, opposing Nehru seemed treason. In *Swarajya* C.R. defended himself (28.2.59). He began with an expression of 'great satisfaction' at 'the general resistance' to any 'attack' on Nehru, for there was 'no unifying force so effective as loyalty and affection.' It was 'God's grace,' C.R. added, 'that there is a good man in India who deserved to be idolised as [Jawaharlal] is.'

'Yet,' C.R. continued, 'there is nothing more important for the ruler of a great, big nation as independent, fearless advice.' Gandhiji and Patel were no longer living to give that advice. 'I, who remain, would be untrue to the trust and love that they had been bestowing to me if, preferring quiet and ease, I kept silent over what I felt.'

The charge that frustrated ambition was his motive was dismissed with the reminder that he had 'held and finished with the highest offices open to anyone' and the assertion, 'God knows that I do not want any office.' (*Swarajya*, 16.9.59).

Alluding to C.R.'s frequent references to the Almighty, Jawaharlal joked that God seemed to be the senior partner of the new party. Also, though Nehru must have been aware that Congress was receiving vastly greater sums from the wealthy, he suggested repeatedly that Swatantra was a party backed by the rich.

This smear was one that C.R. and his Swatantra colleagues sought times without number to remove, but Jawaharlal had chosen an early moment to fasten it, and it stuck. Nehru claimed, too, that it was difficult to know what Swatantra stood for. C.R. urged him to read the 21 points.

So the debate went on, now heated, now reasoned, now fair, now unfair. But the human relationship survived. On C.R.'s first visit to Delhi after the formation of Swatantra, Jawaharlal, a fit 70, ran up the stairs to the second-floor flat where C.R., 81, was staying, and said, 'Rajaji, I have come to see how young you are.' Nehru was naturally curious about the health of his aged but influential foe.

For all its sadness, the Rajaji-Nehru clash had an inevitability to it. Thus far, their decades' old ideological differences had been suppressed — first in the interest of the common struggle for independence and, later, because of the problems that followed Independence and Partition. But the cleavage had to come. Two years after the formation of Swatantra, C.R. gave his version of the root of the ideological disagreement:

> Mr Jawaharlal Nehru returned from Cambridge with notions of how an all-governing interventionist state can force people into happiness and prosperity through socialism.
>
> He sticks to this bias in spite of the demonstration of world experience against it (*Swarajya*, 21.10.61).

From Nehru's viewpoint, C.R. stood for 'merely perpetuating the traditional structure . . . leaving the industrialists to go ahead and do what they like.'[8]

Fearing that in confronting Nehru and Congress C.R. was taking on an impossible task, Rama Rao tried to caution him. Replied C.R. (20.6.59):

> We would have been still a British colony had not the Spanish knights come forward in 1920. We were just Don Quixotes then and many were the good men who thought so and kept back. I hate the present folly and arrogance as much as I hated the foreign arrogance of those days.

By now Rama Rao was ill again. In a letter, C.R. said to him, 'May your fingers continue writing my name and your love for me for yet many more years.' Sending books, money and a doctor from Madras, C.R. encouraged Rama Rao's effort to skip salt. C.R. also informed him of an attempt on his life at the start of a Madras meeting:

> Your dear delightful letter just received proves that salt-free diet improves writing capacity. I was in Allahabad on April 4 and saw [Purshottamdas Tandon] in his sick bed. He talked very cheerfully. 'I have prohibited salt in my food the last 20 or more years' (18.4.60).

> His anger against salt was tremendous. I thought of you all the time and wished you had half that emotion against this enemy of man, salt. But I know how sweet salt is . . .

> Live, live as long as you can . . .

> Somebody will have told you about a man trying to put a knife into me last night. I have not told people, but I have been living long spells wherein every moment I was in danger of being stabbed this way . . . It is so easy to do the thing.

> The man was caught immediately by a policeman. The incident happened just behind me as I was trudging on the loose sand amidst din and enthusiastic crowds . . .

Rama Rao was failing. C.R. wanted to help with his treatment.

> Who would say you were old or ill seeing your beautiful clear and firm handwriting? Please permit me to pay for the Sanatogen and Protinex supplied at Bangalore. I would like to have the feeling that I helped you eat some food now when you need it so much. (18.8.60)

But Rama Rao was beyond nutrients and drugs. When C.R. called on him in the second week of November, the poison had entered his head, and he was incoherent. C.R. asked one of Rama Rao's daughters-in-law to sing a *kirtana* by Purandaradasa. As Rama Rao heard the song of praise, his eyes glistened, and he struggled weakly to bring his palms together in prayer. C.R. helped him do it, and saw peace spreading on his friend's face.

Word that all was over came on 28 November while C.R. was in Belgaum. Travelling by car through the night, C.R. reached Bangalore at dawn, but by then his friend was just a heap of ashes. C.R. walked thrice round that heap.

Their attachment had remained unbroken for 68 years. In a *Swarajya* piece (17.12.60), C.R. recalled its early days:

> We read a lot together, . . . his taste was superb and he guided me like a mesmerist . . . We swore to ourselves, each in his own mind, that we should be friends for life. And so we were, one soul in two bodies and two lives in each body.

The political field to the right of the Congress was not vacant. The Jan Sangh, founded by Shyama Prasad Mookerjee in 1951 and espousing a militant Hinduism, had occupied parts of it, specially in North and Central India. But Swatantra had some advantages. Apart from Rajaji, notable southerners such as Ranga and Menon had joined it. In Masani it had an effective spokesman. Veteran Congressmen such as K.M. Munshi had entered its ranks.

Moreover, its tone being liberal as well as conservative, the new party reached out to moderate Hindus and non-Hindus in ways not available to the Jan Sangh. C.R.'s identification of statism as the menace seemed to click with a number of traders, businessmen and farmers. In Congress's Nagpur resolution the party had an issue which could be exploited, and in Rajaji a leadership that other opposition parties could not rival.

Held in Bombay on 1 August 1959, the first party convention showed several regional parties or factions casting their lot with Swatantra: the Indian National Democratic and Tamilnad Toilers' parties of Madras; the Krishikar Lok Party of Andhra; the Janata and Jan Congress parties of Bihar; a UP Congress faction led by S.K.D. Paliwal and a Punjab one led by Udham Singh Nagoke; and Orissa's Ganatantra Parishad, which was a contender for provincial power.

Aristocrats joining included the Maharawal of Dungarpur, the Raja of Ramgarh in Bihar, the Raja of Manakpur in UP, the Maharajas of Patna and Kalahandi in Orissa, and — the star recruit — the beautiful Maharani Gayatri Devi of Jaipur. The great majority of the former princes, however, sided with Congress, which had the power to remove their privy purses — or, as with the Maharajas of Jaipur and Patiala, to make them ambassadors.

Other eminent recruits to Swatantra included leading businessmen Homi Mody and A.D. Shroff, old warriors like Dahyabhai Patel, the Sardar's son, and the engineer-educator, Bhailalbhai Patel; N.C. Chatterjee, the Bengal lawyer formerly with the Hindu Mahasabha; M. Ruthnaswamy of Madras, once in the Justice party; and outstanding veterans of the civil service such as H.M. Patel, Narayan Dandeker and J.M. Lobo Prabhu.

The comment that Swatantra's leaders were more distinguished than popular[9] was valid. True, Rajaji himself possessed a continuing appeal. As Humayun Kabir, member of Nehru's government, conceded while attacking the new party, 'The only rallying point of the Swatantra party is the personality of Rajagopalachari.'[10] Yet that appeal did not match the magnetism with the masses with which the fates had endowed Jawaharlal.

Apart from lacking in mass appeal, Swatantra was heterogeneous, even if not to the same extent as Congress. Agreement on the evil of statism could not conceal differences. If Rajaji and Munshi proclaimed their roots in Indian culture, and Rajaji unhesitatingly called himself a conservative, Masani and Mody were westernized liberals. Again, Munshi, a Hindi enthusiast, could scarcely warm to Rajaji's campaigns against Hindi, which many of Rajaji's North Indian supporters also found hard to defend.

New Delhi's dismissal of Kerala's Communist ministry, following popular demonstrations against it, showed up a fresh difference. Masani welcomed the centre's decision but Rajaji, unable to disregard the Communists' continuing majority in the Kerala legislature, termed the dismissal unconstitutional. 'I do not like the Communist party but this is not the way to deal with it,' he wrote (*Swarajya*, 20.6.59).

The differences did not trouble C.R., who frequently cited everyone's opposition to statism as well as the party's '21st principle,' conceived by him, which gave members freedom to hold any position on questions not covered by the previous twenty points. As he had said at the opening convention,

> I am totally opposed to giving up English as the official language of our country . . . But I want the majority opinion to prevail . . . Mr Mody will say, 'I am against the prohibition of alcoholic drinks.' I am for state prohibition. But it is not in the Swatantra party [charter]. You are free to hold any opinion on that.[11]

Another lack was of funds, which galled all the more in the context of Nehru's well-publicized charge that Swatantra was 'the rich man's party.' C.R. and his colleagues vigorously advocated a ban on company donations to political parties but Nehru rejected the suggestion: almost all the contributions were going to Congress. In addition, Nehru asserted that he would reject any gifts from a company that also gave money to the Swatantra. Moreover, in a crucial steer, Ghanshyamdas Birla declared, 'Swatantra politics were not good businessmen's politics.'[12]

Most companies became too frightened to give anything to Swatantra. The ones contributing also gave, in almost every case, a much bigger sum to Congress — but, despite Nehru's assertion, no money was in fact returned by Congress. Howard Erdman, an American scholar who made a detailed and critical scrutiny of Swatantra, would state in a 1967 study:

> No one who has seen the party's financial records would conclude that it was generously supported by India's richest men.[13]

Apart from accusing Swatantra of being a party of the wealthy, Nehru also said that it belonged to 'the middle ages of lords, castles and zamindars,' and likely to become 'fascist in outlook.'[14] It was impossible to match Jawahrlal's media reach or to undo the damage his true, false or exaggerated charges caused.

In *Swarajya*'s columns C.R. could argue that fascism's distinctive features were the appeal to the mob and disregard for the constitution, or ask his readers to decide 'who really are the fascists.' (22.8.59). But All India Radio did not broadcast his comment, and the daily Press did not reproduce it.

Nehru was closer to the truth when he said that Rajaji saw virtue in traditional arrangements. Admitting the charge, C.R. argued, 'Survival is a proof of fitness, not of worthlessness,' and added:

> Mr Jawaharlal Nehru used to tell me that he knew the crowd mentality better than I or any of our other colleagues did. This is probably true — not in the sense that he knows what the people want but in the cruder sense of what would please them (*Swarajya*, 4.2.61).

C.R.'s 'principled position' was, however, not likely to attract those, politicians or the moneyed, who were looking for a possible winner.

The creation of Swatantra freed C.R. for verbal jousting.

> Parrots all over, they all shout at the Swatantra party: 'You are only negative, what is your positive?' I have studied some mathematics and I do not much fancy this misuse of important mathematical words . . . Read chapter 20 of the Book of Exodus in the Bible. The famous commandments are all there, all 'negative' (*Swarajya*, 10.9.60).

> Then there is the cheap word reactionary. If to oppose the Congress and the Communist parties is reaction, Swatantra is reactionary. If to fight for fundamental rights is reactionary, Swatantra is reactionary (*Swarajya*, 25.2.61).

When Nehru wondered aloud why Rajaji 'was speaking so much in anger,' C.R. replied (*Swarajya*, 21.10.61):

> Does [Nehru] not realise that a fine cadre of officials have now been made into spineless flatterers and partisans? I see fear enveloping everywhere like a poisonous fog . . .

> I see Chief Ministers, finance and food ministers going about extorting money for the party without fear or shame . . . I happen to remember a time when such things could not be thought of. I see waste on a stupendous scale. Our foreign liabilities are pyramiding up . . .

> I can't help being sad. I am not entirely hopeless. So my grief looks like anger.

The first big test of Swatantra would be the 1962 elections, but its significance was immediately obvious. Noting, from Rashtrapati Bhavan, C.R.'s severe attack on Congress's Nagpur decisions, Prasad wrote in his diary (26.1.59): 'Rajaji commands a respect and hearing which hardly anyone else does in the country.'

Fifteen months later, after a brief meeting with C.R. in Delhi, the President seemed to marvel at C.R.'s passion and to approve of Rajaji's views:

> Rajaji is wonderfully energetic even at the advanced age of 81. He contributes regularly to two Tamil papers. He writes regularly for an English paper also. Besides, he is constantly issuing statements, holding press conferences and addressing large public meetings. Within the last weeks he has toured Bihar, the Punjab, U.P., Delhi and also Calcutta. All that he writes and speaks is as acute and penetrating, as bright and scintillating, as anything that he has ever written or said. There is no sign of any looseness or illogicality anywhere (8.4.60).[15]

One indication of Swatantra's impact was the frequency of Nehru's criticisms. Another was Congress's anxiety to placate Swatantra's likely supporters. The princes were intimidated or cajoled — and peasants were regularly assured, often by Nehru himself, that joint farming would not be forced on them. This was as much a retreat as a clarification, and though it removed a key issue favouring Swatantra, the abandonment of cooperative farming should be regarded, wholly or in part, as a Swatantra achievement.

There were other results. When the party was a year old, C.R. claimed with truth that

> We have released the spirit of criticism. We have hit and wounded, though we have not yet slain, the fear that held the people in its grasp (*Swarajya*, 30.7.60).

Not having become anti-Communist, pro-American or anti-Nehru in any neat or consistent sense, he continued to attack the Americans over the Bomb. And when it became known in November 1959 that China had occupied much of Aksai Chin in Ladakh and cut a road across the territory, and most opposition MPs accused Nehru of serious negligence, C.R. seemed to exonerate Nehru:

> China's misconduct should not be laid on his shoulders . . . It was a pure case of betrayal of him by the leaders of China whom he had trusted, and no fault on his part (*Swarajya*, 5.12.59).

While urging Indians to see China as a long-term threat, C.R. acknowledged China's right to join the UN. Membership there, he explained, was 'a status attached to the actuality of established government, . . . not a prize for good conduct' (*Swarajya*, 28.11.59).

Positions of this kind could be disconcerting for both colleagues and adversaries. Krishna Menon, India's Defence Minister at this time and a favourite of the Indian Left, was right in remarking later that 'the residuum of Rajaji's impact on those who have known him is his uniqueness.'[16] Menon himself, or rather C.R.'s attitude to him, was a perfect instance of this uniqueness. While his Swatantra colleagues disliked Menon intensely, C.R. was often willing to give him the benefit of the doubt.

An Indo-Pak pact offered at this juncture by General Ayub Khan, the Pakistan President, appealed to C.R. 'Pakistan's offer is worth serious consideration,' he wrote, adding, 'There is cause for all the nations south of Chinese borders to be brought together' (*Swarajya*, 5.12.59). He also advocated a more positive attitude towards the USA, which, he thought, might also 'activate Russia' to move in a direction friendly to India (*Swarajya*, 7.5.60). Neither plea was acceptable to Nehru.

A fresh honour had greeted C.R. before he launched Swatantra. His Ramayana earned him a Rs 5,000 award from the Sahitya

Akademi for 'the best work in Tamil in 1955-7.' He waded through illnesses, toured, pacified dissatisfied partymen, and encouraged personalities offering their support.

Premnath, the film actor, was one such. Arriving for a dinner given by the actor in Bombay, Rajaji was welcomed at the door by Premnath's wife, the actress Bina Rai. 'She is a famous star,' Rajaji's aide S.V. Subramaniam informed him. After studying his hostess for a long moment, Rajaji asked, 'Do you mean to say she is a film actress?' 'Yes, she is,' confirmed Subramaniam. 'Really?' Rajaji asked again, adding, 'Surely so much beauty is not required for film acting.'[17]

His boylike curiosity was well-preserved. Thomas Simons, the new American Consul-General, noticed, in 1961, 'the zest and youthful excitement [C.R.] displayed' while showing 'the new car he had just taken possession of.'[18] To John Thompson, an Australian poet who had called on C.R. and later sent him a book of poems, C.R. wrote:

> I was amazed at the volume of courageous poetry that has issued from Australia. Keep your souls God-hungry and you will be blessed (7.9.61).

Lengthening shadows, and the cutting of links with the past . . . C.R. sold the land and house he had acquired in Salem forty or so years earlier to a doctor wanting to build a hospital, for a sum 'far below the market value,' in the doctor's phrase.[19]

Lengthening shadows, and the inevitable quota of tombstones . . . Vedaratnam, the host of the 1930 Vedaranyam battle against the Raj, passed away. C.R. had called him 'a blood brother in political life as far as dear Tamilnad was concerned' (*Swarajya*, 2.9.61).

Three months earlier, Khasa had gone. His lucid, enthusiastic, faith-filled backing, offered without a break for five years, had meant a great deal to C.R. 'Bereaved' was the heading C.R. gave to his note about Khasa:

> The world of journalism in India has lost one of its bravest and best veterans . . . I have lost one who bathed me with his affection and rejuvenated me when I felt weary. He was beloved of all, because he overflowed with love and forgiveness

for all . . . My bereavement is great and I am unable to suppress my self-pity (*Swarajya*, 24.6.61).

Lengthening shadows, and growing grandchildren. A 16-year-old grandson was advised thus:

> You should read at least a dozen of Shakespeare's plays if not all of them. Read books for pleasure . . . Never mind if parts go ununderstood.[20]

Lengthening shadows, and a dinner at Raj Bhavan with Queen Elizabeth, of whose forebears C.R. had been a guest in many a prison and who toured India in 1961 with her husband, the Duke of Edinburgh.

Pothan Joseph replaced Khasa as the *Swarajya* editor. Each issue carried a lead article by C.R. as well as a 'Dear Reader' column in which C.R. commented on sundry national, international and theological subjects.

> *On South Africa and apartheid*, 14.5.60: If they want apartheid, the Boers should carry it forward to its logical end . . . The country should be partitioned off on the basis of the population ratio and white South Africans may have apartheid to their hearts' content. If this division be not possible, then the policy of apartheid must be given up.

> *On a proposal for banning communal parties*, 8.4.61: Now is a trade union . . . [or] an association of cotton merchants less offensive than an association of Jains or Catholics or Muslims or Kayasthas or Brahmins (or Negroes or men of Indian origin in South Africa or of Tamils in Ceylon)? I warn my friends against this foolish and unconstitutional enterprise.

In December 1961, with general elections round the corner, Indian troops entered Goa. The liberation of the enclave the Portuguese had held for centuries was a lucrative election-eve stroke. One of the few Indians to object to the move, C.R. commented that after Goa India had 'totally lost the moral power to raise her voice against militarism' (*Swarajya*, 27.12.61).

Many letters coming to him were destined to be crushed into a ball and flung into the w.p.b. by a practised if slowly weakening hand, but most were dealt with. C.R. would scribble his answer on blank spaces in the letter received; his typist would reproduce it. Even single-sentence replies had a distinctive twist. With some correspondents he was uninhibited or playful. One of them was the English pioneer of All India Radio, Lionel Fielden, a bachelor who had met C.R. often in the thirties and forties and later settled in Italy.

> *C.R. to Fielden about the latter's memoirs*, 4.1.61: What charming poetry have you filled your childhood story with. I am absolutely in love with your grandmother. And then, when the stepmother enters the scene, how delightful! You are a born writer . . . I wish you had not advertised your 'homosexuality'. I am a heterosexual. I wish your grandmother were alive and I could court her.

When Fielden wrote that he saw C.R. as 'a humanitarian who doesn't believe in egalitarianism,' a delighted C.R. replied:

> 22.1.61: You are 'cent per cent' right . . . Strength and energy flow from difference in level . . . Egalitarianism is a fallacy and a fraud. The doctrine of compassion preached by Jesus and the Upanishads of India is the true doctrine of life, not the illusion of egalitarianism or its monster children, envy, hatred and violence . . . Am I getting to be a priest?

> *Fielden to C.R.*, 14.8.62: Thank you for your kindness in seeing my cousins when they were in Madras. They were thrilled to meet you and — like me — thought you by far the most interesting and lively man in all India. They found Jawaharlal dull by comparison with you . . .

> *C.R. to Fielden*, 24.8.62: I am glad to be told that your cousins . . . found me worthy of the time they gave . . . The trouble with J.N. is that he won't take any risk. So he appears dull. He is big and too conscious and anxious about it. I . . . don't care and let go. Anyway I am grateful to your cousins for their partiality.

Ten or so MPs had formed a Swatantra contingent in the existing Lok Sabha, and similar units had emerged in the Bihar, Orissa, Gujarat, Rajasthan and Andhra assemblies. Across India, membership was increasing, but there were some problems. Chatterjee, leading the West Bengal unit, resigned after being told that in the coming elections Bombay would finance only one Lok Sabha seat from West Bengal. The Raja of Ramgarh, who controlled a vote bank in Bihar, clashed with the party's central executive.

As elections drew nearer, the desire to defeat Congress and win some seats through electoral adjustments with non-Communist opposition parties tended to eclipse the anti-statist cause. Resenting a newcomer's intrusion, the Jan Sangh was reluctant to leave seats for Swatantra. However, in Rajasthan, Madras and the Punjab, Swatantra reached constituency-level agreements with, respectively, the Jan Sangh, the DMK, and the Akali Dal.

C.R.'s wooing of C.N. Annadurai, the DMK leader, or Anna, as he was increasingly called, who had courted arrest in defiance of the Rajaji-led ministries of 1937-9 and 1952-4, merits attention. In Annadurai's eyes, C.R. had been an Aryan secretly striving to maintain Brahmin domination over the Dravidians. On his part C.R. had accused the DMK and its parent, the DK, of 'openly preaching a creed of hatred based on ethnological conjectures and unrecorded and unproved historical conflicts.'[21]

Now, however, defeating Congress was the primary aim of both. As C.R. saw it, the DMK had to be assisted, enlisted and if possible moderated; it could not be alienated. In extending his hand to the DMK, C.R. was encouraged by the personality of Annadurai, who possessed mass appeal and a mind seemingly open to new ideas. Though Swatantra and DMK failed to reach a full electoral agreement, Rajaji and Anna hit it off with each other.

Privately and publicly, C.R. urged Anna to abandon the independent Dravidaland that the DK and the DMK had earlier demanded; and with the nationalists in the South and elsewhere he argued that the DMK was not in fact the secessionist demon they feared. He is entitled to his share of the credit for the DMK's formal abandonment of the secessionist aim, which was announced at the end of 1962, following India's conflict with China.

An 83-year-old C.R. threw himself into the election

campaign. As thousands seated on the ground would chant 'Rajaji! Rajaji!', 'a patriarch wreathed in white and carrying his famous cane like some Old Testament prophet' would 'pick his way among them to deliver a delightful drumfire attack.'[22] Congress socialism 'was grinding the individual,' a Congress-Communist contest was no more than 'an Oxford boat race,' and 'the pernicious system of permits, licences, quotas and controls made the Congress party's rich friends richer and the poor poorer.'[23]

He complained about two wrongs. One was the permission, grossly unfair to the other parties, for a Congress flag which was virtually the same as the Indian tricolour. Two, 'the collection of funds for the ruling party's chest [by] prominent ministers' who held the power to promote or ruin industrialists (*Swarajya*, 17.6.61).

Receiving money in Kanpur, Nehru confessed that he was 'a little ashamed,' but, as C.R. pointed out, the Prime Minister 'pocketed the purses given!' (*Swarajya*, 7.10.61).

Two suggestions for the longer term were made by C.R. One was state funding of elections, which would help eliminate 'the overwhelming advantages of money-power.' Added C.R.: 'Elections now are private enterprise, whereas this is the first thing to be nationalised' (*Illustrated Weekly*, 13.8.61).

His second suggestion was that for six months prior to a general election, the President should rule directly, through officials, thereby reducing the capacity of Ministers to influence voting. But fair elections were hardly the ruling party's first concern. C.R.'s complaints and suggestions fell on deaf ears.

'Humble the Congress. Pluck its feathers. Maul its strength.' This was C.R.'s election-eve message to his public. He and others speaking like him were not heeded. In 1957 Congress had polled 46 per cent of the nation's votes; now it secured 44.5 per cent. In the Lok Sabha and most state assemblies it secured comfortable majorities. Swatantra's share of the Lok Sabha vote was 8 per cent, that of the Jan Sangh 7 per cent, of the Communists roughly ten per cent.

In the Lok Sabha, Congress won 361 seats (a loss of ten); the

Communists 29, Swatantra 25, the Jan Sangh and allies 18, and different Socialist factions 18. In 1963, Ranga and Masani would enter the Lok Sabha through by-elections. Until then Deo, the Maharaja of Kalahandi, led the Swatantra MPs.

Swatantra secured a total of 207 seats in the different state assemblies, as against 153 for the Communists, 149 for the Socialists, and 115 for the Jan Sangh. In Madras, the DMK obtained 50 seats and Swatantra 9.

The new party had 50 MLAs in Bihar — Ramgarh had done his bit; 36 in Rajasthan; 26 in Gujarat; 19 in Andhra; and 15 in U.P.

Held earlier, the Orissa Assembly elections had given Swatantra 37 seats out of 140. There, and in Rajasthan, Gujarat and Bihar, Swatantra was now Congress's leading opposition. All in all, while the Congress fortress was not breached, the new challenger had not done too badly.

To an American reporter, C.R. said: 'I will carry on. I will work for a strong opposition in the next general elections.' Meredith Brown of the *Louisville Courier-Journal* noted that these would take place in 1967, when 'the remarkable Mr Rajagopalachari will be 89 years old."

23

Kennedy
1961-63

In the autumn of 1961, the Soviet Union broke a worldwide
pause in nuclear testing by exploding a 50-megaton bomb.
C.R. demanded that India 'ostracize' the USSR, but Nehru was
unresponsive. He was equally cool a few months later when
Bertrand Russell urged him to send, as a gesture of protest, an
Indian ship to the Pacific zone where America had scheduled
'retaliatory' blasts.

Russell's idea clicked with C.R., who told Jawaharlal that
he would like to go to the testing area himself on any ship India
might send!

C.R. to Nehru, 22.4.62: If you are responding positively to
Bertrand Russell's appeal . . . do register me as a civilian going
with the 'resisters.' I do wish the appeal is accepted.

Nehru to C.R., 23.4.62: I admire the crusading enthusiasm of
Bertrand Russell, but I do not see how I can order one of our
warships to go to this place. That would be almost a hostile
act against the United States and might have far-reaching
consequences.

C.R. to Nehru, 25.4.62: Our civil resistance cannot be possibly
treated as an unfriendly gesture . . . We can explain fully our
motive and our friendly attitude. Our opposition would be
only to the tests and not to the government.

Nehru to C.R., 5.5.62: I am afraid I have not yet been convinced by what you have written about sending a ship to Christmas Island . . . Any step of this kind that we take would be considered a hostile act against the United States.

C.R. to Nehru, 8.5.62: I regret to note that I have not been able to persuade you that governments too can offer civil resistance to more powerful governments who seek to act contrary to international law . . .

If we exclude two brief visits to Ceylon and another to Burma when the British ruled it as part of India, C.R. had never travelled abroad. To leave his neighbourhood for the first time at the age of eighty-three and a half, and that too as a civil resister, would have been intriguing. Though that journey did not come about, C.R. soon crossed the oceans — to fight the Bomb.

The journey was a follow-up to a disarmament conference in Delhi which was attended by Indian eminence virtually in its entirety. Nehru, C.R., Prasad, who had just retired as President, Radhakrishnan, who had succeeded Prasad, Jayaprakash Narayan, Zakir Husain, the Vice-President — all took part.

When his turn to speak came, C.R. said he was sorry that Russell's appeal had gone unheeded and added that an Indian initiative was called for. R.R. Diwakar, chairman of the Gandhi Peace Foundation and the conference convener, responded by asking C.R. whether he would be willing, with perhaps one or two others, to visit the leaders of the Big Powers on behalf of the Foundation.

Yes, said C.R., if the Indian government would support such a mission and if he was not expected to respond with silence or evasion to questions about India that might be put to him abroad. If Nehru was uneasy on this score, he would rather not go.

When C.R.'s queries were put to Nehru by Diwakar and Shiva Rao, journalist and former parliamentarian, Jawaharlal expressed willingness to satisfy C.R. on both points. However, he proposed a division of labour, with C.R. calling on the

Western leaders, and U.N. Dhebar, a recent president of Congress, visiting Moscow.

Nehru's view prevailed, but C.R., who obtained the Foundation's sanction for visiting Moscow after America if that proved necessary, warned Krushchev in a letter that he might suddenly turn up at the Kremlin.

He had his overcoat, last used twelve years earlier in Delhi, some pairs of socks and a couple of woollen kurtas pulled out and dry-cleaned, and knee-length semi-woollen pants stitched into his dhotis. The obligatory shots were reluctantly taken. In deference to his age and condition, it was decided that Dr C. Satyanarayana of Madras's General Hospital would accompany C.R.

Diwakar and Shiva Rao were on the delegation with C.R.; in fact, following Nehru's advice, Diwakar was designated 'leader' and C.R. 'chief spokesman.'[1]

On 22 September word came via John Galbraith, the American ambassador in Delhi, that President Kennedy would receive the group on 28 September.

The party flew via London and New York. Meeting the delegation in New York, and noting that the ages of Rajaji, Diwakar and Shiva Rao added up to 223 years, Natwar Singh, the Indian Consul-General, thought, 'Fancy sending three stretcher cases to meet President Kennedy' (*Swarajya*, 3.9.78).

As their plane approached the American capital, C.R. recalled that twenty years earlier Col. Louis Johnson, President Roosevelt's representative in India, had wanted to fly Nehru and C.R. to Washington in a bid to resolve the deadlock in Congress's wartime talks with the British. That trip was not to be, but at 5.00 p.m. the next day he would be meeting one of Roosevelt's successors, the glamorous and, it was said, tough and astute John F. Kennedy, not to seek aid over any Indo-British tangle but to offer aid over the Russo-American one!

Not vanity but a sense of duty had brought him to America. The appointment at the White House was preceded by an 80-minute discussion starting at 3.30 p.m. with a seasoned team led by William Foster, director of the US Disarmament Agency. This exercise exhausted C.R. and almost made him late for the big interview, but it also acquainted him with the hurdles he would need to overcome in his talk with the President.

As their car entered the White House driveway, C.R. said to Shiva Rao, his voice a hoarse whisper, 'What am I going to say to the President? I am so tired.' 'Don't worry,' the faith-giving Shiva Rao replied, 'the right words will come to you.' What followed has been described by Ambassador B.K. Nehru, who had accompanied the delegation:

> We had barely sat down in the waiting room—which was, incidentally, the Cabinet Room of the United States — when the door opened, a young man walked briskly in, shook hands all round and took us into another room a short distance away where flash bulbs popped, television lights shone and batteries of cameramen started taking pictures.

> Rajaji looked up to the man on his left, who was a whole twelve inches taller than he, and said in a very gentle voice, 'Am I in the presence of the President of the United States?' . . . Rajaji had not realised, till the photographing had started, that the young man who had led us in was President Kennedy himself.

Kennedy sat in his rocking chair, with Diwakar and Shiva Rao to his right and Rajaji and B.K. Nehru to his left. Rajaji began disarmingly. He was not pleading, he said, for American disarmament: how could he, when his own government had a policy of armed defence? But the immediate cessation of nuclear tests stood on a different footing. Delicately he introduced the argument that the world as a whole had a right to say to the nuclear powers that they could not, in the name of testing, poison the atmosphere and endanger humanity, now and in the future.

Moreover, America and Russia did not seem too far from an agreement: the Kremlin's refusal to allow inspection was the only hitch. In the absence of an agreement, could not America contemplate a unilateral suspension of all tests save underground ones? Didn't the world need someone with the courage to take the first step?

He had had, Rajaji went on, exchanges on the subject with Krushchev. Though some of these had been disappointing, it could not be denied that the Soviet Union had at one stage announced unilateral cessation. When the Kremlin resumed testing a year ago, Rajaji went on, he had pleaded for its ostracism. Unfortunately, the Indian government could not accept his suggestion.

Yet, faced with American unilateral action, and the global opinion created by such an action, the Kremlin would find it hard not to follow suit, and humanity would be spared the danger of continuous fallout. If the Soviet Union did not repond positively, the USA could legitimately resume testing. B.K. Nehru has written:

> I have had the good fortune of being present when great men have argued their points of view with each other in many parts of the world. But I had seldom seen a case presented with such lucidity of argument, such economy of speech, such felicity of language, such gentleness of manner and such command of facts as Rajaji displayed that day. It was interesting to watch President Kennedy's reactions, for he too was a great admirer of style. One could almost see his eyes open wider and wider in wonder and in admiration of the frail little man who was making this masterly presentation.

Recorded Shiva Rao:

> The minutes sped far beyond the allotted time of twenty-five minutes. Messengers kept coming at regular intervals with notes from impatient aides to remind Mr Kennedy that other appointments were falling behind schedule. The President ignored them all: with a face aglow with admiration he seemed absorbed in the practical wisdom of his Indian visitor. 'Governor,' he said every few moments for a brief intervention . . .

Towards the end, the President said, 'I find the proposals reasonable and I will certainly consider which of them are feasible.' He asked his visitors to wait for good news, and said that it might emerge by January 1963. He was aware, Kennedy went on, of the danger from profilerating tests. The basic problem was of mutual trust. 'Something must be done to build such trust.'

They had been with Kennedy for over an hour but he was in no hurry to send them away. He showed them a writing desk that Queen Victoria had presented to a previous occupant of the White House, gave them a view of his garden, and, taking leave, asked Rajaji to keep in touch.

Kennedy apparently said to Philips Talbot, Assistant Secretary of State, who was present, that the interview 'had a civilising quality about it.' At any rate this is what Talbot afterwards told Shiva Rao.[2] In a gesture normally restricted to a visit by a head of state or government, the White House issued a communique on the talk between 'the President and Mr Rajagopalachari.'

'Was it a fruitful talk?' a reporter asked. 'It was flowerful,' said Rajaji. (This had been Gandhi's reply in 1944 after a meeting with Jinnah.) But it was more than that. Chester Bowles disclosed to the delegation that some of the points C.R. made to Kennedy featured in a State Department discussion two days later.

His fifteen days in America were spent in Washington, New York and Boston. Slowly climbing the steps of the Lincoln Memorial, C.R. stood silently in front of the seated hero and then stretched his arms to touch the marble figure. B.K. Nehru, Rajaji's host in Washington, thought that despite all his reading C.R. seemed surprised by 'the overwhelming affluence of the Western world.' Natwar Singh, the New York host, noted that Rajaji was 'always punctual and a model of tidiness' and that 'the bedroom and the bathroom were kept spotlessly clean.'

Wives of South Indian members of India's missions made the things C.R. was used to eating; he talked — mostly about the Bomb — with interesting scientists and editors, senators and professors, students and diplomats; altogether, it was a satisfactory time in America. It included meetings with Secretary of State Dean Rusk; Adlai Stevenson, the American Ambassador at the UN; U Thant, the UN Secretary-General; Foreign Ministers at the UN including Andrei Gromyko of the Soviet Union; a lunch with a youthful Harvard professor called Henry Kissinger; a session with the editors of the *New York Times*; and more.

'I am a rightist at home,' said C.R., candidly, to Gromyko. 'By which you mean that you want to do the right thing,' said the well-versed Gromyko. They talked very frankly, and it was clear that bridging the Soviet and American positions would be hard work. C.R. was tempted to go to Moscow, but heeded Kennedy's advice to wait.

Zafarulla Khan of Pakistan, the UN President at this time, gave a lunch in C.R.'s honour. Zafarulla has recalled his reaction earlier when his secretary informed him that someone described as Rajaji wished to call on him. 'I recognise only one Rajaji, and he cannot possibly be in New York,' he told the secretary, and asked her to discover 'further particulars of the gentleman who desires to call on me.' When she 'returned with a slip on which Rajaji's full name was spelt out,' Zafarulla asked his secretary to convey that 'if I was given an appointment, I would deem it an honour to call on Rajaji.'

C.R.'s small, fragile frame and the nature of his cause aided his advocacy in the West. The old man in strange apparel was pleading not for a party, country or bloc of countries, but for the whole world's dumb millions. Men of his sort with his sort of aim do not often tread on the carpets of the world's chancelleries. The impact was considerable. He awarded himself fair marks. Writing to his grandson, Gopu, 17 at the time, he said:

> God has helped me to keep good health and to do my work well. Everyone I think who heard me including all the big bureaucrats were impressed, and their conscience is not easy. But God keeps to himself results (8.10.62).

Five days in Britain followed. Rajaji talked with Premier Harold Macmillan and Gaitskell, the opposition leader; with Canon Collins, the peace champion; with Britons who had served in India; and to assorted British and Indian groups.

His host in London, High Commissioner M.C. Chagla, saw that C.R. was curious about 'a particular street.' When Chagla 'laughingly asked why this interest in this particular street,' C.R. replied—Chagla recalls—that he had read about it. 'Though he had tried to visualise it, now that he was in London, he would like to see it as it really was.'[3]

It would have been a mistake, C.R. wrote to his daughter Lakshmi, not to see 'the glories of ancient and modern Rome.' The highlight of three days in Rome was a meeting with Pope John, at which Father Jerome D'Souza, an old friend from Madras, acted as interpreter.

Rajaji sought 'the blessing and encouragement' of the Pope in his mission against the Bomb. The Holy Father offered assurances and said he would pray. Expressing his gratitude, C.R. said he would 'venture also to appeal' for something more. Could there not be, C.R. asked, a Papal plea at a suitable occasion — even, perhaps, at the next Council — for a test-ban agreement? John XXIII said he would 'carefully consider' the idea.

After finding out from Father D'Souza how old Rajaji was, the Pope said to C.R.: 'I am 81 and so your junior.' *C.R.*: 'In wisdom and spiritual knowledge we are children before you.' *The Pope*: 'The secret of keeping young is being ready at all times to answer if the Lord should call us. The coming Council is a great and important event, but it is the Lord's work and I leave it with serene confidence in His Hands.'

The Pope played his part. An encyclical contained a plea for the stoppage of test explosions. C.R. was thrilled. Then, in June 1963, when the Pope died, C.R. paid him a tribute (*Swarajya*, 15.6.63).

> May Mr Kennedy and Mr Krushchev and their advisers be inspired by John the good, whose spirit hovers over us, still pleading.

Responding to many voices, including an eloquent one supplied by C.R., America, the Soviet Union and Britain agreed, at the end of July 1963, on a test-ban treaty. C.R., who sent letters of praise to the leaders of the three powers, wrote to Monica Felton that he was 'delighted beyond expression at what has at last happened.'

'Ours was not,' he said in a letter to Diwakar, 'a case of tilting at the windmills' (9.8.63).

Chester Bowles, who by now was posted again as ambassador to India, wrote to C.R. (9.8.63):

> I am sure that the treaty will be the subject of vigorous discussion in the United States Senate. However . . . I feel confident that President Kennedy will stand firm . . . I might add that this persistence is, in no small measure, due to your eloquent plea for just such a step as this . . . during your visit.

A letter from Kennedy followed. Expressing 'personal thanks' to C.R. for his congratulatory words, the President added (15.8.63):

> Even so limited a beginning cannot help but carry forward the cause of peace for which you have so devotedly laboured.

Visiting Delhi three months later, Rajaji was brushing his teeth one morning when a grandson informed him that Kennedy had been killed. 'It can't be true!' exclaimed C.R.

24

Defiance

1962-69

C.R. was in London when, in a swift move across India's Himalayan border, the Chinese army 'outnumbered, outweaponed, outmanoeuvred and slaughtered' Indian soldiers, as C.R. put it, borrowing a famous phrase.

The defeat outraged the Indian public. The revelation that Indian soldiers in the icy heights were poorly clothed and poorly shod, in addition to being poorly armed, added to the indignation. Asked by Congress MPs to remove Krishna Menon, the Defence Minister, unless he wished to risk his leadership, Nehru — with great reluctance — dropped his protégé.

Though C.R. referred once to the belief that Nehru himself 'had directed the policy' that led to the disaster (*Swarajya*, 10.11.62), he refrained from attempting to force Jawaharlal out. Only Nehru commanded the nation's affection.

In utterances following his return, and at a face-to-face meeting in Delhi, C.R. sought to encourage Nehru the man, while urging a drastic revision of his policies.

[Nehru's] deprecation of any tendency to brutalization of our people's minds was admirable and appropriate . . . Sri Nehru rightly condemns the silly exhibitions of misguided partriots by way of burning effigies and shouting ugly and childish slogans. They do not in the least affect the Chinese; they affect us (*Swarajya*, 24.11.62).

> The Prime Minister is standing up bravely to the reverses we
> have had to suffer. God bless him and give him strength
> (*Swarajya*, 1.12.62).

> Double quick change in policies is called for (*Swarajya*, 24.11.61).

> It is necessary to establish friendly relations with Pakistan ...
> We cannot fight on two fronts ... [Secondly] we must build
> friendship and alliances with Western powers (*Swarajya*,
> 22.11.62).

Much earlier (3.11.62), he had sent a message to President Ayub
Khan: 'Pakistan has a great opportunity to do the grand and
correct thing. I shall not dilate or expand. May God guide you
to do the right thing when Providence has provided the occasion.'[1]

Three years previously, when Ayub made a joint defence
offer to India, Nehru had asked, 'Joint defence against whom?'
Now, when India probed Pakistan's willingness to stand by
India, Ayub asked, 'What about Kashmir?' On Kashmir Nehru
was not prepared to budge.

As for approaching the West, Nehru privately asked for the
West's aid, and it was offered. As Kennedy said in a letter to
C.R. (5.12.62): 'We have given you some military help already
and we are considering your Government's requests for more.'

Prescribing 'a more dynamic military policy' and 'a strategy
that will wrest the initiative from the enemy,' (*Swarajya*, 1.12.62)
C.R. suggested a move towards Taiwan, hitherto an untouchable
in Indian eyes. 'We can bomb Peking from Taiwan,' he had
apparently said to Nehru when the two met on C.R.'s return to
India.[2]

What was dynamic to C.R. may have seemed reckless to
Nehru. Happily for Jawaharlal, pressure for immediate
realignments ceased when, after an easy descent into the
Himalayan foothills, Peking unilaterally returned to the heights.

But it retained bits of captured territory. Nehru's assertion
that India would retrieve these pieces at the border did not
convince C.R. Time would justify C.R.'s cheerless assessment:

> The Chinese have de facto imposed their will and pleasure on
> us and the Prime Minister has resolved to accept it, whatever
> hot and patriotic words may be uttered (*Swarajya*, 16.2.63).

The swoop from the north strengthened C.R.'s view that China's power and possible ambitions constituted a 'menace which is not only big but permanent.' Perceiving stirrings for 'a Chinese empire [in Asia] to rival Soviet Russia in Europe,' C.R. hoped, in response, for 'a system of forces which will produce and maintain equilibrium in Asia' (*Swarajya*, 1 & 22.12.62).

The Chinese withdrawal not being followed by a surrender of the special powers the government had acquired, C.R. rang an alarm.

> 'Bless the baby and save the mother is my motto, sir,' said Mrs Gamp, in Dickens's story of Martin Chuzzlewit. [However,] the motto of all good gynaecologists is that neither the mother nor the baby should be sacrificed . . . Democracy should be preserved as well as national security (*Swarajya*, 19.1.63).

Earlier, when India's defeat became known, he had demanded 'full and accurate news of casualties' and 'correct news about our losses and the reason why' (*Swarajya*, 3 24.11.62).

Morarji Desai, Nehru's Finance Minister, now produced policies that C.R.'s itchy pen was waiting for. He over-taxed; he compelled the diversion of middle-class savings into poor-interest government bonds; and, with his Gold Control scheme, he sought to cure the Indian of his gold-addiction.

Though cordiality existed between him and Desai, C.R. savaged the measures. 'Sadism runs amuck' was his comment on the new taxes, and he foresaw 'fruitless suffering, barren pain' from the compulsory deposit law. But it was the error of Gold Control that most offended him.

A ban on the use of high-purity gold in fresh jewellery, which Desai claimed would reduce the smuggling of gold into India, was the essence of the Desai scheme. Crying 'Dacoity!', C.R. charged that 'the jewels and gold of our womenfolk have attracted . . . greedy eyes.' (*Swarajya*, 1.9.62). As he saw it, 'the yellow metal was . . . the honest and industrious family's village-bank, with no difficult forms and inaccessible counters for the illiterate' (*Swarajya*, 2.2.63).

To him, smuggling of gold was not 'the fault of the people' but the result of the rupee's falling value. One of Desai's follow-up measures amused him:

> I had a notion that [Desai] planned to save our womenfolk from the expensive lure of trinkets, and that his attack on gold was a puritanic taste-reform. But we find now that under his inspiration Government is going to spend public money on a 14-carat-and-below jewellery-making national institute! (*Swarajya*, 6.4.63)

C.R.'s worst fears came true. There was no demand for the 14-carat-jewellery that Desai sought to popularize. Tens of thousands of goldsmiths found they had no work — some committed suicide.

C.R. was not alone in asking for the scrapping of Gold Control and for Morarji's resignation. The latter came, in a curious fashion, in August 1963. Gold Control went three years later.

In May 1963 Congress lost two crucial Lok Sabha by-elections, both fought in Nehru's home state, UP — and lost them to two of Jawaharlal's sharpest critics, Acharya Kripalani and Ram Manohar Lohia. C.R. was jubilant:

> The spell is broken. The tide has turned. The head of the government is no longer a god but a replaceable representative of the people (*Swarajya*, 1.6.63).

Feeling new blood in his veins, he travelled to Rajkot, where, in a third by-election, Masani was battling in a Congress stronghold. Though C.R. experienced 'the heat of a bakery oven' — it was June — he helped Masani win.

As the Opposition's morale rose, that of Congressmen sank. Aware that Congress was declining in Madras as well, Kamaraj came up with the idea that he would resign as Chief Minister and devote himself to party work.

Nehru not only allowed Kamaraj to switch; he applied the Kamaraj Plan, as it was soon called, to many others. All Chief Ministers and Ministers at the centre were asked to 'renounce' office and give their resignations to Nehru, who would accept some and return others.

In the event, Nehru accepted the 'resignations' of four of his ministerial colleagues — Desai, Lal Bahadur Shastri, Jagjivan Ram and S.K. Patil — and two Chief Ministers besides Kamaraj — Kairon of Punjab and Patnaik of Orissa. In the phrase of the day, these men were 'Kamaraj-ed.'

To the masses the exercise was presented as evidence of self-denial in Congress, but C.R. underlined the foot-dragging of some of the Kamaraj-ed and rubbed in the fact that Nehru himself did not go near the sacrificial pyre. Rather the contrary.

> The stunt has proved a farce . . . Sri Nehru was unanimously asked to remain as PM and given discretion and power to order people to the funeral pyre . . . Murder, so to say, has taken the place of the proposed sati (*Swarajya*, 31.8.63).

With guns going silent at the borders, C.R. had felt free to sharpen his criticisms of Nehru. The P.M. was 'playing down corruption.' In his 'permit-licence-quota system, money, unlike water, was flowing upwards,' aggravating disparities in wealth. 'One of the most enlightened and finest national figures in Asia' had been 'sadly transformed into a partyman.' He had 'personal lustre' but was 'not made or brought up' for the tasks of administration. And he was a 'narcissist.' Wrote C.R.: 'Jawaharlal Nehru fell early in life in deep love with his own image, and that passion has not worn off, but has grown with age.'[3]

In January 1964, Nehru had a heart attack. Replying, on her father's behalf, to a wire C.R. had sent, Indira Gandhi said: 'The gesture and the wording are so typical of you. It cheered us both. My father is already much better but will have to rest for some time and pay far more heed to the doctors.'[4]

During his illness Nehru took one major decision: he released Sheikh Abdullah, who had been in detention for eleven years. His people gave the Sheikh a hero's welcome. Then, inviting Abdullah to Delhi and putting him up at the PM's residence, Nehru discussed with him the possibility of a solution to which India, Pakistan and the people of Kashmir might agree.

Predictably, Rajaji welcomed the development and talked

for three hours with Abdullah, who had travelled to Madras to meet C.R. The talks seemed promising:

> Sheikh Abdullah and Kashmir have come into the scene so that a fresh beginning can be made without loss of face or grace.

> We should demonstrate to Pakistan, unmistakably, that the people of Kashmir desire to be affiliated to India. That alone will stop its mouth. To shirk this process, because it may turn out that they want to be unattached either to Pakistan or to India and remain nonaligned but friendly is not quite fair (*Swarajya*, 16.5.64).

Was Nehru prepared, as Rajaji seemed to be, to reopen, even if only partially, the question of Kashmir's accession to India? It looks as if he was, for, fully knowing the Sheikh's mind, he sent him to Pakistan for talks with Ayub. Some Congress leaders voiced indirect but obvious disapproval. Shiva Rao wrote to C.R.

> There is a clear attempt both from within the Cabinet and in Parliament to prevent the Prime Minister from coming to terms with Sheikh Abdullah if it should mean the reopening of the issue of accession. Many of these Ministers have made public statements . . . It is a sign of the diminishing prestige of the P.M . . . (11.5.64).

> *C.R. to Shiva Rao*: I am afraid PM is not now and will not be in the near future strong enough to think and act in defiance of the unfortunate chauvinism choking Delhi (12.5.64).

All the same, Abdullah went to Pakistan, talked with Ayub and phoned Nehru claiming progress. 'Will Ayub come to Delhi?' Nehru asked. Apparently Pakistan's President was willing. Within a week, on 27 May, Jawaharlal died in Delhi of a stroke! Aghast, C.R. knew at once that rapprochement was dead too. Only Nehru could have reconciled India to any change over Kashmir.

So Nehru was dead. How close he and C.R. had been — as comrades in the struggle for liberty, as leaders of Congress's pro-Allies wing in 1940-1, as partners in government from 1946 to

1954, and finally, just before Nehru's death, over Kashmir. And how they had differed — over office acceptance in 1937, over the Pakistan demand in the early forties, and over socialism throughout. For a while they had been rivals or alternatives too. Why else would the Mahatma have said in 1942, 'Not Rajaji but Jawaharlal will be my successor'? And since the mid-fifties they had fought as political enemies.

Newsmen were impatient for C.R.'s reaction. He wrote it out (27.5.64):

> Eleven years younger than me, eleven times more important for the nation, and eleven hundred times more beloved of the nation, Sri Nehru has suddenly departed from our midst and I remain alive to hear the sad news from Delhi — and bear the shock . . . I am unable yet to gather my wits. I have been fighting Sri Nehru all these ten years for what I consider faults in public policies. But I knew all along that he alone could get them corrected . . . A beloved friend is gone, the most civilized person among us all. God save our people.[5]

He had thought of going to the funeral in Delhi. On his word Namagiri had packed his things. Then, picturing the crush of converging multitudes, he changed his mind. Not going would at least save him from any association, alleged or actual, with the intrigues of succession.

Gulzari Lal Nanda, the Home Minister whom the President had named acting Premier, was willing to succeed Nehru. So was Jagjivan Ram. So were Desai and Shastri. Barring Nanda, all had 'renounced' power under the Kamaraj scheme the previous year.

The real contest was between Desai and Shastri. C.R.'s clear preference was for Shastri. In a private letter, he told Lal Bahadur so and added that he would be chosen. The prediction was not difficult to make — Congress's regional bosses had indicated their distaste for Morarji. Kamaraj, who had become party president in the reshuffle his plan had caused, took a private poll of party MPs and announced that Shastri was their choice.

A year before Nehru's death, another occupant of the old guard room had departed: Rajendra Prasad, whose Presidential terms had ended in 1962. Rajaji's Swatantra bid had earned Prasad's admiration. In his tribute Rajaji called Prasad 'a trusty friend, a good soul and an angel on earth,' and added: 'We stood together from the beginning of our adventure for national freedom. Our comradeship and our mutual affection were never disturbed by any misunderstanding whatsoever' (*Swarajya*, 9.3.63).

'We five' was a phrase Nehru had used in 1949 for Patel, Prasad, Azad, Rajaji and himself — the Mahatma's senior team. All except C.R. were now dead. But at 85 C.R. did not seem close to his own departure — he was still capable of climbing unaided to the top berth of a train compartment.

World trends continued to interest or trouble him. Thus 'the calm matter-of-fact way' in which American journals referred to 'pornographic stuff . . . without any nineteenth-century hesitation or revulsion' was 'most alarming' (*Swarajya*, 16.11.63).

Among his visitors was old Dame Flora MacLeod—petite, charming and an engaging conversationalist —, the first woman chief of her ancient Scottish clan. Rajaji had read of her home, Dunvegan Castle, the abode of the MacLeod chiefs, in Boswell's account of his journey with Dr Johnson to the Hebrides. 'How old are you?' he asked Dame Flora. 'Eighty-five.' 'In what month were you born?' She told him. 'Then I can't marry you,' Rajaji volunteered. 'A Hindu is not supposed to marry a woman older than him.'

Periodically, through an advance copy of a *Swarajya* article, C.R. would offer advice to Lal Bahadur Shastri. Occasionally, Lal Bahadur would act on it. When he did not, which was oftener, his apologies were courteously couched.

But he took care not to be isolated. Shortly after he assumed office, Jayaprakash Narayan, as ardent a votary of Indo-Pak amity as C.R., led a goodwill mission to Pakistan and returned with a Kashmir formula that Ayub was evidently willing to consider. Shastri told J.P. that he liked the solution but could not put it across. India's political caste would oppose it, he said.

Valuing J.P.'s efforts, C.R. sent him, via Shiva Rao, his 'respect, hope and affection.' In being true to themselves, Rajaji and J.P. had alienated many Indians. Though Masani's views tallied with Rajaji's, other leading members of Swatantra invoked Principle 21 to voice their disapproval of Rajaji's position on Pakistan and Kashmir. Because of it, Dahyabhai Patel complained, 'our party has become unpopular.' Munshi said that Abdullah's release was a mistake.

> *C.R. to Dahyabhai:* Sri Munshi is wholly wrong about Abdullah. Sri Jayaprakash is right. Keep together and be brave . . . It is a pity I often seem to be a drag on the party. But if you all wish to throw me away and be free to sail with the others, I shall welcome it (23.4.64).

> *C.R. to Masani:* I feel you and I should go on as we have been doing, not shape our views in order to line up with the public view (April 1964).

C.R.'s stand on Hindi was an additional dilemma for his supporters in the North. The Constitution had directed that on 26 January 1965 Hindi should replace English as the official language. However, Shastri declared that English would continue for as long as the South desired. On the other hand, Desai and some other Congress leaders advocated a firm deadline for a switch to Hindi. Crying wolf, Rajaji asked for a suspension of the constitutional directive. The DMK did likewise, in sharper language.

Critics accused C.R. of lacking in patriotism. Warning that imposition of Hindi could rekindle secessionism in the DMK, C.R. wrote (*Swarajya*, 27.2.65):

> English for unity, say I, over and over again. I shall plead for it as long as my breath lasts, for the love I bear for my country.

In May 1965 Pakistan crossed the border in the Rann of Kutch, and Abdullah was rearrested. C.R. termed the latter step 'neither moral nor statesmanlike,' and Abdullah 'a friend of India, not an enemy' (*Swarajya*, 15 & 22.5.65). J.P. spoke similarly, but the two were in a hopeless minority.

China, meanwhile, to C.R.'s great concern, was drawing Pakistan to her side. In a letter (3.6.65), he warned President Radhakrishnan that 'a China-Pak combination' was 'afoot' and added: 'We must divorce Pakistan from China or make the combine a publicly acknowledged arrangement.' For this purpose, he proposed — to Radhakrishnan and also to Chester Bowles, the American Ambassador, and John Freeman, the U.K. High Commissioner — a conference of 'high-grade representatives of America, Britain, Pakistan and India' at which 'the question must be bluntly raised and settled, whether Pakistan intends to collaborate with China.'

Putting Pakistan on the spot was acceptable to the Indian government, but not involving the West in the exercise. C.R.'s proposal was turned down.

Three months later, India and Pakistan were at war. Indian soldiers and airmen gave an excellent account of themselves during three hard-fought weeks and recaptured some of the prestige lost in 1962. The Pakistanis also fought determinedly, but their Patton tanks and quicker planes were worsted by skill on the ground and the Gnat in the air. Prodded by both America and the Soviet Union, the UN obtained a cease-fire.

C.R.'s support to the defence effort was instant and wholehearted. Convinced that China had egged Pakistan on and would long remain a menace, he proposed, at a public meeting in Madras, the recruitment of an army of two million soldiers. It would be an 'anti-Chinese wall,' he said.

However, recalling that 'every day has its separate duties, and so indeed every hour,' he swiftly returned, as did J.P., to the advantages of an Indo-Pak settlement and the shortsightedness of Indian rigidity over Kashmir. When 'firmly accepted truths in the physical sciences' were being modified, 'dogmatism about the liquid truths of political life' bore no sense (*Swarajya*, 9.10.65).

There were demonstrations near C.R.'s house. His arrest was demanded. He replied in *Swarajya* (30.10.65):

> There may be any amount of pressure. I am conscientiously unable to give up my faith in the principle of self-determination. Out of it was born Indian freedom . . .

Our military answer to Pakistan's challenge was as right as it
was successful. Let us never bend our necks to brute force . . .
But let us ever be loyal to fundamental moral principles.

The Madras Chief Minister, Bhaktavatsalam, thought that action
was called for. The Defence of India Rules were invoked, C.R.'s
articles cited as being 'likely to lead the public to question the
territorial integrity of India,' and prosecutions launched against
Sadasivam, *Swarajya*'s publisher — whose wife, M.S.
Subbulakshmi, was raising money for the jawans through her
voice — and Pothan Joseph, the editor. C.R. shot off a letter to
Radhakrishnan:

> Action should be taken against me . . . The truth of the
> matter, viz., that I am to be gagged cannot be hidden from the
> world by such stratagems (1.12.65).

He sent similar letters to Shastri, Home Minister Nanda, and
Bhaktavatsalam. Understanding better than Madras the
implications of silencing Rajaji, the Centre asked Bhaktavatsalam
to withdraw the prosecutions. 'I take it as a victory for freedom
of dissent,' said C.R. (*Swarajya*, 8.1.66).

Shastri, in fact, had become bolder regarding a settlement
with Pakistan. In a letter to Rajaji (15.10.65), he had described
as 'specially important' C.R.'s line about 'the liquid truths in
political life' — one of the lines that made the Madras government
nervous!

Soon after this, Shastri accepted an invitation from Premier
Kosygin of the Soviet Union for an Indo-Pak summit with
Ayub Khan at Tashkent, in Kosygin's presence. Behind the
Soviet initiative lay concern about China's influence over
Pakistan. To Peking's chagrin, Ayub also accepted Kosygin's
invitation.

In a letter C.R. conveyed his blessings to Lal Bahadur. In
Swarajya he wrote (25.12.65): 'May God bless this enterprise and
not allow it to go as one more addition to the limbo of the
might-have-beens, like my formula for satisfying Jinnah's
demands.' And he advised that Shastri should propose an Indo-
Pak zone 'without tariffs or duties or customs of any kind'
(*Swarajya*, 1.1.66).

Opening on 4 January 1966, the summit was close to
breaking down five days later when an almost desperate

intervention by Kosygin turned the tide. Agreement was reached on the vexed question of the return of bits of territory India and Pakistan had gained or lost in the recent conflict, and on rejecting war as a means of solving disputes.

After signing the agreement, Shastri dictated a few letters, including one to Rajaji: 'I am sure you will agree with what we have done in Tashkent and it would get your full support. Trust you are keeping well.'[6] But Shastri was not destined to sign the letter. Within hours he suffered a fatal heart attack.

A stunned C.R. wrote that Shastri's going had 'set a sacred seal on the pledges given at Tashkent' (*Swarajya*, 15.1.66).

Kamaraj and the other Congress chieftains identified Indira Gandhi as Lal Bahadur's most suitable successor. As Nehru's daughter, and as a woman, she would appeal to the masses — with elections only a year away, this was a key consideration. Secondly, as one lacking a political base of her own, she would be dependent on the chieftains. Asking what crime he had committed, Morarji Desai threw his hat in the ring and demanded a vote of Congress MPs. Indira secured 355 preferences, Desai 186.

As alive as the Congress bosses to Indira's vote-getting potential, C.R. was enraged: 'The nation wanted a Prime Minister but the party wanted a mascot and has secured it . . . The Nehru family has come in handy' (*Swarajya*, 29.1.66). He spoke, too, of 'marionettes pulled by wire-pullers,' and a *Swarajya* cartoon sketched Indira as a girl in skirts surrounded by fierce-looking tree-trunks bearing the faces of Kamaraj, Jagjivan Ram and Atulya Ghosh, who was West Bengal's Congress chief. It was captioned, 'Babe in the Woods.'

If he did not fall sick or break his bones, it was in part because of the precautions C.R. took. R.K. Narayan has given us a picture of these, based on a night-stop by Rajaji, 86 at the time, at Narayan's home in Yadavagiri in what was then called Mysore state:

He arrived (*from Tellichery*) nearly at midnight, went to his room, inspected the bed, measured how many steps he would have to take from the bed to the bathroom, asked if the floor was polished, and if the door of the bathroom opened out or in, mentioned the time at which he needed hot water in the morning, and how much — exactly a bucketful, neither more nor less. At six I knocked at his door and found him ready for the day, after a bath and change of dress, busy writing . . . At seven he came to the dining table and breakfasted on one idli and a few spoons of uppumav, finishing it with a small measure of coffee, and left at 7.30 by car for Bangalore.[7]

In 1965 C.R. and Namagiri moved out of the Bazlulla Road house — now too small to contain C.R., Namagiri, Narasimhan, Thangam and Thangam's four grown sons — and into a new house on Naoroji Road in Chetput. This two-bedroom dwelling had the advantage of being almost next-door to Kalki Gardens, where *Swarajya* was produced.

By the middle of 1966 he had five great-grandchildren. Almost all were named by him. Learning that granddaughter Tara had given birth to a boy, he sent her a message, 'Welcome to Vinayak.' The boy was duly named Vinayak. To grandson Ramchandra and his wife Indu, living in Oxford at the time, who were wondering whether the child they were expecting should be born in England or India, he wrote: 'Why should I not have a great-grandchild born in Oxford?' Gopal, learning the vina, was told:

I can't make out *sa* from *pa* any more than I can distinguish a present-day Congressman from a Communist. But keep your voice going along with the vina. If you are shy about the voice, the vina will never enter your bones.

Now and again C.R. would be his age and reminisce. Replying to Mountbatten who had written praising C.R.'s English, he said:

I am flattered. I attribute whatever I have done with English to a Globe edition of Goldsmith's Complete Works and a *Spectator* volume giving all the essays of Addison, Steele and his colleagues in that journal. I read these two books voraciously at the age of 16 and enjoyed it. (3.12.66).

He had not abandoned the hyperbole or the sweeping remark. Asked to recall his impressions of Sarojini Naidu, he termed her, quite simply, 'the sweetest, acutest, kindest, noblest of my dear colleagues.'⁸ And when a Bengali Brahmin wrote wanting to know whether the children of C.R.'s daughter Lakshmi could be deemed Brahmins, he replied:

> I answer your question according to the old law . . . Ramu, my daughter Lakshmi's son is not a Brahmana. My daughter's brahmanhood cannot get down to her son through Devadas Gandhi. But Ramu is better than any Brahmana.⁹

Occasionally, his free-flowing pen gave offence but he could make clean amends, as he did to Balraj Puri who had felt hurt by phrases C.R. had used:

> I accept the rebuke administered by you in your letter . . . I tender my apology. Kind regards. (2.3.66).

A letter written some months earlier could merit a place in any anthology of great apologies. Its recipient was Dr N.B. Khare of Nagpur. Ever since 1938, when the Congress High Command removed him from the Premiership of the Central Provinces, Khare had nursed and poured out great bitterness against Gandhi, C.R. and the Congress movement generally. In June 1965 he sent C.R. a copy of his memoirs in which the ancient grudge was one more spelt out. In acknowledgement, C.R. wrote :

> My dear Doctor Khare, I thank you most sincerely for sending me your autobiography with your autographed inscription. Many years have passed . . . since the historic occasion when you were treated badly by a powerful organization which did not suffer from any lack of arrogance.

> One can now laugh over all the phases of this quarrel and over the various events which display pride, folly, lamentable passion and incompetence. But I can quite understand the proud and honest spirit in you which keeps you still angry, and unforgiving. Most of the people involved are dead . . .

> I have kept no diary or notes and many points are out of my memory . . . I beg of you to pardon me for anything I did in those days which hurt your feelings. You are only four years younger than me. God bless you.

The previous year, as Kamaraj would later recall, Rajaji had gone unexpectedly to Madras's Congress headquarters to greet Kamaraj on his 61st birthday. Pronouncing a blessing on his adversary, C.R. said: 'You should live longer than me.'[10]

He continued to make and challenge phrases:

> *On the licence raj, Swarajya*, 15.1.66: This permit-licence-raj is not a bee in my bonnet but a great big boa-constrictor that has coiled itself around the economy.

> *On Nagas and Mizos, Swarajya*, 12.3.66: Let us drop phrases and headlines about 'dealing firmly with rebels' and such-like, and adopt words encouraging a sense of equality and self-respect . . .

> *On fear and freedom, Swarajya*, 14.5.66: Fear in citizens is the enemy of freedom from domestic misrule. Dear reader, whatever your age and your profession may be, do not murder the truth that arises from time to time in your heart.

After a year of Indira Gandhi's Premiership, fresh elections would be due. Drought, strikes, inflation and riots had damaged Congress's position. C.R. acknowledged Indira's withdrawal of Gold Control and the modest deregulation of industry she announced; and he thanked her for instructing the quick clearance of medicine imported for his needs. But, after a visit by Indira to Moscow, he took her to task for 'allow[ing] the "Imperialists and reactionaries" phrase in the Moscow joint communique' (28.7.66).

And he approached the elections with zest, even though defections and deaths had hurt Swatantra. The potent but self-willed Raja of Ramgarh had to be expelled from the party in 1964. In UP, Paliwal, unable to get along with the Raja of Manakpur, had resigned; two years later, the Raja himself died. Others with stature or influence who had died included V.P. Menon, A.D. Shroff and Udham Singh Nagoke.

But there had been significant accretions, especially in Gujarat and Rajasthan, and in Madras Rajaji had worked out a promising arrangement with the DMK. In these three states, and even more in Orissa, there was a possibility of Swatantra winning a share in power.

Once more Swatantra ran well behind Congress in the race for funds. 'When I go to beg for money,' C.R. complained, 'I find that the industrial companies have given to the Congress five to ten times the dole I could get . . .' (*Swarajya*, 11.2.67).

In August 1966, with elections six months away, C.R. suffered his worst illness in decades. All strength seemed to leave his body and his mind. For the first time in ten years, *Swarajya* appeared without his thoughts, and continued to do so for weeks. But C.R. rallied, and on 29 October the two initials were seen again below the Dear Reader column. Slowly, aided by the therapy of a few hundred daily paces inside the Naoroji Road house, he reacquired some of his energy.

Ever since the 1963 victories of Kripalani, Lohia and Masani, all three of whom were backed by a united opposition, C.R. had striven hard for joint action by Congress's adversaries. In Orissa, Swatantra and the Jana Congress agreed both on a common programme and on seat-sharing. In Rajasthan, Swatantra and the Jan Sangh agreed only on seats.

In Madras, C.R. and Annadurai engineered a DMK-led front where Swatantra had a decidedly junior role. The need to find common ground with other parties affected Swatantra's and even Rajaji's pronouncements. 'Good government' was emphasized more than 'limited government.'

When elections were three months away, J.P. said he was hoping for a non-party government. Seizing on the suggestion, C.R. asked J.P. to take the step that could lead to it:

> In order to further this project, it is necessary that an outstanding personality without any party affiliation should be among those returned to Parliament. I appeal therefore most earnestly to Sri Jayaprakash Narayan to offer himself as a candidate (*Swarajya*, 24.12.66).

C.R. had seen at once that if J.P. and Nehru's daughter both went to the polls, the Indian public would be able, for the first time, to choose a Prime Minister out of two attractive candidates. However, J.P., who was not yet ready to take on Indira Gandhi, expressed his regrets.

All handicaps notwithstanding, C.R. was producing attacking phrases. The use of Defence of India Rules and a spate of amendments had 'killed the Constitution.' Congress policies had let to 'economic sycophancy at America's door and political satellitism under Soviet Russia.'

According to a biographer of Mrs Gandhi, C.R. at this stage was 'ebullient' and giving 'the most damning strictures,' stronger than those of Kripalani or Lohia, though also showing warmth towards Indira as a person.[11] Also noting C.R.'s 'unparalleled zeal to achieve his object of liquidating the Congress,' *The Hindu* asked, 'Is there a Congress leader on the horizon with equal vigour and determination?'

A month before the polling, illness hit C.R. again, frustrating his wish to be 'whirling about all over India' (*Swarajya*, 4.3.67). But he had done his bit, as had others. The result was a significant setback for Congress. Though it again won a majority in the Lok Sabha (280 seats out of 520), Congress's strength there was slashed by almost a hundred seats, and it was humbled and dismissed in eight states, including — to Rajaji's great delight — Madras.

Swatantra's Lok Sabha contingent was doubled from 22 to 44, with Gujarat, Madras and Orissa sending more Swatantra MPs than Congress ones. In Gujarat 66 Swatantra MLAs won as against 26 in 1962; in Rajasthan the improvement was from 38 to 49. In Orissa, Swatantra formed the government, with the Jana Congress as junior partner.

The Congress monopoly was at last over. Sweetest of all, for C.R., were the Orissa and Madras results. Not only was Congress routed in the southern province, Kamaraj lost his seat to a student leader and every central minister contesting from Madras was defeated. 'A virus is sweeping over Madras,' declared Bhaktavatsalam, the defeated Chief Minister, but C.R. saw a 'burst of political health' (*Swarajya*, 18.3.67).

When Annadurai, leading Madras's new DMK Ministry,

asked DMK MLAs to differentiate between party and government and not to pressurize permanent officials, a delighted C.R. said, 'I ask for nothing more of the DMK' (*Swarajya*, 11.3.67).

His room in West Madras contained no TV (not yet brought to Madras) and no radio (his ears were no good for one). It did not even have a desk: he wrote, reclining, on an easy chair, on a clipboard. He kept no library and a minimum of reference books — a large-type Sanskrit Gita, an old leather-bound Bible, some dictionaries. Books lent by others were devoured and returned, and journals sent gratis told him of what was happening in the world.

His bed of hard wood had a foam mattress wrapped in khadi. Next to the bed was an easy chair, a strong reading lamp, a bench and a small table. On the last two rested his reading glasses, a torch, two pocket watches, two old pens, one finely-sharpened pencil, a magnifying glass, an engagement diary, a scribbling pad, and the reference books.

He would rise at 6.30 or so, take his coffee and vitamin pills, glance at the headlines, shave, have his bath and exercise his fingers by washing his hand-towel, exercise his legs with a careful stick-aided walk inside the house or in its small yard, and sit down at 9.00 a.m. or so for his morning meal, call it breakfast or lunch. After a rest, he would write or dictate to Murali (his new secretary) and have him read out any important items in the day's newspapers. He would lie down again till 2.00 or 2.30 p.m. and then, after a tumbler of coffee, write a bit again and, if feeling up to it, receive visitors.

The 'evening' meal would follow and then a dusk-hour drive to the sea-front, where he might walk a few steps or watch boys improvising a game of cricket. Returning home at 6.30 or 7.00 p.m., he would relax in the living room — to which the front-door led — on another hard-wood khadi-covered bed with a foam mattress, his back resting against a high, hard and round pillow.

Narasimhan or Lakshmi, who had moved from Delhi to Madras, and perhaps some grandchildren would call at this stage, which would close with a cup of Complan. Lights were switched off at 8.30 p.m. or 9.00. Assisting her father without pause, cooking and washing for him, available to him round the clock, Namagiri slept six short quick steps away in the living-room.

Of some of his initiatives the Press was totally unaware. Before Congress MPs had re-elected her as Premier, C.R. wrote to Indira Gandhi with a prediction and a suggestion:

> Be assured you will continue . . . You will not be displaced for I still give credit for a moderate modicum of wisdom to your party. But for God's sake do not put some woolly-headed dreamer or V.K.R.V. Rao or any such raw hand as Finance Minister . . . I strongly advise you to persuade and put pressure on Sri Morarji Desai to accept the Finance Minister's place and be Deputy PM also. Forgive my intrusion (2.3.67).

Indira carried out the suggestion regarding Desai but when Rajaji proposed that she should lead a national government — six states were out of Congress's hands, C.R. pointed out, and two or three others were 'held by very slender strings' (13.3.67) — Indira replied that that was not 'a workable proposition.' (18.3.67) An undeterred Rajaji offered her fresh advice:

> The problem cannot be solved unlesss (1) you get rid explicitly of the Fourth Plan . . . (2) you get rid of the spanner in your works, my dear friend Asoka Mehta, sending him if you like as our envoy in Yugoslavia to observe practical socialism and (3) get rid of the Planning Commission along with him (23.6.67).

Despite his warmth towards Zakir Husain, traceable to the Khilafat days of the early twenties, C.R. supported the candidate opposing Husain in the contest for a President to replace Radhakrishnan, whose term was over. This was Subba Rao, who was about to retire as the Chief Justice. Helped above all by Congress's large Rajya Sabha majority, Husain defeated Subba Rao.

The new President was approached by C.R. over the detained Sheikh Abdullah. In *Swarajya* C.R. had written that India could not be called democratic if Abdullah was kept 'in life-long detention' (10.6.67). To Husain, C.R. privately proposed that Abdullah be given power again in Kashmir. If the President did not think this 'quixotic,' he should 'share the idea with Mrs Gandhi.' Four months later he sent the President a reminder and asked if his proposal had gone into the w.p.b.

> All you say, directly or indirectly, is inscribed on my heart. I had soon after getting your first letter discussed it with the people concerned. But as I could not report any progress, I did not write to you . . . I shall continue to follow up your suggestion (30.10.67).

Two months later, the Sheikh was released. Now C.R. publicly suggested his re-installation at the head of Kashmir's government. Indira took time — over seven years — to agree. In February 1975 Abdullah would return as Chief Minister.

As anxious to dethrone Congress as C.R. was Rammanohar Lohia, the brilliant, impassioned Socialist. In May 1967, Lohia called on C.R. and urged him to 'do some fresh thinking . . . on how to make our people work, whether for bread or for . . . change.' His own solution for Indian apathy, Lohia said, was a programme of 'equality through prosperity and prosperity through equality.'

Replying frankly, C.R. said that the slogan of equality was 'an unreal carrot' and would fail. The only way to achieve 'a mass upsurge of industriousness' was through 'just reward for honest labour' and a package of 'incentives, positive and negative.' Lohia recalled an incident of 1934, when Rajaji was a key figure in the Congress high command:

> Rajaji threatened me, of course with a smile and suavity of which he is a peerless master, with a Working Committee resolution which had condemned the Congress Socialist Party and its talk of class struggle. I said that I did not care a tuppence for the resolution . . . I was only 24 at the time. Rajaji answered that he had expected me to swear in Russian currency and he was surprised that I still swore in Brtish currency! (*Swarajya*, 1.7.67)

Five months after their talk, Lohia died. He was 57. C.R. wrote (*Swarajya*, 21.10.67):

> The play is over with Rammanohar Lohia . . . We have lost one of the few honest, dynamic figures in our public life. Lohia detested the passivity of people who desired things but would not work for them. He was angry with people who were not as angry as they should be.

A key factor in his bid to oust Congress was Annadurai or, as he was increasingly called, Anna, the new Madras Chief Minister. A powerful writer and speaker, Anna had put secessionism and anti-Brahminism behind him and was tolerant and open to discussion. Through Anna, C.R. hoped to influence the DMK ideologically, but E.V.R. and the Communists were also wooing the Chief Minister. Unlike some of Annadurai's friends. C.R. was also willing to criticize the Madras government:

> Madras is unique . . . Its present leaders spend more time, energy and imagination in changing names and words in general use than in the substantive business of the state . . . Fresh words have taken the place of 'post office,' 'police station' 'cheque,' 'postcard,' 'bicycle,' etc . . . [But the public continues to] say 'conductor,' 'driver,' 'self-starter,' 'railway station,' etc (*Swarajya*, 24.8.67).

Agreeing on English as the country's link language, C.R. and Annadurai disagreed over the medium of teaching in the colleges and universities of Madras, C.R. preferring English and Anna Tamil. Another difference was over lotteries, which, along with some other state governments, Madras had decided to operate. To C.R., lotteries were an immoral and possibly unconstitutional 'means of robbing the poor' (*Swarajya*, 31.8.68).

But when Annadurai declared that he would call that official 'my best friend who, when he sees me making a mistake, tells me boldly that I am wrong,' C.R. hailed it as 'the most important pronouncement by a Madras Chief Minister in recent times.' (*Swarajya*, 17.8.68). A month later, Annadurai was afflicted by cancer. He was flown to New York for surgery, which was declared successful. C.R. reassured Annadurai:

The skill and care of Dr Miller and the prayers of thousands of men and women have served to put you on the way to recovery. But you have to re-arrange your daily routine . . . You should not convert night into day and day into night . . . You have to avoid all forms of tobacco — snuff, smoking and chewing (24.9.68).

Annadurai to C.R.: I shall ever remember the kind words from you. I am making all efforts to act up to your advice — the snuff habit . . . Though from time to time I feel the anxiety about the political situation in our country, I get confidence from the fact that you are there to guide my colleagues and lead our people . . . The thoughts you have so patiently been sowing have not fallen on barren land . . . (11.10.68).

Shortly after returning to India, Annadurai fell ill again and another operation for cancer was performed. On 3 February 1969 he died. The Tamil country mourned on a scale not seen before — and C.R., roused at 1 a.m. with the news, realized his loss. No one else in the DMK had the stature to remould it. 'Everyone knows how grieved I am and why,' he said. Later he added that the people of Tamilnad had 'lost their good right arm' (*Swarajya*, 15.2.69).

Anna was buried — not cremated — near the beach. As the exhibition of grief continued around the tomb, C.R. recalled a Socrates story:

When he said to the jailor that he was ready to drink the potion of death, the weeping friends of Socrates asked Socrates whether he would like to be cremated or buried. Socrates laughed and told them they might do whatever they liked if they could catch the bird after it had flown away from the cage (*Swarajya*, 8.2.69).

In April 1967, at 88, C.R. underwent surgery for the first time in his life (it was for hernia) and stood it well. A violent attack of hiccups that followed the surgery 'made breathing, eating and sleeping a torture,' (*Swarajya*, 22.4.67) but after ten days the attack passed.

At 89, he surprised newsmen in New Delhi. *The Indian Express* (28.11.67) reported a press conference:

> He was all there: the aphorisms, the arrogance which showed through as he slighted certain questions which were flung at hin, the quickwittedness, the cracks at himself — 'kindly improve my answers when you report this conference' . . . He poured acid on the Communists ('Sir, I do not differentiate between the two groups'), gave the DMK government a good chit, attacked the language bill, jibed at state governors [and] bared his gums at the Congress party.

A year later, he was still in remarkable shape, as the writer Padmalaya Das, interviewing him in Bhubaneshwar, found:

> The curtains parted and a small frail figure stepped in, stumbling a little on the doormat . . . Unaided, Rajaji walked into the room. He . . . sat in a chair and I introduced myself and handed him two pamphlets written by me . . .
>
> And then began the questions. Later I realized that he had asked me more questions than I could ask him . . . He looked very fresh and cheerful. His voice was deep and slow and surprisingly firm and precise . . .
>
> I had typed out a question on a suggestion he was stated to have made for 'a gadget for monitoring the human mind.' . . . As he pored over the piece of paper, I could observe the famous face . . . He has large gentle eyes with heavy lids . . . His skin had a strange glow.
>
> At last he looked up and smiled. 'You can develop the idea yourself,' he said. And I had to laugh.
>
> 'Could you please tell me what you would do if you were compelled to take charge of India?' 'I would first go to a doctor to get younger.' And he really grinned and I burst into laughter.[12]

'Please don't write to me,' he begged of his readers, telling them that his sight prevented him from going through his mail. But he read Tennyson's poems, 'Sixty Years of Power' by Lord Swinton, 'The Divine Flame' by Alister Hardy, and other works, and he re-read Valmiki. 'Tara is the most intelligent and brightest of the womenfolk in Valmiki,' he said, explaining why he named one of his granddaughters Tara.[13]

There had been no diminution in his love of the Epics, for some of his other descendants would be called, in accordance with his wishes, Sita, Govind, Sriram and Kesavan. With the marriages of more of his grandchildren, his clan was getting bigger.

The year 1969 saw the Gandhi centenary — and strife in several parts of India. 'Not a night passes but Gandhiji comes alive in my dreams,' C.R. had written (*Swarajya*, 5.10.68). Writing to grandson Gopu about a classic he had just re-read, C.R. said:

> The sad tenor of the idylls of the King, the corruptions and the tragedy of the Round Table read like an echo of our Congress story in India. Arthur's sword Excalibur was thrown into the lake and so has Bapu's Excalibur been thrown away (18.2.69).

When they live long, dissenters can hear a phrase hard to utter and pleasant to receive — 'You were right.' His age was now conferring this pleasure on C.R. The phrase was used by some who had opposed his stand against Quit India or his Pakistan formula of 1944.

K.R. Karanth, in 1942 an ardent Quit India supporter, now wrote that Rajaji had been prescient in arguing that Britain would give freedom at the end of the war and should not be asked to quit 'when it was fighting for its very existence.'[14] Akshaya Kumar Jain, editor of *Navbharat Times*, wrote:

> Had we acted upon Rajaji's advice (*over the Pakistan demand*) at that time, the country would not have experienced the bloodbath [of 1947] . . . The present-day bitterness would also not have engulfed India and Pakistan.[15]

Hukam Singh, the Lok Sabha speaker from 1962 to 1967, thought that 'Rajaji could see what was coming and could not be avoided,'[16] and in Pakistan Khaliquzzaman reflected that the 1944 Rajaji formula would have been 'far better' than the 1947 arrangement.[17]

There was rethinking, too, on C.R.'s position on the economy. Thus S.C. Sarkar wrote:

> For a number of years Rajaji was campaigning against the failures of . . . 'permit-licence raj.' Few of us who were wedded to the ideals of socialism and economic equality could appreciate the justice of his criticism although in retrospect today few would dare to controvert that criticism. [C.R.'s] long experience had endowed him with an insight of which well-meaning intellectuals had not even the faintest idea.[18]

As he reached and passed the ninetieth milestone, C.R. heard such acknowledgements and was glad. Provided supporters stood firm, he was, he said, prepared to say, 'Life begins at ninety' (*Swarajya*, 23.11.68).

His *Swarajya* and *Kalki* pieces were as interesting as ever. His signed column was, if anything, longer, sharper, richer than before. It asked whether readers realized that Lyndon Johnson had stopped smoking, that the Danes were Europe's leaders in civil aviation, that St. Joseph's College in Trichy was turning out splendid exam results . . . It spoke of the sad final days of Francis Bacon, the current dilemmas of the Beatles, and the foolishness of disbanding traditional regiments of the Indian Army.

The Tamils are told, as they await the change from 'Madras' to 'Tamil Nadu,' that the 'u' at the end of the new name would be infelicitously lengthened when uttered by North Indians, that Tamil Nad would be a better spelling. (But they have long learned to admire him without heeding him, and Tamil Nadu it will be.) They are also told that Chavan rhymes with jawan, not with Ravan; the lesson is called for, for some Tamil papers have made him Chaa-one.

And there are the suggestions, old and new. All India Radio should be run by an autonomous body. The state should bear election expenses. The French should not test their Bomb. Sometimes he was purely, and charmingly, reflective:

> Unquestionably the most beautiful things on earth are the
> flowers and the sweet notes of the birds, sunrise and sunset
> not being of the earth but of the sky. The grandest things are
> the great trees. Man's claim to beauty is only his mind . . .
> (*Swarajya*, 17.5.69).

More frequently he supervised the nation's manners:

> The External Affairs Minister, Mr M.C. Chagla, we are told,
> replied, 'Evidently Mr Mody was saying this on the basis of
> his own weight.' I must very regretfully say that this was
> cheap and in very bad taste . . . The report says the House
> burst into 'applause,' meaning, I suppose, laughter. The MPs
> should have expressed disapproval rather than cheering him
> for his poor joke (*Swarajya*, 17.6.67).

His sarcasm — and sense of moral injury — had full play when,
in 1968, preparations commenced for depriving ex-rulers of the
privy purses guaranteed to them by the Constitution:

> What a fool Rama was, say Congressmen, to give up the
> crown and go to the forest to enable his father to keep his
> word of honour and not break his pledge. 'We break our
> pledges without compunction,' the Congress party says. 'Our
> ideas of morality and honour have marched with the times'
> (*Swarajya*, 27.7.68).

> Sri Jawaharlal Nehru, Sri Vallabhbhai Patel and myself all
> stand to be dishonoured . . . The negotiations regarding the
> privy purses and privileges of the Princes were concluded
> when I was Governor-General and not a mere figurehead.
> Jawaharlal Nehru and Vallabhbhai Patel are gone. But I share
> in the responsibility of maintaining honour in this affair and
> it is my particular and personal duty to protest most strongly
> (*Swarajya*, 16.11.68).

As likely as not, his column referred to the death of
someone famous or significant or near. Martin Luther King and
Robert Kennedy, the assassinated ones; Attlee, who signed away
India; Master Tara Singh ('dear and restless soul'); Deen Dayal
Upadhyaya, president of the Jan Sangh; Sir Homi Mody, Murarji

Vaidya and Charanjit Rai, Swatantra stalwarts; Manu Gandhi, the Mahatma's dedicated grandniece — these and others were farewelled.

He felt no qualms about taking sides in American disputes. He was for Johnson and against the growing ranks of his foes who were demanding withdrawal from Vietnam; and in the end-1968 presidential contest he 'cast his vote,' as he put it in *Swarajya*, for Nixon and against Humphrey. The preference for Nixon was not enthusiastic:

> The whole of América [has] turned isolationist . . . Nixon will be busy with internal problems. North Vietnam will eat Saigon as we dispose of milk chocolates.[19]

While apprehending a day when 'Southeast Asia falls a prey to the Communist powers by American withdrawal,' he was careful not to regard the Chinese people as enemies, and made prescient appraisals:

> The industriousness of the Chinese people, their piety and their adherence to the rules of conduct laid down by Confucius have not ceased to be on account of the black shadow of Communism now upon them. These will shine again when one day . . . the Chinese people are free again. (*Swarajya*, 24.5.69).

He was sure, in fact, that 'years of Communist indoctrination have not brainwashed irredeemably' the Chinese, whom he saw as 'a philosophic as well as a practical race who find their moorings and their bearings in hard work. This great gift of the Chinese people for working hard at the thousand and one things that needed doing in man's daily existence was their surest insurance against their being irretrievably lost to the power games of the politicians' (*Swarajya*, 12.7.69).

When the Czech hopes of 1968 were crushed, he again revealed foresight. 'If the days of Dubcek are numbered,' he wrote, 'the days of Communism are also numbered.' Earlier, during the short-lived Prague spring, he had spoken of 'Czechoslovakia's victorious breach in the walls of Communism' and rejoiced that 'they have not fallen into the fatal trap of violence.'[20] India's official attitude offended him:

> Why should Indira Gandhi be afraid of the word 'condemn' when the Soviet Government was not afraid of committing its monstrous crime? India is not yet a member of the Warsaw Pact (*Swarajya*, 31.8.68).

His religious views and practices may be looked at.

> Whenever I have keenly felt the distress of others, and I pray for their relief, I have found God has answered (*Swarajya*, 18.3.72).

In any three or four consecutive issues of *Swarajya* there was bound to be a piece by Rajaji relating to the Almighty, or on the Gita, or, perhaps, the Bible. No public speech of his omitted a reference to some eternal truth. As Chief Minister he had prayed for rain and the waters did come down. His prayers for opposition unity and Mrs Gandhi's defeat were less successful but he did not blame Providence.

He did not set aside any particular time of day for praying; all his urgings were silent ones; he did not recite any standard verses; and he was opposed to astrology. After joining the Mahatma, he had given up the shikha and the naamam — the hairknot and the forehead mark. What he retained on his person was the annually-replaced sacred thread, first received by him as a boy at a ceremony in the great temple above Tirupati.

Rarely did he visit temples but there were occasions when he sent offerings of money to Tirupati. He adhered strictly to the vegetarianism his tradition prescribed, and occasionally preached it to others, but there were also times when he thought fish and eggs essential to combat malnutrition in India.

His religion was, among other things, a product of thought. In typical passages, he wrote:

> The foundation for science as well as for religion is wonder . . . It is science to find out the answers to wonder through investigation and experiment. When we reach the limit of such investigation and the wonder still remains unanswered, we pass on from wonder to the awe that is worship (*Swarajya*, 22.2.64).

As long as there is suffering in the world, as long as there is the great curiosity to unravel truth, as long as men and women have some intense desire to be fulfilled, as long as there is wisdom in this world, the future of religion is assured (July 1966).

Like many other Brahmins, C.R. believed that genealogy had linked him to the wisdom of ancient India. Thoughts reminding him of his ancestors and of ties with Nallan ('the good') Chakravarti and Ramanuja were pleasant to him. He was proud of the faith and insights of the Hindus of old. No doubt the caste system had been perverted, no doubt untouchability was a shame too deep for words, yet Hindu doctrines seemed to him priceless and made for modern man everywhere:

We have inherited the broadest culture and the most tolerant of all religious creeds (*Swarajya*, 13.11.71).

The children of the rishis of the Upanishads have a mission for the world (*Swarajya*, 12.2.72).

Yet he disavowed any desire 'to plead that the Gita is better or fuller than any other scriptures,'[21] and his respect for other religions and their adherents was noteworthy. He felt Hindus could emulate the average Muslim's trust in God; his *Swarajya* pieces were sprinkled with Biblical quotations and he spoke once of being affected by 'the icon of the crucifix'[22]; and he desired 'all pious Hindus to read the Ganth Saheb either in the original or in good translations.'[23]

'God will not let India down, though He is putting us to hard tests now,' he wrote in 1972 (*Swarajya*, 12.2.72). If his faith sounded sincere, it did not always bubble across from him. His wit effervesced; his faith did not. Often it was faith as duty.

I have written books, stories and fables. But on the whole I am not a man of letters. I have written mostly for causes— propaganda for the abolition of untouchability for instance.[24]

C.R.'s writings may be looked at under four heads: the *Swarajya*, *Kalki*, *Young India* and *Harijan* pieces, in other words his journalistic output; the Ramayana and the Mahabharata; the short stories and fables; and his verses. (These categories exclude, among other items, his commentaries on the Gita and the Kural, as well as the short books he wrote on Socrates, Marcus Aurelius, Ramakrishna and Brother Lawrence.)

His journalistic writing mixed exhortation with observation. The former impinged more on the public consciousness — often it was strong, compelling and controversial stuff. But the latter possesses a sharpness and a sweep that would strike any student of writing. Had he wished to be no more than a mirror of his times he would still have attracted attention.

Offering one man's opinion, W.R. Crocker, the Australian diplomat-writer, placed C.R.'s *Swarajya* outpourings above G.K. Chesterton's contributions in the *Illustrated London News* 'for variety, pungency and interest.'[25]

Rajaji's obituaries — their number growing with him — lighted up the qualities of their subjects in a minimum of graceful and heartfelt lines; and there was at least one person who regretted outliving C.R. because he was denied an obit by Rajaji.[26] The *Swarajya* and *Kalki* pieces written after Pope John, Prakasam and Khasa died and a comment on Tagore suggest in fact that had he had the time C.R. might have made a rare biographer.

In any case he belonged to the highest class as an onlooker, and many would agree with C.S. Venkatachar, civil servant and diplomat, who found Rajaji's 'tête-à-tête with the Dear Reader' a 'model of urbanity, good taste, friendly comment, sane advice, thoughtful reflection.'[27]

The Ramayana won the Sahitya Akademi award for Tamil; in both Tamil and English the Ramayana and the Mahabharata sold in large numbers and continue to be reprinted. In the early 1950s, Ramnath Goenka produced a hundred thousand Tamil copies of Rajaji's Mahabharata on newsprint and sold them within days.

What lay behind the success? Apart from a lucid style and skill in selecting characters and episodes, C.R. reacted as a typical citizen to the paradoxes in which the two Epics abound and which explain, in part, their magnetic appeal. Thus he was as vexed as the man in the street with the Rama who uttered cruel words to Sita. 'Subhadra and Sita walk in our midst and speak a language we understand,' said the *Sunday Statesman* (31.12.72), reviewing one of C.R.'s versions. Contributing to the impact was C.R.'s approach to the Epics. He went to them neither as a scholar nor as an awe-struck worshipper but as a lover of great literature.

None of his short stories (thirty-six were put together in *Stories for the Innocent*) is without a moral. Often they tell of the ruin that liquor or untouchability or caste arrogance brings. All breathe irony and most are sad but a few amuse as well. Virtually all belong to the pre-Independence era and were first written in Tamil.

The characters are from rural South India, the stories almost real-life ones. The strength lies in their plots and characters, not in description. The tragedies unfold naturally. A Madras critic sees in Rajaji 'a mastery of the short-story form' and notes a powerful 'reticence' and 'artistic control.'[28]

'Some of [Rajaji's] characters like Parvati have become part of the popular culture of the Tamils.' Professor K.R. Srinivasa Iyengar, making this observation, categorically places C.R. 'among the masters and makers of modern Tamil prose.'[29] Even if they do not all go so far, most other critics would include Rajaji in any study of this century's Tamil literature.

Poetry was neither a gift C.R. was born with nor a skill he strove to master. Nonetheless, he affected sensitive persons with his rendering in English verse of portions of Kamban's Ramayana. The reaction of the Communist parliamentarian, Hiren Mukerjee, is of interest: 'Much before I had any personal contact with him, I had chanced upon his English translation . . . of Kamba Ramayana. It stirred me and I took an instant liking to one with whom I had little rapport.'[30]

C.R.'s assertion that he was not a man of letters must therefore be rejected. If they had known and read him for any length of time, lovers of the art of writing could not easily dismiss him from their thoughts. 'His voice, his smile are there whenever I put pen to paper with the desire to fit words well to my thoughts,' observes Albert Franklin, an American who had often called on C.R. and followed *Swarajya*.

But the fates denied, or spared, Rajaji a life where he could put all his soul into writing or wit. Action, struggle in fact, was as much, or more, his breath than art; and his art was influenced by his struggles. The people he portrayed in his stories were kin to those he cared and fought for in real life; and while the flesh, blood and heartbeat of his Ramayana and Mahabharata owe a very great deal to Valmiki, Kamban and Vyasa and to his own artistic gifts, they owe something too to the battles C.R. had fought.

Was he then, in essence, a warrior? Or a teacher? A rebel? A statesman? A politician? A sage? All these things and more: this man in a million was at least six men in one. And yet in all his different roles there was something common: a flow of words. Fox (as he was supposed by some to be) or watchdog, farseeing eagle or wise owl, sitting on a throne or pushed (mostly by himself) to a desert, whether standing on a peak or a valley of his undulating life — Rajaji was in each instance a man of words, wise or defiant words, a lawyer's words and those of a patriot, words that provoked and words that consoled, words uttered and words written, prophetic words, sparkling words, indiscreet words, unceasing words . . .

Of course Rajaji was a man of deeds too (and also, despite his disclaimer, a man of letters), but words were very often his deeds and in some ways greater than his deeds. They were his arrows (his quiver was always full), his food, his gifts, his companions.

25

Sparkle

1969-72

When President Zakir Husain died in May 1969, a coterie of provincial bosses — Kamaraj, Nijalingappa of Karnataka, Sanjiva Reddy of Andhra, Atulya Ghosh of West Bengal and S.K. Patil of Bombay — sponsored Reddy for the Rashtrapati Bhavan vacancy. Indira disliked the choice, but Morarji Desai and Y.B. Chavan, boss of the Maharashtra Congress, threw their weight behind Reddy, who, despite Mrs Gandhi's opposition, was named the Congress candidate.

A rebuffed Indira threatened 'consequences.' Writing to her, C.R. asked, 'Why don't you become President yourself, letting Desai take up the Premiership?'[1] Dismissing the gratuitous advice, she loyally put her signature on one of Reddy's nomination papers — and proceeded to work for the success of Vice President V.V. Giri, who had entered the race, and whose fortunes Rajaji had uncannily foreseen and mentioned in a letter to Masani.

> The Congress party will finally be forced to plump for Giri.
> He would be a good rubber-stamp President.[2] (17.5.69).

Swatantra, the Jan Sangh and Charan Singh's Kranti Dal persuaded Chintaman Deshmukh, whom C.R. had approached a decade earlier for leading Swatantra, to be their joint candidate, and instructed their MPs and MLAs to give their second preferences to Reddy. The Left and socialist parties were for Giri, who projected himself as left-of-centre. On Indira's behalf, Congress legislators were urged to vote 'according to their consciences,' i.e. for Giri and not for the Congress candidate, Reddy.

Indira acted boldly. Stripping Desai of the Finance portfolio, she also, in a swift stroke, nationalized the country's top fourteen banks. Overnight, and well before the presidential polling, she became the Left's heroine. Crowds brought to her residence lauded Indira as the saviour of the downtrodden.

In a tantalizingly close finish, Giri edged out Reddy. Deshmukh came a respectable third.

Congress now split, and opposition parties had to decide whether they were against both Congress factions or only one of them. Sensing votes in leftism and strength in Indira, the DMK, which had supported Giri, allied with her.

In the *Swarajya* columns, C.R. was scathing about Indira. Her charge of 'vested interests' opposing her was 'nonsense'. 'Shouts of zindabad raised by admiring crowds' could not 'alter economic laws.' She was guilty of 'socialistic exhibitionism.' Her mind 'had a dictator's bent' — no one else had said that so far about Indira — and she nursed illusions. 'She should not imagine that she alone is modern . . . Outdated socialism is not modernism.'[3]

Chavan switched in Indira's favour and so did Charan Singh, who thereby became Chief Minister of UP. 'To put it mildly,' commented C.R., 'Charan Singh's politics are curious' (*Swarajya*, 21.2.70). Some months later, however, Singh was removed by Mrs Gandhi, who imposed President's rule in UP. Papers to accomplish her ends were flown to Moscow for the signature of Giri, who was on a visit to the Soviet Union. C.R. underlined the fact that Giri 'had put his signature at the point marked in the document sent to him from India without making any enquiry about the other side of the case, and without even caring to go to the [Indian Embassy] to affix his signature' (*Swarajya*, 17.10.70).

When Indira announced a move to amend the Constitution in order to abolish privy purses, C.R. wrote (*Swarajya*, 27.12.69):

> Pledging themselves to break a pledge! Gandhiji would have
> shut his ears in shame. Sardar would be as angry as he could
> ever be, and Jawaharlalji would be horrified and shout, 'Such
> a thing is not done!'

The Lok Sabha sanctioned the amendment but the Rajya Sabha
did not. Indira's response was to 'derecognize' all rulers under
a provision that in the past had enabled a Viceroy to 'derecognize'
a pretender to the throne of a princely state. Giri duly signed a
proclamation and all princely rights at once vanished!

'The Union government has gone berserk,' C.R. cried
(*Swarajya*, 12.9.70). But the Supreme Court declared the order
illegal. Rajaji's comment was, 'The Court has saved India's
honour' (*Swarajya*, 26.12.70).

At the end of 1969, when he turned 91, Rajaji commenced what
was destined to be his last great effort, a bid for 'a genuine and
strong democratic front' (*Swarajya*, 6.12.69) to check the Indira
Congress. First, he pressed Ranga and Masani, who succeeded
Ranga as Swatantra president in 1970, to produce a democratic
bloc in Parliament. Then, in March 1970, he publicly proposed
a 'grand coalition' of Swatantra, the Old Congress and the Jan
Sangh, drawing attention to what he perceived as a change in the
Jan Sangh away from its 'old anti-Gandhian attitude.'

Rajaji had an encouraging talk with Morarji, Kamaraj too
seemed willing to cooperate, and the Old Congress called for
'the consolidation of national democratic forces.' The ancient
campaigner in Madras greeted the appeal with the *Swarajya*
headline, 'My Congratulations to the Old Congress' (11.7.70).

But the Old Congress was neither clear nor united. Ram
Subhag Singh, leader of its group in the Lok Sabha, obstructed
the formation of a three-party bloc in the House. A deeply
disappointed Rajaji wrote to Masani:

> I submit to the decree of Providence . . . I have done my
> utmost and what else is there but to submit to misfortune.[4]

Soon it was a year since he had urged a front. It was nowhere
to be seen. 'Battles are not won riding on snails,' he wrote.
(*Swarajya*, 7.11.70). When Nijalingappa, heading the Old Congress,

expressed the hope that something would 'evolve,' C.R. observed:

> If he asked fellow Darwinians they would tell him how long
> it took for man to evolve out of the ape (*Swarajya*, 28.11.70).

Indira now charged. At the end of December, she announced the dissolution of Parliament and fresh elections. The opposition had no front, no common programme, no common leader and no funds. In vain had the old campaigner shouted and coaxed. Though angry with those who should have come together, he blamed Indira: it was unscrupulous of her to order elections 'a year in advance' to suit her strategy.

Asking Indians to decide 'the single question,' whether they approved of 'Smt. Indira Gandhi's plan to tear up the Constitution and replace democracy by totalitarianism,' he urged her opponents to 'Unite! Unite!' even at the last minute (*Swarajya*, 9.1.71).

To Masani, who was negotiating in Delhi with Nijalingappa and with Atal Behari Vajpayee of the Jan Sangh, C.R. wrote (2.1.71): 'You *must* bring about agreement on a joint appeal to defeat Indira Gandhi.'

After several hiccups, a Grand Alliance of Swatantra, the Old Congress, the Jan Sangh and the Socialists was announced, but the slogan of Indira Hatao could not hide Swatantra's differences with the Socialists or with the Jan Sangh. To reassure those troubled by an alliance with the Jan Sangh, Rajaji said, 'The Swatantra party and the Old Congress will keep the Jan Sangh in order.'[5]

C.R.'s attempts to raise funds from the Rajas came to nothing. Over the vigorous protests of C.R., Indira secured for her party the constitutionally questionable symbol of a cow and a calf, calculated to appeal to the Hindu vote. Ridiculing the Grand Alliance's inconsistencies, Mrs Gandhi also hit upon the slogan of Garibi Hatao, and coasted to an easy victory.

Though not polling more than 43.64 per cent of the votes, her party won 350 Lok Sabha seats. Swatantra went down from 44 seats to 8 and from 8.68 per cent to 3.08 per cent. Masani and Ranga both lost, as did Sanjiva Reddy, S.K. Patil and Ram

Subhag Singh of the Old Congress, and the Socialists Madhu Limaye and Raj Narain. The Jan Sangh was humbled as well. Contesting on the Swatantra ticket from a Madras seat, Narasimhan, too, lost.

In simultaneous elections to the Tamil Nadu Assembly, the DMK, now an Indira Congress ally, routed the Rajaji-Kamaraj alliance. Swatantra and Old Congress circles had expected the opposite, and Kamaraj had joked, 'Rajaji, you had better be ready to become Chief Minister again.' In fact the two had thought of R. Venkataraman, a future President of India, as the Chief Minister.

When he heard over a borrowed radio that the DMK had won 183 seats as against 21 secured by the Old Congress and Swatantra, Rajaji's first reaction was to attack 'the money power of the Indira Congress and the DMK' and 'the stinking permit-licence raj.' Later, he underlined the fact that Swatantra and the Old Congress had polled 59 lakh votes as against 76 lakh votes for the DMK and supporting parties.

'The teacher must go on teaching, whatever may be the difficulties,' he said to the Press. And two days after the results, in a letter to Nijalingappa, he showed an unbelievable willingness to face another long struggle:

> We must organise young men and women as when the Gandhian Congress began ... The enemy now is totalitarianism and we have to fight it as we fought the British.

He attacked an apparent bid by one of Indira's sons for a licence to make an 'Indian' car:

> When Volkswagen of Germany is ready to give small and cheap and, what is most important, good cars to those who want them in India, why should our Government not accept the proposal? ... Adventures in the manufacture of small or big cars are not what tax-payers' money should be spent on. I shall not believe the story about the Prime Minister's son and the small car ... until it is confirmed (*Swarajya*, 25.4. & 5.9.70).

He was equally clear about the proposed cancellation of a cricket series in England against a South African team:

> I do not see why the British people should be deprived of seeing good cricket . . . Shall we succeed in improving the minds and doctrines of people by outcasting them? (*Swarajya*, 6.6.70)

Also in 1970 he relived earlier times when old Khan Abdul Ghaffar Khan of the Northwest Frontier, who was visiting India, called on him. Pothan Joseph retired from *Swarajya* in January 1970 and was succeeded as editor by Philip Spratt, the British-born former Communist with a Tamil wife. Fifteen months later, to C.R.'s grief, Spratt died, and K. Santhanam became editor.

Friends were dying in a ceaseless sequence. And C.R.'s obits were more frequent than ever. That perceptive portrayer, unawed admirer and skilful questioner, Monica Felton died in March 1970 in Madras. Needing an immediate income, she had been free-lancing for a while. In one of her last letters to Rajaji she had said that she hoped 'to write a novel which may possibly make enough money to enable me to try to be a biographer again.'[6] C.R. spoke feelingly if compactly of 'my loss through death of my British author friend Dr Monica Felton to whom I owe so much' (*Swarajya*, 14.3.70).

East Pakistan, meanwhile, was aflame. Though Sheikh Mujib's Awami League had won a majority (160 seats) in the 300-member Pakistan Assembly, General Yahya Khan, the President, refused to install Mujib as Prime Minister. Zulfiqar Ali Bhutto, whose party had won 83 seats in Pakistan's west wing, backed Yahya's refusal. In reaction all of East Pakistan seemed to take to nonviolent civil disobedience. When Mujib and several of his colleagues were seized, the population of East Bengal exploded. Suppression followed but some East Bengalis announced an independent Bangladesh.

J.P. asked Indira to recognize the new nation but C.R.'s advice was to wait a while. He informed *Swarajya*'s readers truthfully that in a 1948 conversation with Mountbatten he had predicted that Pakistan would split in 25 years or so; yet India should not invite the charge of promoting the dismemberment.

He worried about a possible tie-up between Mujib and China. Though he once brought to the notice of his readers 'a rather favourable British appraisal of Chinese Communism,' as he put it (*Swarajya*, 24.1.70), China remained for him the 'crocodile' or 'alligator' that India had to watch.

This assessment, combined with a view that, abandoning Asia, 'America has gone on sick leave,' led C.R. first to urge (in a *Swarajya* piece and in a letter to Premier Kosygin) Soviet arbitration between Yahya and Mujib, and then unreservedly to defend the treaty with the Soviet Union that Indira concluded in August 1971.

The treaty found Swatantra's founder at complete variance with his party, which opposed it. C.R. wrote:

> At one end official America has proved to be a broken reed. At the other end the Chinese menace is growing dangerously. There was, therefore, no alternative for India but to enter into a defensive treaty with the Soviet Union (*Swarajya*, 21.8.71). It was wise to prefer dealing with the Devil to being drowned in the deep sea (*Swarajya*, 4.9.71).

The carnage in East Pakistan was terrible. 'What has happened to General Yahya Khan and his colleagues and rivals?' demanded an outraged C.R. 'Have they lost all adherence to the religion that Arabia gave them? Have they indeed lost all commonsense?' (*Swarajya*, 8.5.71)

Repression caused a vast exodus. By the end of September, nine million refugees had entered India, at the rate of 30,000 a day. Finally, in December 1971, Bangladeshi and Indian forces clashed with Pakistan. Liberation came in days; before long Mujib returned to an unprecedented welcome. The star of Indira soared. Her objective in the East realized, she instructed, at a moment when India held every advantage, a unilateral cease-fire on the western front. Rajaji lauded 'the cease-fire boldly ordered by Smt. Indira Gandhi' and wrote:

> Our Generals and the army, navy and the air force have scored a brilliant triumph . . . Let us be humble in this hour of victory . . . Let us pray that the grace of God may continue to bless the Prime Minister of India (*Swarajya*, 1.1.72).

The 1971 electoral setback led to depletion in Swatantra's ranks and the resignation of Masani from the presidentship. Valuing Masani's keen mind and debating and organizing skills, Rajaji tried hard to retain him in the chair:

> I beg of you to give up your plan to spend your time and energy in cultivating contacts in Europe and writing memoirs . . . There is no one but you to save the party from extinction . . . Give your energy and devotion for one more year and then leave things to God (19.5.71).

However, Masani felt that after the debacle he had no choice except to hand over. Dandeker took over for a while, followed by H.M. Patel; in June 1972, at a General Council meeting that Rajaji attended, Piloo Mody was elected President.

Calling on the old man in Madras, Dandeker suggested a change in the party's name as a means of overcoming the rich-man's-party smear. But the smear would have shifted to any new name; though tempted by it, Rajaji rejected the proposal, which was indicative of the party's sagging morale.

The hardest blow was a change in Ranga's stand. Soon after Indira's Bangladesh triumph, Ranga, one of C.R.'s oldest friends and president of the party for ten years, advocated acceptance by Swatantra of her leadership. Some months later he actually joined the Indira Congress! This was the way to influence Indira, he claimed.

Privately and in *Swarajya*, C.R. contested the reasoning, but he was deeply hurt. Dejectedly, he wrote: 'For a time let religion be our only politics . . . We leave a town when it is infected by plague. So must we vacate politics now' (*Swarajya*, 22.1.72).

But the notion was foreign to his nature. Within days he was commenting on Bhutto, Mujib and Indira, and stoutly proclaiming the Swatantra philosophy. When Ranga formally crossed over, C.R. wrote:

> The people of India cannot continue to give him the respect which he has hitherto enjoyed at their hands. He cannot command the confidence of Smt. Indira Gandhi . . . His defection will not serve him personally [nor] in any way serve the national interest (*Swarajya*, 12.8.72).

A year earlier — six weeks after the poll humiliation — he had countered defeatist currents with a prophecy that would be fulfilled. The policies of Swatantra, he said, were bound to become the Government's policies and programmes, if not now, some years hence (*Swarajya*, 1.5.71). Added C.R.:

> I wish I were young and able to go round all parts of this great and dear land of ours to explain that the Swatantra's is the only true and efficacious programme for driving out squalor and disease.

Following her success, Indira moved to amend the Constitution and abridge the fundamental right to property. When the Old Congress, which was fighting a property case against the Indira Congress, supported the amendment in the name of the poor, C.R. commented:

> The Old Congress is content with defending its ownership and possession of house properties . . . It does not mind what happens to the fundamental property rights of citizens in general (*Swarajya*, 8.1.72)!

Swatantra, declared C.R., would remain 'unalterably loyal' to all the fundamental rights laid down:

> We should defend the Constitution as Winston Churchill defended Britain against Hitler, not surrendering to fear or the prospect of defeat (*Swarajya*, 18.9.71).

The amendment went through, but not without some resistance. Wrote C.R.:

> I am glad the small band of Swatantra party members in the Lok Sabha as well as in the Rajya Sabha voted against the wreckers of the Constitution, undaunted by the massive numbers ranged on the other side (*Swarajya*, 18.12.71).

After another birthday made him ninety-three, he hinted at a revival of the kind of battles he had joined more than half a century earlier — and anticipated the J.P.-led movement of 1974-5:

> We must depend upon ways and means not linked to elections and the hope therefore lies in preparing for non-violent direct

action . . . It is the probability of direct action which will bring about the change that we desire in Smt. Indira Gandhi's convictions (*Swarajya*, 18.3.72).

Recalling some of the men who had had a role in drafting or incorporating the guarantees to citizens, the old soldier vowed:

> Even if all others conspire against the Constitution, I shall not ever let Vallabhbhai Patel, Rajen Babu, K.M. Munshi, Alladi Krishnaswami Iyer and others down, but will protest against the desecration and unwisdom of it as long as my breath lasts (*Swarajya*, 25.9.71).

At 93 he was still the responsible parent. When Lakshmi, 59 at the time, was stricken in the eye, it was C.R. who escorted her to the specialist. After her recovery, Narasimhan, 62, went down with pneumonia and the old father worried intensely until the son was well again.

But life was not only being assailed; it was being renewed. By the end of 1971 he had ten great-grandchildren. And he retained a youthful taste. Finding pleasure in re-reading *David Copperfield*, *Old Curiosity Shop* and *Great Expectations*, he also enjoyed suggesting cartoons for *Swarajya*:

> Cartoon: Indira aiming gun at the clouds, not at the tiger in front, saying, 'I am tackling the social causes that produce communist crimes.'[7]

His brain and nose continued to reach out. Thus, he sent the Tamil Nadu Chief Secretary a formula for resolving a dispute over a mosque coming up in T. Nagar, and educated a joint secretary in the use of honorifics. When a communication from this official referred to the Chief Minister as Dr M. Karunanidhi, C.R. — recipient himself of a dozen honorary doctorates — wrote back:

> It is not the custom to use the appellation Doctor or its abbreviation Dr. when the doctorate is conferred honoris causa and not earned in the regular way . . .[8]

His opinions were as unpredictable as ever, his defence of them as elegant as ever. After reading a large-type edition of *Animal Farm*, he wrote:

> I cannot admire the much-boosted book of George Orwell ...
> Filling up a whole book with animals does not make a fable.
> Aesop knew his animals and knew also how long, or rather
> how short, a fable should be (*Swarajya*, 5.6.71).

He would look back, of course, and on occasion betray a wish to reconstruct the past:

> When the independence of India was coming close upon us
> and Gandhiji was the silent master of our affairs, he had come
> to the decision that Jawaharlal, who among all the Congress
> leaders was the most familiar with foreign affairs, should be
> the Prime Minister of India, although he knew Vallabhbhai
> would be the best administrator among them all ...

> Undoubtedly it would have been better ... if Nehru had been
> asked to be Foreign Minister and Patel made the Prime
> Minister. I too fell into the error of believing that Jawaharlal
> was the more enlightened person of the two ... A myth had
> grown about Patel that he would be harsh towards Muslims.
> This was a wrong notion but it was the prevailing prejudice
> (*Swarajya*, 27.11.71).

On the heels of the 1971 electoral defeat had come another blow — the repeal of prohibition. On a day when uncommonly heavy rains pelted Madras, the aged foe of liquor asked to be driven to Karunanidhi's residence, where he pleaded, 'on behalf of the people,' that the drink ban may continue. As he put it, he returned home 'not with hope but with mental unrest' and took steps to have the withdrawal legally challenged.

The ancient brain was active and sharp. To some of Madras's best advocates C.R. pointed out — with, in his words, 'due diffidence' — the errors in the text of the repeal. For a day or two there was anxiety in the government's camp and the annulment had to be reworded. Then, a massive majority behind him, Karunanidhi crushed C.R.'s resistance.[9]

Put together with love and toil by Sadasivam and his friends, *Rajaji 93* came out as 1971 ended. The volume of recollections by many who had encountered him in the distant or recent past pleased C.R., but he took care, in a Dear Reader para, to reject any implication that his life's work was done:

> The great fuss over *Rajaji 93* seems to order me out of the public scene with this December! But I do not propose to do this and terminate my life of protest, exceptionally long though it has been. We are not masters of our lives in length of days. But when I see the spreading abuses . . . I do not feel inclined to run away from the struggle to improve things, old, weak and incapacitated though I am (*Swarajya*, 13.11.71).

Noticing C.R.'s frustration over Indira's seemingly insurmountable political strength and her apparent disregard for opposing views, a grandson once asked him, simple-mindedly maybe, 'Have you prayed for Indira's change?' Rajaji was silent for some moments and moisture collected in his eyes — perhaps he was reminded of hurts taken and given, or of associations with Jawaharlal and Motilal. Then he changed the subject. But in a subsequent *Swarajya* issue he wrote:

> I have said harsh things about how Smt. Indira Gandhi has come to hold dictatorial power. But . . . let us pray that she may be blessed with strength and purity of spirit and wisdom. There is nothing God cannot bring about if He chooses. Did not Saul of Tarsus became Paul the apostle? (*Swarajya*, 13.11.71)

There was no danger, however, of Rajaji yielding his convictions. In March 1972, dismissing 'climbers' who were willing to 'jump on [Indira's] bandwagon' and 'desert the fight to defend the Constitution,' he added: 'But surrender is not in my book of words and it shall never be' (*Swarajya*, 11.3.72). Three months later he wrote about Indira:

> It appears as if she is in two minds, one being the dictatorship mind and the other crystallizing towards her father's constitutional temperament (*Swarajya*, 3.6.72).

The god of death seemed to be working overtime. Krushchev, Kelappan of Kerala, Syed Mahmud of Bihar, Sri Prakasa of Benares and other servants of the cause of Indian liberty went. C.R.'s trudge into the future was increasingly lonely.

As 1972 began he was weaker. The little washing to exercise his fingers was discontinued, and he ceased giving himself a shave — a Gurkha watchman now did the job every morning. One day in March he fell in the bathroom but all bones including the femur were intact.

He asked himself why he was alive and unharmed. His answer was, to assist 'friendliness between India and what remains of Pakistan' (*Swarajya*, 11.3.72). In four months an Indo-Pak summit took place in Simla and Indira and Bhutto signed a partial agreement. A delighted C.R. called it the Pact of Good Hope and asked for an early second summit for resolving the unsettled issues.

In June he was ill: the skin burned and there was an odd feeling in the stomach. Again he recovered, but he wrote, 'It is God's grace that I continue to live' (*Swarajya*, 30.9.72). He was writing and receiving less than before but Dear Reader unfailingly appeared, even if consisting only of two or three short paragraphs, and callers continued to encounter the chuckle and the grin.

'Ah, you are talking cricket,' he said to Gopala Ratnam, a sports writer, when the latter said he hoped C.R. would live to be a hundred.

In October he said he had 'the fullest confidence in Masani'; after receiving Piloo Mody, Swatantra's new president, the gracious old gentleman wrote, 'Sri Piloo Mody was good enough to call on me.' Also in October, he spoke in his column of his unchanged affection for Ranga, who had joined the ruling party and whose wife had just died.

That month Jayaprakash spoke about the need for a new politics. Rajaji, who for years had tried to involve J.P. politically, was delighted. 'I most warmly welcome Sri Jayaprakash Narayan's statement,' he wrote (*Swarajya*, 14.10.72).

That human nature abounds in contradictions was remarkably proved in C.R.'s case. Humble of heart as he was — Crocker, the Australian diplomat, found in him 'an utter lack of vanity'[10] — he was not humble of mind. Obstinacy was his trait and he knew it. 'I prefer to go down as did Don Quixote,' he had said (*Swarajya*, 24.5.58). Astute in his efforts against both the Raj and its Indian successors, he was also naive (even if sane and farsighted at the same time) in his appeals against the Bomb and for Indo-Pak harmony; and he was simple too in imagining that Indira might exchange the Premiership for Rashtrapati Bhavan. Kind, tender even, in his emotions, he was harsh beyond the call of probity to a friend as close as A.V. Raman.

Very Tamil ('Have you seen Ooty?' was his reaction in Simla when Parasuram, the journalist, remarked on the beauty of the snow-clad Himalayas[11]) but also very universal; frail for decades and going strong in his nineties; a very old man who was very young in curiosity; now despairing, now full of faith, quoting, 'The best is yet to be/ The last of life for which the first was made' (*Swarajya*, 12.1.66); a lover of life resigned to its insignificance; parsimonious ('I never pay for newspapers') — and over-generous, giving a Rs 1,000 tip to a cook Sadasivam had supplied[12]; a closed book, often, to his sons and daughters but opening out without reserve to visitors like Louis Fischer and Monica Felton; a cultivator of detachment who sorrowed deeply; coldly indifferent to hostility and hurt when a short story of his was criticized in an American review — 'I am so sensitive behind all the outward semblance of equanimity,' he had written to son-in-law Varadachari back in 1928; a considerable talker whom General Cariappa found to be 'one of the very few top men of our country who is a good listener'[13]; conservative in belief and theory, impulsive, reckless even, in office; a loyal Hindu accused of a bias in favour of other communities; assailed by orthodox Brahmins and also by anti-Brahmins; passionate advocate of the balanced budget — and proponent, during a seemingly critical moment, of a huge army to which every Indian family would contribute a son; at home in office but a disdainer of votes, too civilized to play to the gallery; a lover of freedom who suspected democracy; a man with no doubts over any issue but with several different opinions on it; the most persuasive opponent of the Raj's legislatures and later their most persuasive champion; scorning theories of nuclear deterrence but trusting in the deterring influence of capital punishment; matching the enemies he made in the South justifying Hindi with the enemies he made in the North resisting Hindi; Congress's great defender who became its leading debunker — C.R. was all that.

'Our dear land' was a phrase that recurred in his *Swarajya* and *Kalki* pieces; it rang true; yet this lover of India was to some 'anti-national' for his opinions on subjects like Hindi, Pakistan, Kashmir, the Nagas and the Sikhs. In 1966, with Nehru dead, Mountbatten referred to C.R. as 'India's greatest living statesman' and Fischer called him India's 'greatest man'[14]; C.R.'s doings reminded Ruthnaswamy, parliamentarian and former vice-chancellor, of the role the Hebrew prophets played; and Lionel Fielden, ex-chief of AIR, wrote that Rajaji was 'the nearest human being to a saint that I have ever known.'[15] Yet there were also those who alleged foxiness and opportunism in C.R.

He could be brusque and tactless. Questioning by the dull and the inquisitive irritated him and he stopped their mouths, and sometimes he made bruising remarks. Yet, as Burke pointed out, 'It is well if when a man comes to die he has nothing heavier upon his conscience than having been a little rough in conversation.' Surely, however, there were additional weights including qualms about the Chief Ministership exercised from a nominated seat and resentment over the 1954 ouster. Then there was the charge that he was 'ever the lawyer.' As Sri Prakasa put it, 'Rajaji . . . can forcibly and convincingly propound an opinion and convincingly establish the opposite only a few months later.'[16] 'Rajaji can convince you against your will,' Rajendra Prasad is said to have remarked.[17]

'*C.R. to seeyar hai*' — 'C.R. is after all a fox' — was a Hindi comment invented against him in the thirties, if not earlier, and used by a few ever since. Some amended the epithet to 'sly fox.' C.R.'s habit of 'retiring' from active politics only to return to office annoyed those benefiting from his 'retirement,' but the initiative to 'return' was, every time, someone else's. While he was pleased to be summoned, it was beyond his or anyone's manipulative capacity to create the necessity for his return. Those grudging his re-entry and charging him with supreme cleverness were in truth foxed by circumstances, not by C.R.

He was independent; he obtained key roles without trying and, at least once, on his own debatable terms; and he was clever. These factors explain why some resented him but do not make him a fox, sly or non-sly. And he was not an opportunist.

Though he disconcertingly altered his opinions — notably on Congress, Hindi and the DMK —, the changes in his stance widened rather than narrowed the distance between him and power.

That there was a personal element in his opposition to Congress has to be granted. According to Indira Gandhi, Rajaji's Swatantra phase was an instance of 'a great man giving to a small party what was meant for a great nation.'[18] If there is some truth in the assessment, it has to be asked whether Congress, and in particular Mrs Gandhi and her father, did not in some measure propel Rajaji towards playing the supposedly smaller role. Moreover, it would be illogical to suggest that in opposing Congress, Nehru and Indira, Rajaji was being unpatriotic or unethical. He may have waged the imperfect fight of an imperfect man, but he also waged what became an essential fight, and did so in memorable style.

He had his share of human limitations and, as we have seen, more than his share of human heterogeneity, but four qualities combined to place him among the uncommon. Firstly, and simply, he was a good man. As Crocker noted, he was free of vanity. In the copy someone gave him of Johnson's life of Alexander Pope, C.R. highlighted a short sentence: 'But let no man dream of influence beyond his life.' 'In twenty-five years' time,' he once said to Monica Felton, 'people will be asking, "Who was Rajagopalachari?"'[19] He was amused by the possibility that troubles many of the great.

There were other facets to this goodness. He made no ill-gotten rupee and concealed no opinion. 'I have kept my record clean,' he claimed, 'and led life honestly throughout. I say what I feel and what appears to be just and right.'[20] He stayed true to his Manga during the fifty-seven years that had passed since she died. He kept greed at bay, as when the doctor in Salem wanted to buy C.R.'s land and house at Salem. And unless we agree with C.R. that reading books was a form of gluttony, we must mark his near-total involvement with public work.

Along with goodness, kindliness. The hurtful remarks that occasionally escaped his lips misrepresented the man who essentially if not uniformly was warm towards friends and gracious to callers. Also, he was punctual with audiences, courteous to correspondents and gentle to his household. He had not once lifted an arm against his children; now they were, some of them, grandparents; in all the intervening years, he had not raised his voice against a servant.

If a dhobi, tailor, cobbler or carpenter was kept waiting at his door, C.R. hated it. 'Time is his only asset. Don't rob him of it,' he would say. Some heard him more attentively than others, but he himself practised what he urged.

The third quality was daring. He had dared orthodoxy in Salem; then, apparently defying commonsense, he had given up his practice; he opposed the Raj when it was powerful, the Mahatma when all of India seemed to lie at his feet, Jawaharlal when Nehru was deemed unassailable and C.R. too old, and finally Nehru's daughter, as securely-placed as her father and as daring as Rajaji himself. In addition, C.R. had coolly asked the White House and the Kremlin to dismantle their Bombs. To him politics was as much the pursuit of the necessary as the art of the possible.

Finally, he sparkled. Jawaharlal's friend and biographer, Chalapati Rau, calling himself C.R.'s 'consistent critic,' also called the subject of his criticisms 'incandescent and magnetic.'[21] Goodness, kindliness, daring and sparkle added up to a greatness made more fascinating by an array of contradictions.

On 8 October the old speechmaker went to Gandhi Mandapam and delivered what was to be his last address, consisting of thirteen short sentences. He asked for 'turning our hearts to humble prayer' (*Swarajya*, 14.10.72). That month the DMK split. M.G. Ramachandran, popular actor and party treasurer, was expelled for opposing the Karunanidhi policies, including the repeal of prohibition. In what would be his last political move, the veteran player backed M.G.R.; and in a final prediction C.R. said that the DMK would be 'the loser in this business' (*Swarajya*, 21.10.72).

Pothan Joseph, who had given valuable support to *Swarajya*, died in November. C.R.'s mind went back to the days of

Khilafat and Gaya when Pothan's brother George had been one of his closest colleagues. 'The world is for me more lonely even than it had been,' he wrote. 'How can I ever find tears enough for George Joseph and Pothan Joseph?' (*Swarajya*, 11.11.72) This characteristic obituary reference would be his penultimate one. In his last obit, on 18 November, C.R. consoled one of the South's leading Swatantrites, G.K. Sundaram, who had lost his mother.

On 12 November C.R. received Richard Wood, Minister for Overseas Development in the UK and, more important for C.R., son of Lord Irwin, the Viceroy who had signed the famous pact with the Mahatma. Wood would prove to be the last in the long line of C.R.'s foreign callers.

Came the 94th birthday. In a short para for Dear Reader, the statesman said he 'prized' the 'good wishes from many friends' and added:

> My call to all people is that there should be a summit meeting as soon as possible . . . to take the Simla accord to its true fulfilment (*Swarajya*, 9.12.72).

This plea for Indo-Pak reconciliation would be his last *Swarajya* piece.

On a morning in early December Namagiri noticed stains on her father's pillow: his mouth had dripped blood during the night. A few days later he shouted from the bathroom. Those rushing in found him seated on a stool and unable to return to his bed. 'I am afraid,' he told Lakshmi later that day.

On 17 December, his illness described as uraemia and dehydration, an ambulance took him away to General Hospital, where he was put on the drip. He seemed to be trying to finger with his free hand the passage for glucose made on his left arm, and a grandson asked him not to. 'Yes, yes,' the man of words replied, 'Let not the right hand know what the left is doing,' adding, after a pause, 'Or is it the other way around.'[22]

'I have been brought here to die,' he said shortly afterwards. Karunanidhi and his ministerial colleagues turned up. Taking the Chief Minister's palm in one hand, with the other the sage stroked Karunanidhi's head and face in blessing, saying, in Tamil, 'I will never withdraw my friendship.' Then he took Nedunchezhian's hand, addressed him by name, and blessed him.

Next morning a grin formed on the aged face when Rajaji was told that he had made the front page again by entering hospital. Informed the following day that the newspapers had reported 'satisfactory progress' by him, he smiled and said, 'I don't trust such unreliable news.'

His curiosity and culture were intact. 'Where are you from?' he asked a young house surgeon. 'Madras,' the doctor replied. 'Which part of Madras?' 'Chromepet, sir.' Weak as he was, he offered his hand to all the doctors who went up to him If their questions were not clear, he would gently ask, 'I beg your pardon?' Once, noticing two nurses, he whispered to a grandson sitting next to his bed, 'Am I properly dressed?'

Telegrams from far and near built a mound. Life was painstakingly defended at General Hospital by doctors and nurses and the former head of state had a room to himself, but the care he was receiving was not private. The people of Madras — whom he had loved and tried to serve — thronged the hospital's corridors and verandas.

On the night of 22 December, C.R. replied, his eyes closed, 'I am happy,' when asked how he felt. At 3.00 a.m., however, he was found to be unconscious and put on oxygen.

A heaving chest was now the only sign of life. As had been done with his father, his father's father and ancestors all the way back to Nallan Chakravarti and beyond, water from the holy Ganga was introduced into his mouth with a copper spoon. Again in accordance with ancient custom, a Vaishnavite priest and Narasimhan (Krishnaswami was too ill to have a part) pronounced into C.R.'s ear the verse of surrender: 'I take refuge in Narayana.'

President Giri, Periyar E.V.R. in his wheelchair, Chief Minister Karunanidhi, a red-eyed Kamaraj, M.G.R. with his jaunty cap, T.T. Krishnamachari, Masani, Ranga and other figures of Indian politics filled the patient's room. In the world outside, other important persons phoned or wired their concern and pondered the tributes they should offer.

'Rajaji Critically Ill,' the *Indian Express* banner headline said the next morning. But the subject had not lost his unpredictability, nor the warrior his fight. He rallied and mouthed some words. Rallying, he stole an additional headline. On the following day, the lead story in the *Express* began, 'Frail old Rajaji staged a remarkable rally yesterday . . .'

After word of deterioration spread on Saturday the 23rd, vast numbers had penetrated General Hospital; they returned on Sunday on hearing that the old sage was, astonishingly, improving. But by Monday morning he was again in a coma. That afternoon, surrounded by loved ones, doctors and nurses, by several of the nation's and Tamil Nadu's leaders and by a segment of the great, winding throng that pressed past his hospital room, the air over him thick with the petition of several choking men and women commending the fleeing soul to God, Chakravarti Rajagopalachari breathed his last. The time was 5.44 p.m., the date, 25 December, Christmas Day. It was also, by the Hindu calendar, the day of the death of the Vaishnava saint, Nammalwar.

Notes

PREFACE

1. Letter from Lionel Fielden to C.R., 14.8.62, Rajagopalachari Papers.
2. See Chapter 4.
3. *Illustrated Weekly*, 13.8.61.
4. *Swarajya*, 25.4.70.

1. MANGA

1. Sir Verney Lovett, *A History of the Indian Nationalist Movement*, John Murray, London, 1921, Ch.1.
2. *Ibid*.
3. Though C.R.'s birthday was at times observed on 8 December, research by T. Sadasivam, who was helped by C.R.'s daughter Namagiri, seemed to establish 10 December as the correct date.
4. Le Fanu, *A Manual of Salem District*, Government Press, Madras, 1883, pp. 128-9.
5. C.R. in *Swarajya*, 17.6.61.
6. C.R. in *Swarajya*, 24.2.68.
7. C.R. in *Swarajya*, 17.12.60.
8. Wenlock to Lord Hamilton; letter 6.2.1896, Wenlock Papers, India Office Library (IOL), London.
9. To the author, in Madras.
10. The father did not wholly dismiss the astrologer's word. Hearing of a prediction that the son of an acquaintance would become a Dewan (Premier of a principality), Iyengar commented: 'That is nothing. My son will become Viceroy.'

11. See Monica Felton, *I Meet Rajaji*, Macmillan, London, 1962, p. 24.
12. *Rajaji 93*, p. 69.
13. Krishna Iyer to author and in *Kalki*, 8.12.57.
14. C.R., *Chats Behind Bars*, Ganesan, Madras, 1931, pp. 46-8.
15. Krishna Iyer in *Kalki*, 8.12.57.
16. C.R., *Chats Behind Bars*, p. 48.
17. Quoted by Masti Venkatesa Iyengar in *Rajaji 93*, pp. 113-4.
18. Rama Rao in *Kalki*, 8.12.57.
19. C.S. Bhasker, Bar-at-law, to author, Bangalore, 1973.
20. S. Vijiaraghavachariar, Salem advocate, to C.R. Narasimhan and K. Vedamurthy, 1973.
21. R. Sundaram, *Bhavan's Journal*, Bombay, 21.12.75.
22. S. Vijiaraghavachariar to Narasimhan and Vedamurthy.
23. T.V. Lakshminarayana Rao, Salem advocate, and C.S. Bhasker, Bar-at-law, to C.R. Narasimhan, 1973.
24. K.S. Ramaswami Sastri, *Rajaji 93*, p. 266.
25. Krishna Iyer to author, Madras, 1973.
26. C.R. in *Young India*, 5. 7. 23; P.T. Venkatachar, advocate, to author, 1973.
27. C.S. Bhasker to Narasimhan and to author.
28. K.N. Sundararajan, son of Narasimha Iyengar, to Narasimhan and Vedamurthy.
29. V.P. Raman in *Rajaji 93*, p. 220A.
30. Diary extracts in *Rajaji*, Hindustan Publications, Madras, 1949.
31. Based on accounts provided to author by C.R., C.R. Krishnaswami, Namagiri, and C. Samachar, and on article by Khasa Subba Rau in *Swarajya*, 5.11.60.

2. HOPE

1. C.R. to Devadas Gandhi, 4.2.20; Devadas Gandhi Papers.
2. C.R. quoted by Khasa Subba Rau, *Swarajya*, 5.11.60.
3. Krishna Iyer in *Kalki*, 8.12.57.
4. Paper by C.R. read before the Salem Literary Society and reproduced in *Indian Review*, Madras, May 1916.
5. Brecher, M., *Nehru*, Oxford, London, 1959, p. 60.
6. Geoffery Ashe, *Gandhi: A Study in Revolution*, Asia, Bombay, 1968. p. 146.
7. Letter of 8.12.49 in Durga Das (ed.), *Sardar Patel's Correspondence*, Navajivan, Ahmedabad, vol.8, pp. 220-2.
8. *The Hindu*, 25.5.17.
9. *The Hindu*, 1.6.17.

10. Station incident described to author by C. Samachar, who was present.
11. From *The Hindu*, 12.5.18 & 16.5.18, and K.S. Venkataraman in *Rajaji*, Hindustan Publications, 1949.
12. *The Hindu*, 2.8.18.
13. See K.S. Venkataraman in *Rajaji*, Hindustan, 1949.
14. *The Hindu*, 14.8.18.
15. Report of 17.7.19 in File 2000M of 1919, Tamil Nadu Archives.
16. E.S. Balasubramania Iyer, the clerk in question, recalling the remark to C.R. Narasimhan and K.Vedamurthy, Salem, 1973.
17. *The Hindu*, July 1918; and C.R., *Chats Behind Bars*, p. 72.
18. Kamaraj in *Rajaji 93*, p. 105.
19. Legh's comment of 17.6.18 and Graham's of 2.8.18 in File 1301M of 1918, Tamil Nadu Archives.
20. File 2000M of 1919, Tamil Nadu Archives.
21. Trial quotes from *The Hindu*, 11.10.18, 10-13.12.18, and 17.1.19.
22. Trichy speech in *The Hindu*, 16.1.19.
23. *Young India*, 8.11.28.
24. Gandhi in *Young India*, 8.11.28.
25. Report of 25.3.19 in Secret File 222 of 1919, Tamil Nadu Archives.
26. Moore's report in Secret File 271 of 1919, Tamil Nadu Archives.
27. C.R. in Secret File 271 of 1919, Tamil Nadu Archives.

3. BATTLE

1. Gandhi to C.R., 3.7.19, *Collected Works of Mahatma Gandhi* (*CWMG*).
2. Phrases in leaflet dated 5.5.19 published by C.R. and contained in Secret File 271 of 1919, Tamil Nadu Archives.
3. Willingdon to Montagu, 9.6.19, in Willingdon Papers, India Office Library, London.
4. Cable dated 19.9.19 in Home (Pol.) B Series, National Archives, New Delhi.
5. Geoffrey Ashe, *Gandhi: A Study in Revolution*, Asia, Bombay, 1968, p. 189.
6. Quoted in Pattabhi Sitaramayya, *History of the Indian National Congress*, AICC, Allahabad, 1935, pp. 319-20.
7. C.R. in *Young India*, 5.4.23.
8. In File 14 of Nov. 1919, Home (Pol.) Deposit, National Archives.
9. Tendulkar, *Mahatma*, vol.1, p. 329.
10. C.R. to Devadas Gandhi, 28.2.20, Devadas Gandhi Papers.
11. In Files 106 and 97 of July 1920, Home (Pol.) Deposit, National Archives.

12. File 97, Home (Pol.) Deposit, National Archives.
13. Tait-C.R. discussion recalled by C.R. in *Report of College Day Celebrations*, Central College Old Boys' Association, Bangalore, 1937.
14. C.R.Narasimhan, *Rajaji 93*, p. 243; and Namagiri to author.
15. Communication of 4.9.20 from the Government of India, in Public and Judicial Records, 1920, India Office Library, London.
16. Quoted in Tendulkar, *Mahatma*, vol. 2, p. 38.
17. C.R. to Devadas, Nov. 1920, Devadas Gandhi Papers.
18. See Knapp, Chief Secretary, Madras, to O'Donnell, Officiating Home Secretary, Govt. of India, 1.2.21, File 43 of 1921, and Marjoribanks, Chief Secretary, Madras, to Home Secretary, Govt. of India, 28.8.21, File 18 of 1921, Home (Pol.) Deposit, National Archives.
19. See Krishnadas, *Seven Months with Mahatma Gandhi*, Ganesan, Madras, 1928.
20. Willingdon to Reading, Sept. 1921, Willingdon Papers, India Office Library, London.
21. Tendulkar, D.G., *Mahatma*, vol. 2, Bombay, 1951 p. 89.
22. C.R., *Chats Behind Bars*, Ganesan, Madras, 1931, p. 50.
23. C.R. to Devadas, 15.12.21, SN 23629, Rajghat Sangrahalaya.
24. Telegram from Gandhi to C.R., Dec. 1921, in Rajghat Sangrahalaya.
25. C.R. to Devadas, 18.21.21, SN 23619, Rajghat Sangrahalaya.

4. JAIL

1. C.R. to Gandhi, 21.12.21, in *Young India*, 12.1.22.
2. Tendulkar, *Mahatma*, vol.2, p. 106.
3. Quoted in C.F. Andrews, 'Heart Beats in India,' *Asia*, March 1930, p. 198.

5. HERO

1. Report by Tasadduq Hussain, Intelligence Officer, File 900/III of 1922, Home (Pol.), National Archives.
2. M. Nehru to S. Satyamurti, 27.11.22, Nehru Memorial Museum & Library (NMML), New Delhi.
3. Rainy to Govt. of India, 7.1.23, File 18 of 1922, Home (Pol.), National Archives.
4. Subhas Bose, *The Indian Struggle*, Asia, Bombay, 1964, p. 82.
5. P.C. Ghosh, *From Nagpur to Lahore*, Abhoy Ashram, Comilla.
6. Prasad in *Swarajya*, Madras, 8.12.62.

7. Reading to Peel, 6.12.23, File 280 of 1923, Home (Pol.), National Archives.
8. Foregoing account from *Young India* issues of Sept.20 & 27, Oct. 4, and Nov. 22, 1923.
9. See article by P.C. Ray in *Rajaji 93*, p. 96.
10. C.R. to Devadas, SN 8155, Rajghat Sangrahalaya.
11. Mahadev Desai, *Diary*, vol.4, pp. 19-20.
12. Gandhi to C.R., SN 8566A, Rajghat Sangrahalaya.
13. Gandhi to C.R., SN 8571, Rajghat Sangrahalaya.
14. C.R. to Devadas, 29.3.24, SN 8629, Rajghat Sangrahalaya.
15. C.R. to Devadas, 12.5.24, Devadas Gandhi Papers.
16. C.R. to Devadas, 29.3.24, SN 8629, Rajghat Sangrahalaya.
17. Tendulkar, *Mahatma*, vol.2, p. 172; and Gandhi to C.R., 6.9.24, in Desai, *Diary*, vol.4, p. 175.
18. C.R. to Gandhi, 24.7.25, SN 8999, Rajghat Sangrahalaya.
19. C.R. to Devadas, 26.9.24, Devadas Gandhi Papers.
20. C.R. to Devadas, 6.10.24, Devadas Gandhi Papers.
21. Wire from C.R. to Gandhi, Nov. 1924, SN 15941, Rajghat Sangrahalaya.
22. Gandhi to C.R., 14.11.24 in Desai, *Diary*, vol.5, p. 22.
23. C.R. to Devadas, 15.1.25, Devadas Gandhi Papers.
24. A.K. Venkatesan in *Rajaji 93*, p. 236A.
25. Ibid.
26. Mahadev Desai, *Diary*, vol.6, pp. 134-41.
27. C.R. to Devadas, 19.7.25, Devadas Gandhi Papers.
28. Mahadev Desai, *Diary*, vol.7, p. 125.
29. C.R. to Devadas, July 1925, Devadas Gandhi Papers.
30. See C.R. to Devadas, 24.12.25, and Desai, *Diary*, vol.8, p. 28.
31. *Young India*, 14.1.26.

6. ASHRAM

1. C.R. to Gandhi, January 1926, SN 10684, Rajghat Sangrahalaya.
2. C.R. to Desai, 20.1.26, SN 10687, Rajghat Sangrahalaya.
3. Account of Morris College meeting from Desai, *Diary*, vol. 8, p.356.
4. Srinivasa Iyengar to C.R., 4.10.26, SN 11334, Rajghat Sangrahalaya.
5. C.R.'s comment related to author in 1973 by Nittoor Srinivasa Rau, who was present.
6. C.R. to Desai, 10.4.27, SN 13274, Rajghat Sangrahalaya.
7. See *CWMG*, 35:32.
8. Tendulkar, *Mahatma*, vol.2, p. 385 & pp.396-7.

9. C.R. quoted in Mahadev Desai, *The Story of Bardoli*, Navajivan, Ahmedabad, 1929, p.266.
10. C.R. to Gandhi, 13.1.28, SN 13050, Rajghat Sangrahalaya.
11. Gandhi to C.R., 27.5.28, SN 13232; C.R. to Gandhi, 31.5.28, SN 13398, Rajghat Sangrahalaya.
12. C.R. to Gandhi, 26.5.28, SN 13391, Rajghat Sangrahalaya; & Gandhi to C.R., 3.7.28, Rajagopalachari Papers.
13. In Desai, *Diary*, vol.7, p.39.
14. Tendulkar, *Mahatma*, vol.2, p.441.
15. C.R. to Gandhi, 18.8.28, SN 15479, Rajghat Sangrahalaya.
16. Gandhi to C.R., 18.10.29, SN 15683, Rajghat Sangrahalaya.
17. Gandhi to C.R., 23.2.29, Rajagopalachari Papers.
18. Marjorie Sykes in *Rajaji 93*, p.75.
19. V. Balasubramanian in *Rajaji 93*, p.219.
20. In his foreword to *Indian Prohibition Manual*, AICC, 1931.
21. Postscript to 'Simplified Marriage,' short story by C.R, in Ashram File, 'Press: 1929-31,' Rajagopalachari Papers.

7. VEDARANYAM

1. From reports of speeches in Ashram File, 'Press: 1929-31,' Rajagopalachari Papers.
2. Tendulkar, *Mahatma*, vol.3, pp.6-7.
3. From reports of speeches in Ashram File, 'Press: 1929-31,' Rajagopalachari Papers.
4. Geoffrey Ashe, *Gandhi*, p.284.
5. SN 16659, Rajghat Sangrahalaya.
6. Ashe, *Gandhi*, p.287.
7. Cotton, Additional Chief Secretary, Madras, to Haig, Home Secretary, Government of India, 4.3.30, File 18 of 1930, National Archives.
8. Thorne to Cotton, Chief Secretary, Madras, 3.4.30, in USS File 687 of 1930, Tamil Nadu Archives.
9. Note by Cotton, Chief Secretary, *ibid*.
10. To Narasimhan and Lakshmi, 14.4. & 16.4.30, Narasimhan Papers.
11. USS File 687 of 1930, Tamil Nadu Archives.
12. From 'The Congress Fight' by C.R. in File 'AICC: 1935,' Rajagopalachari Papers.
13. From article by C.R., 'The Congress Fight,' File 'AICC: 1935,' Rajagopalachari Papers.
14. C.R. to Lakshmi, 30.4.30, C.R. Narasimhan Papers.

15. Confidential Report on the Civil Disobedience Movement (Madras) 1930-1, quoted in B.S. Baliga, *Tanjore District Handbook*, Government of Madras, 1957.
16. Irwin quoted in Brecher, *Nehru*, p.153.
17. Alan Campbell-Johnson, *Viscount Halifax*, p.268.
18. From letter from C.R. dated 24.6.30 in File GO 2617 of 1930, Tamil Nadu Archives.
19. All quotes from *Chats Behind Bars*.
20. Statements by C.R. in Ashram File 'Press 1929-31', Rajagopalachari Papers.
21. Note dated 28.10.30 signed 'G.F.S.' in USS File 699G of 1930, Tamil Nadu Archives.
22. Gandhi to Narandas Gandhi, 16-21.10.30, *CWMG* 44:240.
23. G. Ramachandran, quoting his diary, in *Rajaji 93*, pp.148-9.
24. C.R. to Anderson, 25.12.30, in Ashram File 'Prohibition,' Rajagopalachari Papers.
25. Irwin quoted in Tendulkar, *Mahatma*, vol.3, pp.60-2.

8. STIGMA

1. Recalled by C.R. in *Swarajya*, 1.6.57.
2. Shiva Rao, *India's Freedom Movement*, Longman, 1972, p.238.
3. Ian Stephens, *Monsoon Morning*, Ernest Benn, London, 1966, p.75.
4. Churchill quoted in Madhu Limaye, *Prime Movers*, Radiant, New Delhi, 1985, p.34.
5. Sitaramayya, *History of Congress*, p.786.
6. Tendulkar, *Mahatma*, vol.3, pp.81-2.
7. See *CWMG* 45:379-80.
8. Letter of 24.9.31, SN 17838, Rajghat Sangrahalaya.
9. Letter of 9.5.31, Rajagopalachari Papers.
10. Letter of 24.9.31, SN 17838, Rajghat Sangrahalaya.
11. Circular from Tahsildar in Coimbatore district reproduced in the daily, *Swarajya*, 15.9.31.
12. To Johnson, 21.6.31, to Campbell, 28.6.31, Ashram File 40, Rajagopalachari Papers.
13. C.R.'s rules dated 22.4.31 in SF 733 of 1931, Tamil Nadu Archives.
14. C.R. quoted in Earl of Birkenhead, *Halifax*, Hamish Hamilton, London, 1965, p.307.
15. Tendulkar, *Mahatma*, vol.3, p.138.
16. SN 17609, Rajghat Sangrahalaya.
17. See Gandhi to J.C. Kumarappa, 28.8.31, File 123, Rajghat Sangrahalaya.

18. In Ashram File 20, Rajagopalachari Papers.
19. *Ibid.*
20. Exchange with Boulton, Collector of Salt Revenue, in Ashram File 'Press: 1929-31,' Rajagopalchari Papers.
21. C.R. to Mrs Muthulakshmi Reddi, 10.10.31, Ashram File 21, Rajagopalachari Papers.
22. Resolution of the Tamil Nadu Provincial Conference, Madura, June 6-7, 1931, Ashram File 63, Rajagopalachari Papers.
23. Speech of 20.10.31 in Ashram File 63, Rajagopalachari Papers.
24. Ashram File 61, Rajagopalachari Papers.
25. Letter of 12.11.31 in Ashram File 51, Rajagopalachari Papers.
26. Patel to C.R., 19.11.31, Ashram File 20, Rajagopalachari Papers.
27. Prasad to C.R., 23.11.31, *ibid.*
28. C.R. to S.B. Rath, 10.11.31, Ashram File 21, Rajagopalachari Papers.
29. Letter of 22.11.31 in Ashram File 20, Rajagopalachari Papers.
30. C.R. to Devadas, letter of 2.6.32, Devadas Gandhi Papers.
31. Gandhi to Chhaganlal Joshi, 9.7.32, *CWMG* 50:178.
32. *CWMG* 50:152.
33. *Free Press*, Madras, August 1932.
34. C.R. quoted in Pyarelal, *The Epic Fast*, Navajivan, Ahmedabad, 1932, p.viii.
35. Telegram of 15.9.32, *CWMG* 51:55.
36. From Foreword by C.R. in Pyarelal, *The Epic Fast.*
37. *CWMG* 51:77.
38. Quoted in Pyarelal, *The Epic Fast*, p.227.
39. Quoted in Pyarelal, *The Epic Fast*, p.93.
40. Final quotes from Pyarelal, *The Epic Fast*, pp.205, vii-viii, & 190.

9. SWITCH

1. See Monica Felton, *I Meet Rajaji.*
2. As quoted by C.R. in *Plighted Word*, Servants of Untouchables Society, Delhi, 1937, pp.1-2.
3. Letter of 3.12.31 from the Zamorin to Sir George Stanley, Governor, in USS 813 of 1933, Tamil Nadu Archives.
4. Letters of 17.12.32 and 23.12.32 from Russell to Chief Secretary, *ibid.*
5. Letter of 1.12.32 to Devadas from C.R., Devadas Gandhi Papers.
6. Letter to Devadas, 30.12.32, *ibid.*
7. Talk of 31.1.33 recorded in *CWMG* 53:494.
8. Tendulkar, *Mahatma*, vol.3, p.250.

9. Gandhi-C.R. talks, 1-2 June 1933, in *CWMG* 55:445-8.
10. Brackenbury, Acting Chief Secretary, to Hallett, Home Secretary, Government of India, 22.8.33, Fortnightly Reports of 1933, National Archives.
11. Letters of 12.8.33 sent via P. Sankaran, Sankaran Papers.
12. Messages from C.R. and details of his time in Coimbatore from C.R.'s letters in Sankaran Papers.
13. Devadas Gandhi Papers.
14. Ashram File 'Prohibition: 1934-5.'
15. Ashram File, 'AICC 1934.'
16. Letter of 6.4.34 from Shukla to C.R., ibid.
17. *CWMG* 57:404.
18. Ashram File, 'AICC 1934.'
19. Diary entry in S. Gopal (ed.), *Selected Works of Jawaharlal Nehru,* Orient Longman, New Delhi, 1974, vol.6, p.248.
20. Ashram File, 'AICC 1934.'
21. Dunichand to C.R., 4.5.34, Ashram File, 'Congress Parliamentary Board (CPB) 1934.'
22. *CWMG* 57:396.
23. C.R. to Masani, 24.4.34, Ashram File, 'AICC 1934.'
24. Statement by C.R., *ibid.*
25. C.R. to Ansari, 23.6.34, in Ashram File, 'CPB 1934.'
26. Ashram File 'CPB 1934.'
27. Ashram File 'AICC 1934.'
28. Devadas Gandhi Papers.
29. To Monica Whately, 8.10.34, Ashram File, 'Indian Conciliation Group.'
30. *CWMG* 59:23.
31. *CWMG* 59:268.
32. Leaflet issued by Madras Sanatana Dharma Pracharaka Sabha, 23.10.34, Ashram File, 'CPB-South India, 1934.'
33. Wire dated 17.11.34, ibid.
34. Letter of 23.11.34 in *CWMG* 59:396.
35. Letter to Satyamurti, 12.11.34, Ashram File, 'CPB-South India 1934.'
36. C.R. to T.R. Venkatarama Sastri, 25.1.35, Ashram File, 'CPB 1935.'
37. Jinnah to C.R., 19.3.35, *ibid.*

10. 'FALL'

1. C.R. to Mashruwala, 19.1.35, in Ashram File, 'Gandhi Seva Sangh.'

2. Ashram File, 'Retirement 1935.'
3. *Ibid.*
4. *CWMG* 61:28.
5. Quotes from Ashram Files, 'Retirement' and 'AICC 1935.'
6. Both letters in Ashram File, 'Retirement.'
7. Gandhi to Munshi, *CWMG* 60:421.
8. *CWMG* 61:411.
9. Letter of 30.9.35, Rajagopalachari Papers.
10. Ashram File, 'AICC 1935.'
11. Brackenbury to Home Secretary, Delhi, 3.3.36, Fortnightly Reports of 1936, National Archives.
12. C.R. quoted by Mahadev Desai to Devadas, 6.10.36, Devadas Gandhi Papers.
13. Nittoor Srinivasa Rau told the author in 1973 that he saw C.R.'s remark written on a postcard.
14. All quotes relating to the Rajan episode from *The Hindu*, August 1936.
15. C.R.'s letter in Desai Papers, NMML, New Delhi.
16. C.R. to Mahadev Desai, October 1936, Devadas Gandhi Papers.
17. C.R., *Upanishads*, Hindustan Times Publications, New Delhi, 1937, pp. i and 8.
18. Letter of August 1936, Devadas Gandhi Papers.
19. Rajagopalachari Papers.
20. Related to author in 1973 by P. Ramamurti, the Communist leader, who was present at both conversations.
21. Letter of 14.4.37 in Erskine Papers, India Office Library, London.
22. Nehru quoted in Tara Chand, *History of the Freedom Movement*, Publications Division, vol.3, p.217.
23. Erskine to Linlithgow, 1.5.37, Erskine Papers, India Office Library, London.
24. Gandhi's message quoted in letter of 16.7.37 from Mahadev Desai to G.D. Birla in Birla, *In the Shadow of the Mahatma*, Vakils, Bombay, 1968, p.213.

11. PREMIER

1. Letter of 22.11.38, Erskine Papers, India Office Library, London.
2. Letter of 28.6.37, Zetland Papers, India Office Library, London.
3. File 4144 Home of 16.10.37, Tamil Nadu Archives.
4. C.R. and Erskine quoted in Rutherford to Puckle, 30.6.38, Erskine Papers, India Office Library.
5. Munro to author, 1973.
6. Letter of 20.7.37, Erskine Papers, India Office Library (IOL).

7. Letter of 19.8.37, *CWMG* 66.
8. Letter of 8.12.37, Devadas Gandhi Papers.
9. D. Ramaswami Iyengar to author, Bangalore, 1973.
10. Kher to C.R., 18.7.37, & reply, Kher Papers, NMML, New Delhi.
11. Note of 10.11.37 in File 2602 PWD of 13.12.37, TNA.
12. Letter of 5.8.37, Erskine Papers, IOL, London.
13. Letter of 8.8.37 *CWMG* 66:25.
14. Nehru-C.R. correspondence, Oct. 1937, in S. Gopal (ed.), *Selected Works of Jawaharlal Nehru*, vol. 8, pp.336-7.
15. Recalled to Gopal Gandhi by C.R.
16. Erskine to Linlithgow, 27.8.37; Linlithgow to Erskine, 29.8.37; Linlithgow Papers, IOL, London.
17. Minute in File 94 Public of 18.1.38, TNA.
18. See Erskine to F.H.Brown, 15.3.37, and to Linlithgow, 5.8.37, Erskine Papers, IOL, London.
19. Erskine Papers, IOL, London.
20. See *CWMG* 66:329.
21. 31.1.38, MLAD 4:582.
22. W.G. Lamarque to author, 1973.
23. A. Ramaswami, *The District Gazetteer (Salem)*, Madras, 1967, pp.596-7.
24. Erskine to the King, 27.7.38; the King's secretary to Erskine, 25.8.38; Erskine Papers, IOL, London.
25. See MLAD 4:104ff & 598-9.
26. Letter of 22.11.38 in Erskine Papers, IOL, London.
27. MLAD 5:344.
28. Feb. 1939. MLAD 10:64.
29. *The Hindu*, 16 & 17.7.38.
30. C.R.'s letter to Zetland of 21.12.38 in Erskine Papers, IOL, London.
31. *The Hindu*, June 1938.
32. On 18.8.38. See MLAD 8:333.
33. MLAD 8:342.
34. MLAD 8:342.
35. MLAD 8:344.
36. Note in File 2070 Public of 27.11.39, TNA.
37. Letters of 10.6.38 & 19.10.38 from Erskine to the Governor-General, Erskine Papers, IOL, London.
38. On 18.8.38. MLAD 7:339-41.
39. Letter of 28.12.38, Devadas Gandhi Papers.
40. Note by C.R. dated 8.6.38 in File 2070 Public of 27.11.39, TNA, Madras.
41. MLAD 11:369-70.

42. During debate in March 1939. See MLAD 11:378-82.
43. C.R.'s letter of 21.4.38 in Kher Papers, NMML, New Delhi.
44. Minute by C.R. in File 902 Public of 28.8.38, TNA, Madras.
45. Minute of 2.4.38 in File 1142 Public of 6.7.38, TNA, Madras.
46. In File 187 Public of 1.2.38, TNA, Madras.
47. Krishnaih, member of the Premier's staff, to author, 1973.
48. Quoted in Erskine's letter to the Governor-General, 23.6.38, Erskine Papers, IOL, London.
49. MLAD 9:588 & 703-7.
50. From Linlithgow to Zetland, 23.11. & 13.12.38, Zetland to Linlithgow, 6.12.38 (Zetland Papers, IOL, London), & *The Hindu*, 1.12.38.
51. Gandhi to C.R., 21.5.38, Rajagopalachari Papers.
52. Crombie to author, 23.12.73.
53. Remark of 2.12.38 in MLAD 8:472.
54. On 17.8.38. MLAD 7:203.
55. *The Hindu*, July 1939.
56. See MLAD 13:44ff & 109; & *The Hindu*, 22.7.39.
57. Madras Legislative Council Debates (MLCD), vol.9, pp.94ff.
58. Nehru quoted in Brecher, *Nehru*, p.251.
59. This was Kripalani's view, as communicated to the author in 1975.
60. *Indian Review*, Madras, April 1939.
61. Quoted by G.L. Mehta in *Rajaji* 93:99.

12. HITLER

1. C.R.'s note quoted in letter of 12.4.39 from Erskine to Linlithgow, Erskine papers, IOL, London.
2. Erskine Papers, IOL, London.
3. See Erskine to Linlithgow, 24.4.39, Erskine papers, IOL, London.
4. MLAD 11:370-8.
5. Previous three quotes from MLAD 11:387-9.
6. Note in File USS 1122 of 22.5.39, TNA, Madras.
7. Zetland Papers, IOL, London.
8. C.R. to J.B.L. Munro, 25.12.39. Letter shown to author by Munro.
9. Day to author, letter of 13.12.73.
10. From Erskine's letter to the Viceroy, 26.10.39, Erskine Papers, IOL, London, and *The Hindu*, 26.10.39.
11. Desai in *Harijan*, Oct. 1939.
12. Letter to the King of 19.10.39, Linlithgow Papers, IOL, London.
13. Erskine to Linlithgow, letter of 21.10.39, Erskine Papers, IOL, London.

14. Glendevon, *The Viceroy at Bay*.
15. Erskine to Linlithgow, letter of 10.7.39, Erskine Papers, IOL, London.
16. Erskine's telegram to the Viceroy, 16.9.39, Erskine Papers, IOL, London.
17. Menon, *An Outline of Indian Constitutional History*, Bhavan, Bombay, 1965, p.53.
18. Related to the author in 1973 by B. Shiva Rao, who had conveyed to Nehru the remark made to him by Hydari.
19. Debate excerpts from MLAD 14:36-128.
20. *Ibid.*
21. Letter from Day to author, 13.12.73.
22. Quoted in *Rajaji 93:* 160.
23. Comment in *The Hindu*, end December, 1972.
24. See MLAD 13: 312 & 42.
25. Quoted in *Rajaji 93*:160.
26. Brecher, *Nehru*, p.241.
27. Day to author, 13.12.73.
28. *Ibid.*
29. Reply in File 1672 Public of 9.10.38, TNA, Madras.
30. Morris to author, letter of 21.11.73.
31. MLAD 5:57.
32. In *Rajaji 93:* 204.
33. Reply in File 3551 Home of 29.6.39, TNA, Madras.
34. Saunders to author, 30.11.73; Morris to author, 21.11.73; Day to author, 13.12.73; Khaleeli and Menon in *Rajaji 93:* 177 & 236G.
35. Crombie to author, letter of 23.12.73.
36. MLAD 5:359.
37. Quoted by Butler in Nehru Memorial Lecture, Cambridge University Press, 1966, p.23.
38. Gopal (ed.), *Selected Works of Jawaharlal Nehru*, vol.11, pp.799-800.
39. *Rajaji 93:* 108.
40. Kamaraj to author in an interview in Madras, 7.10.74.

13. COGITATION

1. Letters from Erskine to Linlithgow in November and December 1939, Erskine Papers, IOL, London.
2. Letter of 8.3.40, Erskine Papers, IOL, London.
3. Erskine's and Zetland's remarks in Zetland's letter to Linlithgow, 1940, Zetland Papers, IOL, London.
4. Hope's letter of 5.6.40 in Linlithgow Papers, IOL, London.

5. Quotes taken from Merriam, *Gandhi vs. Jinnah*, Minerva, Calcutta, 1980, pp.68, 81.
6. Letter of 20.7.40 in Nehru, *A Bunch of Old Letters*, Asia, Bombay, 1960, pp.446-7.
7. Gopal (ed.), *Selected Works of Jawaharlal Nehru*, vol.11, p.799.
8. Letter of 18.7.40, Natesan Papers, NMML, New Delhi.
9. Gopal (ed.), *Selected Works of Jawaharlal Nehru*, vol.11, p.800.
10. *Ibid.*, p.178.
11. Letter of 9.9.40, Linlithgow Papers, IOL, London.
12. Discussion of 5.11.40, recorded by Rajkumari Amrit Kaur, in Amrit Kaur Papers, NMML, New Delhi.
13. *The Hindu*, 4.12.40, and eyewitness account to author by C.R. Narasimhan.
14. Letter of 22.1.41, *CWMG* 73:292.
15. Ananthasayanam Ayyangar in *Rajaji 93:*155.
16. Gopala Reddi and T.S. Avinashalingam in *Rajaji 93:*189 & 276; and P.T. Venkatachar to author.
17. Letter from Narasimhan to Tait, 26.5.41, shown to author by Margaret Tait.
18. Related to author by fellow-prisoner P.T. Venkatachar.
19. Linlithgow to Hope, 8.5.41, Linlithgow Papers, IOL, London. Account of the Sikander-Srinivasan initiative given to author by B. Shiva Rao of *The Hindu*, who had passed on Sikander's message to Srinivasan.

14. REBELLION

1. Selected Works of Jawaharlal Nehru (*SWJN*) 11:734.
2. Devadas Gandhi Papers.
3. *CWMG* 75:224.
4. Quoted in C. Rajagopalachari, *The Defence of India*, Rochouse, Madras, 1942, p.24.
5. All quotes from Rajagopalachari, *The Defence of India*.
6. Linlithgow Papers, IOL, London.
7. Quoted by Wavell in Moon (ed.), *The Viceroy's Journal*, Oxford, 1973, p.33.
8. Rajendra Prasad, *Autobiography*, Asia, Bombay, 1957, p.527.
9. Quoted in B. Shiva Rao, *India's Freedom Movement*, Orient Longman, 1972, p.177.
10. Letter of 18.4.42, Linlithgow Papers, IOL, London.
11. Gandhi quoted in letter of 27.4.42 from Pyarelal to Devadas, Devadas Gandhi Papers.

12. Letter of 9.6.42, Linlithgow Papers, IOL, London.
13. Letter of 31.5.42 quoted in *Rajaji 93:* 160.
14. Letter of July 1942 quoted in R. Coupland, *The Indian Problem*, Oxford, 1942, p. 337.
15. Eyewitness account by S. Ramakrishnan in *Rajaji 93:* 213.
16. Quoted in Shiva Rao, *India's Freedom Movement*, p.192.
17. Letter of 5.7.42, Rajagopalachari Papers.
18. Rajagopalachari Papers.
19. Linlithgow Papers, 1942, IOL.
20. Linlithgow's remark recalled by C.R. in *The Hindu*, 10.3.43.
21. Phillips, *Ventures in Diplomacy*, 1952.
22. Entry in Wavell's diary in Moon (ed.), *The Viceroy's Journal*, p.57.
23. Account of talk from Ahmad (ed.), *Speeches & Writings of Mr Jinnah*, vol.2, Peerzada (ed.), *Leaders' Correspondence with Mr Jinnah*, Bombay, 1944, and letter of 14.4.44 from Birla to Devadas Gandhi, Devadas Gandhi Papers.

15. 'MOTH-EATEN'

1. Moon (ed.), *The Viceroy's Journal*, p.78.
2. From Merriam, *Gandhi vs. Jinnah*, Minerva, Calcutta, pp. 92-107.
3. Moon (ed.), *Journal*, p.87.
4. From Merriam, *Gandhi vs. Jinnah*, pp.92-107.
5. *Ibid*.
6. From C. Rajagopalachari, *Reconciliation*, Hind Kitabs, Bombay, 1945.
7. *Ibid*.
8. Gandhi's remark quoted in Pyarelal, *Last Phase* 1:88.
9. From Merriam, *Gandhi vs. Jinnah*, pp.104-5.
10. Khaliquzzaman, *Pathway to Pakistan*, Longman, Lahore, 1961, p.278.
11. Quoted in Merriam, *Gandhi vs. Jinnah*, p.108.
12. Devadas Gandhi Papers.
13. Transcript supplied to author by Pyarelal.
14. From C. Rajagopalachari, *University Addresses*, Hind Kitabs, Bombay, 1949, pp.39-40.
15. From C. Rajagopalachari, *Reconciliation*, Hind Kitabs, Bombay, 1945.
16. See Moon (ed.), *Journal*, pp.98ff.
17. *Ibid*.
18. Quoted in Asoka Mehta and Kusum Nair, *The Simla Triangle*, Padma, Bombay, 1945, p.63.

19. Moon (ed.), *Journal,* p.154.
20. Moon (ed.), *Journal,* p.494.
21. *Ibid.,* p.142.
22. Mehta and Nair, *The Simla Triangle,* p.63.
23. Moon, (ed.), *Journal,* p.156.
24. Letter of 26.8.45, Sarat Bose Papers, Calcutta.
25. Quoted in Durga Das (ed.), *Sardar Patel's Correspondence,* vol.2, p.182 (*SPC* 2:182).
26. Patel to A. Ali, 17.10.45, in Nandurkar (ed.), *Sardar's Letters,* Patel Smarak Bhavan, Ahmedabad.
27. Quoted in Durga Das (ed.), *SPC* 2: 219.
28. Patel to C.R., letter of 22.2.46, *ibid.*

16. FREEDOM!

1. Quoted in Moon (ed.), *Journal,* pp.310 & 399.
2. *Ibid.,* p.
3. See letter of 8.6.46 from Vazirani to Patel, *SPC* 3:105.
4. Comment to the BBC quoted in J. Ahmad (ed.), *Speeches & Writings of Mr Jinnah,* Ashraf, Lahore, vol.2, p.384.
5. See Rajmohan Gandhi, *Patel,* Navajivan, Ahmedabad, 1990, p.366.
6. Quoted in Pyarelal, *Last Phase* 1:251.
7. Cripps's remark of 18.7.46 in the House of Commons quoted in Philips & Wainwright, *The Partition of India,* Allen & Unwin, London, 1970, p.218.
8. Letter of 14.7.46 in Rajagopalachari Papers.
9. Nehru's note dated 15.3.46 in *SPC* 3:242-5.
10. Moon (ed.), *Journal,* p.281.
11. Letter of 1.8.46 in *SPC* 3:248.
12. *SPC* 3:40.
13. Moon (ed.), *Journal,* p.339.
14. Moon (ed.), *Journal,* p.349.
15. Correspondence in July and August 1946 in *SPC* 3: 38, 248-9 & 273-4.
16. Moon (ed.), *Journal,* p.349.
17. *New York Herald Tribune,* 29.10.46.
18. Quoted in Pyarelal, *Last Phase* 1:565.
19. Moon (ed.), *Journal,* p.421.
20. Moon (ed.), *Journal,* p.462.
21. Lady Isobel Cripps to author in an interview in 1973.
22. Rajagopalachari Papers.
23. Mountbatten quoted in Merriam, *Gandhi vs. Jinnah,* p.128.

24. Khaliquzzaman, *Pathway to Pakistan*, p.317.
25. Dharma Vira, *Memoirs of a Civil Servant*, Vikas, Delhi, 1975, p.25.
26. Lamarque quoted in Hunt and Harrison, *District Officer in India*, Scolar, London, 1980, p.244.
27. B.K. Nehru in *Rajaji 93*:97.
28. From the *Hindustan Times*, 27.4.47, 27.9.46, 8.2.47, 4.3.47 & 18.9.46.
29. Reported to author by C.R.
30. N.V. Gadgil, *Government from Inside*, Meenakshi, Meerut, 1968, p.37.

17. CALCUTTA

1. Quoted in *Speeches*, West Bengal Government Press, Calcutta, 1948, pp.1-3.
2. Bimanesh Chatterjee, *Thousand Days with Rajaji*, Affiliated East-West, New Delhi, 1973, p.19.
3. Letter of 26.8.47, Rajagopalachari Papers.
4. Letter of 4.9.47, Rajagopalachari Papers.
5. Letter of 15.9.47, Rajagopalachari Papers.
6. Chatterjee, *Thousand Days*, p.11.
7. Letter of 22.8.47, Devadas Gandhi Papers.
8. Desai to C.R., 17.2.48, C.R. to Desai, 23.2.48, Rajagopalachari Papers.
9. Liaqat to C.R., 27.8.47, C.R. to Liaqat, 31.8.47, C.R. to Singh, 30.9.47, Rajagopalachari Papers.
10. Quoted in C. Rajagopalachari, *Speeches*, Calcutta, 1948, p.47.
11. See Pyarelal, *Last Phase* 2:408.
12. Letter of 8.9.47, C.R. to A.K. Chanda, Rajagopalachari Papers.
13. Letter of 12.11.73 from Mountbatten to author, and author's interview with Mountbatten, 30.10.73.
14. Account of Gandhi-C.R. meeting supplied to author by three eye witnesses, C.R.'s daughters Namagiri and Lakshmi and Gandhi's aide Brijkrishna Chandiwala.
15. Foregoing account of C.R. in relation to Gandhi's assassination based on information supplied to author by Narasimhan, Lakshmi, Singaravelu and Chatterjee; C. Rajagoplachari, *Speeches*, Calcutta, 1948; and newspaper reports.
16. Chatterjee, *Thousand Days*, p.3.
17. C. Rajagopalachari, *Speeches*, Calcutta, 1948, pp.118-9.
18. Rajagopalachari, *Speeches*, Calcutta, 1948, p.117.
19. Mountbatten and C.R. quoted in Campbell-Johnson, *Mission with Mountbatten*, pp.297-8.

20. Quotes from contemporary newspaper reports and from Rajagopalachari, *Speeches.*
21. Chatterjee, *Thousand Days*, p.28.
22. Letter in May 1948 to George Walker, C.R.'s 1937-9 colleague in the Madras Assembly.
23. Letters and Press comment from Rajagopalachari Papers.
24. Prafulla Ghosh to author, 1975.
25. Campbell-Johnson, *Mission with Mountbatten*, p.306.
26. Rajagopalachari, *Speeches*, p.232.
27. Rajagopalachari, *Speeches*, pp.248-9.
28. *Ibid.*
29. *Ibid.*, pp.258-9.
30. *Ibid.*, pp.261-2.

18. PALACE

1. Chatterjee, *Thousand Days*, p.53.
2. Chatterjee, *Thousand Days*, p.91.
3. Letter of 15.5.48 from Fischer to C.R., Rajagopalachari Papers.
4. Menon in *Rajaji* 93:129-30.
5. Related to author by Pyarelal, who was present.
6. Chatterjee, *Thousand Days*, p.86.
7. Alexander in *Rajaji* 93:72E.
8. C.R.-Nizam correspondence published in *Hindustan Times*, 9.9.48.
9. V.P. Menon, *An Outline of Indian Constitutional History*, Bhavan, Bombay, 1965, p.74.
10. Chatterjee, *Thousand Days*, p.57.
11. Ramaswami Iyengar and C.R. Narasimhan to author, 1973.
12. C. Rajagopalachari, *Speeches*, Governor-General's Press, New Delhi, 1950, pp.206-7.
13. Quotes from Rajagopalachari, *Speeches.*
14. Parasuram in *Rajaji* 93:210.
15. In Rajagopalachari, *Speeches.*
16. See *Hindustan Times*, 17.12.48, and letter of 5.12.48 from Nehru to Patel in *Sardar Patel's Correspondence* (SPC) 6:340.
17. Letter of 30.3.49 in *Sardar Patel's Correspondence* 8:7.
18. Letter of 29.10.48 in *SPC* 6:501-2.
19. Letter in August 1949 from N.V. Gadgil to Patel in *SPC* 8:602ff.
20. Letter from C.R. to Mirabehn, 19.10.49, Mirabehn Papers.
21. See Gadgil to Patel, 18.8.49, and Patel to Gadgil, 22.8.49, in *SPC* 8:602ff.
22. Rajagopalachari, *Speeches*, p.233.
23. Letter of 28.6.49 to Mashruwala in *SPC* 8:277-8.

24. See *SPC* 8:266.
25. Letter of 6.1.49 in *SPC* 8:96-7.
26. Episode recalled by C.R. in *Swarajya*, 23.11.68.
27. Letter in Tait Papers, St. Andrews,
28. Chatterjee, *Thousand Days*, pp.79-80.
29. Spratt, *DMK in Power*, Nachiketa, Bombay, 1970, p.38.
30. Rajagopalachari, *Speeches*, pp.331-4.
31. See *SPC* 8:197-216.
32. *Ibid*.
33. Birla and Desai to author, 1973.
34. Mishra, *Living An Era*, Vol. 2, Vikas, 1978, pp.153-61.
35. *Ibid*.
36. *SPC* 8:197-216.
37. *Ibid*.
38. Conversation recalled by C.R. to author.
39. Letter of 31.12.49 in Rajagopalachari Papers.
40. Letter of 26.1.50 in *SPC* 10:77-8..

19. 'MATCHSTICK'

1. Letters to Rama Rao in Feb. and March 1950, Rajagopalachari Papers.
2. Deshmukh in *Rajaji* 93:116.
3. Menon in *Rajaji* 93:130.
4. Gadgil, *Government From Inside*, Meenakshi, Meerut, 1968, p.84.
5. Menon in *Rajaji* 93:130.
6. Chakravarty in *Rajaji* 93:127.
7. Namagiri to author.
8. Namagiri to author.
9. It was revived in 1966.
10. Mullick to author, 1973.
11. Chalapati Rau to author.
12. Mullick to author.
13. Dutt's minute and C.R.'s comment in File 7/40/51 Home (Pol.), National Archives, New Delhi.
14. C.R.'s view cited in note of 17.2.51 by H.V.R. Iengar, Home Secretary, in File 7/13/51, Home (Pol.), National Archives.
15. Iengar's note of 23.2.51 citing C.R.'s view in File 28/2/51, Home (Pol.), National Archives.
16. C.R.'s letter in File 21/1/51, Home (Pol.), National Archives.
17. Minute in File 7/18/51, Home (Pol.), National Archives.
18. In interview to author.
19. Iengar in *Rajaji* 93:133.

20. Mullick to author.
21. Mookerjee-C.R. exchange related to author by R.Venkataraman, who heard it as an MP.
22. From *Towards a Responsible Press*, Publications Division, 1952.
23. *Ibid.*
24. Gadgil, *Government from the Inside*, p.170.
25. Iengar to author, 1973.
26. From lines by C.R. in October 1951, triggered by a farewell party given for him by Hare Krushna Mahtab, a Cabinet colleague, and reproduced in *Swarajya*, 14.6.75.

20. 'DOWNFALL'

1. To R. Chakravarti, 3.3.52, Rajagopalachari Papers.
2. Copy of letter in Rajagopalachari Papers.
3. This and following account based on documents in Rajagopalachari Papers, contemporary newspaper reports, and author's interviews with, among others, Subramaniam, Goenka, Sivaraman and Pattabhirama Rao.
4. Letter in Rajagopalachari Papers.
5. *Ibid.*
6. *Ibid.*
7. Letter of 26.3.52, Rajagopalachari Papers.
8. Remark of 3.7.52 in MLAD II:437.
9. Speech of 9.5.52, MLAD.
10. Proceedings of 28.6.52, MLAD II:45.
11. Pattabhirama Rao to author, 1973.
12. In *Rajaji* 93:184.
13. Remark of 15.7.52 in MLAD III:254.
14. Broadcast of 1.8.52 in Rajagopalachari, *Rajaji's Speeches*, Bhavan, Bombay, 1958, p.56.
15. Quoted in *Rajaji* 93:119.
16. C.R.'s advice repeated by Nehru in letter to C.R., 20.12.52, Rajagopalachari Papers.
17. Assembly speech on 15.3.53, MLAD.
18. Sri Prakasa to C.R., 28.3.53, Rajagopalachari Papers.
19. On 30.7.53, MLAD.
20. See speech by C. Subramaniam, 6.3.54, MLAD XII:651.
21. Pattabhirama Rao, who was present, to author.
22. Letter of 14.9.52 in Rajagopalachari Papers.
23. See *Rajaji* 93:194.
24. Letter of 29.12.52 quoted by Narayan in *Rajaji* 93:171.
25. Nixon, *Memoirs*, Grosset & Dunlap, New York.

26. Note from Ramsey to author.
27. Jotting of 3.4.53 in C.R.'s diary.
28. Raman in *Rajaji 93*:220B.
29. Quoted in *Rajaji's Speeches,* Bhavan, Bombay, 1958, p.96.
30. Narasimhan to author.
31. Tyagi to C.R., 6.9.52, Rajagopalachari Papers.
32. Speech of 29.7.53 in MLAD IX.
33. On 8.8.49. Quoted in *Governor-General's Speeches*:257-9.
34. Speech of 29.7.53. MLAD IX:1736.
35. In the Assembly on 19.12.53. MLAD X:376.
36. *Ibid.*
37. Remark of 21.8.53 in *Rajaji's Speeches,* Bhavan, Bombay, p.165.
38. Assembly statement of 24.12.53 in MLAD X:717.
39. Assembly remark of 29.7.53 in MLAD IX:1732.
40. Ramamurti to author, 1973.
41. C.R.'s words repeated in Mehta's letter to him, 20.8.53, Rajagopalachari Papers.
42. Quoted in Prakasa to Prasad, 16,4,54, Rajagopalachari Papers.
43. *Ibid.*
44. Justice P. Chandra Reddy in *Rajaji 93*:263.

21. WOLVES

1. Statement in Rajagopalachari Papers.
2. In Henry Ramsey papers.
3. Letter from Ramsey to author.
4. Remark of 16.8.45 in Rajagopalachari, *The Voice of the Uninvolved,* National Book Trust, 1960, p.2.
5. To Felton. Quoted in Felton, *I Meet Rajaji (IMR),* Jaico, Bombay, 1964, p.185.
6. Ramsey to author.
7. Based on Felton, *IMR;* C.R., *Voice;* and C.R.'s remarks quoted in *Indian Express,* 7.12.55.
8. Letter from C.R. to Rama Rao, 13.10.55.
9. *Ibid.*
10. Quoted in Gyanvati Darbar, *Portrait of a President,* Vikas, 1974, vol.1, p.111.
11. From letter in Rajagopalachari Papers.
12. Felton, *IMR:* 119.
13. Felton, *IMR:*116.
14. From C.R., *Voice*: 44.
15. Letters of 20.10 & 8.11.58, shown to author by Mirabehn.

22. SWATANTRA

1. H.L. Erdman, *The Swatantra Party and Indian Conservatism*, Cambridge University Press, 1967, pp.68-9.
2. Letter in Deshmukh Papers, NMML, New Delhi.
3. Nehru quoted in Felton, *IMR*:184.
4. Felton, *IMR*:185.
5. Based on Felton, *IMR*:191-3, & Masani, *Against the Tide*, Vikas, New Delhi, 1981, pp.137 ff.
6. Felton, *IMR*:187.
7. In Masani, *Against the Tide*, p.136..
8. Nehru, quoted in Erdman, *The Swatantra Party*.
9. Erdman, *The Swatantra Party*, p.83.
10. Kabir quoted in Erdman, *The Swatantra Party*, p.74.
11. Cited in *Report on Swatantra Party's Preparatory Convention*, Popular, Bombay, August 1959, p.30.
12. Quoted in Erdman, *The Swatantra Party*, p.172.
13. *Ibid.*, p.175.
14. *Ibid.*, p.63.
15. Diary entries in Darbar, *Portrait of a President*, 1:240 & 2:88.
16. Menon in *Rajaji 93*:71.
17. Quoted in article by V.S. Maniam, *The Statesman*, 7.1.73.
18. Simons in *Rajaji 93*:100.
19. Dr Sundaram in *Rajaji 93*:236E.
20. Letter of 15.7.61 to Gopal-Gandhi, RP.
21. C.R. quoted in Erdman, *The Swatantra Party*, p.215.
22. The Canadian journalist David van Praagh in *Rajaji 93*:203.
23. C.R. in *Swarajya*, 25.3 & 13.5.61.

23. KENNEDY

1. Disclosed to the author in 1973 by Shiva Rao who, along with Diwakar, received Nehru's advice. This chapter is based on articles by C.R. & others in *Swarajya;* articles by Zafarulla Khan, B.K. Nehru, Shiva Rao, B.N. Chakravarti, A.B. Nair & Diwakar in *Rajaji 93;* author's interviews with Diwakar, Shiva Rao and Satyanarayana; and notes supplied by Shiva Rao of interviews of C.R. & party with Kennedy, Gromyko, Macmillan & Pope John XXIII.
2. Shiva Rao to author. Kennedy's comment quoted in Shiva Rao, *India's Freedom Movement*, Longman, 1972, pp.243-4, and by Diwakar in *Rajaji 93*.
3. Chagla in *Swarajya*, 9.12.79.

24. DEFIANCE

1. Message for Ayub in letter of 3.11.62 from C.R. to Mahomed Ali, Foreign Minister of Pakistan, Rajagopalachari Papers (RP).
2. T. Sadasivam told the author that he heard this from C.R.
3. From *Swarajya* of 6.4.63, 26.10.63, 11.1.64 & 1.6.63.
4. Letter, RP.
5. In *Swarajya*, 6.6.64.
6. Unsigned letter of 11.1.66 forwarded to C.R. by L.K. Jha, Secretary to the Prime Minister, on 14.1.66, RP.
7. Narayan in *Rajaji* 93:171.
8. To Tara Ali Baig, 9.12.65, RP.
9. To Jyotirmoy Banerjee, 28.4.63.
10. Kamaraj in *Rajaji* 93:105.
11. Uma Vasudev, *Indira Gandhi*, Vikas, Delhi, 1974, p.428-31.
12. Das in *Rajaji* 93:173.
13. C.R.'s remark to Gopal Gandhi about his sister.
14. Karanth in *Rajaji* 93:200.
15. Jain in *Rajaji* 93:175.
16. Hukam Singh to Neerja Chowdhury, Feb. 1980.
17. Khaliquzzaman, *Pathway to Pakistan*, Longman, Lahore, 1961, p.316.
18. Sarkar in *Rajaji* 93:224.
19. Letter to Gopal Gandhi, 7.11.68.
20. Quotes in this para from *Swarajya* issues in August and September, 1968.
21. In *Dipika*, Aug. 1959.
22. To the author.
23. From C.R.'s message to Guru Gobind Singh Foundation, Patiala, 1966, RP.
24. See Ved Mehta in *Rajaji* 93:176; also letter from C.R. to Natwar Singh, RP.
25. Crocker in *Rajaji* 93:87.
26. R.V. Krishna Iyer, official of the Madras legislature and C.R.'s friend from Salem days, as stated to author.
27. Venkatachar in *Rajaji* 93:138.
28. P. Mahadevan in *Swarajya*, 14.12.63.
29. Iyengar to author in Madras, 1973.
30. Mukerjee in *Rajaji* 93:110.

25. SPARKLE

1. Quoted and referred to in *Swarajya* issues, June & July 1969.
2. Quoted in Masani, *Against the Tide,* Vikas, Delhi, 1981, p.298.
3. *Swarajya* issues of 6.9.69, 20.9.69, 18.10.69 and 31.1.70.
4. Quoted in Masani, *Against the Tide,* Vikas, New Delhi, p.313.
5. Letter of 23.1.71, RP.
6. Letter of 15.5.65, RP.
7. Memo for *Swarajya,* 22.8.70, RP.
8. Note to T.V. Venkataraman, Nov. 1971, RP.
9. See *Swarajya,* 24.7. & 7.8.71.
10. Crocker in *Rajaji 93:*87.
11. Parasuram in *Rajaji 93:*210.
12. Sadasivam to author.
13. Cariappa in *Rajaji 93:*26.
14. Mountbatten to C.R., 5.11.66; Fischer to C.R., 19.4.66, RP.
15. Fielden in *Rajaji 93:*172.
16. Sri Prakasa in *Rajaji 89,* Bharathan, Madras, 1967, p.9.
17. Prasad quoted by K.M. Munshi, *Bhavan's Journal,* 3.12.67.
18. To author, New Delhi, 11.3.74.
19. Felton, *IMR:*177.
20. Quoted in Masti Venkatesa Iyengar, *Rajaji,* Bhavan, Bombay,vol.2, p.206.
21. Rau in *Rajaji 93:*275.
22. This and following paras based on incidents and events witnessed by author.

Bibliography

Information for this volume was obtained from private papers; classified government files; files of newspapers and periodicals; correspondence with C.R. supplied by many individuals; letters to the author from officials serving with C.R.; books, pamphlets and other published matter; & a large number of interviews.

Apart from the Rajagopalachari and Devadas Gandhi Papers, the following private papers were consulted: the Pyarelal Papers; the Gandhi Sangrahalya collection in Ahmedabad and New Delhi; the C.D. Deshmukh, Amrit Kaur, S.A.Brelvi, G.A. Natesan, B.G. Kher and Dhirubhai Desai Papers (all at the Nehru Memorial Library, New Delhi); & the Erskine, Linlithgow and Zetland Papers (all at the India Office Library, London).

Letters from & to C.R. were shown to me, or texts supplied, by, among others, the Prime Minister's Office (some Nehru-C.R. letters); the family of Navaratna Rama Rao; Mirabehn; B. Shiva Rao; Henry Ramsey; P. Kodanda Rao; Mahavir Tyagi; J.B.L. Munro; the family of Khasa Subba Rau; and Margaret Tait.

Among officials who sent me written recollections were H.H. Carleston, Bimanesh Chatterjee, Peter Crombie, B.W. Day, W.W. Georgeson, R.B. MacEwen, F.W.A. Morris, D.I.R. Muir, J.B.L. Munro, A.J. Platt and J.F. Saunders.

Newspapers & periodicals studied included *Amrita Bazar Patrika* and *The Statesman*, Calcutta, *Young India* and *Harijan*, Ahmedabad, *Hindustan Times*, New Delhi, and *The Hindu*, *Indian Express* and *Indian Review*, Madras.

Other published material consulted included the following:

Ahmad, J. (ed.), *Speeches & Writings of Mr Jinnah*, Ashraf, Lahore, 1947.

Allana, G., *Quaid-i-Azam Jinnah*, Lahore, 1967.

Ashe, Geoffrey, *Gandhi*, Asia, Bombay, 1968.

Azad, A.K., *India Wins Freedom*, Orient Longman, New Delhi, 1959.

Baliga, B.S., *Tanjore District Handbook*, Government of Madras, 1957.

Bapat, S.V. (ed.), *Reminiscences of Lokamanya Tilak*.

Bharathan, Madras, *Rajaji 89*, 1967, & *Rajaji 93*, 1971.

Birkenhead, *Halifax*, Hamish Hamilton, London, 1965.

Birla, G.D., *In the Shadow of the Mahatma*, Vakils, Feller & Simons, Bombay, 1968.

Bose, Subhas, *The Indian Struggle*, Asia, Bombay, 1968.

Brecher, M., *Nehru*, Oxford, London, 1959.

Campbell-Johnson, Alan, *Mission with Mountbatten*, Robert Hale, London, 1951.

Chand, Tara, *History of the Freedom Movement*, Pub. Div., New Delhi, 1972.

Chatterjee, Bimanesh, *Thousand Days with Rajaji*, Affiliated East-West, New Delhi, 1973.

Coupland, Reginald, *The Indian Problem*, Oxford, 1942.

Darbar, Gyanvati, *Portrait of a President*, two vols., Vikas, New Delhi, 1974.

Desai, Mahadev, *The Story of Bardoli*, Navajivan, Ahmedabad, 1929.

Deshmukh, C.D., *The Course of My Life*, Orient Longman, 1974.

Das, Durga (ed.), *Sardar Patel's Correspondence*, ten vols., Navajivan, Ahmedabad.

Erdman, Howard, *The Swatantra Party & Indian Conservatism*, Cambridge University Press, 1967.

Felton, Monica, *I Meet Rajaji*, Macmillan, 1962; & Jaico, Bombay, 1964.

Gadgil, N.V., *Government from Inside*, Meenakshi, Meerut, 1968.

Gandhi, M.K., *Collected Works of Mahatma Gandhi*, (CWMG) hundred vols., Publications Division, New Delhi.

Ghosh, P.C., *From Nagpur to Lahore*, Abhay Ashram, Comilla, 1930.

Glendevon, *The Viceroy at Bay*, Collins, London, 1971.

Gopal, S. (ed.), *Selected Works of Jawaharlal Nehru*, Orient Longman, New Delhi.

Hindusthan Publications, Madras, *Rajaji*, 1949.

Irschick, *Political and Social Conflict in South India*, University of California Press, 1969.

Iyengar, A.S., *All Through the Gandhian Era*, Hind Kitabs, Bombay, 1950.

Iyengar, Masti V., *Rajaji*, two vols., Bhavan, Bombay.

Jain, A.P., *Rafi Ahmed Kidwai*, Asia, Bombay, 1965.

Khaliquzzaman, Choudhry, *Pathway to Pakistan*, Longman, Lahore, 1961.

Krishnadas, *Seven Months with Mahatma Gandhi*, Ganesan, Madras, 1928.

Lovett, Verney, *A History of the Indian Nationalist Movement*, John Murray, London, 1921.

Masani, M.R., *Against the Tide*, Vikas, New Delhi, 1981.

Mehta, Asoka, and Nair, Kusum, *The Simla Triangle*, Padma, Bombay, 1945.

Menon, K.P.S., *Many Worlds*, Oxford University Press, Bombay, 1965.

Menon, V.P., *The Transfer of Power*, Orient Longman, 1957.

Menon, V.P., *An Outline of Indian Constitutional History*, Bhavan, Bombay, 1965.

Merriam, A.H., *Gandhi vs. Jinnah*, Minerva, Calcutta, 1980.

Mishra, D.P., *Living an Era*, two vols., Vikas, New Delhi, 1975.

Moon, Penderel, *Divide & Quit*, Britain.

Moon, Penderel, *Wavell: The Viceroy's Journal*, Oxford, 1973.

Nandurkar, G.M. (ed.), *Sardar's Letters*, Ahmedabad, 1977.

Narasimhan, V.K., *Kamaraj*, Manaktalas, Bombay, 1967.

Nehru, J., *A Bunch of Old Letters*, Asia. Bombay, 1960.

Nixon, R., *Memoirs*, Grosset & Dundlap, New York.

Peerzada, S.S., *Leaders' Correspondence with Mr Jinnah*, Taj Office, Bombay, 1944.

Prasad, Rajendra, *Autobiography*, Asia, Bombay, 1957.

Publications Division, New Delhi, *The 1921 Movement*, 1971.

Pyarelal, *The Epic Fast*, Navajivan, Ahmedabad, 1932.

Pyarelal, *The Last Phase*, two vols., Navajivan, Ahmedabad, 1958.

Rajagopalachari, C., Articles in *Hindustan Review*, Patna, June & July 1907; 'M.K. Gandhi: His Message to India,'*Indian Review*, Madras, May 1916; *A Jail Diary*, Rochouse, Madras, 1941; *Indian Prohibition Manual*, AICC, Madras, 1931; *Chats Behind Bars*, S. Ganesan, Madras, 1931; *Plighted Word*, Servants of Untouchables Society, Delhi, 1933; *Upanishads*, Hindustan Times, New Delhi, 1937; *The Defence of India*, Rochouse. Madras, 1942; *The Way Out*, Oxford, Delhi, 1943; *Reconciliation*, Hind Kitabs, Bombay, 1945; *Ambedkar Refuted*, Hind Kitabs, Bombay, 1946; *Speeches* (as Governor of West Bengal), West Bengal Govt. Press, 1948; *Speeches*, Governor-General's Press, New Delhi, 1950; *University Addresses*, Hind Kitabs, Bombay, 1949; *Towards a Responsible Press*, Pub. Div., New Delhi, 1952; *Mankind Protests*, All India Peace Council, New Delhi, 1957; *Rajaji's Speeches*, two vols., Bhavan, Bombay, 1958; *The Voice of the Uninvolved*,

NBT, New Delhi, 1960; *Satyameva Jayate*, Bharathan, Madras.
Rajagopalachari, C., and Rama Rao, Navaratna, *Our College — Reminiscences*, undated article about Central College, Bangalore.

Richards, F.J., *Salem*, Government Press, Madras, 1917.

Saiyyid, M.H., *M.A.Jinnah*, Lahore, 1945.

Santhanam, K., *The Trap of Words*, Lalitha, Trichy, 1942.

Shankar, V., *My Reminiscences of Sardar Patel*, Macmillan, New Delhi, 1974.

Shiva Rao, B., *India's Freedom Movement*, Orient Longman, 1942.

Shukla, Chandrashanker, *Conservations of Gandhi*, Vora, Bombay, 1949.

Sitaramayya, Pattabhi, *History of the Indian National Congress*, Padma, Bombay, 1947.

Spratt, P., *D.M.K. in Power*, Nachiketa, Bombay, 1970.

Stephens, Ian, *Monsoon Morning*, Ernest Benn, London, 1966.

Tahmankar, *Lokamanya Tilak*, John Murray, London, 1956.

Tendulkar, D.G., *Mahatma*, eight vols., Bombay, 1951.

Vira, Dharma, *Memoirs of a Civil Servant*, Vikas, 1975.

Index